VIOLENCE IN AMERICAN SCHOOLS:
A Practical Guide for Counselors

Editors

Daya Singh Sandhu, EdD
Cheryl Blalock Aspy, PhD

AMERICAN
COUNSELING
ASSOCIATION

VIOLENCE IN AMERICAN SCHOOLS:
A PRACTICAL GUIDE FOR COUNSELORS

10 9 8 7 6 5 4 3 2 1

American Counseling Association
5999 Stevenson Avenue
Alexandria, VA 22304

Director of Publications
Carolyn C. Baker

Copyeditor
Elaine Dunn

Cover design by Brian Gallagher

Library of Congress Cataloging-in-Publication Data

Violence in American schools : a practical guide for counselors / editors, Daya
 Singh Sandhu, Cheryl Blalock Aspy.
       p.   cm.
    Includes bibliographical references and index.
    ISBN 1-55620-222-9 (alk. paper)
    1. School violence—United States—Prevention.   2. Educational
counseling—United States.   I. Sandhu, Daya Singh, 1943– II. Aspy, Cheryl B.
LB3013.3.V585   2000
371.7′82′0973—dc21   00-021330

DEDICATION

This book is dedicated to all children who are at risk for violence in schools, especially our children, Ravinder (Jason) and Christine.

And to all those children who have been victims of violence, especially John Joseph Wallace, 1980–1999, Dr. Cheryl Aspy's nephew.

Although we know a long list of contributing factors (including individual, familial, and social) and could screen for those, prediction is not an exact science. However, screening along with good clinical judgment by counselors could be the source for identifying children and adolescents who are at risk (Johns, 1998; Myles & Simpson, 1998). Therefore, counselors should have a significant role in the schools as the leaders of the violence prevention teams. This concept recognizes that everyone must be a part of the solution and the counselor is best equipped to provide the skilled leadership that can prevent and remediate school violence.

The purpose of this book is to provide a guidebook for counselors to use to develop their own skills in working with all stakeholders in understanding the etiology of violence, identifying individuals at risk, preventing violence episodes when possible, and remedying the effects of violence in the survivors. The book is divided into six sections grouped by chapters on similar themes. Section I, Defining the Problem, and the three chapters that follow (a) define the problem from a statistical perspective by describing the nature and extent of violence in schools, (b) discuss psychological and cultural characteristics of violent students, and (c) describe school violence from socioecological perspectives.

Section II, The Etiology of Violence in Youths, addresses the source of youth violence. Again this section has three chapters. Chapter 4 examines the characteristics of common student victimization patterns and proposes how to reduce school violence by minimizing the intensity of day-to-day interpersonal conflicts. In chapter 5, the authors explore how masculine thinking is related to recent incidents of school violence. An analysis of male thinking that may force sudden violent actions is presented. Chapter 6 addresses media-created stereotypes that directly or indirectly contribute to school violence. It also offers a profile of potential violent youthful offenders.

School violence prevention strategies are the topics addressed in Section III. It is the largest section in the book and comprises nine chapters. It clearly highlights the importance of prevention. Chapter 7 focuses on the science of violence prevention to create cultures of nonviolence. Various strategies to promote PEACE POWER! are presented. In chapter 8, the author provides a systematic review of violence prevention strategies. A major emphasis is placed on those protective factors that appear to inoculate against the virulent dangers of violence. Chapter 9 discusses the role of virtues that are imperative to prevent, control, and combat school violence. The author vehemently asserts that virtue promotion is a viable intervention strategy to prevent school violence.

Chapter 10 focuses on ecological, social, cultural, and historical factors that lead to violence in society in general and in the schools in particular. This chapter also presents developmental stage information to explain how violence is interpreted by the youth. A comprehensive approach to respond to school violence is delineated. In chapter 11, the authors discuss creative and underused counseling strategies for the prevention of violence in schools. Etiological indicators, predictors, and correlates of school violence are also discussed in addition to many nationally known violence prevention programs such as The Comer Project and The Brave Program. In chapter 12, the authors describe how to train school counselors to prevent school violence. Three different stages—primary, secondary, and tertiary—are described as a framework to conceptualize and implement service delivery. A review of preservice and in-service training issues is also presented.

In chapter 13, the authors provide a comprehensive review of anger management programs for children and adolescents. Because anger is an underlying reason for violence, its management is considered crucial to all prevention efforts. In chapter 14, the author outlines several pragmatic interventions. There is a message of hope that school violence is preventable. Because there is no single cause for school violence, the author asserts that no single program, person, or approach can prevent this violence. In the last chapter of this section, chapter 15, the author describes the current state of school violence programs in the United States. She describes the characteristics of programs that work; more important, she identifies those programs that do not work. The author also explains why some programs are doomed to fail.

Section IV, Violence in Special Populations, starts with chapter 16, which describes the problem of self-violence in the form of adolescent suicide. The author identifies risk factors, stressors that influence suicidal adolescents, assessment, prevention, and intervention strategies. In chapter 17, the author discusses violence against gay, lesbian, bisexual, and transgender, or GLBT, youths. The effects of violence that stunt psychosocial development are identified. The author also discusses strategies that could deter violence against this special population. In chapter 18, the authors discuss hate crimes and their deleterious psychological effects. They also describe counselors' role in preventing these hate crimes.

Section V mainly covers chapters pertaining to violence intervention strategies. This section acknowledges the need for models and techniques to address the aftermath of violence for both the survivors and the perpetrators. For this reason, the focus of these chapters goes beyond prevention into the realm of intervention. These chapters mainly address the issues and concerns on what should be done when violence has already occurred. In chapter 19, the authors discuss correlations between adolescent violence and their alcohol and drug abuse. Behavioral family therapy is proposed as an intervention strategy. Chapter 20 discusses two major questions: How do we differentiate individuals with chronic violent forms of conduct disorder from those having more benign and transitory problems? and Which treatments are more effective for conduct disor-

ACKNOWLEDGMENTS

First and foremost, we would like to thank God Almighty for His help, without Whose Will not even a blade of grass moves in this universe. There are too many persons to be mentioned here who directly or indirectly made the publication of this book a reality. Mere mention of these persons' names is in no way sufficient to compensate them for their help. We will always remain indebted to them.

First, we would like to thank all of the contributors for their hard work, dedication, and chapter contributions. We are also grateful to them for having enough trust in us to serve as their editors. We sincerely appreciate these contributors' profound insights into school violence and violence-related issues. Above all, we are thankful for their cooperation and patience. This bouquet in the hands of readers is the contributors' flowers; we just assembled, arranged, and rearranged them.

We thank Carolyn Baker, Director of Publications at the American Counseling Association, for her encouragement and guidance at every step in the preparation of this book. We also appreciate the editorial work of Elaine Dunn, as well as the anonymous reviewers for their most valuable comments and scholarly suggestions. We would also like to thank Dr. Ronald D. Stephens for taking time from his very busy schedule to write the Foreword to this book.

We also appreciate and thank Don Clothier and Candace Lacy from the University of Oklahoma and Rose Wade and Pamela Hampton from the University of Louisville for their help in the final preparation of the manuscripts for this book. Thanks are also due to Catherine McCliment and Amy Baur, graduate assistants at the University of Louisville, who made numerous visits, too many to count, to the library to find needed materials.

Finally, we thank our spouses Usha and Dave for their moral support and encouragement.

For those we inadvertently missed or who helped us indirectly, please accept our thanks and apology.

Daya Singh Sandhu and Cheryl Blalock Aspy

ABOUT THE EDITORS
AND CONTRIBUTORS

Daya Singh Sandhu, EdD, NCC, NCCC, NCSC, CPC, is chairperson and professor in the Department of Educational and Counseling Psychology at the University of Louisville. He received his BA, BT, and MA (English) degrees from Punjab University, India. After moving to the United States in 1969, he received his MEd from Delta State University, Specialist in English degree from the University of Mississippi, and Doctor of Counselor Education from Mississippi State University. He has more than 30 years of experience in education, both at the secondary and the university levels. He taught English, mathematics, physics, and chemistry in India. In the United States he taught English for 11 years in public schools and also served as a high school guidance counselor and agency testing coordinator for 7 years with the Choctaw Agency, Bureau of Indian Affairs Schools, in Philadelphia, Mississippi. Since 1989, he has taught graduate courses in counselor education and counseling psychology at Nicholls State University and the University of Louisville.

Dr. Sandhu has a special interest in school counseling, multicultural counseling, neurolinguistic programming, and the role of spirituality in counseling and psychotherapy. Previously, he has published four books, *Numerical Problems in Physics, A Practical Guide for Classroom Observations: A Multidimensional Approach, Counseling for Prejudice Prevention and Reduction* (as a senior author), and *Empowering Women for Equity: A Counseling Approach* (as a second author). Dr. Sandhu also edited two more books, *Asian and Pacific Islander Americans: Issues and Concerns for Counseling and Psychotherapy* and *Faces of Violence: Psychological Correlates, Concepts, and Intervention Strategies.*

Dr. Sandhu has also published more than 50 articles in state, national, and international journals. His first book was in Punjabi poetry, *Satranghi Pingh.* Dr. Sandhu is also an experienced presenter and professional workshops trainer. He has made more than 100 presentations at the international, state, and local levels. His presentations have focused on a wide variety of subjects that can be broadly classified under school counseling and multicultural counseling.

Cheryl Blalock Aspy, PhD, MEd, BS, received BS and MEd degrees from Texas Woman's University and a PhD in Measurement, Statistics, and Evaluation from the University of Maryland in 1981. She is a fourth-generation native of Quitman, Texas, and was named a 1999 Distinguished Alumnae Award Recipient of Texas Woman's University.

During the 1980s, she and her husband David Aspy were codirectors of the Carkhuff Institute of Human Technology in Amherst, Massachusetts, where they studied and encouraged the development of effective teaching and counseling models to increase thinking and productivity in classrooms, counseling settings, and organizations.

In 1987, she became the research director at the Department of Family and Community Medicine at the University of Louisville and later accepted a similar position at the University of Oklahoma Health Sciences Center. During her academic medicine career, she has authored or coauthored proposals that were awarded over $2.5 million in funding. Her research addresses the components of an effective doctor–patient relationship, influences on adherence to medication prescriptions, treatment of incontinence, evaluation of teen pregnancy prevention programs, and the effect of intercessory prayer. She also participated in the development of a fellowship for physicians in Humanism in Medicine, the only one of its kind in the United States.

Currently, Dr. Aspy serves as the Educational Director for the Oklahoma Center for Family Medicine Research, directs a Mini-Fellowship in Family Medicine Research, and teaches behavioral medicine to third-year medical students and second-year Family Medicine residents at the University of Oklahoma College of Medicine, where she serves on the Admissions Board. She is the author or coauthor of five books, over 35 articles, and numerous book chapters and monographs and serves on the editorial boards of *Family Medicine* and *The Journal of Invitational Theory and Practice.* She has presented over 50 national and international workshops and seminars on a variety of skill development topics and is an Advanced Trauma Life Support (ATLS®) Educator.

She and her husband have one child, Mary Christine, who is a junior in high school.

Irene Mass Ametrano, EdD, is a professor and program coordinator in the Department of Leadership and Counseling at Eastern Michigan University. She received her EdD in counseling psychology from Rutgers University. She has held leadership positions in the Michigan Counseling Association and served as vice-chair of the Michigan Board of Counseling. She is on the editorial board of *Counselor Education and Supervision.* Her teaching interests focus on community counseling, crisis intervention, and professional issues and ethics. She has worked as a counselor in community mental health and college counseling settings.

David N. Aspy, EdD, is a graduate of the University of Louisville (BA and MA) and the University of Kentucky (EdD) with degrees in Biology, Counseling Psychology, and Educational Psychology, respectively. He is a Professor Emeritus of Counselor Education at Texas Woman's University, has collaborated with Carl Rogers on effective teaching research, and has assembled the world's largest database on classroom interaction. He is a former director of the Carkhuff Institute of Human Technology and is a noted speaker and author of over 20 books and numerous journal articles. He is currently an educational consultant in Edmond, Oklahoma.

Ann L. Bauer, PhD, has worked 19 years in public education—11 years with special education students and 8 years as an elementary school counselor. She received her PhD from Kent State University in 1995 and has been employed as an assistant professor in Jonesboro, Arkansas, since 1997. She was a part of the crisis response when the Jonesboro shootings occurred, and subsequently received training from the National Organization for Victim Assistance. She coauthored a crisis response plan that was accepted countywide and is part of a countywide crisis response team that has been called to work with victims of school tragedies, local crimes, and natural disasters.

Alfiee M. Breland, PhD, is an assistant professor at Michigan State University and a native of Virginia Beach, Virginia. She received a BA in English from Howard University, an MA in Counselor Education from New York University, and a PhD in Counseling Psychology from the University of Wisconsin–Madison. Her internship was completed at Duke University. Her primary research interest includes the effects of "color consciousness" and skin tone variance on African Americans' lives. She currently serves on the board of the *Michigan Journal of Counseling and Development* and was honored as one of *Ebony Magazine*'s 1999 "Young Leaders Under 30."

Yvonne L. Callaway, PhD, is an associate professor in the Department of Leadership and Counseling at Eastern Michigan University. She received her PhD from Wayne State University. She has worked actively in the Michigan Counseling Association and is a past president of the Michigan Association for Multicultural Counseling and Development. Her specialized teaching interests include cross-cultural counseling and group work.

Barbara DeBaryshe, PhD, is a developmental psychologist with interests in the areas of parent–child relations, children's social development, and family stress and coping. In addition to the chapter in this volume, she has published a model of the development of anger regulation in children; this model integrates the influences of physiology, cognition, and interactions with parents and peers. Most of her recent research has focused on how family members cope with economic stress. Populations included in this research are families of displaced workers, families on public assistance, and families of low-wage workers.

M. Sylvia Fernandez, PhD, LPC, NCC, ACS, NCSC, is an associate professor in a School Counseling program at Arkansas State University. She has published and presented in the areas of multiculturalism in counseling and teaching, counselor and counseling supervision, counselor professional identity development, and crisis response and crisis planning. She is a trained crisis responder and has been involved on crisis response teams for over 10 years, including at the Jonesboro, Arkansas, school shootings. Dr. Fernandez holds and has held leadership positions in the Arkansas Counseling Association and the state and national divisions of the Association for Counselor Education and Supervision, Association for Specialists in Group Work, and Association for Multicultural Counseling and Development.

Michael J. Furlong, PhD, is a professor in the Graduate School of Education at the University of California, Santa Barbara. He is affiliated with the American Psychological Association-approved Counseling/Clinical/School Psychology program, the co-coordinator of a National Association of School Psychologists-approved specialist program, and the doctoral specialization in Special Education, Risk, and Disability studies. He is past president of the California Association of School Psychologists, a member of the California Commission on Teacher Credentialing School Violence Advisory Panel, and the California Governor's School Safety Advisory Panel.

Gary G. Gintner, PhD, is an associate professor and coordinator of the Counselor Education Program at Louisiana State University. He has published numerous articles and book chapters on topics such as anger management, differential diagnosis, and treatment planning. His clinical experience includes work in outpatient mental health, inpatient psychiatric care, chemical dependency, and employee assistance programs. Dr. Gintner has been a consultant to several national managed-care companies. He has served as a national workshop presenter for the American Counseling Association and other professional groups.

James P. Griffin, Jr., PhD, is a research assistant professor at the Morehouse School of Medicine and Adjunct Faculty at the Rollins School of Public Health at Emory University. He attended West Virginia University with bachelor's and master's degrees in psychology. He obtained school psychology training at Howard University and obtained his PhD from the Department of Psychology at Georgia State University, where his training was in community and organizational psychology. He is the principal investigator for a National Institute on Drug Abuse-funded substance abuse and violence prevention program for African American young people. He teaches behavioral science courses.

Frederick D. Harper, PhD, is professor of counseling at Howard University and managing editor of the *International Journal for the Advancement of Counselling.* He is also a former editor of the *Journal for Multicultural Counseling and Development* (1991–1995). Dr. Harper is a National Certified Counselor and a member of the American Counseling Association, the American Psychological Association, and the International Association for Counselling. He has presented more than 100 conference papers and has authored more than 90 publications.

Stuart Henry, PhD, is associate dean and director of the Interdisciplinary Studies Program in the College of LifeLong Learning, Wayne State University. Dr. Henry is the author/editor of 18 books and over 100 articles on aspects of crime, deviance, and social control.

Farah A. Ibrahim, PhD, is a professor of Counseling Psychology (Department of Educational Psychology) at the University of Connecticut, Storrs. She has done groundbreaking research on cultural issues in psychology. She has published numerous articles and book chapters in the areas of cultural and gender issues in counseling, assessment issues in cross-cultural research and training, posttraumatic stress disorder, and the minority experience. Dr. Ibrahim's other areas of research include women's achieved identity, depression among North American and Japanese women (with Dr. Hifumi Ohnishi), and South Asian identity development. She has also published about issues relating to Asian American women psychology, the psychology of women, multicultural curriculum development in counseling psychology, issues of violence, drug and alcohol abuse, and suicide in the schools. She is the author (with Harris Kahn) of the Scale to Assess World View©, an instrument that assesses values, beliefs, and assumptions within and between cultures.

Gerald A. Juhnke, PhD, is an associate professor in the Department of Counseling and Educational Development at the University of North Carolina at Greensboro. He is also the director of the department's research and training clinic, a fellow of both the North Carolina Governor's Institute on Alcohol and Substance Abuse and the Center for the Study of Social Issues' Division on Youth Violence and Aggression. Dr. Juhnke is currently review board member and past editor of the *Journal of Addictions and Offender Counseling* and past co-chair of the American Counseling Association's Council of Journal Editors.

James D. Larson, PhD, is professor of psychology and coordinator of the School Psychology Program at the University of Wisconsin–Whitewater. He is a member of the Scientific Board of the Melissa Institute for Violence

Prevention and Treatment and a former school psychologist and director of the Violence Prevention Program with the Milwaukee Public Schools.

Mary K. Lawler, RN, PhD, is assistant extension specialist in family development for cooperative extension at Oklahoma State University in Stillwater, Oklahoma. Dr. Lawler's research interests are in violence prevention, especially dating violence in adolescence and school-related violence. She has presented numerous workshops on how communities can keep schools safe.

Robin Guill Liles, MS/EdS, is a doctoral student in the Department of Counseling and Educational Development at the University of North Carolina at Greensboro. She is also a counselor at High Point Behavioral Health.

Christine T. Lowery, PhD, (Laguna/Hopi) is Assistant Professor, School of Social Welfare, University of Wisconsin–Milwaukee. Dr. Lowery conducts research and has published in the areas of human rights and social justice, Native American women in recovery, Native American elders, and shared power as a framework for professional practice and community building.

Mark A. Mattaini, DSW, ACSW, is associate professor and director of the PhD program, Jane Addams College of Social Work, University of Illinois at Chicago; president of Walden Fellowship, Inc.; chair of Behaviorists for Social Responsibility; and the author/editor of seven books related to serious social issues. His current scholarship and service emphasize youth violence prevention and the construction of cultural systems that support social justice. He consults extensively with community groups interested in the PEACE POWER! strategy.

Donald R. Nims, EdD, is associate professor of counseling in the Department of Educational Leadership, Western Kentucky University, Bowling Green, Kentucky. He is a clinical member and approved supervisor of the American Association of Marriage and Family Therapy; nationally board-certified counselor and mental health counselor; and licensed marriage and family therapist and certified professional counselor in Kentucky. He is a member of the International Association of School Safety Professionals. Dr. Nims is currently project director for the Kentucky Department of Juvenile Justice Group Counseling Certification Program. He has published numerous articles and has made several national presentations in the area of counseling and safety issues.

Mark Pope, EdD, LPC, NCC, NCCC, MAC, ACS, is an associate professor of Counselor Education, Counseling Psychology, and Family Therapy in the School of Education at the University of Missouri–St. Louis. He teaches courses in multicultural counseling, addictions counseling, psychological testing, advanced practice in counseling, and career counseling. His special areas of interest include multicultural career counseling, and he is a past president of the National Career Development Association. Dr. Pope is the author of many books, book chapters, and journal articles and has presented all over the world on counseling issues, including invited presentations in China, Hong Kong, Singapore, and Malaysia.

Sujin Sabrina Rhee is currently a doctoral student in the Counseling/Clinical/School Psychology Program at the University of California, Santa Barbara. Her research interests are in school violence prevention programs and neuropsychology.

Michael Salzman, PhD, is an assistant professor at the University of Hawaii at Manoa in the Department of Counselor Education. He has published in the areas of cross-cultural psychology, intercultural sensitivity training, and prejudice reduction. He has also been working in the areas of violence prevention and the promotion of inclusive school communities. Currently, Dr. Salzman is working on a project designed to identify those behaviors experienced as respectful and disrespectful by students, parents, and teachers in their interactions with each other.

Varrinder Singh Sandhu (Joey) is a senior pursuing a BS in biology and a BA in psychology. He plans to attend medical school in the near future. Varrinder also works at Brooklawn Youth Services, a facility for troubled youths.

Bonita Sharma is currently a doctoral student in the Counseling/Clinical/School Psychology Program at the University of California, Santa Barbara. Her research interests are in school violence risk factors and intervention; juvenile delinquency risk, resiliency, and treatment; grief counseling; school and mental health collaboration; and counseling ethnic-minority youths/families.

Douglas C. Smith, PhD, is an assistant professor in the Department of Counselor Education at the University of Hawaii. Dr. Smith is a licensed psychologist and a nationally certified school psychologist. His research interests are in the areas of children's social and emotional development and in violence prevention and intervention.

Sue A. Stickel, PhD, is an associate professor in the Department of Leadership and Counseling at Eastern Michigan University. She is the author of publications relating to school counseling and school reform. She has served as the editor of the *Michigan Journal of Counseling and Development* and is a past president of the Michigan Association of Counselor Education and Supervision.

xxviii | Violence in American Schools

Jeannine R. Studer, EdD, is a counselor educator and coordinator of the school counseling program at Heidelberg College, Tiffin, Ohio. Prior to her arrival at Heidelberg, she served as a high school counselor. Jeannine has authored numerous articles ranging from aggressive youths to working with students with special needs. She is a Professional Interest Network (PIN) contact person for the American School Counselor Association on the topic of aggressive students. Dr. Studer served as the 1997–1998 Ohio School Counselor Association president and won the 1997 Distinguished Teaching Award for Faculty from Heidelberg College.

Andrew K. Tobias, PhD, NCC, LPC, is an assistant professor at North Carolina Agricultural and Technical State University. He obtained his PhD in School Counseling from the University of Florida. Dr. Tobias also served as an assistant professor for 4 years (1992–1996) at the University of Alabama. He has contributed several articles in publications such as *Professional School Counseling* and *The Peer Facilitator Quarterly.* Dr. Tobias serves as a national and local consultant with school systems on issues such as violence prevention and multicultural awareness.

Joanne M. Tortorici Luna, PhD, DTR, PPSC, is violence prevention coordinator for the Long Beach Unified School District, California. She has consulted for the United Nations Children's Fund (UNICEF), the World Health Organization (WHO), and other humanitarian organizations in the war zones of Central America and South Africa, among other countries. As the UNICEF consultant to the Nicaraguan Ministry of Education, she led the development and implementation of that country's first Peace Education Program. A counseling psychologist, school counselor, and dance/movement therapist, she is a part-time faculty member at California State University, Long Beach, and co-chair of the Counseling Reform Launch Initiative.

Peter Tran is a doctoral candidate in counseling psychology at the Department of Educational Psychology, University of Connecticut, Storrs. He is currently completing his internship in Sacramento, California, and conducting research issues pertaining to homosexual identity and homophobia.

Joe Ray Underwood, PhD, LPC, is a professor of Counselor Education in the Department of Counselor Education and Educational Psychology at Mississippi State University. He is also Director of Mississippi State University Summer Scholars Program.

Vicki Harris Wyatt, PhD, is an assistant professor of Research in the Department of Health Promotions at the University of Oklahoma Health Sciences Center. She holds a BSE in English and Journalism Education; an MEd in Guidance and Counseling; and a PhD in Family Relations and

Child Development. She has expertise as an educator at multiple levels, a parent educator, a family and divorce mediator, an individual and family therapist, and a supervisor of community-based prevention and intervention programs. She is the coprincipal investigator of the Healthy, Empowered, and Responsible Teens of Oklahoma City (HEART of OKC) project, a 7-year teen pregnancy prevention project funded by the Centers for Disease Control and Prevention.

Lissa J. Yogan, PhD, is assistant professor of sociology and acting chair of the Department of Sociology at Valparaiso University. Dr. Yogan has done consulting work and currently teaches on the topics of race, gender, and moral development.

<table>
<tr><td>SECTION

I</td><td>DEFINING
THE PROBLEM</td></tr>
</table>

INTRODUCTION

I sat in the airport in Lexington, Kentucky, on that May 20th afternoon and watched the television in horror with the rest of the world as another school shooting unfolded. This time it was in Conyers, Georgia, a suburb of Atlanta. I wondered about my own daughter's safety in her suburban school not unlike Columbine or Heritage High Schools. How could this happen again? There were other parents watching the monitor that afternoon, and their faces reflected the questions I pondered. What has gone so wrong in the lives of our teens that murder, mayhem, and suicide are plausible options? What is the problem for which violence has become the solution? What can we do to stop the violence?

In this section of the book, we attempt to answer two of these questions. The first chapter, "Violence in Our Schools: A National Crisis" by Donald R. Nims, provides an epidemiological review of school violence and overviews a comprehensive range of response. He suggests, "An effective range of response includes both reactive interventions to use when violence erupts and proactive strategies to prevent violence before it happens by providing training and experience for students, teachers, and administrators in alternative peaceful solutions" (p. 8).

Chapter 2, by Daya Singh Sandhu, Joe Ray Underwood, and Varrinder Singh Sandhu, addresses the psychocultural profiles of violent youths and the therapeutic interventions that counselors may use for prevention and treatment. This chapter provides a lens through which youth characteristics and behavior can be interpreted and assessed for violence potential.

Chapter 3, the final chapter in this section by Vicki Harris Wyatt, addresses the problem of school violence from a social ecology perspective. This theoretical model affirms that there are multiple levels of inter-

23% of students reported being victims of violence in or around their school (Coben, Weiss, Mulley, & Dearwater, 1994). "A Gallup poll showed American parents are most worried about two problems in the schools: violence and gangs, and lack of discipline" (Koklaranis, 1994, p. A1). Kodluboy (1998) quoted Marian Wright Edleman of the Children's Defense Fund as saying, "America has permitted children to rely more on guns and gangs, rather than parents and neighbors, for protection and love" (p. 190).

Studies reveal that teachers who have witnessed violent incidents, fear violence, or cope daily with disruptive students often exhibit symptoms of stress akin to combat soldiers; they can suffer from fatigue, headaches, stomach pains, and hypertension (Kadel & Follman, 1993). In a survey of colleges and university colleges of education, Nims and Wilson (1998) found that most institutions are doing very little to prepare teachers to cope with violence as it occurs in schools. One school teacher reported that he got his training in violence prevention the day a student pointed a gun in his face (Nims & Loposer, 1997). Kadel and Follman (1993) wrote, "Because teachers are given limited training on how to deal with violent students in their classrooms, trying to maintain order and teach class at the same time often leads to stress and feelings of ineffectiveness that fuel teacher burnout and high attrition rates" (p. 63). Contemporary school settings have become battle zones, and the personal safety of teachers and students is not always assured, making it difficult to concentrate on teaching and learning (Nims & Loposer, 1997).

This chapter explores the question of violence in U.S. schools. Current data regarding school safety are presented to explain the impact of violence on the educational process. In addition, a comprehensive range of response is presented, including both reactive and proactive interventions, legal implications, and case examples of what schools are doing.

AN EPIDEMIOLOGICAL
REVIEW OF SCHOOL VIOLENCE

School discipline problems in the 1940s included talking, chewing gum, making noise, and running in the halls. By the 1970s, dress code violations had become the number one disciplinary problem. The 1980s saw fighting on campuses move to the top of the list. However, by the 1990s, weapons in school, gangs, drug abuse, alcohol abuse, and absenteeism were the main issues affecting school discipline (Stephens, 1994). Remboldt (1994) reported that more than 160,000 students stay home from school daily because they are sick of the violence and afraid they might be stabbed, shot, or beaten. Porter (1995) noted that juvenile arrests for murder and other violent crimes have soared over the last decade owing largely to the increase in the availability of guns and drugs.

In 1996–1997, 10% of all public schools reported at least one serious violent crime to the police or a law enforcement representative (*Indicators of School Crime and Safety*, 1998). This translates to an average of 255,000 incidents of nonfatal serious violent crime at school among students 12 to 18 years old and 316,000 nonfatal crimes at school toward teachers during that same period. The Centers for Disease Control and Prevention, in conjunction with the National School Safety Center, estimated that 105 violence-associated deaths occurred on or near school campuses across the nation during the 1992–1993 and 1993–1994 school years combined (Kachur et al., 1996). Other trends are noteworthy. The number of students feeling unsafe at school increased by 50% between 1989 and 1995, the number of students fearing they would be attacked while traveling to and from school rose nearly 100%, and the percentage of students who reported that street gangs were present at their schools increased from 15% to 28% (*Indicators of School Crime and Safety*, 1998). There does appear, however, to be a decease in the number of 12th graders reporting a violent incident involving a weapon (from 5.9% in 1990 to 4.8% in 1996) and a 27% decrease in the number of school killings in the 1997–1998 school year from the 1992–1993 school year (National School Safety Center, 1998).

Even though school safety may be an educational right (Morrison, Furlong, & Morrison, 1998), it appears students and teachers are finding it more difficult to exercise that right. The results of longitudinal research show that, even with a decrease in some measures (number of weapons in schools and the percentage of crime actually caused by juveniles), violence in U.S. schools has steadily increased in both incident and intensity. In the past for some school officials, denial has been an easier choice than accepting the responsibility for directly attacking security problems (Trump, 1997). It is now imperative that we, as a society, accept our collective responsibility of treating school violence as a systemic issue that affects all of us. Only then will we be able to devise successful interventions. Academic excellence in the classroom is only possible in an atmosphere of safety and peaceful coexistence among students and teachers.

SCHOOL VIOLENCE IS A REFLECTION OF SOCIETY

Many professional educators have concluded that school violence is not caused by the school but is a direct reflection of behaviors displayed outside the school (Stephans, 1994) and is the result of social changes in U.S. communities (Pietrzak, Petersen, & Speaker, 1998). These include a lack of family rules, decline in family structure, and a lack of parental supervision. In addition, societal models in the media contribute to school vio-

children spend most of their human contact, become the reflection of this dichotomy.

A COMPREHENSIVE RANGE OF RESPONSE

A problem as complex as school violence requires a response that addresses both the need for safety in the classroom and a means for providing students with new alternatives for more peaceful behavior. Cloud (1997) commented:

> Prevention is the only effective way to neutralize violent and abusive behavior in schools. Intervention is not a long-term solution, because it usually occurs after violent confrontations. Educators must anticipate violent situations and develop policies and procedures which focus on safety and crisis management as much as they do on violence reduction. The emphasis should always be on development of a safe and healthful school environment where discipline has no place. (p. 21)

An effective range of response includes both reactive interventions to use when violence erupts and proactive strategies to prevent violence before it happens by providing training and experience for students, teachers, and administrators in alternative peaceful solutions. Violence is a systemic problem that can invade, pervade, and render whole systems dysfunctional, including family systems, workplace systems, and school systems (Remboldt, 1994). Therefore, a comprehensive, systemic approach is needed to effectively respond to this problem.

Reactive Interventions

Crisis Response Plan
Poland (1997) succinctly pointed out that too often schools have been "caught with their plans down" (p. 155). According to Stephens (1994), schools today face two kinds of crises: the crisis they are currently facing and the crisis that is about to happen. Consequently, school districts need a Crisis Response Plan that describes specific procedures dealing with events such as natural disasters, automobile or bus accidents, death of students and teachers, and other potentially volatile situations (Nims & Loposer, 1997). These plans provide for clear and consistent communication between schools and communities, vital in a time of crisis.

Many school districts have previously lagged behind in crisis planning. They cite obstacles such as the myth that taking action makes a crisis worse; they bring up territorial issues regarding whose responsibility it is; they show a lack of priority in allotting resources and time; and they devote few curriculum units to safety (McIntyre & Reid, 1989). Peterson and Staub (1992), however, emphasized that school administrators have a clear legal obligation to make crisis plans. Several states have enacted legislation to address the area of school crisis planning (Brock, Sandoval, & Lewis, 1995).

The Kentucky Legislature (1998) adopted a law requiring all schools to formulate plans, policies, and procedures regarding safety and discipline in the schools. In addition, this law authorizes the establishment of the Center for School Safety to serve as the central point for data analysis, research, and dissemination of information about successful school safety programs. Stephens (1994) viewed school crisis planning as a constantly evolving task that is a priority in the job description of administrators and other school personnel. Unfortunately, most school crisis planning still takes place only after a tragedy occurs (Poland, 1997).

Crisis plans are contingency policies and procedures for responding to potentially disruptive events. These include response codes for alerting teachers and personnel to lock classrooms, activating on-site crisis teams, contacting law enforcement and other emergency response assistance, working with concerned parents, and preparing for the media. "A thorough plan will detail everything from how to notify parents in the event of a bus crash to steps for keeping students safe if an armed felon is roaming the halls" (Mulrine, 1998, p. 77). It is important not only to have these plans but also to practice them, much as schools schedule a fire or tornado drill. Rather than scare children, these experiences can foster a sense of confidence and security.

Crisis Response Teams
The literature supports the necessity of developing crisis teams (Brock et al., 1995; Johnson & Johnson, 1995; Peterson & Staub, 1992; Poland & Pitcher, 1990; Ruof & Harris, 1988; Slaikeu, 1984; Watson, Poda, Miller, Rice, & West, 1990). Poland (1997) described three levels of team preparation: (a) a building team that meets on a routine basis to review crisis plans, conducts crisis drills and readiness activities, and provides immediate coordinated response in the time of crisis; (b) a district team responsible for coordinated planning and response; and (c) a combination of a district and community team charged with providing and implementing a comprehensive response, particularly when the crisis impacts a larger area. Teams typically include administrative, counseling, security, and health professionals trained in crisis response strategies. Qualities of leadership, teamwork, and responsibility are essential ingredients of successful crisis management (Cornell & Sheras, 1998).

Secure Facilities Design
Crowe (1990) suggested that school design must be assessed through a new perspective that "incorporates an understanding of how the con-

The degree of involvement depends on the size and need of the individual school. Full-time uniformed security staff may permanently patrol the building, or law enforcement officers may drop in to meet and talk to students on an informal basis to foster positive relationships. One such program, BADGES (Be Against Drugs and Guns Entering Schools), is a collaborative effort between city and county police to involve themselves on a more personal level in the lives of students. Very often other students are the first to know when a peer has a gun or knife in his or her possession. Positive relationships with these law enforcement personnel can effectively break the students' code of silence, vital to the awareness of weapons or drugs on campus before an incident takes place. It is important that such security individuals be trained in positive listening/ responding and relationship-building skills.

Confronting Bullying Behavior

Schoolyard bullying is a significant, pervasive, and perhaps the most severely underrated problem within an educational system (Stephens, 1997). Included in bullying behavior is sexual harassment and intimidation. According to Stephens (1997), four out of five students report having experienced some form of sexual harassment in school. Girls, in particular, encounter a learning environment poisoned by sexual harassment (Stein et al., 1993). Recent state and federal court cases serve to bring sexual harassment to the forefront in protecting students' civil rights. According to Hazler (1994), petty teasing, joking, and bullying at school can have devastating effects on students, leading to violent and disastrous consequences for both perpetrators and victims.

Understanding Legal Implications

Students' rights have been addressed in numerous sources (Fischer, Schimmel, & Kelly, 1995; McCarthy & Cambron-McCabe, 1992; Weeks, 1992), and clear guidelines have been delineated with regard to recognizing these rights. In all schools, policies related to the discipline of students must comply with basic guidelines regarding specificity of language and appropriateness of sanctions with regard to the severity of the rule infraction (McCarthy & Cambron-McCabe, 1992).

Investigations using search and seizure must be conducted according to strict constitutional protection of privacy and with the understanding that such actions might result in litigation (Imbed & van Geel, 1995). Inadvertently, teachers can place themselves in jeopardy if they are not aware of the conditions under which a student's person can be searched and property seized (McCarthy & Cambron-McCabe, 1992) and of the roles administrators and police officials assume in such matters (Imbed & van Geel, 1995).

The concept of due process, or fair procedures, undergirds most legal issues related to students. Although minor rule infractions can be addressed with minimal but fair procedures, serious disciplinary cases require extensive due process procedures (Fischer et al., 1995). It is important school districts have clear policies regarding search and seizure, involve law enforcement when appropriate, and document all incidents.

Proactive Strategies

Rather than only reacting in a time of crisis, effective school violence programs seek to positively affect the whole social systemic fabric of the school. Specifically, these approaches are comprehensive and multifaceted; begin in the primary grades and are reinforced across grade levels; are developmentally tailored; and cover appropriate content area. Appropriate content areas include anger management, social perspective taking, decision making and social problem solving, peer negotiation and conflict management, social resistance skills, active listening and effective communication, and information on prejudice, sexism, racism, and male–female relationships (Dusenbury, Falco, Lake, Brannigan, & Bosworth, 1997).

Empathy Skills
Empathy is defined as the ability to deeply grasp the subjective world of another person, to sense and understand another's feelings (Corey, 1991). Violent behavior can be the result of a lack of empathy. Anger from a variety of dysfunctional situations is projected onto another without regard to the consequence to that other person's self-concept and sense of security. Students, however, can be taught empathy by learning to identify and respond appropriately to the feelings of others. Giggans and Levy (1997) emphasized helping students learn the skills and attitudes they need to maintain healthy intimate relationships. Glasser (1986) stated, "To motivate students, schools must concern themselves less with security and survival and more with the ever-pressing psychological need for friendship, freedom, fun and power" (p. 37).

Conflict Resolution and Peer Mediation
Conflict resolution and peer mediation programs encourage students to share responsibility for creating a safe, secure school environment (Stomfay-Stitz, 1994). Lawton (1994) wrote that there are more than 300 violence prevention programs and more than 100 conflict resolution curricula for middle and high school students. One such curriculum, Second Step, reports data suggesting its effectiveness in imputing knowledge related to violence prevention to preschool and kindergarten children (Moore & Beland, 1992). According to Shepherd (1994), conflict resolution programs have made significant inroads to the number of student disputes brought to teachers' and administrators' attention. Conflict resolution and peer mediation provide a win–win process for managing anger by pre-

senting alternatives to confrontation and resolving disruptions produc- tively. These programs share many common elements, including staying in control, finding a time and place to talk, getting all the facts, listening reflectively, sending "I" messages in which the individual expresses how he or she is feeling, looking for win–win situations, and trying it out.

Continuum of Education Programs
One obvious concern is how to successfully address the academic needs of students with severe and challenging behaviors while assuring the safety of all students. Schools are increasingly developing a continuum of education. Rather than immediately suspending or expelling students with behavioral difficulties, schools are accepting the responsibility to dis- cover alternative methods of education. These include in-school suspen- sion, alternative schools, and day treatment. Gootman (1998) described an in-house suspension program that uses anger reduction techniques, builds supportive relationships, and focuses on student resilience.

Peacemaking Curriculum
Any curriculum in school violence prevention must also include strate- gies to proactively take advantage of the excitement and spontaneity chil- dren bring to school. Violence prevention education that includes a class-specific comprehensive educational component as part of a school- wide violence prevention initiative can reduce negative school behaviors, particularly when other supportive curricula and activities are added (Hausman, Pierce, & Briggs, 1996). Farrell and Meyer (1997) found that participation in a school-based curriculum for reducing violence that included building trust, respect, and nonviolent alternatives to fighting resulted in a significant decrease in the frequency of violence and other problem behaviors.

Modeling Trust and Respect
If school personnel are to expect trust and respect from students, they must first be willing to model that same trust and respect toward the stu- dents. Canter and Garrison (1994) described high-risk behaviors that teachers and other school personnel can exhibit that can exacerbate a situation. These include projecting a confrontational "us-against-them" attitude, enforcing discipline "off the cuff" on a case-by-case basis, re- sponding passively or with hostility, and having no outside backup in the event of danger or loss of control (Canter & Garrison, 1994). Adolescents feel that if they are shown any type of disrespect by anyone, they are expected to take action, often violently, to regain that respect (Fatum & Hoyle, 1996). Gootman (1998) wrote, "By listening to these students responsively and nonjudgmentally, and by trying to understand and reit- erate their feelings, we convey the message that they matter" (p. 39). One

does not have to agree with the choices that students make but must respect their right to make those choices. This means establishing friendly, trusting, respectful relationships; having a firm, fair, and consistent classroom discipline plan in effect for all students; responding firmly, fairly, and respectfully; and arranging for in-school backup and a means to summon it (Canter & Garrison, 1994).

Multicultural Awareness

Multiculturalism is a dynamic element in the U.S. educational system. Singer (1994) reported that the key precept in multicultural education is respect for richness of difference and that valuing this diversity is crucial for a democratic society. A multicultural program includes creating an atmosphere of acceptance, fostering social interactions, encouraging open communication, and building the competence of children (Winter, 1994).

Community Involvement

According to Baker (1998), children prone to violence are disadvantaged in their ability to participate meaningfully in the community of the school, thus impeding an important avenue for prevention and intervention. Osher and Warger (1998) included in their characteristics of a school that is safe and responsive to all children a significant effort to involve families in meaningful ways and to develop links to the community. School communities must make parents feel welcome in school, address barriers to their participation, and keep families positively engaged. Schools that have close ties to families, support services, community police, the faith-based community, and the community at large decrease significantly the risk of school violence (Osher & Warger, 1998).

IMPLICATIONS FOR COUNSELORS

School administrators are making a concerted effort to reduce the risk of school violence by finding a balance between implementing more restrictive safety policies and maintaining the positive, challenging atmosphere in which learning takes place. This is particularly important in light of the increasing demands on teachers as well as the social and environmental pressures students bring into the classroom every day. It is in this tenuous atmosphere that counselors must be equipped to respond to the emotional and social needs of students. A comprehensive developmental guidance program in every elementary, middle, and high school is a necessary component of any effort directed at school safety. School counselors must establish themselves as equal players in the educational process. Properly assessing both academic and emotional needs of students and responding to those needs through regular classroom guidance activities, small group counseling, and individual counseling will enable counselors to identify more quickly and intervene with those students at risk of being disengaged and thus prone to violence.

Counselors must also play a part in training those individuals who are directly involved in school safety—bus drivers, security personnel, and law enforcement personnel—in fundamental listening and communicating skills that generate rapport rather than put kids on the defensive. Counseling and psychotherapeutic services provided in collaboration with various children and family mental health services must continue to address the issue of violence in schools. Cutting or decreasing counseling services in schools under the guise of academic necessity only increases the potential for disciplinary problems. As children are developing cognitively and emotionally, they need to be heard. If they are not heard through the empowering process of human relationship building, they will be heard through more volatile means.

Counselors and psychotherapists in the educational milieu have a moral as well as professional obligation to advocate for their part in the education of children. This includes emphasis in building empathetic relationships, teaching productive ways of dealing with anger, and identifying students at risk of failure. In addition, counselors need to assist in the evaluation of programs such as conflict resolution, peer mediation, and drug awareness and education. As long as the research data on such proactive approaches to school safety remain anecdotal, the response to violence will remain primarily reactive. Kohl (1998) wrote, "Schools of hope are places where children are housed and well served . . . where students can work hard without being harassed . . . where the joy of learning is expressed . . . in their sense of being part of a convivial learning community" (p. 332). A comprehensive approach to school violence that effectively balances both reactive interventions and proactive strategies in kindergarten to 12th grade will make a significant contribution to making schools a safe place for all our children.

CONCLUSION

There is no doubt that the much publicized recent episodes of violence in schools across the United States have caused every school counselor, teacher, and administrator to reflect on the question, "Could it happen here?" There is also no doubt that everyone answered the question in the affirmative. A comparison of discipline problems in the 1940s with those in the 1990s is evidence that schools are not immune to the problems in the larger society.

It is essential that every school prepare responses for reaction as well as proaction. Given that prevention is the preferred cure, schools need to be aware of the role that respect and empathy can play in diffusing violence. Counselors can be leaders in modeling the example and by training other staff members. Once a crisis occurs, schools must be able to respond to limit both the immediate and long-term impact. This chapter has provided a range of response in both reactive and proactive postures for counselors as well as teachers and administrators.

REFERENCES

Baker, J. A. (1998). Are we missing the forest for the trees? Considering the social context of school violence. *Journal of School Psychology, 36,* 29–44.

Bender, D., & Bruno, L. (1990). *Violence in America: Opposing viewpoint.* San Diego, CA: Greenhaven Press.

Brock, S., Sandoval, J., & Lewis, S. (1995). *Preparing for crisis in the schools: A manual for building school crisis response teams.* Brandon, VT: Clinical Psychology.

Canter, L., & Garrison, R. (1994). *Preventing conflict and violence in your classroom: Scared or prepared.* Santa Monica, CA: Lee Canter & Associates.

Center to Prevent Handgun Violence. (1990, September). *Caught in the crossfire: A report on gun violence in our nation's schools.* Washington, DC: Author.

Chisholm, J. F. (1998). Understanding violence in the school: Moral and psychological factors. *Journal of Social Distress and the Homeless, 7,* 137–157.

Cloud, R. C. (1997). *Solutions for violence.* Waco, TX: HEALTH EDCO.

Coben, J. H., Weiss, H. B., Mulley, E. P., & Dearwater, S. R. (1994). A primer on school violence prevention. *Journal of School Health, 64,* 309–313.

Corey, G. (1991). *Theory and practice of counseling and psychotherapy.* Pacific Grove, CA: Brooks/Cole.

Cornell, D. G., & Sheras, P. L. (1998). Common errors in school crisis response: Learning from our mistakes. *Psychology in Schools, 35,* 297–307.

Crowe, T. D. (1990, Fall). Designing safer schools. *School Safety,* 9–13.

Dusenbury, L., Falco, M., Lake, A., Brannigan, R., & Bosworth, K. (1997). Nine critical elements of promising violence prevention programs. *Journal of School Health, 67,* 409–414.

Farrell, A. D., & Meyer, A. L. (1997). The effectiveness of a school-based curriculum for reducing violence among urban sixth-grade students. *American Journal of Public Health, 87,* 979–984.

Fatum, W. R., & Hoyle, J. C. (1996). Is it violence: School violence from the student perspective: Trends and interventions. *School Counselor, 44,* 28–34.

Fischer, L., Schimmel, D., & Kelly, C. (1995). *Teachers and the law.* White Plains, NY: Longmans.

Giggans, P. O., & Levy, B. (1997). *50 ways to a safer world.* Seattle, WA: Seal Press.

Glasser, W. (1986). Discipline is not the problem: Control theory in the classroom. *Education Digest, 52,* 36–39.

Goldstein, A. P., & Conoley, J. C. (1997). Student aggression: Current status. In A. P. Goldstein & J. C. Conoley (Eds.), *School violence intervention: A practical handbook* (pp. 3–19). New York: Guilford Press.

Gootman, M. (1998). Effective in-house suspension: How can we modify traditional in-house suspension to be more active, supportive, and effective? *Educational Leadership, 56,* 39.

Gronlund, G. (1992). Coping with Ninja Turtle play in my kindergarten classroom. *Young Children, 48,* 21–25.

Hausman, A., Pierce, G., & Briggs, L. (1996). Evaluation of comprehensive violence prevention education: Effects on student behavior. *Journal of Adolescent Health, 19,* 104–110.

Hazler, R. J. (1994). Bullying breeds violence. You can stop it! *Learning, 22,* 38–41.

Hicks, D. (1992). Ninja Turtles and other super heroes: A case study of one literacy learner. *Linguistics and Education, 4,* 59–105.

Imbed, M., & van Geel, T. (1995). *A teacher's guide to education law.* New York: McGraw-Hill.

Indicators of school crime and safety. (1998). Washington, DC: National Center for Educational Statistics.

Johnson, D., & Johnson, R. (1995). *Reducing school violence through conflict resolution.* Alexandria, VA: Association for Supervision and Curriculum Development.

Kachur, S., Patrick, M. D., Stennies, G. M., Powell, K. E., Modzeleski, W., Stephens, R., Murphy, R., Krensnow, M., Sleet, D., & Lowry, R. (1996). School-associated violent deaths in the United States, 1992 to 1994. *Journal of the American Medical Association, 275,* 22.

Kadel, S., & Follman, J. (1993). *Reducing school violence.* Tallahassee, FL: South Eastern Regional Vision for Education, Florida Department of Education.

Kentucky Legislature. (1998). *The School Safety Act.* Frankfort: The Commonwealth of Kentucky.

Kodluboy, D. W. (1997). Gang-oriented interventions. In A. P. Goldstein & J. C. Conoley (Eds.), *School violence intervention: A practical handbook* (pp. 189–216). New York: Guilford Press.

Kohl, H. (1998). *The discipline of hope.* New York: Simon & Schuster.

Koklaranis, M. (1994, August 28). Area schools get set to open amid big increase in security. *The Washington Times,* p. A1.

Lamberg, L. (1998). Preventing school violence: No easy answers. *Journal of the American Medical Association, 280,* 404.

Lawton, M. (1994). Violence prevention curricula: What works best. *Education Week, 14,* 10–11.

McCarthy, M. M., & Cambron-McCabe, N. H. (1992). *Public school law: Teachers' and students' rights.* Boston: Allyn & Bacon.

McIntyre, M., & Reid, B. (1989). *Obstacles to implementation of crisis intervention programs.* Unpublished manuscript, Chesterfield County Schools, Chesterfield, VA.

Met Life. (1994). *The Metropolitan Life survey of the American teacher 1994. Violence in America's public schools: The family perspective.* New York: Harris & Associates, Inc.

Moore, B., & Beland, K. (1992). *Evaluation of Second Step, preschool–kindergarten; a violence prevention curriculum kit.* Seattle, WA: Committee for Children.

Morrison, G. M., Furlong, M. J., & Morrison, R. L. (1997). The safe school: Moving beyond crime prevention to school empowerment. In A. P. Goldstein & J. C. Conoley (Eds.), *School violence intervention: A practical handbook* (pp. 236–264). New York: Guilford Press.

Mulrine, A. (1998, November 9). Curriculum for crisis: Why your children's school should have an emergency plan. *U.S. News and World Report, 125*, 76–77.

National School Safety Center. (1998). *Nonfatal student victimization: Student reports.* Westlake, CA: Author.

Nims, D. R., & Loposer, N. (1997). Unarmed teachers: The impact of school violence on teacher preparation. *New Directions for Education Reform, 3*(2), 74–86.

Nims, D. R., & Wilson, R. W. (1998). *Violence prevention preparation: A survey of colleges of education and departments of teacher education* (Report No. SP-037-834). Washington, DC: ERIC Clearinghouse on Teaching and Teacher Education. (ERIC Document Reproduction Service No. 418 052)

Osher, D., & Warger, C. (1998). *Early warning, timely response: A guide to safe schools.* Washington, DC: U.S. Department of Education.

Peterson, S., & Staub, R. (1992). *School crisis survival guide.* West Nyack, NY: Center for Applied Research in Education.

Pietrzak, D., Petersen, G. J., & Speaker, K. M. (1998). Perceptions of school violence by elementary and middle school personnel. *Professional School Counseling, 1*(4), 23–29.

Poland, S. (1997). School crisis teams. In A. P. Goldstein & J. C. Conoley (Eds.), *School violence intervention: A practical handbook* (pp. 127–159). New York: Guilford Press.

Poland, S., & Pitcher, G. (1990). Best practices in crisis intervention. In A. Thomas & J. Grimes (Eds.), *Best practices in school psychology* (Vol. 2, pp. 259–275). Silver Spring, MD: National Association of School Psychologists.

Porter, J. (1995, September 26). Report on juvenile crime brings calls for new policies. *Education Week*, p. 6.

Remboldt, C. (1994). *Solving violence problems in your school: Why a systematic approach is necessary.* Minneapolis, MN: Johnson Institute.

Reno, J. (1993, Fall/Winter). A national agenda for children: On the front lines with Attorney Janet Reno. *Juvenile Justice*, 2–8.

Ruof, S., & Harris, J. (1988). Suicide contagion: Guilt and modeling. *Communique, 8*, 16–17.

School Safety Leadership Curriculum. (1993). Westlake, CA: National School Safety Center.

Shepherd, K. K. (1994). Stemming conflict through peer mediation. *The School Administrator, 51*, 14–17.

Singer, A. (1994, December). Reflections on multiculturalism. *Psi Delta Kappa*, 284–288.

Slaikeu, K. (1984). *Crisis intervention: A handbook for practice and research.* Boston: Allyn & Bacon.

Stein, N., Marshall, N. L., & Tropp, L. R. (1993). *Secrets in public: Sexual harassment in our schools.* Wellesley, MA: Wellesley College, Center for Research on Women, NOW Legal Defense and Education Fund.

Stephans, R. (1994, January 15). Gangs, guns, and school violence. *USA Today*, p. A7.

Stephens, R. D. (1994). *Coping with school violence: How to turn schools into safe havens for children.* Westlake, CA: National School Safety Center.

Stephens, R. D. (1997). National trends in school violence: Statistics and prevention strategies. In A. P. Goldstein & J. C. Conoley (Eds.), *School violence intervention: A practical handbook* (pp. 72–90). New York: Guilford Press.

Stomfay-Stitz, A. M. (1994). Conflict resolution and peer mediation: Pathways to safer schools. *Childhood Education, 70,* 279–282.

Trump, K. S. (1997). Security policy, personnel, and operations. In A. P. Goldstein & J. C. Conoley (Eds.), *School violence intervention: A practical handbook* (pp. 265–289). New York: Guilford Press.

Wason-Ellam, L. (1997). Video games: Playing on a violent playground. In J. R. Epp & A. M. Watkinson (Eds.), *Systemic violence in education: Promise broken* (pp. 72–93). Albany: State University of New York Press.

Watson, R., Poda, J., Miller, C., Rice, E., & West, G. (1990). *Containing crisis: A guide to managing school emergencies.* Bloomington, IN: National Education Service.

Weeks, J. D. (1992). *Student rights under the Constitution: Selected federal decisions affecting the public school community.* Athens, GA: Carl Vinson Institute of Government.

Winter, S. M. (1994). Diversity: A program for all children. *Childhood Education, 70,* 91–95.

2 | Psychocultural Profiles of Violent Students: Prevention and Intervention Strategies

Daya Singh Sandhu, Joe Ray Underwood, and Varrinder Singh Sandhu

In recent years, violence in American schools has "become a national public health problem of epidemic proportion" (Flannery, 1997, p. 20). *Youth* and *violence* seem inextricably linked (Eron, Gentry, & Schlegel, 1994). Stephens (1994) believed there were two types of schools in the United States: those that just had a crisis and those that were about to have one. It is estimated that on a daily basis, approximately 100,000 children are assaulted, 5,000 teachers are threatened, and 200 teachers are actually attacked in American schools (Geiger, 1993). Contrary to popular belief, many youth crimes occur in schools and on school grounds (Jenkins, 1997).

About 1.6 million children are generally exposed to physical, emotional, and sexual abuse every year in the United States. Also, more than 1,000 deaths are attributed to these abuses and substantial neglect (Appelbaum, 1999). Violence against children remains a considerable problem. Most of the offenders and violent children were raised in broken homes and disrupted families that are marred by constant family quarreling, domestic abuse, inadequate parenting, erratic punishment, and little parental affection (Flannery, 1997). Neglect, isolation, and physical, verbal, and emotional abuse loom large in such families. If a parent is violent, the trust and attachment between parent and child may be severely strained (Katsikas, Petretic-Jackson, & Knowles, 1996). Children in such families often do not experience the warmth, affection, and caring from their parents that are associated with healthy parent–child relations (Stone, 1995).

Single parenting is another problem that deserves some attention. For example, when a father is missing from home, a young man becomes the *man* of the house. Thus a role reversal takes place in which an immature young man becomes the protector, and the mother and other siblings become the needy. This pattern is quite common in the lives of adolescents who become violent (Garbarino, 1999). Gorski and Pilotto (1993) reported that when compared with children living with both parents, children raised in single-parent homes exhibit higher levels of antisocial, violent behaviors as well as aggression.

There seems to be some truth in the adage, *There are no problem children, only problem parents.* Whereas effective parenting enables parents to encourage and facilitate the development of healthy, well-adjusted children who are prepared to deal with the vicissitudes of life, children raised by problem parents become alienated, frustrated, confused, and violent. There are no emotional ties of love that may anchor these children to any authority figure who may provide them with hope, encouragement, support, and guidance.

In addition to the home environment, there are several major factors that contribute to school violence in America, such as school environments (Watkinson, 1997), negative peer relations (Voydanoff & Donnelly, 1999), gangs (Huff & Trump, 1996), and television (Danish & Donohue, 1996). Also, easy availability of guns (Garbarino, 1999) and alcohol and substance abuse (Doweiko, 1999) exacerbate youth violence. However, this chapter limits its discussion to personality characteristics of violent youths and therapeutic interventions that counselors may use for prevention and treatment.

CHARACTERISTICS OF VIOLENT YOUTHS

Internalizations, Internal Identity, and Violent Worldviews

Isajiw (1990) proposed the concept of subjective identity. This concept explains the process of identity formation as a subjective phenomenon. The basis of one's worldview is this inner identity. Individuals perceive their relationship to the world around them, including nature, other people, and institutions, according to these worldviews that also affect how people think, behave, feel, and define events (Sue, 1978).

Because of internalized physical and psychological pain, abused children develop *violent internal identities* and *violent worldviews*. Their minds become preoccupied with violent thoughts and fantasies. Memories of past traumatic events relating to abuse or neglect cause children to develop *cruel indifference* toward others and suffer from inner confusions. For this reason, these children become preoccupied with violence. They think, feel, and behave violently.

Externally, violent adolescents may appear intact and psychologically sound, but internally they suffer from impaired ego development, dependency needs, and displaced anger (Malmquist, 1990). Thus, it is not uncommon for acquaintances to express their surprise, "We never thought this person could commit such a heinous crime." Framo (1972) suggested that internalized experiences become subidentities and an integral part of the personality. We propose that it is the subidentity of violent persons that remains unchallenged, enabling violent people to elude or escape current therapeutic interventions. For effective interventions, it is important that mental health professionals understand the inner world of these violent youths.

Emotional Characteristics

Perception of Genuine Love
To explain what we mean by genuine love, we chose the attachment theory that conceptualizes "the propensity of human beings to make strong affectional bonds to particular others" (Bowlby, 1977, p. 201). It is the quality of early relationships to the attachment figure that becomes the source of security (Ainsworth, Blehar, Waters, & Wall, 1978), trust, and intimacy. Infants and children internalize experiences with their parents or guardians, which later become *prototypes* for future relationships with others.

On the basis of Bartholomew and Horowitz's (1991) four-category model of attachment styles, Sandhu and Sandhu (1999) developed a typology of four kinds of violent behaviors (see Table 2.1). This classification may be useful to determine if a person is predisposed to violence or not. In summary, there are four types of persons who may engage in different types of violent behaviors.

Pent-Up Anger
Pent-up anger that is due to parental abuse and neglect is the major and integral component of violent youths' internal identity. Perhaps this anger could be best explained in Gorkin's (1997) four I's: injustice, injury, invasion, and intention. The violent persons feel that they are the victims of unfairness, their feelings are injured through disrespect and insult, their privacy is invaded, and they intend to take revenge.

We propose that the frozen, pent-up anger is expressed in three major ways. Some persons express it inwardly and become depressed ("suicidals"); some express it outwardly and become violent ("homicidals"); still others express it both ways, inwardly and outwardly, and thus become "depressed-violents." In summary, suicidal persons kill themselves, homicidal persons kill others, but depressed-violents are the most dangerous, having their own lives on the sleeves to kill as many others as they can. Mark O. Barton's words sum up their sentiments when this chemist and day trader went on a rampage in Atlanta, Georgia to kill his wife, two children, and nine other people: "I don't plan to live very much

Table 2.1 | Nature of Affectional Bonds and Types of Violent Behaviors

Types of Affectional Bonds	Nature of Relationships	Views of Self and Others	Nature of Violent Behaviors
Secure	Comfortable with intimacy and autonomy	Positive views of the self and others	Generally nonviolent (Nonviolents)
Preoccupied	Preoccupied with relationships	Negative view of the self and positive view of others	Violence against self (Suicidals)
Fearful–avoidant	Fearful of intimacy and socially avoidant	Negative views of the self and negative views of others	Violent against self and violent against others (Depressed-violents)
Dismissing avoidant	Dismissing of intimacy, counter-dependent	Positive views of the self and negative views of others	Violence against others (Homicidals)

From "Attachment Styles Among Youth Adults: A Test of A Four-Category Model," by K. Bartholomew and L. M. Horowitz, 1991, *Journal of Personality and Social Psychology, 61,* p. 227. Copyright 1991 by the American Psychological Association. Adapted with permission.

longer, just long enough to kill as many of the people that greedily sought my destruction" (Sack, 1999, p. A1).

Unfortunately, because of the lack of genuine parental love—as perceived by some modern youths—both homicides and suicides have skyrocketed. Each murder committed by a youth is matched with a suicide, approximately 2,300 each year (Garbarino, 1999). In many cases, the depressed-violents who kill others also beg for their own death. Some youths perceive their lives to be so empty and devoid of love that they prefer placid death to painful life. The spontaneously spoken words of Kip Kinkel upon arrest in Springfield, Oregon, "Kill me! Kill me," echo a plea for his own death. Mark O. Barton's letter ended with a similar request, *"You should kill me if you can"* (Sack, 1999, p. A1).

Sadness and Depression
Violent youths may suffer from sadness to severe depression. Their depression is an anger expressed inward toward the self. Mostly, this depression is attributed to the "protracted history of helplessness and exposure to parental figures with diminished positive affective display and interaction" (Kashani & Allan, 1998, p. 25). Psychologically, these

children are crushed to the degree that their lives are full of hopelessness and helplessness. The tragic experiences of their child abuse and neglect evoke pathos and despair.

Emotional Frustrations

The inner lives of abused children and adolescents are dull, dry, and devoid of affection. There are few hopes and dreams; however, there are many hostilities and nightmares. They harbor strong feelings of rejection and injustices. Because their childhood innocence is lost and they are hypersensitive, even their peers' jokes become emotional frustrations and teasing pains. Michael Carneal from Paducah, Kentucky, complained about his classmates teasing him. Luke Woodham of Pearl, Mississippi, lamented, "My whole life I felt outcasted, alone" (A. Rogers, Wingert, & Hayden, 1999, p. 35). There are undeniable decrements of emotional adjustments in these adolescents' lives.

Lack of Empathy

Empathy entails that a person will sense others' feelings *as if* they were her or his own. Empathic individuals can move freely in the inner world of others and sense a deep and subjective understanding of this world without getting lost in it (C. Rogers, 1961). Because empathic people can easily understand others' viewpoints, they are generally more tolerant and become less angry with others' behaviors. Empathic persons also tend to inhibit their aggressive behaviors as they can easily sense pain and distress that these behaviors can cause others (Beland, 1996). Violent youths tend to have a lower level of empathic understanding of others' pains. These children and adolescents lack emotional intelligence—the ability to read emotions in others (Goleman, 1997). They are generally either apathic or antipathic, but not empathic or sympathic.

Callousness

Because these youngsters have not experienced genuine love, violent youths grow up unable to share love with others. Physical cruelty to people and animals does not bother them. On the contrary, they are thrilled by committing heinous acts. Destroying property, setting fires, and stealing from others seem to provide personal satisfaction and enhance self-esteem among their peers who are also engaged in similar criminal activities (Flannery, 1997). Senseless killings become a vehicle to release their built-up anger with a relentless fury. They do not feel guilty or remorseful when they hurt others. Instead, they derive a great satisfaction, as if their mission has been accomplished. Violent youths are emotionally numbed. They have no compassion for others, as they are desensitized by their own deep buried pain and hate hidden in their hearts. For instance, in the Oregon school shootings, Kip Kinkel was deadly calm when he shot his schoolmates, some point-blank. He was so callous that "he put his foot on the back of one kid and shot him four times," said David Willis, a 15-year-old witness (Tims & Meehan, 1998, p. 3).

Social Characteristics

Loners
Violent youths and adolescents are generally alienated and detached. As a result of abuse and neglect, they mistrust others. Erikson (1968) defined *trust* as an "essential trustfulness of others as well as a fundamental sense of one's trustworthiness" (p. 96). Because an abusive parent is rejecting, she or he becomes the source of frustration. This frustration leads to a sense of mistrust that persists throughout the abused child's entire life. Because of weak emotional attachment to parents, these adolescents never learn to develop strong social and emotional ties with others. Mostly, they remain loners, emotionally isolated and emotionally abandoned. Their relationships with others are generally superficial, selfish, and manipulative. On the other side, most people want to distance themselves from this already alienated youth, who is perceived as a troublemaker. This further exacerbates the isolation, and the youth is caught in a never-ending, vicious cycle of rejection.

We propose three types of human relationships. A *primary* relationship is a basic relationship with one's parents, especially the mother. *Secondary* relationships are with other significant others, such as siblings, friends, relatives, and teachers. *Tertiary* relationships are with objects of comfort, pleasure, and power. Unable to make closer or sincere relationships with the first two types, the troubled adolescents make relatively stronger relationships with the third type, such as guns, gangs, alcohol, and drugs.

Belongingness to an Oppositional Culture
This subculture shares similar characteristics with the oppositional culture described by Anderson (1994) and Bourgois (1995). Although oppositional cultures emerge because of violation of a sense of fairness by external controls such as laws and the police (Taylor, 1990), we believe that the subculture of youth violence arose, in part, because of parental neglect, abuse, and other perceptions of unfair treatment. In summary, violence is an effort to achieve retribution, retaliation, restitution, or compensation for perceived wrongs (Tedeschi & Felson, 1994).

A Matter of Honor and Dignity
As gang members, violent youths belong to a subculture with its own special rules for living. Several honor-related qualities such as "machismo, self-esteem, status, power, heart, 'rep'" (Goldstein, 1991, p. 37) are valued and considered of great importance. Because these children have lost their

dignity through abuse, rejection, and neglect, they try to regain it by asserting themselves through hard-core violence.

Power-Seeking Strategies
Personal and social variables determine people's preference for power-gaining strategies while managing conflict situations (Schwarzwald & Koslowsky, 1999). Falbo (1977) identified two kinds of power tactics. One is compromise, persuasion, and bargaining, which are considered rational means. The other is deceit, evasion, and threats, which are viewed as nonrational ways to handle social disputes. With pent-up anger and having antisocial feelings, violent children and adolescents use power tactics that are generally nonrational. To solve problems in their own favor, the alienated youths become highly manipulative and aggressive and may violate all social and legal rules. Aggression by alienated youths is a means to transform their sense of insignificance into a striking power (Flannery, 1997). These children or adolescents may resort to any type of heinous act of carnage and cruelty to have their way. In Littleton, Colorado, Eric Harris and Dylan Klebold decided who may live and who must die. They even asked students if they believed in God. When a female student said "yes," they shot her to death. Perhaps it was to prove that with guns in their hands, they were mightier than God.

Moral and Spiritual Characteristics

Lack of Moral Conscience
Stilwell, Galvin, Kopta, and Padgett (1996) described conscience as the core of personality. In the moral realm, it is with the rules of conscience that a child justifies compliance or noncompliance of various behaviors. Generally, these rules of conscience are authority-derived, peer-derived, or self-derived (Stilwell et al., 1996). Unfortunately, because of ineffective parenting skills, violent children do not derive their moral conscience from their parents. Because of neglect, abuse, and lack of genuine love, either the conscience never develops or it is seriously impaired. Most violent youths lack moral conscience and are easily drawn to the dark side of life, including crime, and other socially prohibited behaviors, such as Satanism and nihilism (Garbarino, 1999).

Spiritual Emptiness: Youth With Murdered Souls
Child abuse, neglect, or the perception of deprived or denied love is responsible for the spiritual emptiness of violent adolescents. Shengold (1989) presented a sad spectacle in an abused child's own words,

> My father beat us so badly he broke bones; my mother put lye in my half-wit brother's oat meal, my mother kept the bedroom door open when she

brought men home . . . love and empathy are never or only intermittently present—cold indifference or destructive hatred reigns. (p. 14)

The terrifying helplessness and rage imposed on young children through parental emotional and physical violence and mental torture cause conditions that Bradshaw (1992) called "a wounded inner child" or a " hurt soul." There is so much internal devastation done to catastrophically abused children that their psyche is terribly mutilated. It seems that their ego is deeply wounded and their soul is departed forever. Shengold (1989) defined the devastation of extreme child abuse as a *soul murder.* Unfortunately, "there are such individuals in our midst, although most of them seem to end up in prisons or mental institutions. Some are violent boys. In such boys, the soul is buried deep under layers of violence and distorted thoughts and emotions" (Garbarino, 1999, p. 35). Miranti and Burke (1998) asserted that "spiritual tendency moves the individual toward knowledge, love, meaning, hope, transcendence, connectedness, compassion, wellness, and wholeness" (p. 162). Exactly the same traits and qualities are missing in violent children. When others might have existential questions about the deeper meaning or purpose of life, the violent children, devoid of spiritual anchors, are preoccupied with their daily survival. They have lost the zest of life and experience degradation of the human spirit.

Cognitive Characteristics

Cognitive Development
Violent children generally have average or above-average intelligence. Some even surpass their peers as genius. Rarely are any of these violent students or young killers mentally retarded (Ewing, 1990). However, they are mostly underachievers, performing poorly in academics and experiencing severe educational difficulties (Bailey, 1994; Myers & Scott, 1998). This is not because they are not intelligent enough, but because they are not motivated to learn and do not actively participate in academic activities.

Good and Brophy (1995) described alienated students as reluctant learners who reject the school and all its activities. Some of them are openly hostile and defiant and create disruptions. Typically, teachers and their peers either are indifferent toward them or reject them. These students are potential dropouts.

Paranoid Thinking
The victims of physical, verbal, emotional, or sexual abuse become more cautious, hypervigilant, and hypersensitive because of psychological trauma inflicted on them. They develop paranoid thinking. If they can't trust their own parents and guardians, naturally they can't trust strangers and their intentions.

Negative Thinking

Violent adolescents generalize their anger to all their activities. They may be geniuses and very creative, but they use their intelligence and talents to carry out destructive activities. Their creativity is a negative creativity. For instance, they are able to understand complicated guidelines to make bombs, find ways to defraud others, and play treachery. Their values, priorities, and motivations are generally deviant and abnormal. Whereas others seek fame, the alienated seek notoriety. Violent children and adolescents are fearless and are not much concerned about shame and self-respect.

Low Frustration Tolerance

Violent students tend to believe that they cannot stand discomfort or frustration. Because of pent-up anger, lack of patience, and inappropriate skills to handle stress, these students resort to violence to handle difficult situations. These students fit the profile of those who suffer from discomfort, anxiety, and depression, a psychological syndrome that Ellis, McInerney, DiGiuseppe, and Yeager (1988) described as *low frustration tolerance*.

Irrational Rationality

All human behavior is adaptive to context (Framo, 1972). From the perspectives of the violent youths, their behavior is purposeful, meaningful, and logical. However, the problem is that their outlook is irrational from a social perspective. For example, Mark O. Barton's rationale for killing his own children is clearly irrational:

> I killed the children to exchange for them five minutes of pain for a lifetime of pain. I forced myself to do it to keep them from suffering so much later. No mother, no father, no relatives. The fears of the father are transferred to the son. It was from my father to me and from me to my son. I had to take him with me. (Sack, 1999, p. A4)

Behavioral Characteristics

Alcohol and Substance Abuse

To soothe the pain of loneliness, neglect, and emptiness, abused and neglected adolescents are subject to violence, and they abuse drugs and alcohol to a much greater degree than other adolescents. Several studies (Clark & Sayette, 1993; Davidson & Ritson, 1993; Helzer, Burnam, & McEvoy, 1991) have reported findings that confirm a positive correlation between substance abuse and negative affect. This negative affect includes feelings such as anger, anxiety, and alienation.

Involvement in Risky Behaviors

Risk taking is a central task for adolescents (Tonkin, 1987). In fact, parents become seriously concerned if their children are too inhibited to take risks

(Kagen, 1991). But the violent youths' involvement in risky behaviors is extreme. Such risky behaviors include aggression and violence, juvenile delinquency, risky sexual behaviors, and consumption of alcohol and drugs. These adolescents may also engage in bullying behaviors and use guns, knives, and other dangerous weapons.

Defiance, Delinquency, Destruction, and Death

Delinquency and defiance are the hallmarks of antisocial adolescents. From simple defiance of authority (parents, teachers, etc.) to destruction of property and other valuable things, to fighting and hurting others, there seems to be a stage-by-stage progression of violent expression in these adolescents. In this sense, violence can be equated to alcoholism and other addictions. *Desensitization* in violence is similar to tolerance in addictions. Infliction of violence is also an expression of power. Delinquents enjoy both addiction and power.

Aggressive youths start exhibiting their delinquent behaviors when they enter elementary school. By the time a student is 8 years old, it is possible to predict the extent of his or her behavior as an adolescent or even as an adult (Eron, Huesmann, Dubow, Romanoff, & Yarmel, 1987; McCord, 1994). During the junior high years, the aggressive and disruptive behaviors increase (Barr & Parrett, 1995; Moffit, 1993). Delinquent behaviors that start with simple defiance may become precursors of serious crimes such as assault or homicide.

THERAPEUTIC INTERVENTION STRATEGIES

The factors that predispose someone to become violent are multidimensional. For this reason, we believe that violence can only be prevented through multidimensional approaches. We propose that the previously developed Multidimensional Model for Prejudice Prevention and Reduction by Sandhu and Aspy (1997) can be adapted to combat violence in schools. The basic premise of this adapted model is that violence is perpetrated, maintained, and perpetuated by a combination of five major factors: (a) individual personality variables, (b) parental practices, (c) peer relationships, (d) educational practices, and (e) social environment. A caring environment, positive expectations, involvement, and a sense of responsibility are the major protective factors needed for violence prevention and intervention.

Counseling or Therapeutic Goals

In the context of a given situation and certain circumstances, a counselor might have some specific goals to help the violent students. In general, the following four major counseling or therapeutic goals are proposed. The first two goals, *catharsis and anger management*, are suggested for immediate intervention. The *enhancement of resiliency* and *empowerment* are proposed as long-term goals.

Emotional Healing Through Catharsis

Catharsis is considered a major factor in emotional or psychological healing (Corsini & Wedding, 1995). In the case of abused and neglected children—who carry inside deep anger, hurt, and hopelessness—it is imperative that they are released from the intense pain through some emotional outlets. Otherwise, the need to express overwhelming feelings of anger, frustration, sadness, and sometimes even depression may result in aggressive behavior. It is generally believed that in counseling the energies clients previously used to repress their traumatic experiences or troubling memories now readily become available through catharsis for their use at the conscious level. Moreover, when clients reunite with previously disowned parts of the self, they feel a great sense of relief (Blatner, 1995; Nichols & Efran, 1985). When alienated adolescents believe that their feelings are understood, they internalize the counselor's acceptance. Thus, their fragmented affect becomes an integrated part of the self at the conscious level (Kosmicki & Glickauf-Hughes, 1997), a real source of emotional relief.

Anger Management

The anger that is caused by child abuse and neglect resides in the deep recesses of violent children's mind, making their everyday life a silent misery. This anger has its own unique characteristics. It is a hybrid of many negative feelings such as rage, repentance, remorse, regret, sorrow, and sadness. As described earlier, anger is at the very core of the lives of violent youths because many of their behaviors, priorities, and values emerge from it. As a result of poorly regulated anger, these adolescents may commit delinquent acts of various types, including damaging property or physically hurting others (Colder & Stice, 1998).

It is important that counselors provide professional help for the anger management of violent adolescents. Anger control training is identified as one of the programs that has shown positive influences on behaviors of antisocial adolescents (Feindler & Guttman, 1994; Zillman, 1993). Recognition of anger triggers, calming techniques, and reflections on anger-provoking events and episodes are generally considered effective anger management strategies (Beland, 1996). Nugent, Champlin, and Wiinimaki (1997) suggested additional strategies such as moral reasoning skills, perspective-taking skills, problem-solving skills, and social skills training to help adolescents manage their anger.

Enhancing Resiliency

Resiliency is the ability of a person to overcome adversity through a set of personal attributes an individual possesses that may help him or her face overwhelming obstacles in life (Barbarin, 1993). Sagor (1996) identified feelings of belonging, feelings of competence, optimism, potency, and usefulness as the characteristics of resilient people. Not only do these resilient people survive, but they also prevail.

Several *protective factors* emerged from resilience research that can be used as immediate or long-term goals for counseling and psychotherapeutic goals. Noonan (1999) identified these factors as high expectations, caring and support, clear and consistent boundaries, life skills training, prosocial bonding, and opportunities for meaningful participation. It is important to note that resilient factors not only are personal characteristics of a child (Garmezy, 1991) but also relate to social contexts where a child develops. Mental health professionals must examine both personal and social characteristics to enhance resiliency of troubled youths.

Using Counseling, Consulting, and Psychotherapy for Empowerment

To modify behaviors of violent adolescents, empowerment has to be considered at two levels: at the personal level and at the social level. At the personal level, empowerment grants a person the ability to direct his or her own life (Aspy & Sandhu, 1999; Stone, 1995). At the social level, empowerment means improvising new social changes and personal capabilities through which people can influence the organizations and institutions in which they live (Dunst, Trivette, & Deal, 1988). To bring about lasting and meaningful changes, it is imperative that changes are made in the self and the system.

To modify destructive behaviors of violent students, counselors must consider changes in the school operating system, such as school policies, discipline, safety procedures, and extracurricular activities, as well as changes in the violent youths' behaviors. In addition to the above discussed goals, it is important that counselors improvise long-term, continuous, and comprehensive goals to effectively change the attitudes of violent youths. Fried and Fried's (1996) program, SCRAPES, is an example of such a model program. Each letter in the acronym stands for a different goal: S = self-esteem and social skills enrichment; C = conflict resolution and mediation skills; R = respect for differences, deprejudicing exercises; A = anger management and assertiveness training; P = problem-solving skills; E = empathy training; and S = sexuality awareness training (p. 159).

The Counselor's Role

Because the problems of violent adolescents are multifaceted, counselors need to focus on various aspects of these adolescents' characters. As discussed earlier, these include their emotional, social, moral, spiritual, and cognitive characteristics. A counselor must make a composite assessment of violent adolescent functioning. The working relationship with the adolescent client is of paramount importance. Counselors should be encouraged to work on these adolescents' pent-up anger, guilt, hostility, and hurts.

While counselors may be active, directive, and didactic, they should also provide comfort and encouragement to heal the wounds of the past. Adolescents in difficulty may manage to put up a facade, but in reality, they have been victimized in the past and now they are in pain. Garbarino (1999) portrayed their plight as follows:

> Some of these boys appear to be tough on the outside. But when I get a glimpse of their inner life, I am deeply touched by their vulnerability and their pain, and I come to see their toughness as a survival strategy, as something that helps them get through another day. In many ways their cold exterior is a defense against overwhelming emotions inside. (p. 22)

Building Therapeutic Relationships

As a caveat, violent adolescents are difficult clients who come to counseling involuntarily and resent counselors for their intrusion. They have little or no motivation to change. They tend to externalize their problems and place blame on others. Normally, they enter counseling or therapy by court orders, angry parents, or school disciplinary referrals (Lennings, 1996).

When dealing with traumatic experiences of the past, abused children become extremely sensitive, angry, and discouraged. Counselors working with this group of clients should be mentally prepared to accept frustrations, failures, and impediments in the counseling process. In addition to C. Rogers's (1961) three necessary conditions of empathy, unconditional positive regard, and genuineness, mental health professionals must have patience, persistence, and perseverance to work with this group and their unique counseling needs.

COUNSELING AND CONSULTING TECHNIQUES

We propose that integrative counseling is a better choice of treatment for violent children and adolescents. Integrative counseling or psychotherapy is characterized by attempts to look beyond and across the confines of single-school approaches in order to see what can be learned from—and how clients can benefit from—other perspectives (Arkowitz, 1992). As space limitations preclude a lengthy discussion, the following concepts, strategies, and techniques are gleaned from different theories of counseling and psychotherapy for demonstration purposes. These desultory strategies to work with the potential violent adolescents are suggestive, rather than an exhaustive, treatment.

Counselors may use any theory or their favorite orientation in which they feel comfortable, competent, and effective. However, we concur with McWhirter, McWhirter, McWhirter, and McWhirter (1998) that Glasser's *reality therapy* is one of the most promising theories of counseling and psychotherapy to deter delinquency and to understand the psychodynamics of violent adolescents. Because this therapy was developed from first-hand experiences with delinquent adolescent girls having similar characteristics as alienated students, it received significant acceptance in school systems. It became even more popular after Glasser's classic book, *Schools Without Failure*, was published in 1969.

Glasser's Reality Therapy

Most recently, Glasser advanced the control theory that forms the basis of this chapter. Glasser (1999) postulated that human behavior originates from within the individual and is always purposeful. Of course, environmental factors influence a person's decisions, but they do not cause his or her behaviors. Internally motivated behaviors are meant to satisfy one or more of the five innate drives: belonging, power, freedom, fun, or physical survival. Glasser also attributed youth violence to poor parent–child and teacher–student relationships.

Glasser's (1965) reality therapy proposed two basic psychological needs of humans as "the need to love and to be loved and the need to feel that we are worthwhile to ourselves and to others" (p. 9). According to reality therapy, people develop a failure identity when either of these two needs is not met. The two major concepts of *love* and *responsibility* are the cornerstone of a person's identity formation.

It is our view that the lack of genuine love and responsibility (or perception of their absence) causes people to become violent. They develop an inner identity that has unique characteristics. Because of different worldviews, behaviors, and priorities of violent persons to meet their five basic drives—belonging, power, freedom, fun, and physical survival—they create a subculture of their own. Generally, this subculture is a culture of violence with special rules for living required of its members. For instance, frustrating experiences and difficult problems are solved with force without considering any other available alternatives. Violence is generally viewed as an appropriate response and serves as a norm of behavior. The members who do not follow the norms are criticized, ridiculed, expelled, or even hurt.

Rational Emotive Behavioral Therapy

From the perspective of rational emotive behavioral therapy of Albert Ellis (1994), irrational beliefs are a major cause of people's disturbance.

The violent behaviors of adolescents can be attributed to five major irrational beliefs. The first is *demandingness* and can be described as a constellation of "musts." Violent adolescents demand that everything must be the way they want it. They get angry or violent when others become obstacles in their way.

The second, *awfulizing*, is a process whereby events are not just bad, they are awful or catastrophic. Because these violent children and adolescents have experienced traumas previously, they are generally ultrasensitive and hypervigilant. They also have apathic or antipathic attitudes toward others and events. They do not get involved and lack motivation. Any challenges of life are awfulizing to them.

Third, *low frustration tolerance* suggests that one cannot stand it when things do not go his or her way. Again, violent adolescents have less stamina to face the vicissitudes of life. They become easily irritated and frustrated. They also lose their temper over matters of minor conflicts and are ready to fight over small differences. These violence-prone adolescents are unable to face stressful events calmly. Stress aggravates their violent feelings and behaviors.

Fourth, *global rating of self and others* is a set of beliefs that assumes a stance of all-or-none thinking. A violent adolescent may develop an irrational belief, "Nobody likes me." This type of thinking makes the adolescent experience feelings of anger, rejection, and dejection.

Fifth, *self-damnation* suggests that "I am a worthless person; I am good for nothing." Violent children constantly ruminate negative thoughts about themselves. Their inner or self-talk keeps reminding themselves, "I am a worthless slob. I have no future. I can't do any thing right." While growing up, they have heard such messages from significant others repeatedly. Now they are convinced about their worthlessness.

The major goal for the counselor or therapist is "minimizing the client's central defeating cognitions" and helping him or her develop "a more realistic, tolerant philosophy of life" (Ellis, 1994, p. 177). They actively dispute clients' irrational beliefs. They may ask clients, "Where is the evidence for your beliefs? Where is it written . . .?" One of the most important techniques of rational emotive behavior therapy is cognitive restructuring and behavioral rehearsal. These techniques can be applied to reframe violent adolescents' attitudes, attributions, values, and expectations concerning aggression and to focus on actual practice in learning how to choose alternative behaviors to avoid violence (Garbarino, 1999).

Gestalt Therapy

One of the key concepts of Perls's (1969) gestalt therapy, unfinished business, focuses on several unexpressed feelings, such as abandonment, anxiety, grief, hatred, pain, rage, and resentment. Most of these feelings become the very core or essence of the internal identity of violent students. It is important that counselors use some techniques of gestalt therapy, such as the empty-chair technique, the rehearsal technique, and playing the projection. The main objective of gestalt therapy is for the client to "gain fuller awareness, experience internal conflicts, resolve inconsistencies and dichotomies, and work through an impasse that is preventing completion of unfinished business" (Corey, 1996, p. 241).

Consulting Strategies

To reduce violence, counselors must involve parents, teachers, administrators, other mental health professionals, and community leaders. To make violence prevention and intervention a success, it has to be a joint collaborative effort. Because violence in schools has become a societal scourge, counselors must adopt a new role of *social change agents*. In this new role of advocacy, school counselors should serve as consultants to help teachers *build a community of learners* in schools. In such a community of learners, teachers and students develop empathic relationships. They listen to one another carefully, share information, explore likes and dislikes, and appreciate strengths and mutual interests (Striepling, 1997).

With multiple challenges and a very high student–counselor ratio, the development of peer helping programs in schools is a necessity. Peer helping programs are designed on developmental principles (Foster-Harrison, 1995) and have an important role to play in violence prevention and intervention. To curb the violence resulting from relationships, bias-related incidents, and other forms of prejudice, counselors can play a pivotal role in implementing peer meditation and conflict resolution training programs in their schools (Simpson, 1998). Johnson (1997) recommended skills-oriented conflict resolution programs in which students are taught small-group and interpersonal skills necessary to resolve conflicts constructively.

Students prone to violence not only should be taught communication skills and problem-solving techniques but also need to practice decision-making skills. Their higher order skills such as critical thinking, empathy, awareness, and management of conflicts must be enhanced (Shulman, 1996).

CONCLUSION

Eron et al. (1994) have an encouraging message for counselors and other mental health professionals. They maintain that violence is not uncontrollable, inevitable, or unrandom. It is something that is learned that can also be unlearned. However, the conditions and causes that lead to violent behaviors, such as homicide, suicide, or both, are multifaceted and interactive. For this reason, they must be confronted at multifarious levels (Heide, 1999). We strongly believe that to curtail school violence, counselors must apply multifocal approaches that involve both microlevel and macrolevel strategies.

REFERENCES

Ainsworth, M. D. S., Blehar, M. C., Waters, E., & Wall, S. (1978). *Patterns of attachment: A psychological study of the Strange Situation.* Hillsdale, NJ: Erlbaum.

Anderson, E. (1994, May). Code of the streets. *The Atlantic Monthly,* pp. 81–94.

Appelbaum, P. S. (1999). Law and psychiatry: Child abuse reporting laws: Time for reform? *Psychiatric Services, 50*(1), 27–29.

Arkowitz, H. (1992). Integrative theories of therapy. In D. K. Freedheim (Ed.), *History of psychotherapy: A century of change* (pp. 261–303). Washington, DC: American Psychological Association.

Aspy, C. B., & Sandhu, D. S. (1999). *Empowering women for equity: A counseling approach.* Alexandria, VA: American Counseling Association.

Bailey, S. (1994). Critical pathways of child and adolescent murders. *Chronicle, International Association of Juvenile and Family Court Magistrates, 1*(3), 5–12.

Barbarin, O. A. (1993). Coping and resilience: Exploring the inner lives of African American children. *Journal of Black Psychology, 19,* 478–492.

Barr, R. D., & Parrett, W. (1995). *Hope at last for at risk youth.* Boston: Allyn & Bacon.

Bartholomew, K., & Horowitz, L. M. (1991). Attachment styles among youth adults: A test of a four-category model. *Journal of Personality and Social Psychology, 61,* 226–244.

Beland, K. R. (1996). A school wide approach to violence prevention. In R. L. Hampton, P. Jenkins, & T. P. Gullotta (Eds.), *Preventing violence in America* (pp. 209–231). Thousand Oaks, CA: Sage.

Blatner, A. (1995). The dynamics of catharsis. *Journal of Group Psychotherapy, Psychodrama, and Sociometry, 37,* 157–166.

Bourgois, P. (1995). *In search of respect: Selling crack in El Barrio.* New York: Cambridge University Press.

Bowlby, J. (1977). The making and breaking of affectional bonds. *British Journal of Psychiatry, 130,* 201–210.

Bradshaw, J. E. (1992). *Homecoming: Reclaiming and championing your inner child.* New York: Bantam Books.

Clark, D. B., & Sayette, M. A. (1993). Anxiety and the development of alcoholism: Clinical and scientific issues. *American Journal on Addictions, 2,* 59–76.

Colder, C. R., & Stice, E. (1998). A longitudinal study of the interactive effects of impulsivity and anger on adolescent problem behavior. *Journal of Youth and Adolescence, 27,* 255–274.

Corey, G. (1996). *Theory and practice of counseling and psychotherapy* (5th ed.). Pacific Grove, CA: Brooks/Cole.

Corsini, R. J., & Wedding, D. (1995). *Current psychotherapies* (5th ed.). Itasca, IL: Peacock.

Danish, S. J., & Donohue, T. R. (1996). Understanding the media's influence on the development of antisocial and prosocial behavior. In R. L. Hampton, P. Jenkins, & T. P. Gullotta (Eds.), *Preventing violence in America* (pp. 133–155). Thousand Oaks, CA: Sage.

Davidson, K. M., & Ritson, E. B. (1993). The relationship between alcohol dependence and depression. *Alcohol and Alcoholism, 28,* 147–155.

Doweiko, H. E. (1999). *Concepts of chemical dependency* (4th ed.). Pacific Grove, CA: Brooks/Cole.

Dunst, C. J., Trivette, C. M., & Deal, A. G. (1988). *Enabling and empowering families: Principles and guidelines for practice.* Cambridge, MA: Brookline Books.

Ellis, A. (1994). *Reason and emotion in psychotherapy: A comprehensive method of treating human disturbances* (Rev. ed.). New York: Carol Publishing Group.

Ellis, A., McInerney, J. F., DiGiuseppe, R., & Yeager, R. J. (1988). *Rational-emotive therapy with alcoholics and substance abusers.* Boston: Allyn & Bacon.

Erikson, E. H. (1968). *Identity, youth, and crisis.* New York: Norton.

Eron, L. D., Gentry, J. H., & Schlegel, P. (Eds.). (1994). *Reason to hope: A psychosocial perspective on violence and youth.* Washington, DC: American Psychological Association.

Eron, L. D., Huesmann, L. R., Dubow, E., Romanoff, R., & Yarmel, P. W. (1987). Aggression and its correlates over 22 years. In D. Crowell, E. Evans, & C. O'Donnell (Eds.), *Aggression and violence: Sources of influence, prevention, and control* (pp. 249–262). New York: Plenum.

Ewing, C. P. (1990). *When children kill.* Lexington, MA: Lexington Books.

Falbo, T. (1977). The multidimensional scaling of power strategies. *Journal of Personality and Social Psychology, 35,* 537–548.

Feindler, E., & Guttman, J. (1994). Cognitive–behavioral anger control training. In C. Leroy (Ed.), *Handbook of child and adolescent treatment manuals* (pp. 170–199). New York: Lexington Books.

Flannery, R. B., Jr. (1997). *Violence in America: Coping with drugs, distressed families, inadequate schooling and acts of hate.* New York: Continuum.

Foster-Harrison, E. S. (1995). Peer helping in the elementary and middle grades: A developmental perspective. *Elementary School Guidance and Counseling, 30,* 94–104.

Framo, J. (1972). Symptoms from a family transactional viewpoint. In C. J. Sager & H. S. Kaplan (Eds.), *Progress in group and family therapy* (pp. 271–308). New York: Brunner/Mazel.

Fried, S., & Fried, P. (1996). *Bullies and victims: Helping your child survive the schoolyard battlefield.* New York: Evans.

Garbarino, J. (1999). *Lost boys: Why our sons turn violent and how we can save them.* New York: Free Press.

Garmezy, N. (1991). Resiliency and vulnerability to adverse developmental outcomes associated with poverty. *American Behavioral Scientist, 34,* 416–430.

Geiger, K. (1993, January 14). *Violence in the schools.* Statement presented at a news conference given by the president of the National Education Association, Washington, DC.

Glasser, W. (1965). *Reality therapy.* New York: HarperCollins.

Glasser, W. (1969). *Schools without failure.* New York: Harper & Row.

Glasser, W. (1999). *Choice theory: A new psychology of personal freedom.* New York: Harper Perennial.

Goldstein, A. P. (1991). *Delinquent gangs: A psychological perspective.* Champaign, IL: Research Press.

Goleman, D. (1997). *Emotional intelligence.* New York: Bantam.

Good, T. L., & Brophy, J. E. (1995). *Contemporary educational psychology* (5th ed.). White Plains, NY: Longman.

Gorkin, M. (1997). The four faces of anger. *Treatment Today, 9*(3), 57–58.

Gorski, J. D., & Pilotto, L. (1993). Interpersonal violence among youth: A challenge for school personnel. *Educational Psychology Review, 5,* 35–61.

Heide, K. M. (1999). *Young killers: The challenge of juvenile homicide.* Thousand Oaks, CA: Sage.

Helzer, J. E., Burnam, A., & McEvoy, L. T. (1991). Alcohol abuse and dependence. In L. N. Robins & D. A. Regier (Eds.), *Psychiatric disorders in America* (pp. 81–115). New York: Free Press.

Huff, C. R., & Trump, K. S. (1996). Youth violence and gangs: School safety initiatives in urban and suburban school districts. *Education and Urban Society, 28,* 492–503.

Isajiw, W. W. (1990). Ethnic-identity retention. In R. Breton, W. W. Isajiw, W. E. Kalbach, & J. G. Reitz (Eds.), *Ethnic identity and equality* (pp. 34–91). Toronto, Ontario, Canada: University of Toronto Press.

Jenkins, P. H. (1997). School delinquency and the school social bond. *Journal of Research in Crime and Delinquency, 34,* 337–367.

Johnson, D. W. (1997). *Reaching out: Interpersonal effectiveness and self-actualization* (6th ed.). Englewood Cliffs, NJ: Prentice Hall.

Kagen, J. (1991). Etiologies of adolescents at risk. *Journal of Adolescent Health, 12,* 591–593.

Kashani, J. H., & Allan, W. D. (1998). *The impact of family violence on children and adolescents.* Thousand Oaks, CA: Sage.

Katsikas, S., Petretic-Jackson, P., & Knowles, E. (1996, November). *Long-term sequel of childhood maltreatment: An attachment theory perspective.* Poster session presented at the annual meeting of the Association for the Advancement of Behavior Therapy, New York.

Kosmicki, F. X., & Glickauf-Hughes, C. (1997). Catharsis in psychotherapy. *Psychotherapy, 34,* 154–159.

Lennings, C. J. (1996). Adolescent aggression and imagery: Contributions from object relations and social cognitive theory. *Adolescence, 31*(124), 831–840.

Malmquist, C. P. (1990). Depression in homicidal adolescents. *Bulletin of the American Academy of Psychiatry and the Law, 18*(1), 23–36.

McCord, J. (1994). Aggression in two generations. In L. R. Huesmann (Ed.), *Aggressive behavior: Current perspectives* (pp. 241–254). New York: Plenum.

McWhirter, J. J., McWhirter, B. T., McWhirter, A. M., & McWhirter, E. H. (1998). *At-risk youth: A comprehensive response for counselors, teachers, psychologists and human service professionals* (2nd ed.). Pacific Grove, CA: Brooks/Cole.

Miranti, J. G., & Burke, M. T. (1998). Spirituality as a force for social change. In C. C. Lee & G. R. Walz (Eds.), *Social action: A mandate for counselors* (pp. 161–176). Alexandria, VA: American Counseling Association.

Moffit, T. E. (1993). Adolescence-limited and life-course-persistent antisocial behavior: A developmental taxonomy. *Psychological Review, 100,* 674–701.

Myers, W. C., & Scott, K. (1998). Psychotic and conduct disorder symptoms in murders. *Journal of Homicide Studies, 2,* 160–175.

Nichols, M. P., & Efran, J. S. (1985). Catharsis in psychotherapy: A new perspective. *Psychotherapy, 22*(1), 46–58.

Noonan, C. (1999). Brief interventions foster student resiliency. *Education Digest, 64*(8), 36–39.

Nugent, W. R., Champlin, D., & Wiinimaki, L. (1997). The effects of anger control training on adolescent antisocial behavior. *Research on Social Work Practice, 7,* 446–462.

Perls, F. (1969). *Gestalt therapy verbatim.* Moab, UT: Real People Press.

Rogers, A., Wingert, P., & Hayden, T. (1999, May 3). Why the young kill. *Newsweek,* 32–35.

Rogers, C. (1961). *On becoming a person.* Boston: Houghton Mifflin.

Sack, K. (1999, July 31). Atlanta gunman left chilling letter. *The Courier-Journal,* pp. A1, A4.

Sagor, R. (1996). Building resiliency in students. *Educational Leadership, 54*(1), 38–43.

Sandhu, D. S., & Aspy, C. B. (1997). *Counseling for prejudice prevention and reduction.* Alexandria, VA: American Counseling Association.

Sandhu, D. S., & Sandhu, V. S. (1999). *Nature of affectional bonds and types of violent behaviors: Implications for counseling and psychotherapy.* Unpublished manuscript.

Schwarzwald, J., & Koslowsky, M. (1999). Gender, self-esteem, and focus of interest in the power strategies by adolescents in conflict situations. *Journal of Social Issues, 55*(1), 15–32.

Shengold, L. (1989). *Soul murder: The effects of childhood abuse and deprivation.* New Haven, CT: Yale University Press.

Shulman, H. A. (1996). Using developmental principles in violence prevention. *Elementary Guidance and Counseling, 30,* 170–180.

Simpson, C. (1998). *Coping through conflict resolution and peer mediation.* Center City, MN: Hazelden.

Stephens, R. D. (1994). Planning for safer and better schools: School violence prevention intervention strategies. *School Psychology Review, 23,* 204–216.

Stilwell, B., Galvin, M., Kopta, S., & Padgett, R. (1996). Moral valuation: A third domain of conscience functioning. *Journal of the American Academy of Child/Adolescent Psychiatry, 35,* 230–239.

Stone, S. J. (1995). Empowering teachers, empowering children. *Childhood Education, 71,* 294–295.

Striepling, S. H. (1997). The low aggression classroom: A teacher's view. In A. P. Goldstein & J. C. Conoley (Eds.), *School violence intervention: A practical handbook* (pp. 25–45). New York: Guilford Press.

Sue, D. W. (1978). Eliminating cultural oppression in counseling: Toward a general theory. *Journal of Counseling Psychology, 25,* 419–428.

Taylor, C. S. (1990). *Dangerous society.* East Lansing: Michigan State University Press.

Tedeschi, J., & Felson, R. B. (1994). *Violence, aggression and coercive actions.* Washington, DC: American Psychological Association.

Tims, D., & Meehan, B. T. (1998, May 22). The shooting: Methodical violence leaves 4 dead, 22 hurt. *Today From the Oregonian* [Online]. Available: http://www.oregonlive.com/todaysnews/9805/at052201.html.

Tonkin, R. (1987). Adolescent risk-taking behavior. *Journal of Adolescent Health Care, 8,* 213–220.

Voydanoff, P., & Donnelly, B. W. (1999). Risk and protective factors for psychological adjustment and grades among adolescents. *Journal of Family Issues, 20,* 328–349.

Watkinson, A. M. (1997). Administrative complicity and systematic violence in education. In J. R. Epp & A. M. Watkinson (Eds.), *Systematic violence in education: Promise broken* (pp. 3–24). New York: State University of New York Press.

Zillman, D. (1993). Mental control of angry aggression. In D. Wegner & J. Pennebaker (Eds.), *Handbook of mental control* (pp. 370–392). Englewood Cliffs, NJ: Prentice Hall.

3 | A Social Ecology Approach to Violence in American Schools

Vicki Harris Wyatt

At 8:00 a.m. on a fall morning, an upset and concerned school counselor from a rural school telephoned a professional at a local youth organization. The school counselor needed someone to come to one of her rural high schools to talk with the students and teachers about teen suicide. A 16-year-old girl had attempted suicide the day before. The result was nearly fatal. In fact at the time of the phone call, the teenage girl was still listed in critical condition. The doctors were not yet able to determine the extent of the damage to the young woman's brain, liver, and kidneys. The school counselor reported that this teenage girl had attempted suicide in the past, but no attempts were this serious. Everyone thought she was doing okay.

In this small rural school, the students and teachers were stunned. This popular, high-achieving student, the daughter of a professional in the community, was attractive and funny. Why her? The students, the teachers, the counselor, and the parents all questioned how they missed the warning signs. This young woman survived without serious physical damage. Her cries for help were heard. Not only did the teen need help, so did her siblings, her parents, her teachers, and her fellow students. This individual's problem situation became a community problem. Once the teen had healed physically and was home, the parents and siblings along with the teen began family counseling sessions recommended by the school counselor.

A suicide prevention and crisis intervention specialist presented a 1-day workshop for the students and the teachers to educate them on the warning signs and the myths surrounding suicide. Additional sessions were scheduled to help answer other questions from the students and teachers. One young woman's suicide attempt brought a community together. This event changed the lives of many individuals. This school and community were fortunate to have a school counselor who used her resources to get help for the young woman, her family, and the others in the school and community affected by this tragedy. This story has a happy ending because people at all levels of the situation were committed to examining the situation, making necessary changes, and moving forward.

The purpose of this chapter is to summarize the literature concerning the perspectives of violence to and among youths using a social ecology framework. Often schools are viewed as the change agent in the community, and the school counselor appears to be viewed as the person with solutions to children's problems. However, as the previous scenario demonstrated, there are multiple levels of interaction in a system. To reduce the incidence of violence in schools, multiple levels of factors that influence violence are examined from a social ecology framework.

THEORETICAL PERSPECTIVE
FOR EXAMINING SCHOOL VIOLENCE

Regarded as a major contributor to the advancement of the human ecology perspective, Bronfenbrenner (1979) integrated ideas from ecological theory and Lewin's (1935) field theory to formulate the ideas in his book *The Ecology of Human Development*. The ecological perspective assumes that for most behaviors there are multiple causes that occur at all levels of the individual's social ecology rather than single causes (Small & Kerns, 1993). Bronfenbrenner viewed the individual as embedded in a microsystem of roles and relations, a mesosystem of interrelations between two or more settings, an exosystem of external settings that do not include the individual, and a macrosystem or culture.

The microsystem is "a pattern of activities, roles, and interpersonal relations experienced by the developing person in a given face-to-face setting with particular physical, social, and symbolic features that invite, permit, or inhibit, engagement in sustained, progressively more complex interaction with, and activity in, the immediate environment" (Bronfenbrenner, 1993, p. 15). The mesosystem is defined as "the linkages and process taking place between two or more settings containing the developing person. Special attention is focused on the synergistic effects created by the interaction of developmentally instigative or inhibitory features and processes present in each setting" (Bronfenbrenner, 1993, p. 22). The exosystem is defined as "the linkages and process taking place between two or more settings, at least one of which does not contain the developing person, but in which events occur that indirectly influence processes within the immediate setting in which the developing person lives" (Bronfenbrenner, 1993, p. 22). The macrosystem is defined as "the overarching pattern of micro-, meso-, and exosystems characteristic of a given culture, subculture, or other extended social structure, with particular reference to the developmentally instigative belief systems, resources, hazards, lifestyles, opportunity structures, life course options, and patterns of social interchange that are embedded in such overarching systems" (Bronfenbrenner, 1993, p. 25).

Ecological theory suggests that it is necessary to identify risks and protective processes at several levels of the human ecology, including the individual, family, peer, school, work, and community settings. According to Bronfenbrenner (1993), children are shaped not only by their personal attributes but also by the ever-widening environments in which they develop. Children are influenced first by their family, but also by their peers, school and work settings, and communities. The ecological risk/protective theory contends that human development is shaped by a multitude of processes. These processes exist in multiple levels of human ecology.

Two paradigms have gained prominence for addressing youth issues (Bogenschneider, 1996). The epidemiological risk-focused model used to address prevention of heart and lung disease (Hawkins, Catalano, & Miller, 1992) argues that human development is influenced by multiple risk processes and that reducing or eliminating identified risks will prevent youth problem behaviors (Bronfenbrenner, 1986; Hawkins et al., 1992; Segal, 1983). Bogenschneider (1996) identified the second paradigm as the resiliency or protective process approach, which suggests that conditions can be created to facilitate positive youth development. Numerous children exhibit resilient behaviors and attitudes so the circumstances and characteristics that encourage their health-promoting competence can be studied.

Bogenschneider (1996) proposed the ecological risk/protective theory as a framework for understanding human development and extracted 12 principles from the model to help practitioners build prevention programs, policies, and community capacity around positive youth and family development. The principles outlined by Bogenschneider (1996) are as follows:

1. Identify the real issues or problems facing local youth;
2. Establish well-defined goals targeting the risks and protective processes associated with youth issues and problems;
3. Address comprehensively both risks and protective processes in several levels of the human ecology;
4. Collaborate with community or neighborhood stakeholders;
5. Educate coalition members about relevant theory and research concerning adolescent development, prevention programming, and community process;
6. Structure the plan to the community, thereby reducing risks that exist locally and building protective processes that do not exist;
7. Involve the target audience in program design, planning, and implementation;

8. Be sensitive to cultural, ethnic, and other forms of diversity in the neighborhood or community;
9. Intervene early and continuously;
10. Select developmentally appropriate prevention strategies;
11. Anticipate how changes in one part of the system may affect changes in the system or other settings; and
12. Evaluate effectiveness by monitoring changes in risk and protective processes.

Bronfenbrenner's ecological model of human development can assist "in efforts to generate hypotheses about causation, about unintended consequences, and about alternative avenues for intervening in social and personal problems" (Garbarino, Schellenbach, & Sebes, 1986, p. 297).

LEVELS OF ANALYSIS

The transition to adolescence is a time of increasing psychological vulnerability for youths (Harter, 1990). However, even in the face of multiple risks, many children exhibit remarkable resilience. This phenomenon led researchers and practitioners to shift from thinking only about risk and pathology to asking what processes protect these children (Werner, 1990). Protective processes are individual or environmental safeguards that enhance children's ability to resist stressful life events and promote adaptation and competence (Garmezy, 1983; Steinberg, 1991; Werner, 1990). Because the terms *resiliency, invulnerability,* and *stress resistance* imply characteristics of the individual, the phrase *protectiveness process* is more accurate because it denotes aspects of both the individual and the environment (Werner, 1990).

Bogenschneider (1996) described the various levels of analysis. At the individual level of analysis, the risk processes are antisocial behavior, alienation or rebelliousness, and early initiation. The protective processes include well-developed problem-solving skills and intellectual abilities, self-esteem/self-efficacy, and personal responsibility; well-developed social and interpersonal skills; and religious commitment. At the family level of analysis, the risk processes are poor parental monitoring; distant, uninvolved, and inconsistent parenting; and unclear family rules, expectations, and rewards. The protective process is a close relationship with at least one person. The risk process at the peer level of analysis is an association with peers engaged in high-risk behaviors, and the protective process is having close friends. At the school level of analysis, the risk processes are school transitions, academic failure, and low commitment to school. The protective processes are positive school experiences. At the work-setting level of analysis, the risk process is long work hours, and the protective process is required helpfulness. At the community level of analysis, the risk processes are low socioeconomic status, complacent or permissive community laws and norms, low neighborhood attachment, community disorganization, high mobility, and media influences. The protective processes include belonging to a supportive community and bonding to family, school, and other social institutions. (See Figure 3.1.)

Figure 3.1 | Bogenschneider's (1996) Level of Analysis

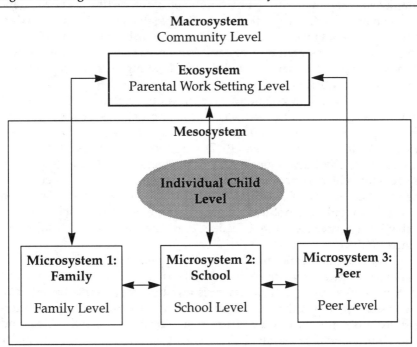

One limitation of the protective focused approach is that from a pragmatic community development perspective, promoting health or wellness is less effective in mobilizing parents, community leaders, and policymakers than is attacking problems or crises (Bogenschneider, 1996). Until parents recognize that risky behavior may compromise their children's development, mobilizing communities around youth issues will be difficult.

SPECIFIC TARGET AREAS

Two target areas that have been specifically linked to youth violence include family violence and juvenile delinquency. Both of these areas exert a powerful influence on the lives of children that has a far-reaching impact on their potential for violence.

Family Violence Impact

Research by Daly and Wilson (1988a, 1998b, 1992) found that acts of family violence occur according to a fairly well-specified set of characteristics. The tendency toward violence in a given family interaction is relatively low when compared with the high number of interactions between family members, yet the proportion of all violence that is familial is considerable. The rate of violent family interactions differs by relationship and life stage. Biosocial research by Daly and Wilson has shown how reproduction, parental investment, sexuality, and bonding help to explain this seeming contradiction.

Spousal abuse is a common form of family violence. Most spousal homicides result because of male sexual proprietaries or jealousy, and female jealousy seems to be related to resource provision (Daly & Wilson, 1988b). Weitzman and Dreen (1982) described "psychosocial traits" of spouses in violent interspousal relationships in the context of the couple system in which behaviors manifest themselves through interactions between the couple. Giles-Sims's (1983) model of wife battering noted that if a woman does not leave a man after the first violent incident, her behavior functions as positive feedback and increases chances of the violence recurring.

Child abuse and child murder statistics appear to follow similar evolutionary biological predictions. Parent–offspring conflict seems to be most prevalent when parental investment is low. Infancy, paternal uncertainty, stepparenting, low offspring quality, scarce resources, and parental alternatives are common characteristics that contribute to child abuse and child murder statistics (Daly & Wilson, 1992).

Child killing is dramatically age related. Studies by Daly and Wilson (1988a, 1988b) have found that consistent with the biological prediction, most child murders occur in the first year of a child's life, which is also the time of lowest accumulated parental investment. The murder of adolescents is virtually nonexistent, which reflects the importance of parental investment or the fact that adolescents can fight back. Parenting adolescents involves considerable parental investment. Because parents may not want to make any further emotional investment in their child, poor-quality children tend to be at particular risk for abuse and neglect (Barash, 1976).

For a child to have a stepparent is a definite risk factor, because stepchildren are 40 times more likely to be abused than are children being raised with both biological parents (Troost & Filsinger, 1992). Independent of socioeconomic status, maternal youth, family size, or abuser personality, stepparents are much more likely than biological parents to be abusive. Abusive parents discriminate within their own families and will abuse their stepchildren while not harming their biological children (Troost & Filsinger, 1992).

Many believe that aggression is learned by observing the behavior of others and its positive or negative consequences. Because learning is more likely to occur when models of behavior are perceived as having high status, competence, power, and exposure (Bandura, 1977), parents, who typically are viewed in this way by their children, are one of the main sources of learning for children. According to social learning theory, children who observe parents using violence observe not only the violent behavior but also emotional triggers for violence, circumstances of violence, and consequences of violence (Bandura, 1977). These observations are significant factors that influence behavior. Whether the observed behaviors and associated cognitive patterns are learned depends on both the observed consequences of the behavior and the expected outcomes of using the behavior.

Children who observe family violence used as coercion may interpret violence as having positive consequences. For example, a child who witnesses a father hit a mother may observe the deference shown by the mother toward the father and other outcomes consistent with the father's wishes. Children who are abused may acknowledge the controlling effect that the abuse has on their behavior. In contrast, children who have not observed family violence have not seen any useful positive consequences associated with a family member's violence. Children of violent parents tend to use violence because they have observed more useful positive than negative consequences of their parents' use of violence and have formed positive outcome expectations for using the behavior. The child would probably not use violence if the child observed more negative than positive consequences associated with the violent acts and if the child formed negative outcome expectations for using violence.

People in situations involving violence often do not use negotiation, verbal reasoning, self-calming strategies, or listening skills. Adults who use violence to resolve conflict typically lack constructive strategies for conflict resolution, and children with violent parents do not usually witness constructive ways of resolving conflict or observe the positive consequences associated with these tactics (Smilkstein, Aspy, & Quiggins, 1994). Children who do not witness family violence tend to have more opportunities to observe and learn constructive conflict resolution skills.

Family factors seem to be the most powerful predictors of aggressive behavior in children. Two broad areas of family characteristics have been identified as being associated with serious aggressive and antisocial behavior and include parental management skills and family relationship characteristics. Parental management skills refer to supervision and discipline practices (Tolan & McKay, 1996). Gerard and Buehler (1999) found

that poor parenting quality, the most consistent predictor of youth problem behaviors, is detrimental to youth well-being regardless of other positive familial processes and resources considered important to youth
adjustment (i.e., cooperative styles of addressing conflict or high socioeconomic status). Poor monitoring skills and harsh discipline practices
have been consistently linked to childhood aggression (Loeber & Dishion,
1983; Patterson, Chamberlain, & Reid, 1982).

Parenting skills and coercive family interactions have been found to
account for 30–40% of the variance in level of antisocial behavior in children (Tolan & McKay, 1996). Family relationship characteristics refer to
day-to-day interaction patterns and qualities of interpersonal relations
(Loeber & Stouthamer-Loeber, 1987; Patterson, Reid, & Dishion, 1992;
Tolan, Cromwell, & Brasswell, 1986). A series of studies suggest that families with children who exhibit high levels of antisocial behavior (a) tend
to have a greater frequency of parental disagreement; (b) are characterized by less differentiation between parents' and children's influence on
family decisions (with power distributions in favor of the children); (c) are
characterized by less expression of positive affect and more expression of
negative affect; (d) tend to experience more misperceived communication;
and (e) tend to be relatively less willing to compromise (Loeber &
Stouthamer-Loeber, 1987; Tolan et al., 1986). These characteristics have
also been reflected in studies that have found families of delinquents to
have lower cohesion (Tolan, 1988), poorer organization and more disagreement about family beliefs (Reiss, 1981), and less communication
(Alexander, Barton, Schiavo, & Parsons, 1976) than families whose children did not exhibit delinquent behaviors.

Media researchers have reasoned that whatever direct effects televised
violence has on children, the effects would be moderated by the nature of
the family viewing environment (Fitzpatrick & Ritchie, 1992). The family
environment influences the child's use of various forms of media, including television, by way of family norms that emphasize either conformity
to authority or open expression of ideas and active engagement in debate
(Fitzpatrick & Ritchie, 1992). Curtner-Smith and MacKinnon-Lewis (1994)
recommended that parents should insist on being informed of their
child's whereabouts, activities, and peer association. Parents of young
teens should increase the parental monitoring by asking the child about
his or her plans and following up to see that the child complied with specified rules, such as abiding by curfew.

Juvenile Delinquency Impact

Juvenile delinquency is a complex construct, and the processes that contribute to violent juvenile crime differ from those associated with nonviolent crime. Youths who begin their delinquent activity at age 15 or later

("late bloomers") are primarily influenced by susceptibility to negative peer pressure, poor parental monitoring, and few opportunities to contribute positively to the community (Moffit, 1993; Steinberg, 1987).

"Early starters" are adolescents who begin their criminal careers before age 15 and tend to become more frequent offenders and commit violent crimes (Patterson & Yoerger, 1993; Steinberg, 1987). Early starters are also considered antisocial at the preschool stage, primarily as a result of harsh, inconsistent discipline. This early aggressiveness leads to rejection by peers, trouble with teachers, and poor school performance. Gelles (1991) questioned whether there is a continuum of violence or distinct behaviors. Strategies for preventing violent juvenile crime target different risk and protective processes than do ones aimed at nonviolent crime.

Youth maladjustment is defined as the relative inability of youths to engage appropriately in interpersonal relationships in work, play, and academic activities over time with relative freedom from damaging social behaviors and burdensome emotions (Trotter, 1989). Buehler, Krishnakumar, Anthony, Tittsworth, and Stone (1994) explained that this definition focuses on the youth's ability to match emotional and behavioral responses to demands across time, people, and settings. Maladjustment is a multidimensional construct involving externalizing behavior problems (e.g., aggression, hyperactivity, and delinquency), internalizing behavior problems (e.g., depression, anxiety, and withdrawal), and academic failure.

Deviant acts such as violent behaviors are considered to be natural tendencies instead of learned behaviors. Friedman and Rosenbaum (1988) stated that if "the proclivity toward deviant behavior is inherent in human nature and constant across all individuals" (p. 364), then conformity to environmental factors requires an explanation. Also, if there is only one moral order, then participation in any behavior outside the conventional moral order is considered deviant behavior (Nye, 1958; Reiss, 1951).

Social bonding prevents a person from deviating from conventional behavior and, according to Hirschi (1969), is generated through the influence of four elements: attachment, belief, commitment, and involvement. *Attachment* is defined as affective ties with people and institutions likely to express conventional norms. *Belief* refers to the acceptance of central social values of the society. *Commitment* is theorized as the participation in and favorable evaluation of "conventional" activities (e.g., school, work, religion, sports). *Involvement* refers to the amount of time spent participating in these socially defined conventional activities. Hirschi theorized that social bonds prevent deviant behavior by imposing behavioral restrictions, but when social bonding weakens, children no longer feel the need to exhibit conventional, prosocial, and normative behavior. Attachment to family is considered necessary for the internalization of normative behaviors (Hirschi, 1969; Menard, Elliott, & Wofford, 1993).

Adolescents attached to their parents are more likely to believe in society's rules and to be committed to activities promoted by society (Foshee & Bauman, 1993). The rules and activities supported by society are usually promoted by parents, even those parents who participate in deviant behaviors. If an attachment bond is not formed, then the adolescent is not as likely to feel an obligation to follow parental and societal rules or to participate in activities promoted by parents and society. Exposure to family violence tends to preclude parental attachment and interferes with the development of the child's belief and commitment bonds. Parental attachment is lower among victims of sexual abuse (Fromuth, 1986), incest (Harter, Alexander, & Neimenyer, 1988), and child abuse (Magai, Distel, & Liker, 1995) than it is among children who are not victims. A decrease in social bonding is related to other adolescent problem behaviors, such as crime, delinquency, substance use, and sexual behavior (Foshee, Bauman, & Linder, 1999).

INTERVENTIONS FOR LEVELS OF ANALYSIS

As ecological theory would predict and a growing body of research indicates, most problem behaviors have no single cause. Risk and protective processes are not confined to any one part of the adolescent's world. Successful programs address both risk and protective processes at several levels of the human ecology to create a comprehensive, multifaceted effort.

Hammond and Yung (1993) applied a public health framework to identify intervention opportunities in host-related factors (person and behavior), agent-related factors (weapon or other instrument), and environment-related factors (social, economic, and cultural influences). Intervention strategies can be classified in many ways, but most of the individual/family-oriented interventions are biological or cognitive behavioral and focus on enhancing social skills and problem-solving skills in juveniles (Tate, Reppucci, & Mulvey, 1995) and modifying parenting and discipline strategies used by their parents (Dishion & Andrews, 1995).

Reid and Eddy (1997) noted the trend toward influencing community-level factors with individually oriented interventions. Hawkins, Arthur, and Olson (1997) reviewed promising community mobilization, media, and policy interventions aimed at reducing antisocial behavior and found several key characteristics of successful programs. They use a broad-based approach, target multiple issues in multiple domains, and address behavior in its social context, including coordinating strategies across social domains (Mulvey, Arthur, & Reppucci, 1993; Tolan & McKay, 1996; Slaby, 1998).

Local community residents tend to be the best resources for bringing about change in their neighborhoods. Involving local citizens in the planning stage helps ensure that prevention programs fit the community, promotes local ownership, and engenders commitment to seeing that the program is implemented and maintained. Prevention programs are more likely to be successful if they are ecological and deal with the child as part of the family and the family as part of the school and community (Lerner, 1995; Schorr, 1991). Families, schools, and community organizations seem to function best when each is supportive of the other (Bronfenbrenner, 1986).

The risk and protective approach serves to break complex, seemingly overwhelming problems into manageable pieces, which helps individuals overcome the sense of hopelessness that often pervades adolescent concerns. According to interviews of 17 Youth Futures coalition members, the two most important determinants of the success of coalitions are (a) the composition of the local coalition, specifically, its representativeness and collective power to access resources and influence policy and program development, and (b) the coalition's support from stakeholders in the community, including civic leaders, youths, parents, churches, and business groups (Bogenschneider, 1996). Training on the most effective prevention strategies helps coalitions work strategically by focusing their efforts on activities with the greatest potential payoff. By identifying resources and supports that are already in place and those that are missing, coalitions can target prevention strategies on the gaps at the local community level.

Researchers and practitioners, however, struggle with the developmental implications for the timing and process of intervention (Coie et al., 1993). Risk factors must be mapped to the appropriate developmental periods (Reid & Eddy, 1997). Although the general maxim of "earlier is better" holds for violence and antisocial behavior, research has begun to specify the hypothesized process by which risk factors relate to the target condition and what role they play at particular developmental periods (Cicchetti & Toth, 1992; Kazdin, 1993). Recent reviews of early parent–child education programs have documented a reduction in delinquency into late adolescence (Yoshikawa, 1994; Zigler, Taussig, & Black, 1992). Although significant progress has been made in the development of preventive interventions for younger children, few primary prevention programs exist for adolescents; most programs focus on treatment of identified adolescent offenders (Guerra, Attar, & Weissberg, 1997).

For any problem behavior, the earlier the onset, the more severe the consequences (Dryfoos, 1990). Program implementation should begin early, because even the most successful prevention programs are not effective after youths have begun drinking or become sexually active (Howard & McCabe, 1990). Youth involvement can make programs more credible and attractive to young people. Program planners need to be sensitive to differences in assumptions, values, and expectations that usually exist across communities. Adolescents change as they mature, as do the influences on their development. Changes during the adolescent stage of development occur faster and greater than at any other time except during the infant stage (Steinberg, 1991). Prevention programs can be more effective by taking these changes into account and recognizing the implications for program timing, type, and focus. Conflict resolution or peer mediation programs are usually more effective when implemented with students between sixth and ninth grades at the stage when peer pressure peaks, rather than later in adolescence when the influence of peer pressure declines (Steinberg, 1991).

In any ecological system, changing one part will usually affect the entire system (Segal, 1983). The likelihood of extinguishing one behavior is enhanced if alternative behaviors are available. To be effective, a prevention program must be initiated several years prior to the onset of the problem behavior. Practitioners first need to assess the extent to which programs have reduced risks and enhanced protective processes and then wait several years after initiation of the programs to do outcome evaluations. Evaluation should strive to be multidimensional not only by assessing effects on individuals but also by assessing the effects on community programs and policies and their institutionalization in the community.

Intervention at the family level has shown significant promise in reducing the emergence of serious antisocial behavior. Early displays of antisocial behavior are a serious public health issue. Urban areas have crime rates 4 to 10 times higher than the national average, with the violent crime rate highest among inner-city African American and Latino young men (Fingerhut & Kleinman, 1990; Hammond & Yung, 1991). The prevention of antisocial behavior has become a national priority because of the increased incidences of violence. Unfortunately, Tolan and McKay (1996) found that family intervention programs are less successful in involving families who are of low socioeconomic status, experience more stressors, and have fewer social resources. Children from these segments of society who are more at risk for serious behavioral difficulties receive the least focus from program planners.

Eccles and Barber (1999) found clear evidence that adolescent participation in extracurricular activities during the high school years helps to provide a protective context in terms of both academic performance and involvement in risky behaviors. Participation in sports, school-based leadership, school-spirit activities, and academic clubs predicted increased school attachment as well as the likelihood of being enrolled full time in college at age 21 (Eccles & Barber, 1999). Participation in prosocial activities was related to lower alcohol and drug use, as well as to lower levels at both Grades 10 and 12, and participation in performing arts served this same function for male adolescents (Eccles & Barber, 1999).

Eckert (1989) explored the link between peer-group identity and activity involvement. As children move through adolescence, they become identified with a particular group of friends, and being a member of a "crowd" helps structure both what teenagers do with their time and the kinds of values and norms to which they are exposed. Over time, the adolescent's personal identity, peer group, and activities can mold his or her course through adolescence. The peers involved in similar activities become the adolescent's peer crowd, which often develops an activity-based culture, which, in turn, provides the adolescent with the opportunity to identify with a group having a shared sense of style. Extracurricular activities can facilitate adolescents' developmental need for social relatedness and can contribute to the adolescent's identity as an important and valued member of the school community.

Delinquent behavior emerges from environmental and person-centered factors. Negative school-related experiences, poor academic and social skills and resources, and a poor quality of family life were all found to have an association with higher levels of delinquent behavior, directly or indirectly, and in the case of academic performance and social skills, both effects were found. Higher levels of alienation were associated with higher levels of delinquency, and that relationship was found to be mediated by association with delinquent peers. However, alienation was not identified as a necessary mediating variable.

Clinical and developmental research has identified a number of individual and family factors that place adolescents at risk for violent behavior (Tolan & McKay, 1996). The individual-level factors deemed important include social cognitive components, such as attitudes and beliefs favorable toward aggression, poor problem-solving skills, and disruptive behavior patterns during the early years (Guerra & Slaby, 1990; Tremblay, Pagnai-Kurtz, Masse, Vitaro, & Pihl, 1995), as well as lack of adequate supervision, skills deficits, and violent behavior in the household (Widom, 1991).

Researchers have also identified community or contextual factors that place adolescents at risk for violent behavior (Lowry, Sleet, Duncan, Powell, & Kolbe, 1995). These include media portrayals and sanctioning of violence, availability of alcohol and drugs, access to weapons, and poor economic conditions (e.g., low socioeconomic status, poverty, lack of opportunity). Guerra et al. (1997) explained that chronic stress and a violent environment that are characteristic of inner-city communities are critical factors that increase the risk of youth violence and impact the effectiveness of preventive interventions. The development of violence prevention programming has traditionally followed the prevention–intervention cycle of moving from research-based demonstration programs to community implementation. Although significant study has been conducted on the content of interventions, critical issues of implementation and evaluation remain understudied.

Part of the difficulty in evaluation occurs when bringing demonstration projects into the community. Kendall and Southam-Gerow (1995) described three types of factors (individual, professional, and research) to explain some of the outcome differences between research-based and community-based intervention outcomes. Individual factors include the nature of the individual's problems and his or her expectations for outcome. Professional factors include both theoretical and practical differences in the training and worldview of those implementing the research project versus community-based professionals. Studies of effective programs often point to the "dynamic leader" who makes the program successful, and these critical characteristics may not be available for multisite implementation of a program staffed by the design team.

Research factors that affect transportability include the isolation of research from community input (Henggeler, Schoenwald, & Pickrel, 1995). Unfortunately, researchers have often failed to identify, operationalize, and assess key characteristics of the community context that affect program process and outcome (Mulvey & Woolard, 1997) because of the difficulty required to balance the core components of a violence prevention program with the flexibility necessary for implementation in a variety of settings. Organization and implementation issues are key in considering the factors that influence a community's selection of strategies as well as their readiness for implementation (Hammond & Yung, 1993; Hawkins et al., 1997).

INTERRELATIONSHIPS ACROSS LEVELS OF ANALYSIS

The counselor alone cannot address all the issues related to school violence, but through a multidisciplinary approach, the incidence of violence in American schools may be reduced. Youth problems are much too complex and the solutions much too comprehensive for any one agency or organization to address alone (Albee, 1983). Also, the lack of a clear definition of "youth violence" contributes to the problem of exporting successful intervention strategies (Reppucci, Woolard, & Fried, 1999). Targeted behaviors or screening criteria for interventions may range from conduct disorder and antisocial behavior to aggressive behavior (e.g., fighting), to delinquency and crime (e.g., court involvement, convictions), to institutional placement (e.g., correctional centers, mental hospitals, schools; Mulvey et al., 1993; Tate et al., 1995). Another difficulty with youth interventions is that because of the pressure to respond immediately to youth violence, well-intentioned programs that lack a clear theoretical base or evaluative component have been implemented in schools.

It is clear, however, that youth violence affects a substantial proportion of society despite attempts to contain it. The Federal Bureau of Investigation (FBI) crime statistics have documented increasing rates of juvenile crime in every major offense category between 1988 and 1992, which suggest that considering the size of the juvenile population in the United States, juveniles are committing disproportionately more violent crime than are adults (Snyder & Sickmund, 1995). Reviewing data from the Centers for Disease Control, Bureau of Justice Statistics, and the FBI over the past 29 years, Lowry et al. (1995) documented stable offending rates for the whole population and increasing rates of offending and victimization for persons under 18. Beyond criminal justice statistics, studies of delinquency and self-reports of offenses indicate that some form of offending is a common component of adolescence for most juveniles, particularly males (Elliott, 1994; Moffit, 1993). Schwartz (1999) stated that although no recent nationwide study of the real extent of youth violence is available, small-scale and regional studies indicate that youth violence is increasing slightly.

In the 1990s, principles of community mobilization and development have increasingly been used in health and wellness promotion efforts. These programs involve local citizens to identify health needs and implement initiatives to improve the health of neighborhood residents. One dimension of the health promotion and prevention efforts is the use of multiple settings for health care and health education, including the community, the workplace, schools, churches, and traditional health care settings. By increasing the number of settings available for information about health care, the chances of reaching alienated individuals increase (Mullen et al., 1995). Mediating social structures such as churches and neighborhoods play an important role in linking individuals to health care and health education, especially by increasing social support, advocating for health programs, and supplying financial resources (Eng & Hatch, 1991; Sutherland, Hale, & Harris, 1995). Linking agents who connect community residents to health care and health education is important in enlisting community participation and increasing social support, especially among isolated and disenfranchised groups (Eng & Young, 1992).

To deal specifically with violence in schools, President Bill Clinton signed the 1994 Gun-Free Schools Act, mandating a 1-year expulsion for students who bring weapons to school and bolstering the "zero-tolerance" policies already in existence in some school districts (Schwartz, 1999). The federal government and most states provide funding for prevention activities through anticrime and education legislation. These include antigang programs and other very focused prevention education, along with more general recreational activities.

Many local community agencies focus on breaking family cycles of violence. For the most effective long-term interventions, a range of family services is provided at the local community level through the collaborative efforts of religious and recreational organizations; social service, public housing, and health agencies; the business community; the schools; and law enforcement agencies. For example, programs in parenting skills and family relationships, particularly those focusing on nonviolent living skills and recovery from substance abuse, can protect children from learning violence at home. Other programs include conflict resolution, anger management, and divorce mediation.

Out-of-school programs (either independently operated or school-sponsored) keep youths constructively engaged when their families are unavailable and provide them with attention from caring adults and good role models. These programs keep youths away from negative influences on the street and offer educational enrichment, assistance with schoolwork, and help for children to develop positive values. The most effective violence prevention programs focus on the prevention goals of the local schools and those that serve as extensions of school prevention activities.

Community campaigns to supplement school programs against gangs are crucial because gang membership cuts across school lines. In fact, there is gang activity in all 50 states now. Effective antigang programs include crisis intervention teams comprised of the police, probation officers, and community leaders; intensive community, family, and youth education programs; alternative youth activities; and a long-term commitment.

School antiviolence policies and programs range from general educational improvement efforts to interventions that target specific types of illegal or antisocial behavior. The most effective programs and policies are directed by an administration that clearly understands the local needs and has provided money in the budget to specifically meet those needs. Community intervention strategies involve parents in a variety of roles as well as community leaders. Community initiatives are directed not only at preventing violence but also at punishing and rehabilitating the juvenile offenders. A primary goal for all communities is to have school policies at the district level, the school level, and the classroom level that promote a safe, nonviolent school community.

Consistent with the notion that development occurs in context, consensus seems to be emerging that the most appropriate place for solving problems is where they occur—in communities. The burgeoning of local collaborative efforts has led some to call the 1990s the "decade of community coalitions for children" (Lerner & Miller, 1992).

CONCLUSION

In writing this chapter, I am reminded of the pain on many young faces and many faces aged beyond their years resulting from some personal experience with violence. One strong memory is the face and voice of a mother in her early 20s who had suffered many broken bones from abuse by her father, including a broken tailbone caused by a kick from his steel-toed boot. In telling this story, the young mother's face and voice did not show any emotion until she told about her mother watching and not doing anything. "Why didn't she leave him? Why did she stay and let him hurt us?" she asked. While this young mother was telling about her past, she was living in a battered woman shelter trying to protect herself and her 5-year-old son from her abusive husband.

I am also reminded of the pain of a family who went to work one day entrusting their elementary-age children to a teenage babysitter, the daughter of a friend and neighbor. A handgun left out by the babysitter's older brother was picked up by one of the children, who did not realize it was real. The gun discharged and the other sibling died. The pain of two families for different reasons, the pain of the individuals, the pain of the school friends and teachers, and the pain of the community were monumental. Even when people do all the right things and teach their children to be safe and provide them a family environment absent of family violence, a tragedy almost too unbearable to know can happen, and the rest of one's life is changed. No matter where the violence occurs, children in our schools are affected.

REFERENCES

Albee, G. W. (1983). Advocates and adversaries of prevention. In N. Garmezy & M. Rutter (Eds.), *Stress, coping, and development in children* (pp. 309–332). New York: McGraw-Hill.

Alexander, J. F., Barton, C., Schiavo, P. S., & Parsons, B. F. (1976). Impact of family systems intervention on recidivism and sibling delinquency: A model of primary prevention and program evaluation. *Journal of Consulting and Clinical Psychology, 44,* 656–664.

Bandura, A. (1977). *Social learning theory.* Englewood Cliffs, NJ: Prentice Hill.

Barash, D. P. (1976). Some evolutionary aspects of parental behavior in animals and man. *American Journal of Psychology, 89,* 195–217.

Bogenschneider, K. (1996). An ecological risk/protective theory and building prevention programs, policies, and community capacity to support youth. *Family Relations, 45,* 127–138.

Bronfenbrenner, U. (1979). *The ecology of human development: Experiments by nature and design.* Cambridge, MA: Harvard University Press.

Bronfenbrenner, U. (1986). Ecology of the family as a context for human development: Research perspectives. *Developmental Psychology, 22,* 723–742.

Bronfenbrenner, U. (1993). Ecology of cognitive development. In R. H. Wozniak & K. W. Fischer (Eds.), *Development in context: Acting and thinking in specific environments* (pp. 3–44). Hillsdale, NJ: Erlbaum.

Buehler, C., Krishnakumar, A., Anthony, C., Tittsworth, S., & Stone, G. (1994). Hostile interparental conflict and youth maladjustment. *Family Relations, 43,* 409–416.

Cicchetti, D., & Toth, S. L. (1992). The role of developmental theory in prevention and intervention. *Developmental Psychopathology, 4,* 489–494.

Coie, J. D., Watt, N. F., West, S. G., Hawkins, J. D., Asarnow, J. R., Markman, H. J., Ramey, S. L., Shure, M. B., & Long, B. (1993). The science of prevention: A conceptual framework and some directions for a national research program. *American Psychologist, 48,* 1013–1022.

Curtner-Smith, M. E., & MacKinnon-Lewis, C. E. (1994). Family process effects on adolescent males' susceptibility to antisocial peer pressure. *Family Relations, 43,* 462–468.

Daly, M., & Wilson, M. (1988a). The Darwinian psychology of discriminative parental solicitude. In D. W. Leger (Ed.), *Comparative perspectives in modern psychology* (pp. 91–144). Lincoln: University of Nebraska Press.

Daly, M., & Wilson, M. (1988b). Evolutionary social psychology and family homicide. *Science, 242,* 519–524.

Daly, M., & Wilson, M. (1992). Who kills whom in spouse killings? On the exceptional sex ratios of spousal homicides in the United States. *Criminology, 30,* 189–215.

Dishion, T. J., & Andrews, D. W. (1995). Preventing escalation in problem behaviors with high risk young adolescents: Immediate and one-year outcomes. *Journal of Consulting and Clinical Psychology, 63,* 538–548.

Dryfoos, J. G. (1990). Community schools: New institutional arrangements for preventing high-risk behavior. *Family Life Educator, 8,* 4–9.

Eccles, J. S., & Barber, B. L. (1999). Student council, volunteering, basketball, or marching band: What kind of extracurricular involvement matters? *Journal of Adolescent Research, 14,* 10–43.

Eckert, P. (1989). *Jocks and burnouts: Social categories and identity in the high school.* New York: Teacher College Press.

Eng, E., & Hatch, J. W. (1991). Networking between agencies and Black churches: The lay health advisor model. *Prevention in Human Services, 10,* 123–146.

Eng, E., & Young, R. (1992). Lay health advisors as community change agents. *Family Community Health, 15,* 24–40.

Fingerhut, L. A., & Kleinman, J. D. (1990). International and interstate comparisons of homicide among young males. *Journal of the American Medical Association, 263,* 3292–3295.

Fitzpatrick, M. A., & Ritchie, L. D. (1992). Communication theory and the family. In P. G. Boss, W. J. Doherty, R. LaRossa, W. R. Schumm, & S. K. Steinmetz (Eds.), *Sourcebook of family theories and methods: A contextual approach* (pp. 565–589). New York: Plenum Press.

Foshee, V. A., & Bauman, K. E. (1993). An assessment of the temporal order among the elements of the bond in Hirschi's control theory: A study of adolescent smoking initiation. *Journal of Adolescent Research, 9,* 88–104.

Foshee, V. A., Bauman, K. E., & Linder, G. F. (1999). Family violence and the perpetration of adolescent dating violence: Examining social learning and social control processes. *Journal of Marriage and the Family, 61,* 331–342.

Friedman, J., & Rosenbaum, D. P. (1988). Social control theory: The salience of components by age, gender, and type of crime. *Journal of Quantitative Criminology, 4,* 363–381.

Fromuth, M. E. (1986). The relationship of childhood sexual abuse with later psychological and sexual adjustment in a sample of college women. *Child Abuse and Neglect, 10,* 5–15.

Garbarino, J., Schellenbach, C. J., & Sebes, J. M. (1986). Conclusion: The prognosis for troubled youth in troubled families. In J. Garbarino, C. J. Schellenbach, J. M. Sebes, & Associates (Eds.), *Troubled youth, troubled families* (pp. 293–308). New York: Aldine de Gruyter.

Garmezy, N. (1983). Stressors of childhood. In N. Garmezy & R. Rutter (Eds.), *Stress, coping, and development in children* (pp. 43–84). New York: McGraw-Hill.

Gelles, R. J. (1991). Physical violence, child abuse, and child homicide: A continuum of violence, or distinct behaviors. *Human Nature, 2,* 59–72.

Gerard, J. M., & Buehler, C. (1999). Multiple risk factors in the family environment and youth problem behaviors. *Journal of Marriage and the Family, 61,* 343–361.

Giles-Sims, J. (1983). *Wife battering: A systems theory approach.* New York: Guilford Press.

Guerra, N. G., Attar, B., & Weissberg, R. P. (1997). Prevention of aggression and violence among inner-city youths. In D. M. Stoff, J. Breiling, & J. D. Maser (Eds.), *Handbook of antisocial behavior* (pp. 375–383). New York: Wiley.

Guerra, N. G., & Slaby, R. G. (1990). Cognitive mediators of aggression in adolescent offenders: II. Intervention. *Developmental Psychology, 26,* 269–277.

Hammond, W. R., & Yung, B. R. (1991). Preventing violence in at-risk African American youth. *Journal of the Health Care for the Poor and Underserved, 26,* 1–16.

Hammond, W. R., & Yung, B. R. (1993). Psychology's role in the public health response to assaultive violence among young African-American men. *American Psychologist, 48,*142–154.

Harter, S. (1990). Self and identity development. In S. S. Feldman & G. R. Elliot (Eds.), *At the threshold: The developing adolescent* (pp. 352–387). Cambridge, MA: Harvard University Press.

Harter, S., Alexander, P. C., & Neimenyer, R. A. (1988). Long-term effects of incestuous child abuse in college women: Social adjustment, social cognition, and family characteristics. *Journal of Consulting and Clinical Psychology, 56,* 5–8.

Hawkins, J. D., Arthur, M. W., & Olson, J. J. (1997). Community intervention to reduce risks and enhance protection against antisocial behavior. In D. M. Stoff, J. Breiling, & J. D. Maser (Eds.), *Handbook of antisocial behavior* (pp. 365–374). New York: Wiley.

Hawkins, J. D., Catalano, R., & Miller. (1992). *Communities that care.* San Francisco: Jossey-Bass.

Henggeler, S. W., Schoenwald, S. K., & Pickrel, S. G. (1995). Multisystemic therapy: Bridging the gap between university and community-based treatment [Special section: Efficacy and effectiveness in studies of child and adolescent psychotherapy]. *Journal of Consulting and Clinical Psychology, 63,* 709–717.

Hirschi, T. (1969). *Causes of delinquency.* Berkeley: University of California Press.

Howard, M., & McCabe, J. B. (1990). Helping teenagers post-pone sexual involvement. *Family Planning Perspectives, 22,* 21–26.

Kazdin, A. E. (1993). Adolescent mental health: Prevention and treatment programs. *American Psychologist, 48,* 127–141.

Kendall, P. C., & Southam-Gerow, M. A. (1995). Issues in the transportability of treatment: The case of anxiety disorders in youths [Special section: Efficacy and effectiveness in studies of child and adolescent psychotherapy]. *Journal of Consulting and Clinical Psychology, 63,* 702–708.

Lerner, R. M. (1995). *America's youth in crisis: Challenges and choices for programs and policies.* Thousand Oaks, CA: Sage.

Lerner, R. M., & Miller, J. R. (1992). *Integrating human development research and intervention for America's children: The Michigan State University model.* East Lansing: Michigan State University, Institute for Children, Youth, and Families.

Lewin, K. R. (1935). *A dynamic theory of personality.* New York: McGraw-Hill.

Loeber, R., & Dishion, T. J. (1983). Early predictors of male delinquency: A review. *Psychological Bulletin, 94,* 68–99.

Loeber, R., & Stouthamer-Loeber, M. (1987). The prediction of delinquency. In H. C. Quay (Ed.), *Handbook of juvenile delinquency* (pp. 325–382). New York: Wiley.

Lowry, R., Sleet, D., Duncan, C., Powell, K., & Kolbe, L. (1995). Adolescents at risk for violence. *Educational Psychology Review, 7,* 7–39.

Magai, C., Distel, N., & Liker, R. (1995). Emotional socialization, attachment, and patterns of adult emotional ties. *Cognition and Emotions, 9,* 461–481.

Menard, S., Elliott, D. S., & Wofford, S. (1993). Social control theories in developmental perspective. *Studies on Crime and Crime Prevention, 2,* 69–87.

Moffit, T. E. (1993). Adolescence-limited and life-course-persistent antisocial behavior: A developmental taxonomy. *Psychological Review, 100,* 674–701.

Mullen, P. D., Evans, D., Forster, J., Gottlieb, N. H., Kreuter, M., Moon, R., O'Rourke, T., & Strecher, V. J. (1995). Settings as an important dimension in health education/promotion policy, programs, and research. *Health Education Quarterly, 22,* 329–345.

Mulvey, E. P., Arthur, M. W., & Reppucci, N. D. (1993). The prevention and treatment of juvenile delinquency: A review of the research. *Clinical Psychology Review, 13,* 133–167.

Mulvey, E. P., & Woolard, J. L. (1997). Themes for consideration in future research on prevention and intervention with antisocial behaviors. In D. M. Stoff, J. Breiling, & J. D. Maser (Eds.), *Handbook of antisocial behavior* (pp. 554–562). New York: Wiley.

Nye, F. I. (1958). *Family relationships and delinquent behavior.* New York: Wiley.

Patterson, G. R., Chamberlain, P., & Reid, J. B. (1982). A comparative evaluation of a parent training program. *Behavior Therapy, 13,* 630–650.

Patterson, G. R., Reid, J. B., & Dishion, T. J. (1992). *Antisocial boys: A social interactional approach* (Vol. 4). Eugene, OR: Castalia.

Patterson, G. R., & Yoerger, K. (1993, October). *Differentiating outcomes and histories for early and late onset arrests.* Paper presented at the annual meeting of the American Society of Criminology, Phoenix, AZ.

Reid, J. B., & Eddy, J. M. (1997). The prevention of antisocial behavior: Some considerations in the search for effective interventions. In D. M. Stoff, J. Breiling, & J. D. Maser (Eds.), *Handbook of antisocial behavior* (pp. 343–356). New York: Wiley.

Reiss, A. J. (1951). Delinquency as the failure of personal and social controls. *American Sociological Review, 16*, 196–207.

Reiss, A. J. (1981). *The family's construction of reality*. Cambridge, MA: Harvard University Press.

Reppucci, N. D., Woolard, J. L., & Fried, C. S. (1999). Social, community, and preventive interventions. *Annual Review of Psychology, 50*, 387–418.

Schorr, L. B. (1991, January). *Successful programs and the bureaucratic dilemma: Current deliberations*. Speech presented at the National Center for Children in Poverty, Columbia University School of Public Health, New York.

Schwartz (1999). *An overview of strategies to reduce school violence* [On-line]. New York: Eric Clearinghouse on Urban Education. Available: http://ericweb.tc. columbia.edu/digests/dig115.html.

Segal, J. (1983). Utilization of stress and coping research: Issues of public education and public policy. In N. Garmezy & M. Rutter (Eds.), *Stress, coping, and development in children* (pp. 239–252). New York: McGraw-Hill.

Slaby, R. G. (1998). Preventing youth violence through research-guided intervention. In P. Trickett & C. Schellenbach (Eds.), *Violence against children in the family and the community* (pp. 371–399). Washington, DC: American Psychological Association.

Small, S., & Kerns, D. (1993). Unwanted sexual activity among peers during early and middle adolescence: Incidence and risk factors. *Journal of Marriage and the Family, 55*, 941–952.

Smilkstein, G., Aspy, C. B., & Quiggins, P. A. (1994). Conjugal conflict and violence: A review and theoretical paradigm. *Family Medicine, 26*, 111–116.

Snyder, H. N., & Sickmund, M. (1995). *Juvenile offenders and victims: A national report*. Washington, DC: Office of Juvenile Justice Delinquency Prevention.

Steinberg, L. (1987). Familial factors in delinquency: A developmental perspective. *Journal of Adolescent Research, 2*, 255–268.

Steinberg, L. (1991). *Adolescent transitions and alcohol and other drug use prevention. Preventing adolescent drug use: From theory to practice* (Office of Substance Abuse Prevention Monograph 8). Washington, DC: U.S. Department of Health and Human Services.

Sutherland, M., Hale, C. D., & Harris, G. J. (1995). Community health promotion: The church as partner. *Journal of Primary Prevention, 16*, 201–216.

Tate, D. C., Reppucci, N. D., & Mulvey, E. P. (1995). Violent juvenile delinquents: Treatment effectiveness and implications for future action. *American Psychologist, 50*, 777–781.

Tolan, P. H. (1988). Socioeconomic, family and social stress correlates of adolescent antisocial and delinquent behavior. *Journal of Abnormal Child Psychology, 16*, 317–331.

Tolan, P. H., Cromwell, R. E., & Brasswell, M. (1986). Family therapy with delinquents: A critical review of the literature. *Family Process, 25*, 619–650.

Tolan, P. H., & McKay, M. M. (1996). Preventing serious antisocial behavior in inner-city children: An empirically based family intervention program. *Family Relations, 45*, 148–155.

Tremblay, R. E., Pagnai-Kurtz, L. Masse, L. C., Vitaro, F., & Pihl, R. O. (1995). A bimodal preventive intervention for disruptive kindergarten boys; its impact through mid-adolescence. *Journal of Consulting and Clinical Psychology, 63*, 560–568.

Troost, K. M., & Filsinger, E. (1992). Emerging biosocial perspectives on the family. In P. G. Boss, W. J. Doherty, R. LaRossa, W. R. Schumm, & S. K. Steinmetz (Eds.), *Sourcebook of family theories and methods: A contextual approach* (pp. 677–714). New York: Plenum Press.

Trotter, B. B. (1989). *Coparental conflict, competition, and cooperation and parents' perceptions of their children's social–emotional well-being following marital separation.* Unpublished doctoral dissertation, University of Tennessee, Knoxville.

Weitzman, J., & Dreen, K. (1982). Wife beating: A view of the marital dyad. *Social Casework, 63,* 259–265.

Werner, E. E. (1990). Protective factors and individual resilience. In S. J. Meisels & J. P. Shonkoff (Eds.), *Handbook of early childhood intervention* (pp. 97–116). Cambridge, England: Cambridge University Press.

Widom, C. S. (1991). Childhood victimization: Risk factor for delinquency. In M. E. Colton & S. Gore (Eds.), *Adolescent stress: Causes and consequences* (pp. 201–221). New York: Aldine de Gruyter.

Yoshikawa, H. (1994). Prevention as cumulative protection: Effects of early family support and education on chronic delinquency and its risks. *Psychological Bulletin, 115,* 28–54.

Zigler, E., Taussig, C., & Black, K. (1992). Early childhood intervention: A promising preventive for juvenile delinquency. *American Psychologist, 47,* 997–1006.

THE ETIOLOGY OF VIOLENCE IN YOUTHS

INTRODUCTION

What happened at school today? That question most often answered by children returning from school with the reply, "Nothing," can be a good thing. One day when my daughter was in middle school, the answer was, "Emily got a black eye!" My shock only increased when I heard the whole story of a how a young man had claimed the hallway as his own, stuck out his fist, and hit everyone who got in his way who did not duck in time. Unfortunately, Emily had been in this latter category.

Emily was not the kind of child to be involved in violence, and this incident left not only her parents but many others as well more than a little concerned about the safety of their children. "It can't happen here," we thought, but it had. The reasons for that day's violence could have been understood, anticipated, and prevented, if only someone had paid attention. This section is devoted to answering, "Why do some children become violent?"

Most studies of school violence are conducted from the perspective of the perpetrator. In chapter 4, the first chapter of this section, Michael J. Furlong, Bonita Sharma, and Sujin Sabrina Rhee report the results of a cluster analysis of victim subtypes to examine the characteristics of common student victimization patterns on school campuses. Their results provide insight into potential interventions for various types of victimization.

In chapter 5, Lissa J. Yogan and Stuart Henry explore masculine engenderment and its relationship to school violence. We have long been aware of the gender disparity between males and females for violence. For youths under age 18, 85% of all those arrested for violent crime are males; for homicide and nonnegligent manslaughter, the male-to-female ratio is

9:1. The rate of suicide reflects a similar gender disparity in violence, with teenage boys ages 10–14 experiencing 3.3 times the suicide rate of teenage girls, and rates for teenage boys ages 15–19 are 5.6 times the rate for teenage girls. These statistics are a result of many factors that are discussed in this chapter, and interventions are recommended to reduce the prevalence of male violence.

The final chapter in this section, chapter 6, by Alfiee M. Breland addresses the effects of the media on violence from the premise that the media has created stereotypes that have served to develop the public understanding of the youthful violent offender. Furthermore, these images have diverted school officials from recognizing the true violent offenders in their midst. Finally, this chapter describes the components of programs that have succeeded in correctly identifying and assisting potential violent offenders.

In a disease model, etiology or pathogenesis must be derived from good theory. In this section, we provide background information for several theoretical models that drive theory development. This step is crucial to the process of designing interventions that are effective in changing the course of the disease and preventing violent behavior to manifest. That is where our hope for effective behavior change lies.

4 | Defining School Violence Victim Subtypes: A Step Toward Adapting Prevention and Intervention Programs to Match Student Needs

Michael J. Furlong, Bonita Sharma, and Sujin Sabrina Rhee

One of many lessons that have been learned from the tragic shootings on school campuses is that extreme forms of violence often have their origins in interpersonal relationship disputes and minor conflicts and hassles that occur frequently in schools (Dwyer, Osher, & Warger, 1998). One component of a comprehensive strategy to prevent more serious forms of violence on school campuses is to implement programs that minimize the frequency and intensity of day-to-day interpersonal conflicts at school. This chapter contributes to this objective by using cluster analysis to examine the characteristics of common student victimization patterns in schools.

GENERAL RESEARCH ON VIOLENCE VICTIMIZATION

Research examining childhood victimization suggests that frequent victimization can disrupt the course of development and is associated with symptomatology over the course of the life span (Terr, 1991). Although investigations examining long-term consequences of school violence are infrequent, other youth violence studies have found that inner-city school-age children exposed to extreme violence (e.g., witnessing physical assault, knife attacks) on a frequent basis suffer negative developmental outcomes, such as withdrawn and negative social behavior, less supportive interpersonal relationships, lowered academic achievement, and heightened risk of future aggression (Bell & Jenkins, 1993; Richters & Martinez, 1993; Shakoor & Chalmers, 1991). Exposure to more chronic but less severe forms of violence also has been found to have negative effects and is a risk factor for future aggressive behavior (Finkelhor & Dzuiba-Leatherman, 1994), a finding that has implications for milder forms of school violence as well.

Outside of the school context, it is known that early childhood experiences with violence in the home can have profound effects on the development of aggressive and violent behaviors. Adults who, as children, witnessed violence in their family have been found to be at increased risk both of physically abusing their spouses or intimates and of being the victim of abuse (Jaffe, Wolfe, Wilson, & Zak, 1986). Children as young as 1 to 3 years of age who have been physically abused at home were found to be more than twice as likely than nonabused children to physically assault their classmates and adult caretakers at school (George & Main, 1979). Also closely related, depression in youths has been linked to witnessing or personally being a victim of violent events (Freeman, Mokros, & Poznanski, 1993).

Given the negative developmental outcomes associated with chronic exposure to violence, the findings of Boney-McCoy and Finkelhor (1995) are particularly important. They used a national telephone sample of youths ages 10 to 16 years and found that over one third reported having been the victims of one or more forms of assault in any setting (i.e., simple and aggravated physical assaults, sexual assaults, attempted kidnappings, and parental violence). An increased prevalence of sadness, posttraumatic stress disorder symptoms, and school problems was associated with a wide range of victimization. Victims of sexual assault showed particularly high levels of symptomatology.

SCHOOL VIOLENCE VICTIMIZATION

Current Use of the Term *School Violence*

It is somewhat peculiar that educational researchers have not been at the forefront of discussion about school-site violence and safety issues (Furlong & Morrison, in press). *School violence* as a term has come to reflect broad community concerns about youth violence and how that violence affects the schooling process; the term has utility because it reflects societal values that schools should be a special place of refuge and nurturance for children. Given this, researchers and practitioners need to consider the many complex precursors of violent–aggressive behavior occurring at schools, how to prevent it, and how to reduce its impact when it does occur. An important but neglected part of this task is to better understand who is victimized at schools and which types of victimization they experience. In this chapter, we consider school violence to encompass a range of behaviors from mild (e.g., verbal taunts) to severe (e.g., physical assaults, social rejection), all of which cause harm. (For reviews of the incidence of school violence, see Cornell & Loper, 1998; Furlong, Morrison, Bates, & Chung, 1998.)

Despite a growing body of research that has examined general school violence trends, the research has typically focused on the perpetrators of aggressive acts. Relatively few studies have shed light on the victim himself or herself. Some information about victimization has come from the Centers for Disease Control and Prevention's Youth Risk Behavior Surveillance Survey (YRBS), which has been administered biannually since 1991 (Kann et al., 1998). As with many school violence studies, the YRBS has examined univariate relationships with specific victimization items. As an epidemiological study, its goal is to estimate the population base rates of four conditions: (a) fighting, (b) theft, (c) being threatened or injured with a weapon, and (d) fear of being harmed at school or on the way to/from school. To our knowledge, no one has yet examined the co-occurrence of these victimization experiences using YRBS data. Our own analysis of the YRBS data from 1997 (Centers for Disease Control and Prevention, 1999) showed victimization at school is common among secondary school students, with about one third of female students and one half of male students reporting at least one of these four types of victimization in a typical school month. In addition, 9th and 10th graders report more victimization than 11th and 12th graders. Despite the exposure of many youths to victimization experiences, a relatively small number (between 0.5% and 1.0% across Grades 9 to 12) report experiencing all four types of victimization assessed by the YRBS.

In a series of related studies, Furlong and his colleagues have examined the distinguishing characteristics of school violence victims. In one investigation, Furlong, Chung, Bates, and Morrison (1995) compared characteristics of students who reported being victims of multiple types of violence (top 5% of all students) with those who reported no victimization. The results showed that multivictims were more likely to be males, to perceive the school campus to be more dangerous, and to be more hostile than their nonvictim counterparts. In addition, the multivictim group tended to have less satisfying and positive peer interactions, a lower sense of school attachment or belonging, fewer strong connections to teachers, and more worries about school violence. Multivictims also tended to have lower academic achievement and negative attitudes toward school and achievement in school. Furlong et al. noted that the associations between level of victimization and social and attitudinal effects were more pronounced than the association with actual school performance.

Serious forms of violence victimization are not as common on school campuses as the general public may believe; however, it is sufficiently documented that violence victimization is widespread and there are victims at each and every school in the United States. Given the base rates derived from the YRBS, it can be estimated that at a high school with 2,000 students, there are likely to be 60 to 70 students who experience multiple forms of victimization in a given month. There is clearly a need for all schools to carefully consider these students' needs. Despite this widespread victimization, there is no evidence that schools systematically implement victim support programs. Furthermore, fundamental information is unknown about the types and combinations of victimization that occur and how specific knowledge about victim subtypes might influence prevention and intervention programs.

Are Some Students More Vulnerable to School-Site Violence?

Berkowitz (1990) asserted that victims are often considered to be scapegoats for displaced aggression because of their perceived qualities as well as because they are available and safe targets. Because of this, displaced aggression is especially likely to be directed against persons from groups that are associated with the aggressor's perceived source of the frustration or dislike. Although victims do not cause or deserve their victimizing experiences, they may have traits or exhibit behaviors that provoke others who are primed for aggression. Consistent with Berkowitz's formulation, Morrison, Furlong, and Smith (1994) found that students who stand out on campus, for example, those in special education resource or leadership classes, experience more victimization than other students. Similarly, Dodge and Schwartz (1997) showed that aggressive young males often misread social cues and have a bias toward attributing hostile intentionality to other youths, and this leads to a vicious cycle of their victimizing others and in turn being victimized themselves.

In another study examining victimization and associated characteristics of victims, Finkelhor and Asdigian (1996) found that specific characteristics of victimized youths increased the potential victim's target vulnerability: (a) characteristics that make the youth easier to victimize (e.g., physical weakness or psychological distress); (b) target gratifiability or features that make the target a good source of gratification (e.g., female gender for crime of sexual assault); and (c) target antagonism or features that increase the victimizer's anger (e.g., acts associated with specific ethnic or group identities that may ignite hostility or resentment). Finkelhor and Asdigian indicated that specific characteristics of a potential victim are viewed as markers and are "congruent" with the motives, needs, and gratification of violent offenders.

Within the school context, bullying is the most common type of serious school violence (Batsche & Knoff, 1994; Hoover, Oliver, & Hazler, 1992; Limber & Nation, 1998; Williams, Chambers, Logan, & Robinson, 1996).

Smith et al. (1999) defined bullying as both verbal and physical intimidation and attacks carried out systematically over time by one person (or a group of people) to a specific victim. This is to distinguish it from episodic schoolyard fights that do not evolve into a chronic pattern. Of particular interest, these researchers provided a description of the bully victim. Bully victims are not randomly selected but tend to possess traits (e.g., undersized, overweight, and lacking assertiveness) that may foster others' negative perceptions of them. Bullies select victims in part because the victim appears weak and vulnerable to them (Olweus, 1997), a pattern suggested also by Berkowitz's (1990) aggression model.

A perspective that has been offered by bully researchers is that there are two types of victims: passive and provocative (Olweus, 1997). Passive victims usually are characterized as (a) more anxious and insecure than other students; (b) more cautious, sensitive, and quiet; (c) possessing low self-esteem; and (d) lonely and abandoned at schools. Olweus stated that the characteristics of passive victims are not provocative, and bullying encounters are not a consequence of these students' behavior. These students do not value violence and, if they are boys, tend to be physically weaker than other boys at school (Smith et al., 1999). Bullying victimization appears to occur in part because these youths send signals to potential aggressors that they are insecure and weak and will not retaliate when attacked, threatened, or insulted. In contrast, Olweus (1978) described another group of victims, the provocative victims, who display a combination of both anxious and aggressive reaction patterns. These youths tend to have problems with concentration, they tend to have a high energy or activity level, and their behaviors often provoke other students to engage in negative aggressive actions. These patterns suggest that grouping all victims of school violence into one category misses important differences among victim subtypes.

PURPOSE OF THIS STUDY

This study was conducted to provide researchers and practitioners with information about the patterns of victimization that occur on school campuses in a typical month. We reason that empirically supported information about student reports of being victimized at school and the patterns of this victimization will help inform educational practitioners who are interested in customizing intervention programs to meet the varying needs of students.

Given what is known about the occurrence of antisocial behavior and victimization in community settings, it seems likely that similar patterns will be found for school-site violence victimization. We know that a sizable group of students report that they are not victimized at school

(Brener, Simon, Krug, & Lowry, 1999; Furlong et al., 1995). It is also known from previous research that those who experience no violence victimization at school in a given month are markedly different from those students who experience multiple types of victimization (Furlong et al., 1998). To date, however, a more complete scope of victimization that occurs on school campuses has not been examined. What types of victimization patterns occur, and how prevalent are they in a large sample of students? Do some students only experience verbal taunts in the absence of physical aggression, or are both inexorably linked? What are some other subtypes, if any, of victimization experienced by students, for example, those who report that they have been exposed to or threatened by someone with a weapon? This chapter explores the types of violence victimization that students report experiencing at school in a typical month. Cluster analysis procedures were used to derive empirically based victimization subtypes.

METHOD

Participants

Responses of 9,723 students to the California School Climate and Safety Survey (CSCSS) were used for this study. There were slightly more female than male students (5,479 female and 4,244 male). The sample was ethnically and racially diverse, with European Americans being the largest group (41%), followed by Latinos (36%), Asian Americans (9%), African Americans (6%), and Native Americans (3%). A small group of the students (5%) did not complete the race/ethnicity identification question. Students in the sample included 643 fifth graders, 1,249 sixth graders, 1,604 seventh graders, 1,718 eighth graders, 1,229 ninth graders, 1,228 tenth graders, 1,075 eleventh graders, and 977 twelfth graders. The students attended schools located in urban, suburban, and semirural areas of central and southern California.

School Violence Victimization Measures

The CSCSS is a self-report questionnaire developed to measure general school campus climate and personal safety-related experiences (Furlong et al., 1998). The CSCSS was originally developed as a needs assessment tool to help schools develop and evaluate school violence prevention and intervention programs (Morrison & Furlong, 1994).

Victimization Index
The victimization index used in this investigation was derived from items that asked students to indicate if they had personally experienced any of

the 21 types of violence victimization at the school site during the 30 days preceding administration of the CSCSS. In preparation for this analysis, we reexamined the content of all the 21 victimization items and decided to eliminate 6 items from this analysis because the items were determined to be too ambiguous. The remaining 15 items were logically organized into four victimization subscales: (a) verbal threats, (b) physical attacks, (c) sexual victimization, and (d) weapon exposure/threat. To verify this logical organization of the items, we asked 20 graduate students in school psychology (at the master's and doctorate level, who were unaware of the purpose of the study) to Q sort each of these 15 items into one of the four victim categories. Results showed that these raters concurred with the original item grouping (80% to 100%) for all items except one: "You were cut with a knife or something sharp by someone trying to hurt you." This latter item was excluded from the analyses. Thus, the final victimization index included 14 items. The specific items were as follows: (a) *verbal threats* (total score = 0–4)—"Another student threatened to hurt you," "Someone yelled bad words, cursed at you," "You were bullied, threatened, or pushed around by gang members," and "Someone tried to scare you by the way they looked at you"; (b) *physical attacks* (total score = 0–4)—"You were grabbed or shoved by someone being mean," "You were punched or kicked by someone trying to hurt you," "You were hit with a rock or another object by someone trying to hurt you," and "You had personal property stolen"; (c) *sexual victimization* (total score = 0–2)—"Someone made unwanted physical sexual advances toward you" and "Someone sexually harassed you (made unwanted sexual comments to you)"; and (d) *weapon exposure/threat* (total score = 0–4)—"You personally saw another student with a gun on campus," "You personally saw another student on campus with a knife or razor," "You were threatened by a student with a gun and you saw the gun," and "You were threatened by a student with a knife and you saw the knife."

Other Measures

Other indexes, previously developed as part of the CSCSS, were used in this study to compare and contrast characteristics of students in different victimization subtypes. These measures have been used in previous studies of victimization (Bates, Chung, & Chase, 1997; Furlong et al., 1995, 1998). These measures include (a) perceived safety, (b) perceived danger, (c) hostility, (d) interpersonal trust, (e) belonging to school, (f) teacher connections, (g) peer connections, (h) like/dislike school, (i) average course grades, and (j) preoccupation with school violence. For indexes with more than one item, the mean response across all items was used in the analyses. Therefore, the range for all index scores is from 1 to 5, reflecting the Likert scale used in the response choices.

Perceived safety was assessed using the item, "I feel perfectly safe at this school," and measured students' sense of personal safety.

A *personal danger* index examined students' attitudes and beliefs about the occurrence of dangerous activities on campus, a more general perception of campus danger. Students were asked to indicate how frequently seven types of situations (weapons possession, drug use, bullying, vandalism, alcohol consumption, fights, and theft) happened on their school campus using the following 5-point scale: *not at all* (1), *a little* (2), *some* (3), *quite a bit* (4), and *very much* (5). Previous reliability analysis with the total sample showed an interitem reliability of 0.80 (Furlong et al., 1995).

A Hostility subscale from the Buss and Perry Aggression Inventory (Buss & Perry, 1992) was used as a measure of generalized expectations for negative interpersonal outcome and includes six items (e.g., "I sometimes wonder why I am so bitter about things" and "I know friends talk about me behind my back"). These items were randomly inserted throughout the school climate portion of the CSCSS. Again, a 5-point Likert response scale (1 = *strongly disagree* to 5 = *strongly agree*) was used. Reliability analysis computed on the total sample in the Furlong et al. (1998) study indicated an interitem reliability of 0.65 for this scale.

Interpersonal trust was measured by one item: "You can really trust people at this school." A 5-point Likert response scale ranging from 1 = *strongly disagree* to 5 = *strongly agree* was provided.

School attachment was assessed by asking about the students' belonging to school and their like or dislike of school. The items "I feel I belong at this school" and "I am comfortable talking to teachers about problems I might have" assessed sense of belonging. Both items used 5-point Likert scales ranging from 1 = *strongly agree* to 5 = *strongly disagree*, and the responses were combined for the analyses. Another item asked: "How do you feel about going to school?" It included: *I like school very much* (1), *I like school quite a bit* (2), *I like school* (3), *I don't like school very much* (4), and *I hate school* (5). This item was analyzed separately.

Peer and teacher connections assessed the quality of students' school social relationships. They were asked how many other students they considered to be good friends (peer connections) and how many teachers they would be able to talk to about their problems (teacher connections). The response choices were 0, 1, 2, 3, and 4 or more.

To assess *preoccupation with school violence (worry)*, we asked students to indicate which of the following they were *most* worried about: (a) getting good grades, (b) violence in school, (c) being accepted by peers, (d) violence in the neighborhood, or (e) getting along with parents or other family members. This forced-choice item was used to assess preoccupation or worry about school violence.

To estimate academic achievement (course grades), we asked students to state their average course grades; the responses included mostly As, mostly Bs, mostly Cs, mostly Ds, or mostly Fs.

Survey Procedures

Data were gathered from 1 of 26 elementary, middle, junior, and senior high schools involved in developing school safety plans during the 1994–1995 and 1995–1996 school years. Negative consent was allowed at the time of survey administration. Classroom teachers administered the survey to students during one class period. Students recorded their responses on a computer-scanable form. We reviewed all response sheets and tabulated those with responses to all victimization items, as required by cluster analysis procedures. In addition, all respondents passed two validity check items that were randomly inserted among the violence incidence items. The validity check items represented possible but highly unlikely situations (e.g., "I took ten field trips in the previous months"). Students who responded positively to these items were not included in the analyses because they were considered to have given inaccurate or careless responses about their violence victimization. The questionnaire was also available in Spanish, and a few students chose to use the translated version.

Cluster Analysis

Although clustering procedures are commonly used in research, there are no clear guidelines to aid in selecting cluster procedures or in choosing the optimal number of clusters or subgroups derived from the data. It has been shown that even randomly generated data can yield subgroups when subjected to clustering procedures. Because of this, it was important to replicate and verify the number of meaningful clusters derived from this sample. Therefore, we obtained three randomly selected subsamples of 125 students (475 students in total) who indicated that they had experienced at least one victimization event. To explore the number of clusters within these samples, we completed a hierarchical cluster procedure using Ward's procedure for each of the three subsamples (the computations for this type of cluster analysis are complex and can be completed only with relatively small subsamples). The four victimization subscale scores were transformed into standard scores for this analysis.

Ward's procedure builds clusters by successively joining an individual case or cluster to other cases or clusters and so on until, at the final step, all cases are grouped into one cluster. Of interest are how many meaningful subgroups or clusters are present in the data. Replicated across the three subsamples, five, six, or seven clusters produced possible solutions. On closer examination of the number and pattern of students placed into these clusters, we found that the five- or six-cluster solutions left out one or two distinct groups; we thus decided that the seven-cluster solution appeared to provide the best fit for the data.

A limitation to the hierarchical procedure is that once an individual is placed into a cluster, he or she cannot be moved to another cluster as the clustering procedure continues. Thus, a K-means cluster procedure was completed next because it uses an iterative process that allows individuals to be moved between clusters if needed to improve the solution. For the K-means procedure, the mean victimization subscale standard scores for the 125 students in the third Ward (hierarchical) cluster solution were used as the starting points to classify all 9,723 participants into the seven-cluster solution. This resulted in the grouping of the entire sample of victims into one of seven clusters, with the nonvictim group automatically being the eighth cluster.

RESULTS

Across all 9,723 participants, 22% reported they did not experience any victimization events, 45% reported one to three events, 25% reported three to seven events, and 7.3% reported eight or more events (total score range = 0 to 14). On the basis of these responses, seven subtypes of school violence victimization emerged in addition to the rationally formed nonvictim cluster. (Cluster means, standard deviations, and z scores are available from the authors upon request.)

We conducted a discriminant analysis to examine the relative contribution of each of the four victimization subscales to cluster membership. As expected, the results of the discriminant analysis were significant, approximate $F(40, 3190) = 79.55$, $p < .01$, and resulted in the accurate (re)classification of 97.2% of the students across all clusters (100% accuracy for Clusters 7 and 8). The largest number of classification changes was in Cluster 2, with 125 students moving from Cluster 2 (low victimization) to Cluster 1 (nonvictims). Other moderate classification changes involved 71 students in Cluster 3 being moved to Cluster 4 and 46 students in Cluster 6 being moved to Cluster 7. The largest classification change (Cluster 2) moved youths to a cluster with a lower victimization level, whereas the other changes mainly moved youths only one cluster up to groups with slightly more elevated victimization levels. This pattern of results suggests that the empirically derived victim clusters have good internal cohesion with few changes in classification.

Description of Victimization Clusters

General demographic information and more specific cluster characteristics are presented in Table 4.1. Following are general descriptions of each of the eight clusters and their pattern of high and low scores for the victimization and other variables.

Cluster 1 (Nonvictims, n = 2,087, 21.5%)
The youths in this cluster reported no incidents of victimization. The ethnicity of students in Cluster 1 was similar to that of the total sample. The mean score for peer connections was highest for this cluster, indicating that nonvictimized students reported having more good friends at school compared with students in other clusters. Also, the highest percentage (94%) of students reported getting C or better grades when compared with other subtypes. When asked about their feelings about school, 76% said they generally liked school, and 24% said they either disliked or hated school. On the safety and school attachment indexes, students in this cluster had the highest mean scores. They tended to perceive more personal safety at school and also had a stronger sense of belonging to their school. They also expressed high trust of people at their school (interpersonal trust: $M = 2.99$; highest of all clusters).

Cluster 2 (Low Victimization, n = 1,989, 20.5%)
This group was characterized by their reports of low levels of all four types of victimization. Their profile was similar to the nonvictim cluster except that these students reported some victimization. The majority (92%) of students reported doing average or above average in school, and most (94%) felt like they had two or more friends at school. This group had the second highest mean for the safety and school attachment subscales, which shows that they felt secure at school and had solid connections and a sense of belonging.

Cluster 3 (Moderate Verbal Threats, n = 1,336, 13.7%)
This group of youths had a majority of female students (61%), which compares with the gender distribution in the total sample of 55–45 in favor of females. Moderate levels of verbal threat and low levels of other types of victimization characterized students in this group. Most (93%) reported getting average or above average grades in school. Students in this group seemed to have a lower rate of truancy (23%) than that of other groups. About 1.9% (lowest rate) of students reported being in a gang or associating with its members. Students in this cluster generally liked school, felt safe at school, and reported having friends at school.

Table 4.1 | Characteristics of Students by Victim Cluster

Characteristic (and Statistic for Entire Sample)	Cluster 1 Non-victims	Cluster 2 Low Victimization	Cluster 3 Moderate Verbal Threat	Cluster 4 Sexual Harassment	Cluster 5 Moderate Verbal & Weapon Exposure	Cluster 6 High Verbal & Physical Threat	Cluster 7 High Verbal, Physical Threat & Sexual Harassment	Cluster 8 Pervasive Victim
N = 9,723	n = 2,087	n = 1,989	n = 1,336	n = 1,138	n = 936	n = 1,416	n = 456	n = 365
Gender (56% female, 45% male)	66% female, 34% male	58% female, 42% male	61% female, 39% male	79% female, 21% male	43% female, 57% male	30% female, 70% male	54% female, 46% male	75% male, 25% female
Ethnicity (%)								
Caucasian (43.0%)	40.0	44.5	46.8	46.6	35.0	53.2	47.4	26.6
African American (5.9%)	3.9	4.5	4.7	7.9	8.1	5.3	9.0	13.3
Latino (38.0%)	42.9	38.8	33.6	34.5	46.7	24.7	28.8	43.1
Native American (3.3%)	2.9	2.8	3.0	3.1	2.2	5.4	6.4	5.8
Asian American (9.8%)	10.3	9.5	11.9	7.9	8.0	11.4	8.3	11.3
Peer connections (M = 3.59)	3.66	3.63	3.60	3.56	3.56	3.53	3.51	3.47
Friends (% having 2+ friends at school)	94	94	93	92	91	92	92	79

Grades (% with Grades C or higher)	94	92	93	90	87	92	87	77
Truancy (self-reported, %)	29	26	23	41	39	22	35	52
Gang membership (self-reported, %)	3	3	2	5	6	4	8	19
Receive free school lunch? (%)	34	33	35	20	30	35	24	33
Like school? (% yes)	76	73	71	65	65	60	57	50
Like school? ($M = 3.00$)	2.81	2.91	2.96	3.11	3.13	3.18	3.27	3.45
School attachment ($M = 6.12$)	6.56	6.40	6.19	5.82	5.89	5.91	5.36	5.08
Interpersonal trust ($M = 2.68$)	2.99	2.86	2.65	2.49	2.50	2.60	2.21	2.15
School climate ($M = 31.50$)	33.7	32.97	32.26	29.41	30.12	31.32	27.38	25.32
Perceived safety ($M = 20.77$)	22.52	21.66	21.01	20.40	19.84	19.45	17.89	16.2
Hostility ($M = 23.19$)	21.06	22.29	24.23	23.59	23.35	25.46	26.28	25.01
Personal danger ($M = 11.97$)	10.46	11.24	12.17	12.64	12.45	13.05	14.2	14.36

continues

Table 4.1 | continued

Characteristic (and Statistic for Entire Sample)	Cluster 1 Non-victims	Cluster 2 Low Victimization	Cluster 3 Moderate Verbal Threat	Cluster 4 Sexual Harassment	Cluster 5 Moderate Verbal & Weapon Exposure	Cluster 6 High Verbal & Physical Threat	Cluster 7 High Verbal, Physical Threat & Sexual Harassment	Cluster 8 Pervasive Victim
$N = 9{,}723$	$n = 2{,}087$	$n = 1{,}989$	$n = 1{,}336$	$n = 1{,}138$	$n = 936$	$n = 1{,}416$	$n = 456$	$n = 365$
Teacher connections ($M = 2.93$)	3.04	2.98	2.94	2.88	3.04	2.99	2.93	3.15
Worry most about (%)								
1. Getting good grades (60.4%)	66.2	63.8	56.8	60.6	64.3	49.8	49.3	45.6
2. Violence in your school (11.3%)	9.4	11.4	11.6	7.9	10.5	16.1	13.0	20.2
3. Being accepted by peers (12.1%)	9.4	9.7	15.0	13.5	9.3	15.4	18.8	18.8
4. Violence in neighborhood (5.5%)	5.0	4.9	5.9	3.5	5.3	9.3	4.9	7.4
5. Getting along with parents (10.8%)	9.9	10.3	10.8	14.6	10.5	9.3	13.9	8.0

Cluster 4 (Sexual Victimization, n = 1,138, 11.7%)
This group was characterized by moderate to high reports of sexual harassment with some verbal threats. A significant proportion were female (79%), and this is understandable given that female students tend to experience sexually explicit verbal taunts at school. A large number of students (41%) reported truant behaviors. Sixty-five percent of the youths in this cluster reported they liked school, whereas 35% reported that they disliked school.

Cluster 5 (Moderate Weapon Exposure and Verbal Threats, n = 936, 9.6%)
Higher rates of weapon exposure and verbal threats and low rates of other victimization characterized this cluster of students. Thirty percent of these students said they received free or low-cost lunches at school. Students in this group had the second highest rate (39.9%) of self-reported truant behaviors (skipping classes or entire schooldays). There was a higher proportion of African Americans and Latinos in this group when compared with the ethnic distribution of the entire sample. About 6% of the youths reported being a gang member or associating with gang members. When compared with groups with lower levels of victimization, fewer students (87%) reported getting grades of C or better.

Cluster 6 (High Verbal Threats and Physical Threats, n = 1,416, 14.6%)
High levels of verbal and physical threat types of victimization characterized students in Cluster 6. The ethnic distribution did not match the original sample because there was a larger percentage of Caucasians (53%) and Asian Americans (11%) and fewer Latinos (25%). This group had more male (70%) than female (30%) students and the lowest rate of reported truant behavior. The mean score on the personal danger index was 13.05, which indicates some concern about general campus danger and the potential of dangerous acts occurring on campus. Individuals in this cluster also had a lower sense of personal safety when compared with the clusters that had lower rates of victimization. Sixteen percent reported being primarily concerned about violence at their school.

Cluster 7 (High Verbal and Physical Threats and Sexual Harassment,
n = 456, 4.7%)
High rates of verbal threats and physical threats, a moderate rate of sexual harassment, and a lower rate of weapon exposure characterized this group. Gender was about equally distributed in this cluster (54% female and 46% male). A number of these students (35%) reported truancy problems, and 8% reported being a gang member or associating with gang members. Compared with the previous six clusters, fewer students in this cluster reported positive feelings about school and had a lower sense of school attachment (school attachment index subscale: *M* = 5.36). About 57% of these students indicated that they generally liked school, but 43%

reported they disliked or hated school. This group had the highest average score on the hostility index, which indicates that they had negative expectations for interpersonal relationships. Also, this group had the second highest mean score on the danger index, which implies that they anticipated that dangerous and violent acts would occur on their school campus. Thirteen percent of these students indicated that they were most concerned about violence on their school campus, 19% were concerned about being accepted by peers, and 14% were concerned about getting along with their parents. These students also did not feel that they could really trust people at their school (interpersonal trust subscale: $M = 2.21$). A promising marker, however, is that this group tended to feel that they could turn to an average of about two or three teachers for help when needed.

Cluster 8 (Pervasive Victimization, n = 365, 3.8%)

This cluster was characterized by high levels of all types of victimization except sexual harassment (low level). The group comprised 273 male (75%) and 92 female (25%) students. A relatively lower percentage (79%) of students reported having two or more good friends at school, and fewer students (77%) reported getting C or higher grades. More than half of these students reported truant behaviors (52%). This cluster had the highest percentage (19%) of students who reported being either a gang member or a friend of a gang member. The school attachment mean ($M = 5.08$) was the lowest among all eight clusters. This may indicate that these students had a lower sense of belonging to their school and tended to not like school as much. Similarly, these students did not have a strong sense of trust in other people at their school (interpersonal trust subscale: $M = 2.15$) and had a much lower sense of personal safety at school (perceived safety subscale: $M = 16.72$) than students in the other clusters. This group also had the highest mean ($M = 14.36$) on the danger index, which implies that they were more likely than students in other clusters to feel that dangerous and violent acts would occur on their school campus. Although the majority of students in Clusters 1 through 7 reported being most worried about their school grades, only 46% reported being worried about grades in Cluster 8, and 20% (highest across all clusters) reported being most concerned about violence on their school campus. Another 19% indicated that they were worried about being accepted by peers, 7% worried about violence in their neighborhood, and 8% worried about getting along with their parents. On a positive note, these students still thought that they could turn to an average of about three teachers for help when necessary.

SUMMARY AND IMPLICATIONS FOR PRACTICE

In this chapter we presented information about the negative developmental outcomes known to be associated with exposure to violence and to violence victimization. We have argued that because of the special, intimate relationships that students have with peers, teachers, administrators, and mental health professionals, the effects of school violence victimization can be compounded. Schools are places where individuals expect to be safeguarded, and when this expectation is violated, it has the potential to undermine basic feelings of interpersonal trust and to disrupt the learning process (Furlong & Morrison, in press; Morrison & Furlong, 1994). It is for this reason that educators must be particularly mindful of the types and patterns of victimization that occur on their campuses. Given their background and training, we argue that counselors and other mental health professionals are well positioned to support schools' violence efforts designed to prevent victimization and to minimize its impact when it does occur. We have further argued that knowledge of school violence victim subtypes provides a starting point to consider violence victim support programs.

Sometimes, victims experience violation and exploitation and respond to this victimization by drawing on available resources and resilience to positively cope with it. Another response may be that victims withdraw and experience diminished self-esteem and social self-efficacy. Yet, others may react to these affronts by seeking to "level the score" and by taking revenge or retribution (Kingery, Pruitt, & Heuberger, 1996; Lockwood, 1997). Insidiously, the last response can lead to a chronic perpetration–retribution cycle that has no easy or clear exit. The results of the study presented in this chapter indicate that students do indeed experience different types and intensities of victimization at school and that the victimization patterns are associated with different ways of experiencing school.

Consistent with the results of the YRBS national study, we found that a majority of students report experiencing some form of victimization in a typical school month. Although this finding is discouraging, upon closer inspection we found that 55.7% of all students were in Clusters 1, 2, or 3, all of which had no or low levels of victimization. Students in these three clusters indicated experiencing nothing more than verbal taunts, name calling, or attacks. This is not desirable, but it is hopeful to find that these students generally reported positive attitudes and continued to be engaged interpersonally and academically at school. This raises the important point that even as educators seek to minimize exposure to social and physical harm on campuses, this will not always be possible. The students in Clusters 1, 2, and 3 showed that their exposure to mild or moderate verbal taunts did not appear to have had negative impacts on their schooling process, and their available coping resources and assets were sufficient. However, it is likely that these students may witness aggression at school and may at times become a victim of random violence. A prevention program could address these possibilities.

The results of this cluster analysis replicated many other studies showing that male students are most likely to be victimized on school campuses. However, it was also found that whenever sexual victimization behaviors were involved, female students' victimization increased. Cluster 4, in particular, had 79% female membership, the only one with such a large gender discrepancy in favor of female students. It is an important finding that this sizable proportion of students (11.7%) also reported high rates of truancy and dislike of school. In addition, when verbal and physical threats occurred in combination with sexual victimization (Cluster 7: high verbal threats, physical threats, and sexual victimization), there were more female (54%) than male (46%) students. This is in direct contrast to strong male representation in all other clusters that included high levels of physical attacks (Clusters 6 and 8). Emphasizing the negative impacts of the victimization reported by students in Cluster 7, about two fifths of them disliked school, they had a low sense of attachment to school, and they were developing hostile, untrusting cognitions about their interpersonal relationships at school. Although sexual victimization involves female more than male students, it is notable that many male students also reported this type of victimization. We did not inquire about this directly in our questionnaire, but it raises questions about whether some male students are being victimized because of their sexual orientation. A final issue to consider when examining sexual victimization on campuses is how the school helps students manage intimate relationships. It is noteworthy that a number of the school-related multiple-victim homicides that occurred during the late 1990s involved boys who were reported to have felt rejected by a girlfriend. Given the negative effects of sexual victimization on a student's schooling experience and the potential, however slight, for extreme physical violence, school mental health practitioners need to examine how their school violence prevention and intervention programs address dating relationships, date rape, gay and lesbian issues, and harassment behaviors.

Among the many implications of this study are the victimization patterns that emerged for Cluster 6 (high verbal and physical threats). This group had a male–female ratio of 3:1 and comprised 14.1% of all the students. Even though these students had high levels of verbal and physical threat experiences, they generally had a positive attitude about school. They had a low rate of truancy and at least moderately positive levels of involvement and attachment to school. However, they perhaps rightly expressed worries about the level of danger and safety at their schools. These youths were not generally involved with gangs and felt they were performing adequately in their classes. The youths in Cluster 6 present as those who may be picked on repeatedly but are not aggressive themselves. This is in contrast to the small subset of students in Cluster 8 (pervasive victimization). These youths report high levels of verbal attacks, physical attacks, and weapons exposure, and perhaps not surprisingly they have a male–female ratio of 9:1. This group of high-risk students reports the most negative school-related outcomes. They have the poorest attachment to school, have low levels of interpersonal trust, and are the most likely to report being associated with a youth gang. As a group, they are the most likely to be worried about violence at school and to perceive school as a dangerous place. Although this is a relatively small group (a high school with 2,000 pupils might expect to have 50 to 70 of these students), there are enough of them to potentially negatively affect a school's climate. One can imagine that a general conflict resolution program implemented on a school campus would not address the needs of the students represented in Cluster 8. It is likely these students will require comprehensive interventions that involve various public and private community agencies.

CONCLUSION

School violence prevention programs typically focus on breaking the retribution cycle at the point of violence activation, not at the point of victimization. An exception to this practice is Olweus's (1997) work. Of particular relevance to violence prevention programs is a study reported by Lockwood (1997). He found that when asked why they had been in a fight, 84% of the youths provided a rationale justifying their use of violence. These justifications included (a) retaliation for harmful behavior (28.8%), (b) the other youth's behavior was offensive (17.7%), (c) self-defense to stop victimization (13.6%), and (d) helping a friend (12.6%). Even when unjustified explanations were offered, they included being blinded by anger into action (6.6%) and being "pushed" into violence by another youth (5.6%). Lockwood concluded that most of the violent incidents described by these youths involved situations in which they perceived themselves or others to be victimized and that their actions were justified as an act of retaliation. They did not believe that their actions were inappropriate. One can imagine the limited impact that a violence prevention or conflict management program would have on similar youths when these programs emphasize peaceful negotiation but the youths' beliefs promote justified retaliation. Lockwood's findings are particularly important for a comprehensive school violence program that includes a victim support component because they suggest that perceptions of victimization will be widespread, even among the perpetuators of violence. This study clearly shows that student victims of violence are not a monolithic group but have a broad range of experiences with differing impacts on their schooling outcomes. Educators implementing school violence prevention and intervention efforts should consider the diversity of victimization experience on their campuses as part of their comprehensive school safety planning efforts.

REFERENCES

Bates, M., Chung, A., & Chase, M. (1997). Where has the trust gone? The protective role of interpersonal trust and connections with adults in the school. *California School Psychologist, 2,* 39–52.

Batsche, G. M., & Knoff, H. M. (1994). Bullies and their victims: Understanding a pervasive problem in the schools. *School Psychology Review, 23,* 165–174.

Bell, C. C., & Jenkins, E. J. (1993). Community violence and children on Chicago's southside. *Psychiatry: Interpersonal and Biological Processes, 56,* 46–54.

Berkowitz, L. (1990). *Biological roots: Are humans inherently violent?* In B. Glad (Ed.), *Psychological dimensions of war.* Newbury Park, CA: Sage.

Boney-McCoy, S. F., & Finkelhor, D. (1995). Psychosocial sequelae of violent victimization in a national youth sample. *Journal of Consulting and Clinical Psychology, 63,* 726–736.

Brener, N. D., Simon, T. R., Krug, E. T., & Lowry, R. (1999). Recent trends in violence-related behaviors among high school students in the United States. *Journal of the American Medical Association, 282,* 440–446.

Buss, A. H., & Perry, M. (1992). The aggression questionnaire. *Journal of Personality and Social Psychology, 63,* 452–459.

Centers for Disease Control and Prevention. (1999). *National YRBS data files and documentation.* Atlanta, GA: Author. (http://www.cdc.gov/nccdphp/dash/yrbs/datareq.htm)

Cornell, D. G., & Loper, A. B. (1998). Assessment of violence and other high-risk behaviors with a school survey. *School Psychology Review, 27,* 317–330.

Dodge, K. A., & Schwartz, D. (1997). Social information processing mechanisms in aggressive behavior. In D. M. Stoff & J. Breiling (Eds.), *Handbook of antisocial behavior* (pp. 171–180). New York: Wiley.

Dwyer, K., Osher, D., & Warger, C. (1998). *Early warning, timely response: A guide to safe schools.* Washington, DC: U.S. Department of Education.

Finkelhor, D., & Dzuiba-Leatherman, J. (1994). Victimization of children. *American Psychologist, 49,* 173–183.

Freeman, L. N., Mokros, H., & Poznanski, E. (1993). Violent events reported by normal urban school-aged children: Characteristics and depression correlates. *Journal of the American Academy of Child and Adolescent Psychiatry, 32,* 419–423.

Furlong, M. J., Chung, A., Bates, M., & Morrison, R. (1995). Who are the victims of school violence? *Education and Treatment of Children, 18,* 282–298.

Furlong, M. J., & Morrison, G. M. (in press). The SCHOOL in school violence: Definitions and facts. *Journal of Emotional and Behavioral Disorders.*

Furlong, M. J., Morrison, R., Bates, M., & Chung, A. (1998). School violence victimization among secondary students in California: Grade, gender, and racial–ethnic incidence patterns. *California School Psychologist, 3,* 71–87.

George, C., & Main, M. (1979). Social interactions of young abused children: Approach, avoidance, and aggression. *Child Development, 50,* 306–318.

Hoover, J. H., Oliver, R., & Hazler, R. J. (1992). Bullying: Perception of adolescent victims in midwestern USA. *School Psychology International, 13,* 5–16.

Jaffe, P., Wolfe, D. A., Wilson, S., & Zak, L. (1986). Emotional and physical health problems of battered women. *Canadian Journal of Psychiatry, 31,* 625–629.

Kann, L., Kinchen, S. A., Williams, B. I., Ross, J. G., Lowry, R., Hill, C. V., Grunbaum, J., Blumson, P. S., Collins, J. L., & Kolbe, L. J. (1998). Youth Risk Behavior Surveillance–1997. *MMWR, 47*(No. SS–3), 1–89.

Kingery, P. M., Pruitt, B. E., & Heuberger, G. (1996). A profile of rural Texas adolescents who carry handguns to school. *Journal of School Health, 66*(1), 210–214.

Limber, S. P., & Nation, M. (1998). *Bullying among school children.* Washington, DC: Office of Juvenile Justice and Delinquency Prevention.

Lockwood, D. (1997). *Violence among middle school and high school students: An analysis and implications for prevention.* Washington, DC: U.S. Department of Justice, Office of Justice Programs, National Institute of Justice.

Morrison, G. M., & Furlong, M. J. (1994). From school violence to school safety: Reframing the issue for school psychologists. *School Psychology Review, 23,* 236–256.

Morrison, G., Furlong, M. J., & Smith, G. (1994). Factors associated with the experience of school violence among general education, leadership class, opportunity class, and special day class pupils. *Education and Treatment of Children, 17,* 356–369.

Olweus, D. (1978). *Aggression in the schools: Bullies and whipping boys.* Washington, DC: Hemisphere.

Olweus, D. (1997). Tackling peer victimization. In D. P. Fry & K. Bjoerkqvist (Eds.), *Cultural variation in conflict resolution: Alternatives to violence.* Mahwah, NJ: Erlbaum.

Richters, J. E., & Martinez, P. (1993). The NIMH community violence project: I. Children as victims of and witnesses to violence. *Psychiatry: Interpersonal and Biological Processes, 56,* 7–21.

Shakoor, B. H., & Chalmers, D. (1991). Co-victimization of African-American children who witness violence: Effects on cognitive, emotional, and behavioral development. *Journal of the National Medical Association, 83,* 233–238.

Smith, P. K., Morita, Y., Junger-Tas, J., Olweus, D., Catalano, R. F., & Slee, P. (Eds.). (1999). *The nature of school bullying: A cross-national perspective.* New York: Routledge.

Terr, L. (1991). Childhood traumas: An outline and overview. *American Journal of Psychiatry, 148,* 10–20.

Williams, K., Chambers, M., Logan, S., & Robinson, D. (1996). Association of common health symptoms with bullying in primary school children. *British Medical Journal, 313,* 17–19.

5 | Masculine Thinking and School Violence: Issues of Gender and Race

Lissa J. Yogan and Stuart Henry

That men commit more crimes and more violent acts than women is perhaps no surprise. Popular stereotypes of men as competitive, dominant, and aggressive and women as cooperative, subordinate, and passive suggest this difference, and it has a strong basis in fact: "The male crime rate exceeds that of females universally, in all nations, in all communities, among all age groups, and in all periods of history for which statistics are available" (Hagan, 1998, p. 72). The gender disparity between males and females for violent crime is even greater than for property crime. In 1996, for youths under age 18, 85% of all arrestees for violent crime were males (Bureau of Justice Statistics, 1998).

Thus while it might be shocking, it should not be surprising that overtly violent acts are committed by teenage boys. The real shock of the recent teenage violence is that it is now happening in suburban and rural schools. Places that were formerly deemed safe have lost their sense of security. Parents, educators, and school children are worried that serious school violence can happen anywhere. Indeed, it seemingly has. Since 1997, there have been several school shootings and related deaths: 25 in 1997, 42 in 1998, and, to date, 24 in 1999, in all 211 since 1992. These recent shootings have been committed by White boys on their classmates and teachers. They have occurred in places thought to represent the ideals of American society, places in which families and communities took pride, places reflecting their economic achievements and sense of community. To such communities and the nation, the eruption of such violence is terrifying. Citizens long to answer the question, why is this happening here? The broader questions to ask are why teenage boys commit such high rates of violent crime compared with teenage girls, and is there something about the intersections of class, race, and gender in youths that produce different outcomes? Furthermore, is there something about the changing social and cultural landscape of American society that is providing the formative context for these different and frightening developments?

Before this recent spate of incidents, school violence was largely seen as an issue of troubled inner-city schools and of African American and Latino boys who have historically suffered discrimination. Indeed, between 1992 and 1994, 50% of school homicides were committed by African Americans (Kachur et al., 1996). Violence in urban schools was seen as an angry response to structural inequalities in American society: poor conditions, dilapidated and decaying neighborhoods, and hopeless opportunities in life. Such "normal" school violence was largely collective and gang related. Yet, the most recent incidents have not occurred in the inner cities, nor have they been perpetrated by minority youths. They have been committed by young White males acting alone or in pairs, living in middle- or upper-income communities, and frequently having come from intact families. Because these young men come from stable, desirable families and communities, indeed, several from the structurally privileged classes, much of the national-level discussion has focused on American society's "toxic culture" and deficient gun laws.

Yet, if gun laws and media-based violence alone were responsible for this new wave of school shootings, it seems likely that at least some of the violence would have been committed by teenage girls who are also exposed to the same toxic culture. To date, that has not been the case. And why, if culture and guns are to blame, does "normal" school violence (i.e., the violence appears to have been around for generations, including fighting and intimidation, gangs, bullying, and threats) seem to take a different form from these recent high-profile school massacres? It is our view that these new violent acts cannot be explained in isolation from the society in which they develop. Thus this chapter explores the social context shaping the development and thinking of young men and how masculine thinking is related to the recent incidents of school violence committed by White males in places formerly assumed to be safe institutions of learning. We begin our analysis with an examination of how teenage boys think and how that might lead them to decide on violent action as the solution to a moral dilemma or personal conflict.

GENDER DIFFERENCES IN THINKING
IN A CHANGING CAPITALIST SOCIETY

Kohlberg (1980a) wrote: "Today the major problem in developing youth is privatism; its major educational solution is participation" (p. 459). He went on to describe privatism as the philosophy of "look[ing] out for number one" (Kohlberg, 1980a, p. 461). Kohlberg worried that such a philosophy could undermine the attainment and even understanding of his

Stage 4 principles that served to maintain society's social order through violating rules or harming others. Today, 20 years later, it appears that he was right to be worried. The principles that serve to maintain society have seemingly weakened. The White youths who recently turned their violence onto their schools and themselves appear to have exhibited a Stage 2 level of moral reasoning, a lack of concern for their classmates, and an alienation from institutional schooling.

Stage 2 reasoning is characterized as an instrumental relativist orientation (Kohlberg, 1980b). At this stage, "right action consists of that which instrumentally satisfies one's own needs and occasionally the needs of others. Reciprocity is a matter of you scratch my back and I'll scratch yours, not of loyalty, gratitude, or justice" (Kohlberg, 1980b, p. 91). Violent students who act from a Stage 2 level of moral reasoning frequently conclude that their acts are justified because other students acted against them; thus they have a need for revenge or power over others. Clearly such thinking does not see value in doing what that person's family, community, or nation would see as right (Stage 3), nor does it take into account the rules necessary for the maintenance of social order (Stage 4).

In Kohlberg's original research, only males were studied. When females were later included, they clustered around Stage 3, the level at which concern for interpersonal expectations is expressed. Gilligan (1982) suspected that women were equally capable of exhibiting high levels of moral reasoning but that the orientation on justice and rights of Kohlberg's theory did not sufficiently address the context of women's lives. Gilligan found that women potentially experience three stages of moral development that are based on issues of caring and personal relationships. In the first stage, women make decisions based on caring for themselves and use egocentric reasoning. At the second stage, women make decisions on the basis of caring for others and often engage in self-sacrifice or complete lack of focus on self. At the third stage, women come to understand that a good moral decision is one that integrates concern for self with concern for others.

Gilligan (1982) saw gender socialization as the explanation for differences in the ways that men and women reason. This explanation was verified by Pratt, Golding, and Hunter (1984). They found that men who were defined as masculine exhibited moral reasoning based on the ideals of justice and fairness. Women who were identified as feminine exhibited reasoning based on issues of caring. Gender differences in moral orientation seem to stem from gender differences in socialization. Socialization is influenced by parents and the media in the context of the wider social structure of a changing capitalist society that has increasingly alienated its members.

Gender roles that are constructed initially on the basis of economic production contribute to alienation. Gender is an important status that is

symbolized through specific behaviors, styles of dress, and ways of acting. These symbols of gender determine whom people interact with and
the way in which they interact. Constructing gender in a rigid or narrow
manner that denies women from being aggressive and tough and that
restricts men from being the primary nurturer or demonstrator of feelings
alienates individuals from each other and from their own humanness.

Bonger (1916) applied a Marxian analysis to issues of crime and violence. He argued that capitalism spreads an impoverishment of humanity
to all members of society, regardless of their class position. Bonger said
that crime is an acting out of a "criminal thought." The criminal thought
and the willingness to act on it are more likely when a society promotes
"egoism" than when it promotes "altruism." As Kohlberg and others have
noted, American society is seen as increasingly me-oriented; it promotes
egoism more than altruism. Along these same lines, the dominant feature
of masculinity that we discuss later is the notion of autonomy and toughness—which directly contrasts with altruism. However, women are still
taught that appropriate feminine behavior and thinking are based on
ideals that are more closely linked to altruism than egoism. Thus, Bonger's
analysis helps explain why women are less likely to engage in criminal
behavior than men.

As capitalism has transformed the 20th century, there has been further
impoverishment of the humanity of society. In the late 1980s and early
1990s, the United States changed from a predominantly manufacturing
economy using skilled labor to a labor-intensive, service-oriented one.
The result was less high-paid manufacturing jobs and more low-paid service jobs. This changing nature of work left many unemployed, including
White men (highly educated and those with only a high school diploma).
For them, the rules of the game had seemingly changed. No longer could
it be assumed that college education or loyal work would be rewarded
with lifetime employment. Also perceived as threatening White men's
position in the labor force is the policy of affirmative action that emerged
out of the 1960s civil rights and women's movements. By the 1990s, affirmative action became an increasingly important issue in state and
national elections as Whites declared that hiring practices involved quo-
tas that effectively discriminated against White men (Schaefer, 1998). But
this belief in the existence of "reverse discrimination" has never been verified. However, reality might not matter in the social construction of a
gender-related or race-related problem. Such is the perception of alienation from their fellow humans that White males came to believe that
they, as a group, are entitled to a privileged position.

In its most extreme version, this has been termed *White supremacy*. If
White men believe that their traditional ways of establishing relationships
(through work and then marriage) are threatened or that an education no
longer guarantees them a good job, then it is likely they will act on these
beliefs no matter what the actual data or statistics reveal: "If . . . . [people]

define situations as real, they are real in their consequences" (Thomas & Thomas, 1928, p. 572). Thus, even though many women and minorities might see society as politically dominated and economically controlled by White men, if White men believe their power or social identity is threatened, they will act as if it is. If White boys lose faith in the power of education to provide them with good jobs, it is likely that they will become alienated from institutional schooling. In this sense, White males may be doubly alienated. If they believe that society is now discriminating against them, they will see no reason to engage in moral reasoning that upholds the laws and norms of society. In essence, the thinking and action of White males is based on their perception of the social world, but as Marx had pointed out, it is also shaped by that world as they are constituted through it. As late 20th-century capitalism merges into the postmodernist information age, the very alienation and anomie that the founding sociologists described have intensified. There has been an economic polarization between low-income service jobs and high-tech, high-paying information jobs. Thus, recent social critics such as Jean Baudrillard (Poster, 1988) argue that in a postmodern consumer society, meaningful social relationships are almost nonexistent. Postmodern culture, says Baudrillard, involves social relations without content, fixed meaning, or substance.

Some have described this culmination of capitalism's worst features as producing a "broken world," and they claim that it is the very cultural context of this world that shapes the formative years of today's youths (Staples, 2000, p. 31). Staples argued that in the consumerist world, "relationships are secondary, acquisition is primary . . . individuals become little more than functionaries to fulfill each other's symbolic needs and not persons of worth and value" (Staples, 2000, p. 32). This results in violence in the schools as "our deeper yearning for significance" goes unmet. Traditionally, males have met their needs through work relations; however, not only have these become devalued, but there has been a growing tendency, driven by the women's movement, for men to become more nurturing and less masculine.

Today, the perception of an alienated, empty, and changing world appears to be the backcloth that has led young White males to violent expressions of anxiety and uncertainty over their role and place in society. Part of the problem may be that patterns of socialization, which themselves are shaped by the wider social structure, are not aligned with the changing structural and cultural conditions identified earlier.

AGENTS OF SOCIALIZATION AND THE CONSTRUCTION OF GENDER AND RACE

Socialization is "the lifelong process through which individuals learn their culture, develop their human potential, and become functioning members of society" (Lindsey, 1994, p. 48). Socialization is an uneven process that takes place in many areas and with many different groups and individuals. People are primarily socialized by their families, schools, media, and peers. Socialization is powerful because it is a form of social control (Lindsey, 1994) designed to ensure that members of any given society act in normatively approved ways.

The social constructionist model of gender argues that the meaning of femininity and masculinity varies from culture to culture and within any one culture over time (Kimmel & Messner, 1995). Masculinity and femininity also vary within any one society by the types of cultural groups that compose it. Thus, gender is constructed differently by socioeconomic class, race, and age. Although some generalizations can be made regarding the meaning of masculinity and femininity in the United States, there are different norms, behaviors, and practices associated with being a White male than are associated with being a Latino or African American male.

Being a "real male" is the subject of the recent work of Pollack (1998), who claimed that the mandate from society that boys reject nurturing roles and come to associate masculinity with negative expressions is causing a crisis for boys. He called society's mandate to be tough and independent the "boy code." Pollack said that this code is in conflict with the late 20th-century value of American society that men become more nurturing, take on more of the familial and domestic responsibilities, and exhibit more "sensitivity":

> We now say that we want boys to share their vulnerable feelings, but at the same time we expect them to cover their need for dependency and *hide* their natural feelings of love and caring behind the mask of masculine autonomy and strength. It's an impossible assignment for any boy, or, for that matter, any human being. (Pollack, 1998, pp. 12–13)

Yet, parents, peers, the media, and schools persist in the socialization techniques that reinforce fairly rigid gender roles and tell boys that the way to become masculine is to develop their strength and independence, not their relationships and communication skills.

Masculinity: Shame, Strain, and Violence

Handling shame may be one of the key differences between boys and girls that helps explain boys' likelihood of using violence when handling emotional situations. According to Jordan (1989) and Pollack (1998), shame can be described as the feeling state that accompanies emotional disconnection. Pollack (1998) said that humans feel stupid and vulnerable when embarrassed or humiliated and want to hide or isolate themselves. Such experiences lead to emotional disconnection or "shame." No one enjoys these feelings, thus both boys and girls will work to hide them. Yet, Pollack said that whereas girls are shame-sensitive, boys are shame-phobic. Shame often accompanies adolescence in girls and can lead to the silencing of their voices in middle school and high school. Pollack believed, however, that boys are attuned to shame at a much earlier age because the requirements of becoming masculine are more rigid than those for becoming feminine, and because boys are pushed to separate from their mothers and the sense of caring and goodness that their mothers often represent. He said that boys will do almost anything to avoid a loss of face: "Rather than expose themselves to this kind of potent embarrassment, boys, in the face of suffering shame, engage in a variety of behaviors that range from avoidance of dependency to impulsive action, from bravado and rage-filled outbursts to intense violence" (Pollack, 1998, p. 33).

Agnew (1995) developed a related argument. He said that youths are not only goal seeking but pain avoiding, so long as there are legitimate opportunities to avoid pain. But if these escape routes are blocked, strain may result in anger and frustration:

> Adolescents who are abused by parents, for example, may be legally unable to escape from home. Or adolescents who are harassed by teachers may be unable legally to escape from school. This inability to escape from painful situations, or this blockage of pain avoidance behavior . . . creates pressure for corrective action, with delinquency being one possible response. (Agnew, 1995, pp. 115–116)

Certainly we have read and seen evidence of rage-filled "corrective action" and intense violence in Littleton, Colorado, where the two shooters in the Columbine High School massacre were described as boys who had been rejected and made fun of by athletes and other students at school. We have seen impulsive action by the boy who shot six classmates in Conyers, Georgia, after his girlfriend broke up with him. The link between shame, masculinity, and violence is apparent in these recent incidents of school violence. But why are these highly visible incidents of teenage White male violence occurring in high schools? Is it just a convenient place to attack those who have in some way shamed these White youths, or is it the case that schools themselves contribute to this problem? It appears that schools are often a part of the problem but could also be a significant part of the solution to school violence. We examine how schools create an environment that alienates boys, and in the final section of this chapter we discuss how schools, with the help of school counselors, can become part of the solution to the problem of school violence.

Schools, Socialization, and Alienation

Schools are the major agent of secondary and continuing socialization, yet schools can also be perceived as alienating institutions. Schools influence children's identities for numerous years, and

> unfortunately, many schools unwittingly socialize children into acquiring one set of values, to the virtual exclusion of the other. The stereotype is that in filling breadwinning roles, boys will need to be taught the value of competitiveness. In filling domestic roles, girls will need to be taught the value of nurturance. Though both may be positive traits, they are limited or truly accepted by, only one gender. (Lindsey, 1994, pp. 64–65)

This trend of emphasizing only one aspect of being fully human is repeated in many ways. And as Marx emphasized, fragmentation of self can result in alienation from self and from the institutions that socialize this fragmentation.

The sense of self-esteem that is socialized and developed in school is accomplished through different activities for boys and girls. For girls, popularity with boys is linked to prestige. Although many feminists may wish that this were not the case, and correctly point out that girls form a sense of self that is dependent on the approval of boys, this also has a positive value: The human aspect girls develop may help them in many future interactions with both genders. Girls gain prestige through successful interactions with others that focus on caring and taking the role of the "other." Indeed, this is precisely what Marxist feminists object to in that it trains girls to be reproducers and repairers of compliant labor for the capitalist economy (Alleman, 1993).

Coleman's (1961) classic findings that boys' prestige with both genders rests on their athletic accomplishments are still highly relevant. Messner (1987) found that if a boy does not measure up to his peers in terms of athletic prowess or physical deeds, his self-esteem suffers. According to the values promoted by ideals of masculinity and embodied in the boy code, academic achievement is no real substitute for athletic rewards. Thus in school, athletic skills, which often include denial of pain, substitution of aggression for emotion, and the value of using physical violence against others (i.e., football), become the route to increased self-esteem and prestige among peers for boys. Boys develop the individual part of selfhood, are capable of violence, and are encouraged to deny human feelings of fear, pain, and so on. These are not skills that will help them interact or develop close intimate relationships with a variety of people, though they are skills that may help them resist oppression. Girls' popularity with boys and boys' athletic skill development are tangential to learning to read, write, and do arithmetic—the manifest function of schools. How are boys and girls affected by schools in the actual academic learning environment?

For several years now, attention to gender in schools has focused on the ways in which schools shortchange girls. Women are rarely mentioned as making meaningful contributions to history, science, or government, and curriculum material is filled with stereotyped portrayals of men and women. Although girls in elementary school are confident and assertive, they leave adolescence and middle school with a poor self-image. Over the past 20 years, the focus has been on how schools and educational processes fail to help girls fully develop. Ironically, the assumption during this time has been that schools are only harming girls. This does not seem to be a safe or valid assumption. It now appears that the rigid gender socialization that is present in schools also causes significant harm for boys.

The harm that schooling causes boys is harder to notice at first because of boys' tendency to brag and because many of the most publicized academic stars in math and science are boys. While it may be true that boys outnumber girls in the top 10% of math and science performers, one study found that in relation to reading and writing skills, boys outnumbered girls at the bottom of the scales by a margin of two to one (Hedges & Nowell, 1995). Being able to read and write well are skills that U.S. Secretary of Education Richard Riley (1997) claimed are linked to children's education and career achievement: "Teachers will tell you that . . . [poor readers] often get down on themselves . . . become frustrated, and often head down the road to truancy and dropping out. Then things can get worse: Some . . . begin to make the wrong choices about drugs." Becoming frustrated, increasing truancy rates, and increasing alienation were demonstrated by Harper and Purkey (1993), who found eighth-grade boys 50% more likely to be held back a grade than girls, and by high school, two thirds of all special education students are boys. Boys also constitute 71% of school suspensions and have more difficulty "adjusting" to school life. Pollack (1998) wrote, "Overwhelmingly, recent research indicates that girls not only feel more confident about themselves as learners but also show more vigor in the steps they take toward developing meaningful careers" (p. 235). If it is true that boys suffer a large crisis in terms of their development as learners, why has the majority of recent national attention focused on girls?

A major reason that recent attention has focused on girls' development and self-esteem is due to the work of Gilligan (1982) and Pipher (1994), which revealed when girls do not feel self-confident at school they are less likely to speak in classes and their emotional and academic growth decline. Another reason might be due to the nature of tests previously used to measure self-esteem. These tests have traditionally asked very direct questions such as "Do you feel that you are good at math?" Boys, more than girls, have a tendency to answer such questions in a way that indicates their knowledge of what society would like to hear. Pollack (1998) said that boys are likely to answer direct questions about ability in ways that will make them sound self-confident (a mandate of the boy code) regardless of the truth of their answers.

Studies indicate that boys' sense of self as a good learner is at risk and that self-esteem as a learner is more a matter of gender than race. Thus, it can be said that schools appear to be causing a crisis in self-esteem for both boys and girls. Yet, the crisis for boys is not mitigated by their gender role expectations. Rather, it is heightened by the strict code of masculinity. Whereas girls can still feel successful if they simply graduate high school, marry, and raise a family, boys face the pressure to excel at athletics, obtain a good career, and provide for their future families. All this is to be accomplished by boys without expressing self-doubt, fear, anxiety, or the need to have help from others.

One of the significant ways in which boys are socialized and also alienated from schools is through the discipline process. The message "boys will be boys" is often communicated by parents, grandparents, and friends. It is a message that encourages boys' early adventures and allows them to be more physical at play than their female counterparts. Yet, when boys enter school, they often hear a contradictory message: that they must sit passively for hours and not explore their physical environment with others. Many educators cast boys as the "bad or difficult kids" and simply send them to the principal's office when they exhibit the "boys will be boys" type of behavior. Other educators attempt to make sure that boys follow appropriate gender-typed behavior. Often, little boys are discouraged from dressing up as a woman, crying when their feelings are hurt, or engaging in play around domestic-type toys. Pollack (1998) said that "boys at school are often perceived as 'little (testosterone-driven) monsters' whose 'aggression' must be controlled and disciplined rather than as vulnerable little boys who must be nurtured and encouraged" (p. 243).

The connection between teachers and boys may grow farther apart during the teen years when boys begin to physically mature. At this time, boys may be physically intimidating, and it becomes harder for teachers to see the vulnerable part of the masculine body in front of them. Teachers who are also socialized by society and the media may become blinded to the rigid code of masculinity that dictates much of adolescent male behavior. They may even feel intimidated or physically threatened by teenage boys. In situations that call for a response, teachers may be inclined to use the school's discipline process rather than hold a conversation with the boy and try to see behind the mask of masculinity.

In short, gender stereotyping continues when children enter schools. For girls, this process calls them to question themselves and their thoughts and achievements. Yet girls often attribute their academic failing to themselves and thus try harder. For boys, this stereotyping suggests they exhibit toughness in athletics, deny academic failings, and attribute their struggles to behavioral difficulties. School is not a place that encourages boys to try harder. It is a place that asks them to deny their feelings, and it provides a rather narrow avenue of gender-appropriate achievement. It is also a place that says (through the large number of discipline cases that involve boys) that not achieving is typical and in fact somewhat accepted if you happen to be a boy. Not surprisingly, therefore, when alienation generated by frustration and anger knows no outlet, resistance to pain can come through aggressive, violent reactions against all who symbolize the cause of the pain. If the cause of the pain is "the popular boys and girls," or even the school itself, then that is where violence will likely be directed, if for no other reason than to make the pain stop. Yet the question remains, why does the socialization that defines violence as morally wrong not keep violence at bay? Part of the reason for this stems from the effect of peers.

Peer Socialization, Subculture, and Neutralizing Morality

As children move outside the home and interact with other children, peers play an increasing role in their socialization. "Both gender segregation and the influence of peer groups increase throughout the school years, exerting powerful influences on children" (Lindsey, 1994, p. 62). Brinn, Kraemer, Warm, and Paludi (1984) found that boys in particular are tenacious in their gender role attitudes and exhibit strong masculine preferences through preadolescence.

For those youths who have become alienated from conventional institutions or who failed to form bonds to conventional morals and laws, peers become a major force of influence. However, the influence of peers is rarely to the exclusion of other socialization but forms an intertextual discourse from which individual youths make decisions. In the school context, this discourse is manifest through cliques, some of which reflect an accentuation of dominant societal values, some of which reflect subcultural values, and all of which reflect the hierarchy of inequality of the wider society, including its intergroup conflicts. Take Columbine High as an example:

> Circulating around the noisy jock center are the preps in their Abercrombie & Fitch, cheerleaders giggling near the water fountains, computer geeks, skaters, thespians, and debate-teamers. Gangsta pretenders in huge pants and Starta jackets hang out by the pay phone near the main entrance with their pagers. And then there are all the low-status outsider cliques: punks, goths, stoners, the now infamous Trench Coat Mafia and anybody else who cannot belong to a clique as that term is understood. (Wilkinson & Hendrickson, 1999, p. 49)

As in the wider society, conflicts between different subcultural groups and the system in general can be particularly intense when one group, in close proximity to another, feels relatively and unjustly deprived. This situation can be aggravated when the more successful group holds the less successful in contempt. In understanding the way these school cliques reflect the wider society's inequalities and how that can become converted into sufficiently focused hate that justifies violence and even murder, the work of David Matza on neutralization of morality is instructive.

NEUTRALIZING MORALITY:
THE SIGNIFICANCE OF DENYING THE VICTIM

One of the central points that emerged from the work of David Matza (1964) and Gresham Sykes (Matza & Sykes, 1961; Sykes & Matza, 1957) was that delinquent youths are morally ambivalent. This ambivalence stems in part from their socialization experience in the conventional society and in part from their socialization experience among their peers. Matza argued that youths remain both in conventional culture and in subcultures and exercise choice over their action in relation to the demands of both. Again Columbine is illustrative. While Eric Harris hated many things, including liars and country music, he particularly hated racists, athletes with attitudes, and flag burners; yet he saw no reason why, counter to law and American values, such people should not die. Thus, Harris was both consistent with, and contradictory to, American values.

Matza and Sykes's theory is cognizant of this ambivalence. They argued that most youths are not full-fledged gang members but "mundane delinquents" who are remorseful and have a conscience, differentiating between victims and admiring law-abiding citizens and values. Delinquents are aware of the difference between right and wrong and choose to engage in harmful behavior only under certain circumstances. Moreover, the source of these circumstances, which permit youths to engage in wrongs, stems not necessarily from negative subcultures, though it may be reinforced there, but from the underbelly of mainstream society: from its subterranean values. According to Matza and Sykes, these exist side by side with other values and are part of what gets communicated through the socialization process, especially in schools:

> When a teacher presents the class material on social studies she or he teaches the knowledge content of the subject; when the teacher deals with the students with favoritism, using gender or racial bias, or emphasizes grades as more important than understanding, she or he sends a different message. Students learn how society works. They learn that there are public statements and private practices; they learn that beneath the rhetoric, what matters is getting ahead by whatever means, including cheating if necessary. . . . Simply by learning and being socialized into conventional values and norms, adolescents are simultaneously socialized into the negation of those values. (Lanier & Henry, 1998, p. 147)

This certainly describes the recent perpetrators of school violence who come from middle- and upper-class homes yet also interacted with peers, albeit "outsiders."

IMPLICATIONS FOR COUNSELING

Structural and cultural forces create conditions of alienation and anomie that fragment community and leave individuals isolated. But these forces are mediated by race and gender. Socialization processes reflect and reinforce these differences. In particular, their effect is to accentuate the isolation of boys and men, while preserving the connectedness and community of girls and women. Moral development, which occurs through interaction and socialization, produces the capability of making judgments that do not result in harmful outcomes. However, socialization of youths simultaneously sends ambiguous messages that provide the seeds for moral neutralization, regardless of a person's generalized level of moral development. Depending on their race and gender, youths respond differently to these conditions and social processes.

Structurally oppressed and ecologically insulated, alienated minority male youths focus their anger and frustration on each other in their neighborhoods. They act collectively through gangs and justify their victimization of others in relation to harms caused to themselves historically, institutionally, or interpersonally. Their school violence is more stable and controlled as they are more subject to surveillance. White males, in contrast, who have historically come to expect a relatively privileged life, but who are also socialized to "do their gender" through individual acts of violence, react alone or in pairs. Their violence tends to be extreme, homicidal, or suicidal and is taken out on the system or on those who seem to succeed where they have failed. Finally, female alienated youths, through both socialization and control, internalize their anger on themselves. This is manifest through acts of self-destruction through food, smoking and drugs to lose weight, and depression. Short of a social and cultural revolution, how can counselors help to reduce school violence?

Newmann (1981) said the key is in creating educational institutions that help students expend energy in ways that enhance their engagement with schoolwork, people at the school, and the physical setting itself, but in ways that promote community and social integration rather than reinforcing the wider social processes of alienation. Thus, the basis for our recommendations for counselors rests on what we have outlined throughout this chapter. The concept of masculinity taught to White youths, coupled with structural and cultural changes in American society, has led to thinking that results in violent action. Schools need to provide an environment that helps boys reconnect with the feminine side of themselves and ultimately to others and the institution of school.

A national longitudinal study found that the largest factor (other than closeness within families) that protected youths from violence, drug abuse, and emotional distress was "perceived school connectedness" (Resnick et al., 1997). Jenkins's (1997) research on 754 middle school students supports the finding that the school as an instrument of socialization can play a major role in delinquency prevention by strengthening the bond between students and the educational process. Jenkins found that personal background characteristics, family involvement in schooling, and ability grouping influence the strength of the school bond. Importantly, commitment to school and a belief in the fairness and consistent enforcement of school rules were the most important predictors of school crime.

Helping boys connect to schools is critical if we are to reduce the incidence of school violence. How can this connection be fostered by school counselors? One of the biggest problems facing school counselors is lack of time. In 1997, as the incidence of school violence began to increase, there was a demand by the American Conference of Mayors to add 100,000 more counselors to American schools. Counselors do not have the time to meet one-on-one with all the students who are assigned to them. Any work that will be effective in addressing the problems of alienation and school connectedness will have to be done in groups, and there is some evidence that this is more effective.

Peer-Facilitated Groups

Groups are an ideal environment for helping students develop their moral thinking. And groups that help facilitate moral development do not have to initially be led by the overtaxed counselors themselves. Indeed, Kohlberg's (1980a) concept of the "just community" suggests that a participatory form of group structure is the most productive for furthering moral development. Selman and Schultz (1988) found when comparing relationships between teenage peers with relationships between teens and adults, "adolescents may more readily develop reciprocal or collaborative strategies in the context of their interactions with peers, and then perhaps transfer these skills to negotiations with adults" (p. 222). The implications for school counselors is that their work with large groups of boys may best involve the use of peer facilitators prior to involvement with a counselor (Locke & Zimmerman, 1987).

What kind of work should peer groups attempt? The ability to take the role of another is critical to the development of maturity and moral reasoning (Kohlberg, 1969, 1984). As we have seen, youths subscribe to multiple perspectives and may have trouble determining the best perspective from which to make sense of the event. Involvement in peer groups enables youths to hear their own voice (and perspective) and experience the reactions of others to their viewpoints. As they experience others' reactions, they learn to "take the role of another," and they start to synthesize their multiple perspectives. Importantly, at least one voice (ideally that of the peer facilitator) should be at a stage or level above that of the troubled youth. On the basis of Kohlberg's work, it has been found "that exposing individuals through moral discussions to the reasoning of those who were more developmentally advanced was most successful in stimulating the development of moral reasoning when the arguments were presented at a level just beyond the individual's current level of functioning" (Hayes, 1994, p. 263).

In addition to helping students increase their level of moral development, such peer groups can help students connect with other students as well as develop their own sense of individuality. The goal for counselors is to help youths achieve a sense of competence in dealing with troubling situations, to integrate themselves with others who will listen to them and challenge them in a way that supports moral development, and ultimately to disconnect from negative peer groups and organizations and get involved with more positive institutions (what school, it is hoped, will come to represent). At a minimum, counselors need to hear the voices of students who claim that the school is supporting some groups' exercise of power and domination over others and attempt to bring that to the attention of school administrations.

Cooperative Work in Nonathletic Settings

A sense of communality is important in reducing alienation (Newmann, 1981). Traditionally, school instruction has discouraged cooperative work among students, and dialogue among students in class is often seen as a discipline problem rather than a form of shared learning. Individual effort is difficult to evaluate in group projects, so most teachers use this method sparingly. Schools do not try to schedule classes in such a way as to promote or strengthen peer friendships and in some cases deliberately try to separate an individual's peer group members (Newmann, 1981).

Cusick (1973) pointed out that the strong peer culture that exists in schools is often a reaction to and based on the peer group's alienation from the institution. It is not a positive model of communality, and it only reinforces the alienation that youths feel. Alternative forms of communality could be developed if students were taught and expected to lend support to one another and function in groups to accomplish academic goals, provide recreation, offer service to the community, and care for the school. Communal groups should also include other members of the school. Generally, students only interact with adults in the school in terms of the specific functional area in which that adult works. Thus, they only see cafeteria workers when they eat lunch. They only see the counselor when taking a college placement test or when they are in trouble. They only see the custodian before or after school. All of these workers are a part of the community of school. Schools can create a broader sense of community if they ask students to become involved in and give assistance to the tasks that are a part of the overall institution's functioning.

> Narrow role specialization is likely to threaten integration because individuals express only a small part of themselves in these relationships. . . . Cooperative work with a broader range of peers and adults will increase the potential for an integrated experience in school, and student contributions to other individuals and to the group should increase a sense of communality. (Newmann, 1981, p. 554)

It is our suggestion that school counselors help educate the school as to the benefits of communal groups and then help organize such groups. Rather than using traditional means for dealing with students who are perceived as discipline problems, counselors could begin to try and help these students become more involved with the school. Using these students, rather than always picking the "best and brightest" students to be office aids, help do media work, or do tutoring, might help boys develop a sense of other and form a bond with a broader range of adults and peers.

The Validity and Need for All-Male Classes

A second way that counselors can help male youths is to promote or even teach a few all-male classes that focus on the socialization and gender development of boys, perhaps as part of a sociology, psychology, or social studies curriculum. Such classes could also be offered in an all-female form for girls. When boys are not surrounded by girls, they may be less likely to feel the need to brag, tease, and bluster. They may not feel as competitive or as vulnerable. In coeducational settings, it appears that boys may fear that teachers or other students will make fun of them if they do not behave in ways that are deemed "masculine." They are less likely to discuss poetry, ask a question that could be perceived as "stupid," and engage in any course work or method that is labeled as feminine (Pollack, 1998).

From the research on academics, the case for holding reading and writing classes in single-sex form can easily be made. However, we feel that because much of the impetus for school violence comes directly from internalizing the rigid codes of masculinity, school counselors should consider teaching or helping create classes in the field of sociology or psychology that focus on gender development and are taught in single-sex classes.

Examining Our Own Ideas About Gender Roles

Our final recommendation is that all school counselors look inward before they begin to suggest any changes at their school. Gender and racial bias can be insidious. It is so pervasive in U.S. culture that it blinds many of us to the full capacity of men and women, or to the same humanness of individuals who have been identified as belonging to different cliques. It also prevents us from seeing how our adherence to role expectations has led to violence. School counselors need to see beyond gender-linked thinking to effect any changes that will help reduce school violence. Thus, the most important step school counselors can take is to learn more about the ways that gender and race influence the thinking of school children. Counselors must then work to eliminate their own biases and stereotypes and help create groups and programs at schools that will promote humanness, integration, and community.

Finally, although school counselors cannot be held responsible for the macrolevel structural changes in society, economy, and culture, they can take steps to mitigate these forces. They can insert themselves between the youths, the outside world, and the school to provide students with an understanding of the political economy of which they are all a part. They can serve as an interactive buffer to the alienation that society produces, and they can constructively suggest ways that this might be minimized, including designing exit strategies, even to the point of facilitating transfers of students who "hate" their school.

CONCLUSION

In this chapter, we have argued that high-profile school violence, like violence in general, is directly related to intersections between structural inequalities, gender, and race, and that this confluence of social forces provides the formative context of youths' thinking processes and moral referents. We examined Kohlberg's (1980b) model of moral development, which was developed and researched primarily on White male participants, and then Gilligan's (1982) gender-informed challenge to this model. Here we showed the negative effects on both men and women of constructing polarized gender roles in a capitalist society. We saw the importance of class relations in capitalist societies in mediating social processes, socialization, and microlevel cognitive processes. We examined how these have changed in contemporary American society, the fragmentation and alienation that they have produced, and the differing effects these intersections of class, race, and gender have had on male and female thinking, and particularly on the construction of masculine identity. We explored the development of masculine identity through the process of socialization, mindful of Pollack's (1998) work on real male gender construction. We linked this and its denial through contemporary culture to the internalization of shame and anger that builds when adolescent boys are unable to escape their gender construction. Consistent with Agnew's (1995) revised strained theory, we argued that this can easily translate into violence as a solution to internal pain and suffering. We turned to an examination of the alienation effects of agents of socialization, particularly the school and peers, and found that these contribute to the problem by reinforcing harmful and rigid gender constructions that harm boys as well as girls. Matza's (1964) theory of moral neutralization was used to show that morality established and influenced by socialization can also be negated by that same process. Finally, we used the knowledge provided by this analysis to examine how school counselors might effect change that will ultimately reduce student alienation and school violence. We conclude that school counselors can make a difference, but the difference they make must be supported by major changes in the social and moral order, as well as the social forces that constitute them. Without such changes, school violence will remain a recurrent feature of our times.

REFERENCES

Agnew, R. (1995). The contribution of socio-psychological strain theory to the explanation of crime and delinquency. In F. Adler & W. S. Laufer (Eds.), *The legacy of anomie theory: Advances in criminological theory* (Vol. 6, pp. 113–137). New Brunswick, NJ: Transaction Publishers.

Alleman, T. (1993). Varieties of feminist thought and their application to crime and justice. In R. Muraskin & T. Alleman (Eds.), *It's a crime: Women and justice* (pp. 3–32). Englewood Cliffs, NJ: Prentice Hall.

Bonger, W. (1916). *Criminality and economic conditions*. Boston: Little, Brown.

Brinn, J., Kraemer, K., Warm, J. S., & Paludi, M. A. (1984). Sex-role preferences in four age levels. *Sex Roles, 11,* 901–910.

Bureau of Justice Statistics. (1998). *Sourcebook of criminal justice statistics 1997.* Washington, DC: U.S. Department of Justice, Office of Justice Programs.

Coleman, J. S. (1961). *The adolescent society: The social life of the teenager and its impact on education.* Glencoe, IL: Free Press.

Cusick, P. A. (1973). *Inside high school: The students' world.* New York: Holt, Rinehart & Winston.

Gilligan, C. (1982). *In a different voice: Psychological theory and women's development.* Cambridge, MA: Harvard University Press.

Hagan, F. (1998). *Introduction to criminology: Theories, methods and criminal behavior.* Chicago: Nelson-Hall.

Harper, K. L., & Purkey, W. W. (1993). Research in middle level education. *National Middle School Association, 17*(1), 79–89.

Hayes, R. L. (1994). The legacy of Lawrence Kohlberg: Implications for counseling and development. *Journal of Counseling and Development, 72,* 261–267.

Hedges, L. V., & Nowell, A. (1995). Sex differences in mental test scores, variability, and numbers of high-scoring individuals. *Science, 269,* 41–45.

Jenkins, P. H. (1997). School delinquency and the school bond. *Journal of Research in Crime and Delinquency, 34,* 337–367.

Jordan, J. (1989). *Relational development: Therapeutic implications of empathy and shame* (Stone Center Working Paper Series, Work in Progress No. 39). Wellesley, MA: Wellesley College, Stone Center.

Kachur, S. P., Bearman, P. S., Blum, R. W., Bauman, K. E., Harris, K. M., Jones, J., Tabor, J., Beuhring, T., Sieving, R., Shew, M., Bearinger, L. H., & Udry, J. R. (1996). School-associated violent deaths in the United States, 1992 to 1994. *Journal of the American Medical Association, 275,* 1723–1729.

Kimmel, M. S., & Messner, M. A. (1995). *Men's lives* (3rd ed.). Needham Heights, MA: Allyn & Bacon.

Kohlberg, L. (1969). Stage and sequence: The cognitive–developmental approach to socialization. In D. Goslin (Ed.), *Handbook of socialization theory and research* (pp. 347–480). New York: Rand McNally.

Kohlberg, L. (1980a). Educating for a just society: An updated and revised statement. In B. Munsey (Ed.), *Moral development, moral education and Kohlberg* (pp. 455–470). Birmingham, AL: Religious Education Press.

Kohlberg, L. (1980b). Stages of moral development as a basis for moral education. In B. Munsey (Ed.), *Moral development, moral education and Kohlberg* (pp. 2–98). Birmingham, AL: Religious Education Press.

Kohlberg, L. (1984). *Essays on moral development: The philosophy of moral development* (Vol. 2). New York: Harper & Row.

Lanier, M. M., & Henry, S. (1998). *Essential criminology.* Boulder, CO: Westview Press.

Lindsey, L. L. (1994). *Gender roles: A sociological perspective* (2nd ed.). Englewood Cliffs, NJ: Prentice Hall.

Locke, D. C., & Zimmerman, N. A. (1987). Effects of peer-counseling training on psychological maturity of Black students. *Journal of College Student Personnel, 28,* 525–532.

Matza, D. (1964). *Delinquency and drift.* New York: Wiley.

Matza, D., & Sykes, G. (1961). Juvenile delinquency and subterranean values. *American Sociological Review, 26,* 712–719.

Messner, M. A. (1987). The meaning of success: The athletic experience and the development of male identity. In H. Brod (Ed.), *The making of masculinities* (pp. 193–209). Boston: Allen & Unwin.

Newmann, F. M. (1981). Reducing student alienation in high schools: Implications of theory. *Harvard Educational Review, 51,* 546–564.

Pipher, M. (1994). *Reviving Ophelia.* New York: Grosset/Putnam.

Pollack, W. (1998). *Real boys: Rescuing our sons from the myths of boyhood.* New York: Random House.

Poster, M. (Ed.). (1988). *Jean Baudrillard: Selected writings.* Stanford, CA: Stanford University Press.

Pratt, M. W., Golding, G., & Hunter, W. J. (1984). Does morality have a gender? Sex, sex role and moral judgment relationships across the adult life span. *Merrill-Palmer Quarterly, 30,* 321–340.

Resnick, M. D., Bearman, P. S., Blum, R. W., Bauman, K. E., Harris, K. M., Jones, J., Tabor, J., Beuhring, T., Sieving, R., Shew, M., Bearinger, L. H., & Udry, J. R.

(1997). Protecting adolescents from harm: Findings from the national longitudinal study on adolescent health. *Journal of the American Medical Association, 278*, 823–832.

Riley, R. W. (1997, September 4). [Testimony of Secretary Richard W. Riley before the Senate Labor, Health and Human Services and Education Subcommittee of the Senate Appropriations Committee.]

Schaefer, R. T. (1998). *Racial and ethnic groups* (7th ed.). New York: Addison-Wesley.

Selman, R., & Schultz, L. (1988). Interpersonal thought and action in the case of a troubled early adolescent: Toward a developmental model of the gap. In S. Shirk (Ed.), *Cognitive development and child psychotherapy* (pp. 207–246). New York: Plenum.

Staples, S. (2000). The meaning of violence in our schools: Rage against a broken world. *Annals of the American Academy of Political and Social Science, 567*, 30–41.

Sykes, G., & Matza, D. (1957). Techniques of neutralization: A theory of delinquency. *American Sociological Review, 22*, 664–670.

Thomas, W. I., & Thomas, D. (1928). *The child in American society.* New York: Knopf.

Wilkinson, P., & Hendrickson, M. (1999, June 10). Humiliation and revenge: The story of Reb and Vodka. *Rolling Stone*, 49–54, 140–141.

6

The "True" Perpetrators of Violence: The Effects of the Media on Public Perceptions of Youthful Violent Offenders

Alfiee M. Breland

Increasingly, violence in U.S. schools is a topic of great concern. Recent incidents in places like Springfield, Oregon; Pearl, Mississippi; Jonesboro, Arkansas; Littleton, Colorado; and Fort Gibson, Oklahoma, inform us that a significant number of American youths consider aggressive, physical violence to be the appropriate means for solving their often powerful emotional problems. Indeed, "according to a National School Board Association survey of 700 schools, school violence is worse now than it was 5 years ago" (Petersen, Pietrzak, & Speaker, 1998, p. 332). In response to these occurrences, counselors, psychologists, teachers, and other school administrators scramble to better understand the problem of school violence. Many believe it is imperative that both the true magnitude (or lack thereof) of the problem of school violence and the factors that contribute to the occurrences of violence be determined. All too often, school officials are left with many questions regarding the contributing factors of these heinous crimes against the children, schools, and communities. Furthermore, because of the inconsistent nature with which schools in the United States compile statistics on the occurrences of violence, we are left to speculate on the magnitude of the problem and the answers to the many probing questions that underlie the problem.

Numerous factors have been described as contributing to the rise in youth violence in U.S. schools. In the minds of many, factors such as single-parent homes, media images, video games, movies, and drug and

The author would like to thank Karen Lowenstein Damico for her assistance in preparing this chapter.

alcohol abuse serve as the "spark" that light the flame of school violence (Pietrzak, Petersen, & Speaker, 1998). In addition, school officials have attempted to determine the environments and qualities of the violent youthful offender reeking havoc on the schools and communities. In doing so, officials have often touted research suggesting that the young person most likely to act out violently is one who is male, is of low socio-economic status, is a member of a minority group, has low self-esteem, and does not perform well in school (Chisholm, 1998; Pietrzak et al., 1998). Given this profile of the violent youthful offender, it is no wonder that so many seemed unprepared for the tide of school violence that swept the United States in the latter part of 1998. Indeed, "violence within suburban and rural schools has eroded the perception that its occurrence is an 'inner city phenomenon' and that 'good' schools are havens from serious crime" (Chisholm, 1998, p. 138).

It is the problem of racial stereotyping that I believe contributes so greatly to the misperceptions of who exactly is "lying in wait" to inflict violence upon the schools. Furthermore, I believe that schools and com-munities have allowed these stereotypes to influence both what acts are considered to be violent and which children are labeled as "at risk" for violent behavior. It is important to note that by missing the signals given by the children who did inflict violence upon their schools in recent months, the schools and communities missed their opportunities to pro-tect loved ones from the violence that later ensued.

I am certainly aware that it may seem odd to interject issues of stereo-typing and multiculturalism into a discussion on school violence, yet I think it is imperative to do so. If we do not begin to address the con-tributing factors and symptomatology of violent youthful offenders, we will never be prepared to develop programs to curb the violence occur-ring in schools.

Given the aforementioned ideas, the focus of this chapter is to provide insight into the real questions to be asked and answered regarding the "true" perpetrators of school violence. Specifically, this chapter addresses the general topic of recent occurrences of school violence perpetrated by youths, along with the effect of stereotypes on perceptions of potential youthful offenders. This chapter also addresses media-created stereotypes that have served to develop the public understanding of the youthful vio-lent offender and the manners in which current media images have allowed school officials to overlook the true violent offenders in their midst. In addition, this chapter offers a more accurate profile of the youth-ful violent offender, as well as the familial and personal traits to be used in determining who the at-risk children are. Finally, the essential compo-nents of programs that have succeeded in correctly identifying and assist-ing potential violent youthful offenders are offered. It is hoped that this chapter will enlighten those who interact with youths such that they may more carefully consider their target populations and devise more appropriate means of working with young people to end violence.

RECENT INCIDENTS OF SCHOOL
VIOLENCE PERPETRATED BY YOUTHS

With the advent of multiculturalism and cultural diversity awareness, counselors and other school officials began to address how the students' differences might be incorporated into an ameliorated school and interpersonal environment. As laudable as efforts over the last 20 years have been however, we continue to live in a society heavily driven by prejudice and stereotypes.

How prejudice and stereotypes affect perceptions of violent youth offenders should be a topic of discussion when authorities consider means of addressing youth violence to curb and ultimately end it. Unfortunately, such attention to diversity is not always considered. In this section, I reflect on the perceptions of youthful offenders that the media encourages and that school officials and mental health professionals adhere to with regard to determining which children are most likely to be a threat to public safety. It is hypothesized that media projections of lower income and minority youths as violent offenders often lead authority figures to target the wrong youths in violence prevention efforts. Recent incidents such as the school shootings in Pearl, Mississippi and Springfield, Oregon attest to this fact and suggest that school officials are indeed targeting the wrong populations. For example, note the words of Governor John Kitzhaber of Oregon (where Kipland Kinkel killed 1 person and injured 23 others in school): "All of us should look at how we have failed as a society and how this could happen in the heart of Oregon" (Egan, 1998, p. A1).

In a school in Jonesboro, Arkansas, where Mitchell Johnson and Andrew Golden killed one teacher and four classmates, a teacher stated, "This is not supposed to happen at Westside" (Bragg, 1998, p. A20). Bragg, who prepared the article from which this excerpt was taken, commented that the "attack left experts grasping for explanations" (p. A20). Similarly, King and Murr (1998) described the "shock value" of the three shootings in Jonesboro, Arkansas; Springfield, Oregon; and West Paducah, Kentucky. In their treatise on the rash of school shootings, they quoted psychologist Michael Flynn, who asked the question, "Has it taken middle-class kids shooting each other to realize something is wrong?" (King & Murr, 1998, p. 33). In other articles describing the more widely publicized occurrences of school violence in 1998, Labi (1998) labeled Jonesboro "a monstrous anomaly" (p. 29), and Lacoyo (1998) called these "schoolboy massacres" a possible "aberration" (p. 38). These descriptions seem plausible only on critical examination of society's belief that these acts of well-planned senseless violence can only be attributed to "urban crime," "ghetto culture," and a societal vision of what the violent offender looks like (Blank, Vest, & Parker, 1998). Even with statistics that indicate that murder rates in general have dropped in cities and suburbs across the United States (Witkin, 1998) and more relevantly for teen homicide in the same areas of the United States (Blank et al., 1998), many persist in the belief that the numerous occurrences of school violence in the past year are aberrations. The scenes caused by killers such as Michael Carneal (West Paducah, Kentucky), Mitchell Johnson (Jonesboro, Arkansas), Andrew Golden (Jonesboro, Arkansas), Kip Kinkel (Springfield, Oregon), Eric Harris and Dylan Klebold (Littleton, Colorado), and Seth Trickey (Fort Gibson, Oklahoma) persist in the minds of many as not befitting society's explanations of violence. Indeed, these young White perpetrators of violence do not conform to a societal stereotype that describes who commits violent acts. Next, I examine whom indeed are viewed as perpetrators of violence.

MEDIA IMAGES AND VIOLENT OFFENDERS

With regard to whom the public, and more specifically school officials, see as the true perpetrators of violence, Hall (1992) wrote that the violent offender is considered "most menacing," of an "imposing" figure, of skin "necessarily dark," and to have a face that reveals a "look of angry lust." In stark contrast to this image, Cloud (1998) characterized Mitchell Johnson as "a sensitive, soft thirteen-year-old" and Kip Kinkel as small for his age. Regarding Michael Carneal, various writers described him as a "smallish ninth-grader" (Bragg, 1998), "skinny and bespectacled" (Pedersen & Van Boven, 1997), and "timid-looking" (Prichard, 1998). King and Murr (1998) began their coverage of Kip Kinkel with a description characterizing him as a "15-year-old . . . innocent look that is part Huck Finn and part Alfred E. Neuman—boyish and quintessentially American" (p. 32). As a final example, note that Blank et al. (1998) commented on Andrew Golden that "he looks less like a bully than like a bully's victim" (p. 20). It is interesting the ways in which the media sends subliminal messages to the public, and de facto to school officials, in their use of such language. Indeed, even in the midst of powerful evidence that these children are cold-blooded killers, most are still characterized as all-American boys who went astray. It is almost as if the media would like the public to believe that these children are not the people to fear; rather it is the people of lower socioeconomic status and from minority groups who pose the greatest threat to public safety. The general message conveyed by the media (and absorbed by the public) is summarized in the words of Principal Bill Bond of Heath High in Paducah: These young, White, middle-class killers do "not fit the mold of what our society says an angry person should be like" (Pedersen & Van Boven, 1997, p. 30). This statement begs the question, "Then what persons do fit the mold of what an angry person should look like?"

THE MEDIA-CREATED PROFILE
OF THE VIOLENT OFFENDER

In addressing the question of what physical traits the "typical" angry person possesses, many stereotypes abound. Chisholm (1998) eloquently delineated "the perception linking violence primarily with poverty, pervasive unemployment, the uneducated, and disenfranchised ethnic groups" (p. 139). She commented on the specific "association between violent perpetrator and 'Black'" (p. 139) that continues to pervade society's notions of who are violent offenders. Furthermore, writers such as Bridges and Steen (1998) reported that "persons of color, despite having similar offense histories, are perceived differently than Whites, often as presenting images of threat and danger" (p. 555). In addition, Duncan (1976) posited that "one of the stereotypes most frequently applied to blacks is that they are impulsive and given to crimes and violence" (p. 591).

Hall (1992) also wrote of the societal stereotype of the African American male as "a . . . beast with a penchant for violence aimed at the European-American community" (p. 77). In one example, he discussed the fabrications of a White Boston businessman, Chuck Stuart, who claimed that he and his pregnant wife were robbed and shot by an African American man. Willie Bennett, a poor African American male, was "caught" and charged despite the fact that a member of the accuser's family emerged to detail a plot of deception and murder that Chuck had invented. The investigation ended when Chuck committed suicide. Hall concluded that the majority group of society needs to somehow rationalize or justify historical and present treatment of minorities; there is a need to stereotype minorities as representing something to be feared. The historical denigration by the dominant culture is validated by a "web of pernicious myths about the . . . African American" (Greene, 1994, p. 12).

When questioning how these stereotypes are formed, we need look no further than the media to understand how it is that the public comes to such biased conclusions regarding what violent offenders look like. Specifically, it is often the television and print media that provide us with vivid images of violent offenders and their crimes. Often, it is the "television news [that] makes an indelible impression because of its visual impact and its tendency . . . to shape and stabilize the meanings experienced from the symbols of language" (Tait & Perry, 1994, pp. 195–196). In particular, the stereotypes that are associated with people of color, especially African Americans, are quite pervasive. One need only view popular television programs such as "COPS" or even the evening news to determine that "television [often] presents African Americans to the viewing public as deviant, threatening, and unintelligent subhumans" (Tait & Perry, 1994, p. 195). In studies conducted by Entman (1990), he determined that "76% of all local TV stories about Blacks fell into the categories of crime or politics" (p. 332). In his analysis of 1 week of local Chicago newscast stories, "the key categories were crimes of violence explicitly reported as committed by blacks" (Entman, 1990, p. 336). For the week studied, six of eight lead stories were of violent crimes committed by African Americans. Furthermore, Entman (1990) observed that the accused African American criminals were "usually illustrated by glowering mug shots or by footage of them being led around in handcuffs" (p. 337), whereas none of the accused violent White criminals were shown in "mug shots or in physical custody" (p. 337). He also cited evidence to support the idea that whereas Whites' perspective on certain events dominated the broadcasts, the voices of African Americans did not directly narrate incidents. Overall, Entman (1992) concluded that, given the manners in which both Black and White offenders were portrayed, "there were differences in the visual treatment that may tend to reinforce whites' fears" (pp. 349–350). In general, there exists strong evidence to support the notion that African Americans are often associated with violent crime in the United States. Therefore, it should come as no surprise that many in the general public, and by extension in the schools, believe that the acts of children like Andrew Golden and Kip Kinkel constitute "out of the ordinary" behavior.

THE EFFECTS OF STEREOTYPES ON INTERVENTIONS WITH VIOLENT OFFENDERS

So how are these media-created and reinforced stereotypes acted on in school officials' interactions with violent offenders? The following examples offer some plausible explanations.

When young violent offenders are caught in the act, how are they typically dealt with? Whaley (1998) cited more evidence that "the stereotype of black people as violent is still quite pervasive" (p. 48) and concluded that African Americans are dealt with in much more severe manners than their White peers. Whaley referred to a study that found that violent Black adolescents were predominantly sent to local correctional facilities, whereas violent White adolescents were sent to mental health hospitals. This study offers compelling evidence for the notion that young White violent offenders are behaving in aberrant manners, therefore requiring psychological assistance. Conversely, young African American violent offenders are viewed as behaving in manners "typical" of their group, hence the need to "lock them away" to protect the public. Similarly, in an analysis of 453 violent incidents in a Connecticut state psychiatric hospital for adolescents, the number of violent acts committed by non-White patients equaled the number of violent acts committed by White patients, yet staff restrained non-White patients almost four times as often as they restrained White patients (Bond, DiCandia, & MacKinnon, 1988). In seeking to explain why such was the case, Bond et al. (1988) suggested that "sanction usage reflects racial discrimination by White staff" (p. 455). In Duncan's (1976) previously mentioned study, White participants viewed and judged a videotape of an ambiguous shove by African Americans as more violent than the same act as performed by Whites. These examples point to the idea that African American and other non-White violent offenders are often considered to be more dangerous than their White counterparts, thereby requiring more drastic measures of intervention.

By the same token, it is quite possible that because African American and other non-White offenders are viewed so differently by the public, those behaviors typically associated with each group might be often viewed differently. Take, for example, the violent act of bullying. In a review of the literature on school bullying, Batsche and Knoff (1994) asserted that approximately 15–20% of American school children suffer from being bullied by peers. Unfortunately, because the generally accepted definition of violence in U.S. schools is "acts of assault, theft, and vandalism" (Batsche & Knoff, 1994), those children engaged in the act of bullying their peers are overlooked. It has been asserted that there is a sort of acceptance of childhood fighting and bullying and that such is often a necessary evil in childhood development (Batsche & Knoff, 1994). The problem with this passive attitude toward bullying is that the potential exists to send a positive reinforcement message to the children engaging in bullying. Indeed, in research conducted with school officials in school districts from inner-city, urban, rural, and suburban settings, it was found that "perceptions of campus violence were not associated with the presence of bullying and to a lesser extent harassment, forms of school violence that receive intense attention in other countries" (Furlong, Babinski, Poland, Munoz, & Boles, 1996, p. 34). What is particularly interesting about the findings of this study is that of the 123 school psychologists who responded to the survey, 45.6% of those from inner-city schools reported having very big problems with school violence, whereas 5% or fewer of those from suburban and rural settings reported having a very big problem with violence in the schools. The significance of this finding is that there were no reported significant differences in the amount of bullying occurring in all of the school districts surveyed. In another study of 291 school officials, 63% reported that they themselves had been verbally threatened or intimidated by students and that they perceived 37% and 38% of White and African American students, respectively, as the perpetrators of violence in their schools. The findings of these and similar studies might lead one to believe that people are quite selective in what they believe constitutes violent behavior. Furthermore, when these types of findings are coupled with one's notions of what racial and ethnic groups of children commit which acts, it is almost a foregone conclusion that one is dealing with the children in very different manners. Indeed, it is quite likely that because we as a society perceive certain violent acts to be more heinous than others, we send a mixed message to children that indicates that as long as they possess the right physical traits and perform the right violent acts, we will overlook their behavior. This disregard for what is generally considered nonthreatening violent behavior can only serve to reinforce the behavior, thereby allowing children to progress to more severe types of violent acts. As an example, note the numerous descriptions of Mitchell Johnson (implicated in the Jonesboro shootings) as a "swaggering bully." Is it possible that had Mitchell been reprimanded earlier in his life for bullying that he might not have escalated his behavior to include the horrible act of murder?

The aforementioned examples offer some ideas regarding how society and school officials differentiate the treatment of youthful violent offenders. It is quite possible that, on the basis of the physical characteristics of and the particular crime committed by a juvenile violent offender, vastly different means of reprimand are used.

A MORE ACCURATE PROFILE
OF THE YOUTHFUL VIOLENT OFFENDER

Lowry, Sleet, Duncan, Powell, and Kolbe (1995) noted that, "without a comprehensive and standardized school violence reporting system, it is impossible to identify trends in school related homicide" (pp. 23–24). These researchers also noted that most children between the ages of 12 and 19 who were victims of crime were victimized by people of their own race and that 78% of the school districts responding to the survey of the National School Boards Association cited occurrences of student assaults on other students. Other studies have reported similar results with regard to the wide variety of students who engage in violent activity. In a 1996 study, drawn from 4,500 students in California and Oregon, 58% of urban and 52% of nonurban area adolescents had engaged in some form of violent behavior (Ellickson, Saner, & McGuigan, 1997). It therefore stands to reason, given the aforementioned statistics (i.e., school districts nationwide report incidents of student violent crimes against other students, and people are usually assaulted by people of their own race), that there exists no physically racial prototype of the violent offender and that any child with certain influences is capable of violence.

Given that we now have some idea regarding how we formulate stereotypes of violent youthful offenders, it is imperative that we turn our focus away from physical characteristics and direct our energy toward understanding the real traits of a youthful violent offender. The question we might ask is, "Which young people should be labeled as 'at-risk'?"

Chisholm (1998) asserted that there are significant family characteristics that offer insight into who will become a violent offender. Specifically, she stated that "much research on family violence has determined a direct relationship between severity of childhood abuse and later victimization of others" (p. 142). Other research has concluded that violent youths are more likely than their peers to have experienced concurrent public health concerns, including substance use and abuse, poorly developed self-concept and/or esteem, and poor academic motivation and involvement (Ellickson et al., 1997). It is quite possible, therefore, to correctly surmise that school officials pay attention to their students' family interactions, peers, and communities when determining who is at risk. That of course is not to say that certain racial/ethnic or socioeconomic communities are at risk, rather that children, families, and communities demonstrating poor patterns of behavior are more likely to have children who are at risk. It is clear that the nation as a whole and individual communities are aware of many of the patterns that contribute to youth violent behavior; what is unclear is how we seem to be unable to look beyond stereotypes to address the true problems and concerns.

ESSENTIAL COMPONENTS
OF SUCCESSFUL PROGRAMS

The body of this chapter focused on the manners in which the nation as a whole and school officials have incorrectly surmised who the violence-prone young offenders are. In this section, I move toward identifying and recognizing those elements of programs that have been successful in labeling and assisting the violent youthful offender. By delineating these elements, it is my hope that concrete strategies can be provided to assist in identifying and helping the violence-prone young people.

At various points in this chapter, I have attempted to convey a clearer picture of what components contribute to youths acting out in violent manners. In doing so, the following elements were listed as factors to be addressed when determining who is at risk for violence: family interaction patterns, human development issues, cultural issues, media images, and stereotypes. With those factors in mind, I now complete an overview of the elements essential to a successful school violence prevention program. Keep in mind that the programs identified as successful in curbing school violence address the various characteristics of violence-prone youths (as well as the misconceptions) that school officials harbor about certain young people.

In June 1998, the "Safe Schools, Safe Students" study was released. This study surveyed 84 national programs developed to stem the tide of school violence. The following elements were listed as essential pieces of successful programs: activities that assist in the establishment of school norms against violence, aggression, and bullying; family, peer, and community training and involvement with the school; physical plant changes in the school that foster a positive environment; interactive teaching; and culturally sensitive material (Portner, 1998). Further reviews of other violence prevention programs appear to make similar claims regarding which elements are essential to truly preventing violence from occurring. In a review of violence prevention programs, Larson (1994) emphasized the importance of cultural sensitivity by stating, "Clearly, school based programs for the prevention of violent behavior must be sensitive to the unique causative and maintenance features in the population to be served" (pp. 160–161). Furthermore, he asserted that sound prevention training programs will focus on skill development and family involvement/ training with the at-risk child. Other research on violence prevention in the schools suggests all of the aforementioned ideas and adds that school planning, which includes establishing a positive school climate and fostering relationships between schools and communities, is an essential component to violence prevention (Poland, 1994; Stephens, 1994). Overall, it appears that the best programs in the United States have the same general foci. It is imperative that school officials and other concerned individuals learn to adapt the recommended strategies to fit their individual environments. Just as I assert that there is no one profile to fit the potential youthful violent offender, there exists no one program to meet the needs of all schools in the country.

CONCLUSION

I have attempted to offer a different perspective on how potential youthful violent offenders are identified. Unfortunately, because we live in a society rife with stereotypes, we too often make assumptions about those young people prone to violent acts. Because many of the predictions regarding who is at risk are based on racial stereotypes, we are often at a loss to explain the motivations behind the supposed random acts of violence that strike affluent and nonminority communities. When presented with the facts of the various perpetrators' behavior prior to their acting out, it is clear that many warning signs existed. However, until we can understand and acknowledge that any child, regardless of racial origin or socioeconomic status, is capable of violence, we will continue to live with the delusion that it can only happen to "those people," and we will continue to wonder, as did the people of Jonesboro, Paducah, Pearl, Littleton, and Fort Gibson: "How could this happen here?"

It behooves school officials to consider the available research that will assist them in determining the traits of the potential violent offender and the best practices for dealing with such children before they are able to strike out. If school personnel are willing to acknowledge and address these biases, they can pave the way for more accurate assessment, prevention, and intervention.

REFERENCES

Batsche, G. M., & Knoff, H. M. (1994). Bullies and their victims: Understanding a pervasive problem in the schools. *School Psychology Review, 23*, 165–174.

Blank, J., Vest, J., & Parker, S. (1998, April 6). The children of Jonesboro. *U.S. News & World Report*, 16–22.

Bond, C. F., Jr., DiCandia, C. G., & MacKinnon, J. R. (1988). Responses to violence in a psychiatric setting: The role of patient's race. *Personality and Social Psychology Bulletin, 14*, 448–458.

Bragg, R. (1998, March 25). Five are killed at school; boys, 11 and 13, are held. *The New York Times*, pp. A1, A20.

Bridges, G. S., & Steen, S. (1998). Racial disparities in official assessments of juvenile offenders: Attributional stereotypes as mediating mechanisms. *American Sociological Review, 63*, 554–570.

Chisholm, J. F. (1998). Understanding violence in the school: Moral and psychological factors. *Journal of Social Distress and the Homeless, 7*, 137–157.

Cloud, J. (1998, July 6). Of arms and the boy. *Time*, 58–62.

Duncan, B. L. (1976). Differential social perception and attribution of intergroup violence: Testing the lower limits of stereotyping of Blacks. *Journal of Personality and Social Psychology, 34*, 590–598.

Egan, T. (1998, May 22). Oregon student held in 3 killings; one dead, 23 hurt at his school. *The New York Times*, pp. A1, A20.

Ellickson, P., Saner, H., & McGuigan, K. A. (1997). Profiles of violent youth: Substance use and other concurrent problems. *American Journal of Public Health, 87*, 985–991.

Entman, R. M. (1990). Modern racism and the images of Blacks in local television news. *Critical Studies in Mass Communication, 7*, 332–345.

Furlong, M., Babinski, L., Poland, S., Munoz, J., & Boles, S. (1996). Factors associated with school psychologists' perceptions of campus violence. *Psychology in the Schools, 33*, 28–37.

Greene, B. (1994). African-American women. In L. Comas-Diaz & B. Greene (Eds.), *Women of color: Integrating ethnic and gender identities in psychotherapy* (pp. 10–29). New York: Guilford Press.

Hall, R. (1992). African-American male stereotypes: Obstacles to social work in a multicultural society. *Journal of Multicultural Social Work, 1*(4), 77–89.

King, P., & Murr, A. (1998, June 1). A son who spun out of control. *Newsweek,* 32–33.

Labi, N. (1998, April 6). The hunter and the choirboy. *Time,* 28–37.

Lacoyo, R. (1998, April 6). Toward the root of the evil. *Time,* 38–39.

Larson, J. (1994). Violence prevention in the schools: A review of selected programs and procedures. *School Psychology Review, 23,* 151–164.

Lowry, R., Sleet, D., Duncan, C., Powell, K., & Kolbe, L. (1995). Adolescents at risk for violence. *Educational Psychology Review, 7*(1), 7–39.

Pedersen, D., & Van Boven, S. (1997, December 15). Tragedy in a small place. *Newsweek,* 30–31.

Petersen, G. J., Pietrzak, D., & Speaker, K. M. (1998). The enemy within: A national study on school violence and prevention. *Urban Education, 33,* 331–359.

Pietrzak, D., Petersen, G. J., & Speaker, K. M. (1998). Perceptions of school violence by elementary and middle school personnel. *Professional School Counseling, 1,* 23–29.

Poland, S. (1994). The role of school crisis intervention teams to prevent and reduce school violence and trauma. *School Psychology Review, 23,* 175–189.

Portner, J. (1998, July 8). Violence-prevention guide, drills follow year of shootings. *Education Week,* 14.

Prichard, J. (1998, October 6). Teen asserts mental illness, admits guilt in school shooting. *Lansing State Journal,* p. A3.

Stephens, R. D. (1994). Planning for safer and better schools: School violence prevention and intervention strategies. *School Psychology Review, 23,* 204–215.

Tait, A. A., & Perry, R. L. (1994). African Americans in television: An Afrocentric analysis. *Western Journal of Black Studies, 18,* 195–200.

Whaley, A. L. (1998). Racism in the provision of mental health services: A social–cognitive analysis. *American Journal of Orthopsychiatry, 68*(1), 47–57.

Witkin, G. (1998, May 25). The crime bust. *U.S. News & World Report,* 28–37.

SCHOOL VIOLENCE PREVENTION STRATEGIES

INTRODUCTION

The call came in at 8:15 a.m. There was a bomb, the caller said, hidden in the high school. The signal went out over the intercom. Without missing a word in her presentation, the teacher walked calmly to the classroom door and locked it. The telephone rang, and the teacher nodded confidently to the students who watched her face intently. Attempting to keep the fear out of her own response, she described the situation. A bomb threat had been called in. Everyone should remain calm. The police and bomb units would be on site shortly. No one would enter or leave the classroom until the all-clear was sounded. It was April 22, 1999, 2 days after the Columbine High School tragedy in Littleton, Colorado.

The dogs carefully inspected every scent in the high school, and by 11:30 a.m. the police were sure that there was no bomb. The all-clear was sounded, and students rushed from their classrooms for bathrooms and water fountains and some to call parents. They were afraid; they were relieved. They were strained by the morning's events. Many went home. They were forever changed. They had lived a morning fearing that at any moment an explosion would snuff out their young lives.

This event was not unique. It happened all across the United States in the week following the Columbine shootings. Although no other violence erupted that week, the threat was very real, and plans for massacres were discovered and thwarted. Teachers, administrators, and counselors in every school were asking, what can we do to prevent such a tragedy from happening here?

The purpose of this section is to address prevention from the broadest of perspectives. We have included nine chapters, the largest section in the book, and rightly so. Prevention is the preferred mode of treatment.

The section begins, in chapter 7, with a description of the PEACE POWER! Toolkit by Mark A. Mattaini and Christine T. Lowery, which addresses the process for constructing a culture of nonviolence. In chapter 8, Ann L. Bauer, who was involved as a counselor with the Jonesboro, Arkansas, shootings, addresses violence prevention from a systematic perspective. David N. Aspy suggests in chapter 9 that violence can be prevented by a process that supports and encourages the development of virtues in children and youths.

In chapter 10, Farah A. Ibrahim and Peter Tran propose a model for eradicating school violence that involves the community, school, and the home and that takes a psychoeducational approach to reshape the beliefs and assumptions in a community that provide the models for children and youths. Frederick D. Harper and James P. Griffin, Jr., describe in chapter 11 several creative and underused counseling strategies that can be effective in preventing school violence. The role of counselor training in providing leadership in violence prevention is described in chapter 12 by Sue A. Stickel, Irene Mass Ametrano, and Yvonne L. Callaway.

The final three chapters in this section explore prevention from unique perspectives. In chapter 13, Douglas C. Smith, James D. Larson, Barbara DeBaryshe, and Michael Salzman discuss anger management for youths in detail and describe what is effective for various subtypes. In chapter 14, Andrew K. Tobias extends the role of the counselor as a leader in providing practical solutions for school violence using interventions at the administrative, teacher-focused, curricular, community, legal, student-focused, physical plant, and parent-focused levels. And finally, in chapter 15, Mary K. Lawler reviews 20 published programs for violence prevention that have been researched and found to be effective.

This section provides a compendium of prevention strategies that can be applied across multiple ages and geographic areas. The tools for addressing violence prevention are available and can make a difference in the lives of our children. They are the muscles behind our hope that children and youths can achieve healthy development in our schools without the fear of violence.

7 | Constructing Cultures of Nonviolence: The PEACE POWER! Toolkit

Mark A. Mattaini and Christine T. Lowery

In response to recent high-profile violent attacks in schools, concern with youth violence has intensified, and many in society find themselves asking, "What's wrong with these kids?" and "Who is to blame?" Children and youths are safer in school than almost anywhere else, including their homes, but there is still reason for deep concern. Three thousand children are murdered annually (only about 1% at school; Kaufman et al., 1998). Young people between the ages of 12 and 24 years are victims of violent crimes at least 2 million times a year (Perkins, 1997); children of color as well as gay and lesbian youths are particularly at risk, mirroring the general experiences of oppression in which their lives are grounded. School and youth-serving organizations are better positioned than any other social institution to contribute to reducing these rates.

The heart of the problem lies in the deep reliance of U.S. society on coercive and adversarial processes (Sidman, 1989). Violence is the extreme of a coercive continuum, in which threat and punishment are often used to induce people to act, or not to act, as others want (Lowery & Mattaini, in press). The legal system, corrections, residential treatment, the welfare system, the school system, and, sadly, even families often rely extensively on threats and sanctions to maintain order. Coercive processes do not lead to the education and healing that many other cultures recognize are essential to maintaining and strengthening the human web (Ross, 1996). Many young people, however, have experienced no alternative to coer-

Mark A. Mattaini and Christine T. Lowery are with the PEACE POWER! Working Group. Contributors to the PEACE POWER! strategy have included Wendy Chin, Jennifer DiNoia, Karen Herrara, Kyung Nam Lee, Helen Perez, Dawn Rannie, Janet Twyman, and Frank Wood. Anthony Biglan of the Oregon Research Institute and Dennis Embry of Paxis, Inc., in Tucson, Arizona, have also made important contributions to our thinking.

cive power and have learned no other way to influence their worlds. Violence reflects not just a deficit in anger management or conflict resolution repertoires (although these are sometimes important); rather violence and threats of violence are often means for exercising some power and control in an otherwise unmanageable world.

THE SCIENCE OF VIOLENCE PREVENTION

An enormous amount of research has recently been devoted to violence, and youth violence in particular. Although popular media sometimes indicate that little is really known about the problem and how to prevent it, a great deal has actually been learned. In a comprehensive review, the American Psychological Association (1993) explored what is known about the causes of such violence and the approaches for prevention and intervention. They noted:

> Effective intervention programs share two primary characteristics: (a) they draw on the understanding of developmental and sociocultural risk factors leading to antisocial behavior, and (b) they use theory-based intervention strategies with known efficacy in changing behavior, tested program designs, and validated, objective measurement techniques to assess outcomes. (American Psychological Association, 1993, pp. 53–54)

The National Research Council prepared a four-volume report on understanding and preventing violence that included a range of data-based recommendations, while also clarifying the limitations of current knowledge and areas in need of further research (Reiss & Roth, 1993). A recent review of the state of knowledge from the perspective of the science of behavior also suggests specific data-based strategies (Mattaini, Twyman, Chin, & Lee, 1996). All of these data suggest that coercive acts, including violence, are selected at three interlocking levels: the biological, the experiential, and the sociocultural. In the section that follows, potentiating factors at each of these levels are briefly explored.

Biological Factors

Despite popular media presentations, most violence is not the result of genetics, brain pathology, or mental illness. Genetic explanations for the overall incidence of violence in geographic areas and populations are dismissed even by sociobiologists, who note that genetic change simply does not occur quickly enough to account for the differential rates and patterns observed. Variations in innate propensities for violence are probably universal among cultures, but some manage these better than others. More important are immediate levels of such neurotransmitters and hormones as serotonin, dopamine, cortisol, and norepinephrine (Embry & Flannery, 1999; http://www.bfsr.org/violence.html).

Among children and youths, levels of those brain chemicals and over time even the structure of the brain are highly sensitive to environmental transactions. Changing the brain state in ways consistent with reducing violence requires high levels of social contact and reward and low levels of threat or coercion (Embry & Flannery, 1999). For older youths, or those who have experienced significant trauma, prophylactic environments that structure such experiences intensively over long periods of time are likely to be required. For this reason, those who work with significantly delinquent youths indicate that those problems should be viewed as significantly disabling conditions, requiring long-term support (Wolf, Braukmann, & Ramp, 1987). The most powerful available preventive strategies operating on the biobehavioral substrata of behavior involve enduring changes in the cultures (organizations, families, and communities) that structure young people's experiences.

Experiential Factors

All human behavior, including violent behavior, is rooted in biological activity. Coercive and violent repertoires are not organized primarily at the physiological level, however, any more than other complex behaviors like driving a car. Threatening, attacking, and punishing are shaped and maintained largely through experience with the social and physical environment. Although there are many qualifications that need to be made, basically such behavior is *functional*—it continues to occur because it somehow "works" for the individual in his or her world. Ultimately, violence and other coercive repertoires are maintained because they provide access to positive conditions and events, produce escape from or avoidance of aversive conditions or events, or both. Our working group has identified a number of specialized functional classes of violent and coercive behaviors ranging from maintaining social status in the peer group to escaping economic embarrassment (Mattaini, Lowery, Herrera, & DiNoia, 1999; Mattaini et al., 1996). These analyses indicate that "single-focus" prevention programs are unlikely to be adequate. For example, anger management programs are likely to be very useful with one cluster of violent actions (in which the function of the behavior is relieving an aversive physiological condition), but only marginally so for the others. Effective violence prevention programming needs to provide youths with alternatives for at least most of the more common functional clusters.

Sociocultural Factors

While individuals can acquire coercive repertoires on the basis of personal experience alone, many of those repertoires are also learned in the course of experience with transactional networks, ranging from the microculture of the family, to peer cultures, to sociocultural processes at a national level. Extensive accumulated data make clear that observing coercive and violent behavior, particularly when such action "works" and produces few obvious problems for the initiator, has a powerful modeling effect for many youths. When youths observe parents, siblings, peers, older youths, police officers, school authorities, employers, and government officials relying heavily on coercive processes within a supporting sociocultural matrix, it should not be surprising that youths often turn to similar strategies. One of the paradoxes of modern society, in fact, is that we commonly rely on socially sanctioned coercive threats, violence and punishment to reduce coercive threats, and violence and punishment by others. It need not be this way. Ross (1996), for example, described a Canadian First Nations perspective on punishment and incarceration as seen by community leaders assembled to deal with serious interpersonal crimes including sexual abuse:

> Promoting incarceration was based on, and motivated by, a mixture of feelings of anger, revenge, guilt, and shame on our part, and around our personal victimization issues, rather than in the healthy resolution of the victimization we were trying to address. Incarceration . . . actually works against the healing process, because "an already unbalanced person is moved further out of balance." . . . The threat of incarceration prevents people from coming forward and taking responsibility for the hurt they are causing. It reinforces the silence, and therefore promotes rather than breaks, the cycle of violence that exists. (p. 38)

Sociocultural factors, ranging from media violence to justice policy, have profound effects on the level of violence in society.

THE PEACE POWER! STRATEGY

Over the past several years, the PEACE POWER! Working Group and other researchers have developed and begun testing strategies for constructing cultures of nonviolent, noncoercive power in schools, community organizations, and other networks. Because many factors contribute to violence, many approaches can contribute to solutions (e.g., Embry & Flannery, 1999; Goldstein & Glick, 1987; Mayer, 1995; Prothrow-Stith, 1987; Walker, Colvin, & Ramsey, 1995; Wolfe, Wekerle, & Scott, 1997). Many of the existing programs focus primarily on work with youths themselves, which can certainly be useful (and is discussed below as an adjunct to the PEACE POWER! strategy). Well-validated behavioral theory suggests, however, that the primary power for affecting the incidence and prevalence of violence lies in changing the social matrices within which youths are embedded (Biglan, 1995).

Many positive practices can be encouraged in the home, school, and community cultures with which youths are involved. Implementation and maintenance of programs are more likely, however, if they are simple, flexible, and adaptable to local conditions (Fawcett, Mathews, & Fletcher, 1980). Our emphasis, therefore, has been to identify a small number of broadly applicable, empirically validated, and theoretically powerful core practices to be encouraged in local programs. For example, Mayer and his colleagues (Mayer, Butterworth, Nafpaktitis, & Sulzer-Azaroff, 1983) implemented a program in elementary and junior high schools in Los Angeles County two decades ago, applying the central practices recommended here. This project produced dramatic reductions in vandalism costs (often an accessible marker variable for the range of antisocial behaviors) and improved discipline significantly. Mayer et al. (1993) later implemented a dropout prevention program that relied on similar methods and produced similar, very strong outcomes.

Embry and Flannery (1999) extended Mayer's work in developing the PeaceBuilders™ program for work with elementary-age children. Their preliminary results indicated reductions of disciplinary actions and violence of between 50% and 60%; 77% of participating teachers indicated that the program made their jobs easier (see http://www.peacebuilders.com). The PEACE POWER! strategy, which targets primarily middle and high school students, has obtained similar social validity data, with school staff indicating that the practices outlined below are valuable for improving school climate (Mattaini et al., 1999) and community services workers agreeing on their utility.

The four data-based, interlocking practices in which the PEACE POWER! strategy is grounded are shown in Figure 7.1. These core practices can structure a wide range of programs, adapted to fit local needs, for work with preadolescent and adolescent youths within their social worlds. The four core practices are discussed briefly.

1. **Recognize Contributions and Successes.** Recognition and reinforcement of contributions to the community and of positive actions is the heart of constructing a new culture, whether it be the microculture of the family or the larger cultures in organizations and communities (Mattaini, 1999; Sidman, 1989). Cultures of recognition change brain chemistry in ways consistent with achievement and cooperation (increasing rates of available serotonin and dopamine in critical regions of the brain) and inconsistent with antisocial behavior. Children and youths who are richly rewarded for personal successes, and especially for contributing to the collective good, have no need for the "dopamine fix" (Embry & Flannery, 1999) associated with aggression. High levels of recognition can dramati-

Figure 7.1. | The core interlocking PEACE POWER! practices. (The PEACE POWER! logo is a registered service mark, reprinted here with permission of Mark A. Mattaini. This logo may be used freely in community programs so long as the service mark holder is noted.)

cally change the atmosphere in an organization, home, or community. A quantitative behavioral principle (the matching law) indicates that high levels of recognition for prosocial acts will naturally and dramatically reduce the level of antisocial acts. Such recognition is seldom provided at adequate rates without specific programming, however, and many youths experience very low rates of praise, recognition, and reward (Connolly, Dowd, Christe, Nelson, & Tobias, 1995). Disruptive youths, in particular, often experience far more reprimands than recognition events. Those young people are at very high risk for depression, escalating antisocial behavior, and avoiding contact with adults and prosocial peers. Carefully designed programs can shift relative levels of recognition without demanding excessive staff time (see below).

2. Act With Respect. Acting with respect (for oneself, others, and the earth) is incompatible with coercion and oppression, reduces the level of interpersonal threat experienced in the community, and builds recognition of the value of every member of the community. An atmosphere of respect reduces threat as well, changing the neurobiological balance (e.g., maintaining low levels of norepinephrine and cortisol) and helping to remediate the effects of histories of traumatic stress. The general approach required is to reduce the prevalence of all forms of coercion, from apparently minor but cumulative insults to serious bullying and punitive, inconsistent disciplinary procedures maintained by formal systems. The goal is to increase the rate of respectful actions while decreasing disrespectful ones, and by doing so reduce the need to constantly scan for possible threats.

Behavioral theory and research consistently indicate that eliminating behavior is less likely to produce lasting results than constructing alternatives, so the PEACE POWER! strategy primarily emphasizes the shaping and support of respectful repertoires, including empathy and assertiveness. Indigenous value systems (Ross, 1996) arrive at much the same conclusion: The most useful approach is not so much to punish infractions, but rather to assist the offender to learn to act more respectfully and experience the positive consequences, which leads to the healing of relationships (see *Make Peace* below).

3. Share Power to Build Community. Shared power is a construct that emerges from Native American thought and experience and is supported by state-of-the-art behavioral science (Lowery, 1999; Lowery & Mattaini, in press). Organizations that institutionalize the sharing of power minimize dominance hierarchies by acknowledging that everyone has something valuable to bring to the table. In a community of shared power, each person's differing powers are recognized, each has a strong voice, each contributes, and each shares responsibility for collective outcomes. A culture of shared power emerges from reinforcement and respect and brings the potential power of diverse gifts and resources to the collective. For youths and the adults around them, the sharing of power teaches that there are nonviolent, noncoercive ways to influence one's world and leads youths to discover and create their own power. Note how much more useful this strategy is than one that relies on telling youths to "just say no" to violence, without offering alternative sources of power. The collective sharing of power, in concert with respect, also moves toward inclusion and away from the alienation and isolation often associated with violence.

Sharing power in building community is consistent with the emerging literature supporting service learning for youths. Positive outcomes associated with structured community-service activities include increased self-confidence, increases in moral reasoning, improved academic performance, and decreases in disciplinary problems. Interestingly, the advantages for "youths at risk" may be particularly strong. Youths constitute an important reservoir of often-untapped behavioral potential for the community. As Finn and Checkoway (1998) asked, "What would happen if society viewed young people as competent community builders?" (p. 335).

4. Make Peace.   One of the most common approaches to violence prevention is conflict resolution or peace making (see, e.g., the "Resolving Conflict Creatively" program; Aber, Brown, Chaudry, Jones, & Samples, 1996). By themselves, conflict resolution programs are of some value, although not a complete response to youth violence, in part because not all violence involves conflict narrowly defined. In some cases, attending to conflicts rather than prosocial behavior may paradoxically increase the rate of such conflict.

In addition, finding solutions to particular conflicts is clearly not enough. Indigenous cultures teach us that what is crucial is not so much reaching an ideal solution but rather restoring relationships that have been damaged by the conflict, which may extend quite far out into the social web (Ross, 1996). Making peace then is not primarily a problem-solving process but rather a healing process. The data supporting such approaches are impressive. In New Zealand, for example, the Family Group Conference process, based on traditional Maori practice, is now being used for all but the most severe criminal offenses for youths from the ages of 14 to 16 (MacElrea, 1994). Within the context of an overall program that constructs a respectful and rewarding reality in which youths are active, empowered participants, conflict resolution and healing skills can be a useful fourth component. Because human society is built on networks of relationships, healing processes are critical to healthy communities, which in turn support positive action by youths.

The four core PEACE POWER! practices are not separate and independent; they are multiple, interwoven strands that structure an empowered culture of nonviolence. The key to the PEACE POWER! strategy is to embed these practices deeply in the cultural web within which youths live their lives, so everyone uses the language, everyone is reminded often of the practices, and everyone recognizes and reinforces others for using them. The PEACE POWER! strategy is not a curriculum, nor is it a structured program. It is not "owned" by or licensed from an outside group. Rather, it involves sharing information about the science that underlies violence and prevention, elaborating the basic practices associated with prevention, and providing a toolkit from which tools and techniques can be selected, creatively combined, and adapted in ways consistent with local interest, values, and resources. In the following section, we offer illustrative examples of such tools for supporting each of the core practices.

TOOLS FOR LOCAL PROGRAMS

In this section, we briefly introduce some of the tools the PEACE POWER! Working Group has developed and begun testing over the past several years to increase the rates of core PEACE POWER! practices. We focus here particularly on tools for use in schools and other organizations, but we also mention certain materials and techniques for family and community application, because an integrated project that involves all of these interlocking cultures is likely to be far more effective than piecemeal efforts. (Many of the specific tools discussed, and a draft manual outlining programmatic options, are available at cost on the World Wide Web, at http://www.bfsr.org/PEACEPOWER.html.)

Recognize Contributions and Successes

Recognition for positive action is the most powerful behavior-change strategy ever discovered. Group, as opposed to individual, recognition and rewards are particularly powerful with preadolescents and adolescents and can be structured seamlessly into regular school and community activities. Specific recognition arrangements need to be creatively adapted for every setting; no single process will work everywhere. Some approaches, however, have demonstrated their utility in a broad range of settings.

In developing their program two decades ago, Mayer and his colleagues (Mayer et al., 1983) discovered that oral praise is often discounted by youths but that most of them have little exposure to written praise (D. D. Embry, personal communication, June 1997). In Mayer's work, as well as in the PeaceBuilders program (Embry & Flannery, 1999), written Praise Notes and public posting of those notes on Praise Boards therefore were used as a primary programmatic approach. *Recognition Notes* and *Recognition Boards* may be the single most powerful intervention available for use by youth-serving organizations, perhaps surprisingly, far more powerful than disciplinary arrangements, for example.

Recognition Notes can also be combined with weekly or daily *Recognition Circles* in which oral recognition is shared among all participants. *Home Notes* in which teachers provide parents (many of whom have primarily experienced negative communications from academic staff, particularly if their children have struggled in school) with regular feedback regarding the positive steps their children have taken are also very well received and begin to build an additional programmatic bridge to the home. *Family Recognition Boards,* erasable white boards on which family members can mutually note positives experienced from each other, can be used to further extend the practice of recognition into the home. Using these tools, the people involved can tailor the form and wording of recognition in ways that are consistent with cultural differences, and they can select those actions and contributions for recognition that are culturally valued.

At a larger community level, media outlets are often willing and even eager to become involved in violence prevention efforts. The Peace-Builders program in Tucson, Arizona, for example, has successfully recruited local media to provide daily recognition to youths and other community members for contributions on news programs. Businesses may also be interested in sponsoring community recognition events if approached, as well as in providing small incentives (e.g., movie passes) that may sometimes be incorporated into prevention programs.

Act With Respect

In an environment in which people generally treat each other respectfully, the level of threat and of the physiological arousal and scanning that result from threat is low. Acting with respect involves a number of repertoires, from acting assertively to actively passing up opportunities to criticize (e.g., "Give Up Put-Downs"; Embry & Flannery, 1999). One important step for promoting such practices discussed is to embed language describing them deeply into daily life. The PEACE POWER! Pledge (http://www.bfsr.org/pledge.html), for example, can be incorporated into each school day, turning attention to the practices every day. Note that giving up "put-downs," force, and weapons are specifically addressed in the pledge.

Homework modules that youths can use to guide them in interviews with important adults in their lives (parents, grandparents, or others) about the meaning and importance of respect can again bridge the school–home gap, and copies of the pledge (or something similar) can be provided to families as well as to other community networks, especially churches, for dissemination. Given the availability of firearms in U.S. society, pledges to give up weapons may be particularly important. Many youths carry weapons for "protection"; overall, this practice is counterproductive, and activities like those suggested here may be helpful for opening youth–adult dialogues around this issue.

Acting with respect is often best learned through scheduled role-play and discussions. There are also commonly many opportunities to practice appropriate behavior through incidental teaching (see, e.g., the Corrective Teaching process developed at Boys Town: http://www.boystown.org).

Many other activities can increase respect for oneself, others, and the natural world. These range from youth and police dialogues to structured life and leadership skills training (described below) and may emphasize locally relevant considerations, including tolerance for persons of particular races, ethnicities, varying sexual orientations, abilities, and social groups, as well as generally useful skills such as appropriate assertiveness.

Share Power to Build Community

One issue that has often been mentioned in recent years, usually immediately after violent incidents that draw national attention, is the alienation and isolation from adults that many young people face. "Adolescence" is a 20th-century invention, a time when young people are seen by adults and themselves as having no important cultural place or function. In addition, adults are now often less available than ever before, and many young people live primarily in a culture of adolescents. The Papago Indians told anthropologist Ruth Underhill in the early 1930s that the way to raise healthy children was to "draw the children into your own life. Give them from birth love, companionship, and responsibility" (Underhill, 1979, p. 90). The contrast with contemporary U.S. society could hardly be starker.

Young people often do not recognize their own gifts and talents and may have few opportunities to create and develop their own power and their own ways of contributing to the collective. PEACE POWER! programs can greatly expand such opportunities. As a beginning, plans for such programs can easily include Youth Boards, as well as youth representation as full members in central planning groups, for example, those working on school violence prevention.

"Conferencing" of various types is another way to offer youths "seats at the table." Conferencing involving youths in leadership roles (as well as organizational staff at multiple levels) is a demonstrably effective way to deal with school discipline problems (McCold, 1997; McDonald, Moore, O'Connell, & Thorsborne, 1995). Groups of young people can also be involved in improving school culture and settings in many ways that are important to them, from improving physical conditions to involvement in menu planning and development of disciplinary policies. These and other creative alternatives provide youths with ways to develop and test their gifts in a matrix of shared power in which the gifts of all are valued. Effective collectives help everyone to find and deepen their gifts and powers, in an interlocking network of recognition and respect.

Make Peace

As noted earlier, "making peace" involves much more than agreeing on solutions to particular conflicts; conflict resolution needs to focus particularly on healing the relationships involved. In addition, skills training alone may not result in changes in people's day-to-day functioning. Many people know how to "control their tempers" with their supervisors, for example, but may not use those skills at home. Structured tools and processes appear to be particularly helpful in moving toward generalization and maintenance of skills learned.

As an example, a great deal of research has examined ways to resolve conflicts in families. Serna, Schumaker, Sherman, and Sheldon (1991) found, as did earlier research, that parents and youths could learn communication and problem-solving skills in structured programs, but they also discovered that these were seldom used in real family conflicts, even when additional practice was conducted in the home. What Serna and her colleagues found did work, however, was the use of a structured family conferencing format (building on the earlier work of others, particularly the Teaching Family model) in which family members first completed written cards as part of a structured process in the home; use of skills was maintained when the cards were later faded. The *PEACE POWER! Making Peace Card* relies on this and related research. This erasable white board lists five steps for "making peace" when an issue arises and is completed by the family as they problem solve. Preliminary testing by our group indicates that families can be taught to use this tool through modeling and initial guidance and can then use it on their own. It can simply be wiped clean after each use, actually a useful metaphor for healing. The tool was developed for wider use, however, because the process can also be used in conflict resolution programs and classroom settings at school and in other youth-serving settings. In fact, the best arrangement would probably involve using the same tool in multiple systems in the child's life.

In organizations and communities, as mentioned above, *family group conferencing* is a demonstrably effective approach for resolving serious conflict and promoting healing in schools and communities (McDonald, Moore, O'Connell, & Thorsborne, 1995). This approach has proved very effective in schools; further information, manuals and other materials, and training are readily available (see, e.g., http://www.realjustice. org).

YOUTH COUNSELING

Concurrent work with youths can certainly extend efforts to change the cultural matrices within which youths live their lives. Consistent with the constructive approach discussed in this chapter, a primary approach for such counseling is skills development. The PEACE POWER! materials emphasize eight clusters of life and leadership skills, as shown in Figure 7.2.

These empirically supported skills roughly map onto the overall PEACE POWER! strategy, with skills shown in each sector of Figure 7.2 contributing to the practices in the same sector in Figure 7.1. For example,

Figure 7.2. | Life and leadership skills for youths. From Mark A. Mattaini and the PEACE POWER! Working Group, 1999, *PEACE POWER! Working Manual*, Chicago: Walden Fellowship, Inc. Copyright 1999 by Mark A. Mattaini. Reprinted with permission.

"Find a Passion" involves finding activities that produce high levels of recognition and reward, and "Assert Yourself" and "Honor Diversity" emphasize skills to increase respectful action.

Life and leadership repertoires are best learned through a process of modeling, rehearsal, and social feedback; groups offer a natural modality for such processes. Other standard group work techniques, including exercises, structured discussions, use of teams, and group incentives, work well as part of such a program. Not all may require emphasis in all settings or with all groups, and time may not permit attention to all. As usual, there needs to be substantial room for tailoring the programming to local needs, interests, and resources. (More detail regarding each cluster of skills can be found in the *PEACE POWER! Working Manual:* http://www.bfsr.org/PEACEPOWER.html.) Intensive individual services can also be provided for youths who are particularly high risk for coercive and antisocial behavior, to assist them to develop alternative ways to influence their worlds (Mattaini, in press).

ORGANIZATIONAL SUPPORTS
FOR PEACE POWER!

Experience suggests that administrative support, particularly the active involvement of the principal or an equivalent administrator, is crucial to establishing and maintaining effective preventive programs, although certainly an individual teacher or classroom can act as a pilot and catalyst for adoption of the PEACE POWER! strategy. A consistent overall discipline plan providing positive structure is an important framework within which the power of recognition is intensified (see, e.g., Connolly, Dowd, Christe, Nelson, & Tobias, 1995). The physical environment of the school can also contribute to school atmosphere for good or for ill; damage from vandalism and graffiti tends to feed on itself, for example, and even the level of ambient noise affects the level of aversive stress experienced. A particularly useful program component is public organizational self-monitoring, including data on disciplinary referrals and problems, but particularly emphasizing the incidence of positive practices in the environment, such as the number of recognition notes completed and the number of peace-making agreements made (and kept!). Finally, staff training in handling residual aggressive and potentially violent incidents can be helpful. This should be seen as the last, rather than the first, emphasis of programming, because it can increase attention to negative behavior and reduce attention to positive behavior. A number of useful materials are available for such training (e.g., Goldstein, Palumbo, Striepling, & Voutsinas, 1995; Wood & Long, 1991).

CONCLUSION

We know a great deal about the factors that shape violence and coercion and those that can promote alternatives. If what we already know were widely applied, the incidence of socially damaging behaviors could be dramatically reduced. Those affected are our children, and the data suggest there is power in a strategy such as the one described here—power to transform the children's worlds, power to protect them, and power to participate with them in constructing a less coercive world. This is PEACE POWER!

REFERENCES

Aber, J. L., Brown, J. L., Chaudry, N., Jones, S. M., & Samples, F. (1996). The evaluation of the Resolving Conflict Creatively Program: An overview. *American Journal of Preventive Medicine, 12*(Suppl. 2), 82–90.

American Psychological Association. (1993). *Violence and youth: Psychology's response.* Washington, DC: Author.

Biglan, A. (1995). Translating what we know about the context of antisocial behavior into a lower prevalence of such behavior. *Journal of Applied Behavior Analysis, 28,* 479–492.

Connolly, T., Dowd, T., Christe, A., Nelson, C., & Tobias, L. (1995). *The well-managed classroom.* Boys Town, NE: Boys Town Press.

Embry, D. D., & Flannery, D. J. (1999). Two sides of the coin: Multilevel prevention and intervention to reduce youth violent behavior. In D. J. Flannery & C. R. Huff (Eds.), *Youth violence: Prevention, intervention and social policy* (pp. 47–72). Washington, DC: American Psychiatric Press.

Fawcett, S. B., Mathews, R. M., & Fletcher, R. K. (1980). Some promising dimensions for behavioral community technology. *Journal of Applied Behavior Analysis, 13,* 505–518.

Finn, J. L., & Checkoway, B. (1998). Young people as competent community builders: A challenge to social work. *Social Work, 43,* 335–345.

Goldstein, A. P., & Glick, B., with Reiner, S., Zimmerman, D., & Coultry, T. M. (1987). *Aggression replacement training.* Champaign, IL: Research Press.

Goldstein, A. P., Palumbo, J., Striepling, S., & Voutsinas, A. M. (1995). *Break it up: A teacher's guide to managing student aggression.* Champaign, IL: Research Press.

Kaufman, P., Chen, X., Choy, S. P., Chandler, K. A., Chapman, C. D., Rand, M. R., & Ringel, C. (1998). *Indicators of school crime and safety, 1998* (Report No. NCES 98-251/NCJ 172215). Washington, DC: U.S. Departments of Education and Justice.

Lowery, C. T. (1999). The sharing of power: Empowerment with Native American women. In L. Gutierrez & E. Lewis (Eds.), *Empowerment with women of color.* New York: Columbia University Press.

Lowery, C. T., & Mattaini, M. A. (in press). Shared power in social work: A Native American perspective. In H. Briggs & C. Corcoran (Eds.), *Foundations of change: Effective social work practice* (2nd ed.). Chicago: Lyceum.

MacElrea, F. W. M. (1994). Restorative justice: The New Zealand Youth Court—A model for development in other courts? *Journal of Judicial Administration, 4.*

Mattaini, M. A. (1999). *Clinical intervention with families.* Washington, DC: NASW Press.

Mattaini, M. A. (in press). *PEACE POWER: Youth violence prevention.* Washington, DC: NASW Press.

Mattaini, M. A., Lowery, C. T., Herrera, K., & DiNoia, J. (1999). *Youth violence prevention: A behavioral review.* Manuscript submitted for publication.

Mattaini, M. A., & the PEACE POWER! Working Group. (1999). *PEACE POWER! Working manual.* Chicago: Walden Fellowship, Inc.

Mattaini, M. A., Twyman, J. S., Chin, W., & Lee, K. N. (1996). Youth violence. In M. A. Mattaini & B. A. Thyer (Eds.), *Finding solutions to social problems: Behavioral strategies for change* (pp. 75–111). Washington, DC: American Psychological Association.

Mayer, G. R. (1995). Preventing antisocial behavior in the schools. *Journal of Applied Behavior Analysis, 28,* 467–478.

Mayer, G. R., Butterworth, T., Nafpaktitis, M., & Sulzer-Azaroff, B. (1983). Preventing school vandalism and improving discipline: A three-year study. *Journal of Applied Behavior Analysis, 16,* 355–369.

Mayer, G. R., Mitchell, L. K., Clementi, T., Clement-Robertson, E., Myatt, R., & Bullara, D. T. (1993). A dropout prevention program for at-risk high school students: Emphasizing consulting to promote positive classroom climates. *Education and Treatment of Children, 16,* 135–146.

McCold, P. (1997). *Restorative justice: An annotated bibliography.* Monsey, NY: Criminal Justice Press.

McDonald, J., Moore, D., O'Connell, T., & Thorsborne, M. (1995). *Real justice training manual.* Pipersville, PA: Piper's Press.

Perkins, C. A. (1997). *Age patterns of victims of serious violent crime* (No. NCJ-162031). Washington, DC: U.S. Department of Justice.

Prothrow-Stith, D. (1987). *Violence prevention curriculum for adolescents.* Newton, MA: Educational Development Center.

Reiss, A. J., Jr., & Roth, J. A. (Eds.). (1993). *Understanding and preventing violence.* Washington, DC: National Academy Press.

Ross, R. (1996). *Returning to the teachings: Exploring aboriginal justice.* Toronto, Ontario, Canada: Penguin.

Serna, L. A., Schumaker, J. B., Sherman, J. A., & Sheldon, J. B. (1991). In-home generalization of social interactions in families of adolescents with behavior problems. *Journal of Applied Behavior Analysis, 24,* 733–746.

Sidman, M. (1989). *Coercion and its fallout.* Boston: Authors Cooperative.

Underhill, R. (1979). *Papago women.* New York: Holt, Rinehart & Winston.

Walker, H. M., Colvin, G., & Ramsey, E. (1995). *Antisocial behavior in school: Strategies and best practices.* Pacific Grove, CA: Brooks/Cole.

Wolf, M. M., Braukmann, C. J., & Ramp, K. A. (1987). Serious delinquent behavior as part of a significantly handicapping condition: Cures and supportive environments. *Journal of Applied Behavior Analysis, 20,* 347–359.

Wolfe, D. A., Wekerle, C., & Scott, K. (1997). *Alternatives to violence: Empowering youth to develop healthy relationships.* Thousand Oaks, CA: Sage.

Wood, M. M., & Long, N. J. (1991). *Life space intervention: Talking with children and youth in crisis.* Austin, TX: Pro-Ed.

8 | Violence Prevention: A Systematic Approach

Ann L. Bauer

For the last decade, increasing attention has been brought to the issue of violent behaviors in a school setting. This increasing attention to the issue of violence in schools came to a head in the 1997–1998 school year with a series of tragic occurrences in such places as Paducah, Kentucky; Pearl, Mississippi; and Jonesboro, Arkansas, where children became mass murderers. We had a sharp reminder that this problem had not gone away in spring 1999 when the Littleton, Colorado, shooting occurred, and again in the fall with the shootings in Fort Gibson, Oklahoma. School counselors would seem to be in a unique position to effectively impact this tragic trend. However, without a broad-scale approach, this could easily become just one more societal dilemma handed to schools and counselors to fix. Administrators, teachers, and counselors express dismay at the wide variety of issues already piled on their plate with limited time and resources to address this heaping plateful of urgent problems. Adding the risk of fatal violence to this pile requires some careful thought as to how best to approach all of these problems in an economical and effective way. One approach that meets these requirements is to manage the school as a system in ways that encourage resilience.

During the 1980s, a great deal of research was done to identify children "at risk" for school failure, drug use, early sexual experience, violence, and so on. Certain red flags were identified, such as low socioeconomic status, abusive homes, and one parent who had been incarcerated. As the ability to identify at-risk children became more precise, researchers also identified children who had many strikes against them but survived, even thrived. Efforts were made to discover the protective factors present in these children's lives that appeared to inoculate them against the virulent dangers active in their lives. This research avenue offers hope for an economical and effective approach to prevention because the protective factors appear to be similar whether prevention efforts are aimed at violence, early sexual experience, or drug and alcohol use.

RESILIENCE RESEARCH

Several major studies have been conducted to examine these assets that protect children from the effects of living risky lives. Werner (1989, 1992) and her colleagues in Hawaii have been involved in a long-term study of resilience within a large poverty sample for the last four decades. They have identified a pattern of three types of protective factors: individual attributes; warm and connected relationships within the family; and external support available from school, church, or work.

In a summary of resilience research, Garmezy (1992) clarified these factors further. The personality characteristics associated with resilience include activity level, reflectiveness in a new situation, possessing cognitive skills, and responding positively to others. Families that are warm and cohesive encourage resilience, as does access to a caring adult. External support can come from a supportive teacher, a caring agency, or a church or other religious institutions.

Leffert and her colleagues (Leffert et al., 1998), associated with the Search Institute in Minneapolis, Minnesota, surveyed a large aggregate of youths in Grade 6 through Grade 12 during the 1996–1997 academic year. This research examined 40 protective factors or assets that have been sorted into external and internal categories. External assets include support from family, school, or neighborhood; the sense of empowerment that comes from being useful; boundaries and expectations; and constructive use of time. Internal assets are characterized by a commitment to learning, possessing positive values such as caring and responsibility, possessing social competencies such as planning and decision making, and having a positive self-identity. (For a complete chart of these 40 assets and their definitions, see Table 8.1.) The presence or absence of these assets is a powerful influence on behavior, and this influence can be seen functioning in a cumulative fashion. The more assets students possess, the less likely they are to indulge in risky behaviors. The reverse also holds true; the possession of fewer assets is highly associated with an increase in unhealthy behaviors such as drug use and early sexual experimentation.

RESILIENCE AND VIOLENCE PREVENTION

As mentioned previously, prediction and prevention of violence has become an urgent issue in U.S. schools. Dykeman, Daehlin, Doyle, and Flamer (1996) found three personal characteristics predictive of future violence: impulsivity, lack of empathy, and an external locus of control. If one were to take these negative indicators and reverse them into positive protective factors, they might read like this: good impulse control, empa-

Table 8.1 | Search Institute's 40 Developmental Assets

External Assets

Support
1. **Family support:** Family life provides high levels of love and support.
2. **Positive family communication:** Young person and her or his parent(s) communicate positively, and young person is willing to seek advice and counsel from parents.
3. **Other adult relationships:** Young person receives support from three or more nonparent adults.
4. **Caring neighborhood:** Young person experiences caring neighbors.
5. **Caring school climate:** School provides a caring, encouraging environment.
6. **Parent involvement in schooling:** Parent(s) are actively involved in helping young person succeed in school.

Empowerment
7. **Community values youth:** Young person perceives that adults in the community value youth.
8. **Youth as resources:** Young people are given useful roles in the community.
9. **Service to others:** Young person serves in the community one hour or more per week.
10. **Safety:** Young person feels safe at home, school, and in the neighborhood.

Boundaries and Expectations
11. **Family boundaries:** Family has clear rules and consequences and monitors the young person's whereabouts.
12. **School boundaries:** School provides clear rules and consequences.
13. **Neighborhood boundaries:** Neighbors take responsibility for monitoring young people's behavior.
14. **Adult role models:** Parent(s) and other adults model positive, responsible behavior.
15. **Positive peer influence:** Young person's best friends model responsible behavior.
16. **High expectations:** Both parent(s) and teachers encourage the young person to do well.

Constructive Use of Time
17. **Creative activities:** Young person spends three or more hours per week in lessons or practice in music, theater, or other arts.
18. **Youth programs:** Young person spends three or more hours per week in sports, clubs, or organizations at school and/or the community.
19. **Religious community:** Young person spends one or more hours per week in activities in a religious institution.
20. **Time at home:** Young person is out with friends with nothing special to do two or fewer nights per week.

Internal Assets

Commitment to Learning
21. **Achievement motivation:** Young person is motivated to do well in school.
22. **School engagement:** Young person is actively engaged in learning.
23. **Homework:** Young person reports doing at least one hour of homework every school day.

continues

Table 8.1 | continued

24. **Bonding to school:** Young person cares about her or his school.
25. **Reading for pleasure:** Young person reads for pleasure three or more hours per week.

Positive Values

26. **Caring:** Young person places high value on helping other people.
27. **Equality and social justice:** Young person places high value on promoting equality and reducing hunger and poverty.
28. **Integrity:** Young person acts on convictions and stands up for her or his beliefs.
29. **Honesty:** Young person tells the truth even when it is not easy.
30. **Responsibility:** Young person accepts and takes personal responsibility.
31. **Restraint:** Young person believes it is important not to be sexually active or to use alcohol or other drugs.

Social Competencies

32. **Planning and decision making:** Young person knows how to plan ahead and make good choices.
33. **Interpersonal competence:** Young person has empathy, sensitivity, and friendship skills.
34. **Cultural competence:** Young person has knowledge of and comfort with people of different cultural/racial/ethnic backgrounds.
35. **Resistance skills:** Young person can resist negative peer pressure and dangerous situations.
36. **Peaceful conflict resolution:** Young person seeks to resolve conflict nonviolently.

Positive Identity

37. **Personal power:** Young person feels he or she has control over things that happen to me.
38. **Self-esteem:** Young person reports having high self-esteem.
39. **Sense of purpose:** Young person reports that my life has a purpose.
40. **Positive view of personal future:** Young person is optimistic about his or her personal future.

Note. From *The Asset Approach: Giving Kids What They Need to Succeed.* Copyright 1998 by Search Institute, Minneapolis, Minnesota. Reprinted with permission. All rights reserved by Search Institute.

thy, and an internal locus of control. Dykeman et al. also suggested that positive peer relationships may help protect against violent behaviors.

As a part of their general research on resilience, Leffert et al. (1998) examined the effects of the number of assets present as well as specific factors that would appear to buffer youths from engaging in violent acts. In their survey, 61% of youths with 10 or fewer assets had been violent, whereas only 6% of those with more than 30 assets had demonstrated violent behavior. The possession of certain assets was particularly associated with an absence of violent behaviors. Mirroring the suggestion of Dykeman et al. (1996), Leffert et al. reported that positive peer influence was the most significant predictor of decreased report of violence. The second most powerful influence reported was the ability to peacefully resolve conflicts. School engagement also made an important contribution to reduction in violence.

Leffert et al. (1998) offered an important caveat that is echoed in the work of Werner (1989). While it is tempting to take these results and turn them into a silver bullet or magic solution, it would be unwise to do so. In her longitudinal study, Werner found that the relative importance of protective factors shifted across the decades. Leffert et al. (1998) pointed out that the effects of these protective factors are cumulative and that none of them work in isolation.

THE BENEFITS OF A WELLNESS
APPROACH TO PREVENTION

There are several positives to viewing at-risk children from the resilience perspective. Taking the other perspective, a problem-centered approach, can lead to a sense of hopelessness. It is difficult for school counselors to have much impact on preventing risk factors such as divorce, an incarcerated parent, or separation from a caregiver in the first year of life. However, looking at protective factors as the building blocks in healthy development makes it possible for school counselors to work to foster positive peer relationships, teach conflict management skills, and engage students in the education process.

Furthermore, the problem-centered focus on intervention can lead to bewildering and conflicting demands on a school counselor's time. He or she "should" work to prevent tobacco, drug, and alcohol abuse; prevent teenage pregnancy and suicide; and eliminate violence. These shoulds, all vitally important, compete for time and resources. Resilience research puts all the pieces together and provides a positive avenue to deal with all of these issues in an economical and efficient way. Looking at the glass as half full is not only more hopeful but also potentially more effective.

SCHOOLS AS CARING COMMUNITIES

To this point, this chapter has followed the pattern of most research in violence prevention. I have concentrated on the characteristics of potentially violent children and factors that they may or may not possess that lead to overcoming stressful life events. It is reasonably comfortable to list risk factors such as divorce, separation from mother, or a father who is absent or incarcerated. It is less comfortable, and fewer researchers discuss, the inadvertent ways those in the school community may have contributed to the violence that has erupted in schools. The stakes have been raised to such frightening proportions that it might be time to turn that intense gaze on the school communities and the manner in which the "way they have always done things" has potentially become a part of the problem. In the belief that comfortable denial does not foster healthy problem solving, the next topic to be discussed is the ways that schools may have functioned as part of the problem.

Because caring and supportive ties are suggested as being associated with healthy development by resilience research, I first discuss whether schools as they are currently structured tend to function as caring and connected communities. I begin with some thought proposed by Noddings (1984, 1988) about a morality based on caring relationships and the ways this might play out in the community that is a school. Ridley and Walther (1995) discussed some thoughts and research on the subject of creating a positive school environment. Following that, I turn to Baker's (1998) perspective of schools as systems that may inadvertently foster violence, and I finish the discussion of schools as caring communities by talking about the part school counselors might play in such a system.

Noddings (1984) suggested that schools have largely been managed under a legalistic moral approach that can function to remove caring from the equation. She proposed that truly moral behavior grows out of a sense of oneness with the other, which could be summarized in the statement, "I am so connected to you that if I hurt you, I also hurt myself." This would seem to be the essence of empathy. A morality based on empathy would lead one to do what is moral not because it is "the right thing to do" but because it is the "caring thing to do." A moral education would thus be an education that was conducted in a moral, and thus caring, way.

One of the remarkable features of the recent school killings was the way in which the killers appeared to feel no connection with those they attacked. Rather than crimes committed in the heat of passion and anger, the shootings in Jonesboro, Arkansas and those in Littleton, Colorado appeared to be cold-bloodedly planned and executed. It was almost as though the killers' victims were not real to them; certainly, this would appear to be the antithesis of what Noddings (1984) viewed as ethical behavior. It is also interesting to note that empathy, the opposite of cold detachment, has been suggested as an important protector against violence (Dykeman et al., 1996). In addition, caring as a positive value is one of the assets proposed by the Search Institute (Leffert et al., 1998). The killers in the schools behaved in ways that appeared devoid of caring and empathy. Certainly, it makes sense to suppose that if they had possessed those characteristics they could not have behaved in the way that they did.

This philosophical discourse about morality could be seen as a nice discussion for the front porch as we sip ice tea except for the imperative call for our attention represented by these school killings. Somehow members of the school community have felt so little empathy, so little connection and caring that they are killing teachers and students in a cold and calculated way. This issue of the presence or absence of caring has become one of life-and-death importance.

Do schools demonstrate caring in the way that they go about the business of educating? Noddings (1984) suggested that a mother's way of caring has been missing from this educational process. This way of caring seeks to foster growth, as a mother shapes a child who will mature into someone who will be a responsible citizen, a productive worker, and a caring spouse and parent. Noddings proposed that in putting the curriculum ahead of the student, schools become tempted to behave in uncaring ways. In 1988, Noddings warned against the danger that an overemphasis on achievement presented to the development of nurturing, caring relationships. Certainly, this emphasis and this danger have not diminished but rather have increased in the decade since her article was published.

If one uses the metaphor suggested by Noddings (1984, 1988) of the different approaches to parenting of fathers and mothers to examine the educational process, one can see how out of balance this process has become. The archetype of fathering implies setting expectations for achievement and rules with consequences for both good and bad behaviors. The archetypal mother nurtures, protects, and attends to the needs of her children. In reality, both approaches need a bit of the other to be successful. A father gone too far can be perceived as cold, disconnected, and critical, whereas the extremes of mothering appear indulgent and enmeshed. Indeed, research on parenting styles that lead to the best outcomes for children reveals that the preferred parenting style for either gender is a blend of both; this preferred style combines the setting of expectations and boundaries with a caring and connected relationship (Franz, McClelland, & Weinberger, 1991).

Following the proposed metaphor of education as good parenting, the best approach to education would demonstrate caring and respect while setting boundaries and expectations. It is frighteningly easy while in the pursuit of academic achievement and improved test scores to lose sight of students whom we are attempting to educate. If we must reach objectives five, six, and seven today, we have far too little time to connect to students in a caring way. As an examination of the history of education reveals, the pendulum swings too far before it swings back too far in the other direction, seldom resting in the center. Perhaps it is time to consider that schools may have gone too far in the fathering direction, creating an environment in which students perceive the process as cold, uncaring, and rejecting.

In the manner of caring parent figures striving to meet the needs and wants of students, it might be worthwhile to ask the students themselves what they want and need. Indeed, Ridley and Walther (1995) suggested a curious blind spot in the discourse about designing positive learning environments—that the students are not asked this question very much. In their book titled *Creating Responsible Learners*, Ridley and Walther (1995, pp. 12–13) compiled a list of students' answers to the question drawn from motivational research:

- Acceptance, a feeling of worth, and respect for their school and non-school identities
- Belonging and bonding with fellow students
- Choice, shared ownership, and involvement in determining class direction
- Personal responsibility, autonomy, and independence
- A positive personal relationship with teachers
- Purposeful and challenging schoolwork
- Confidence in their ability to understand and learn
- Active engagement and involvement rather than boredom
- Creative work
- Personal goal achievement
- Fun while learning
- Numerous opportunities for mastery
- Recognition for effort and success
- Trust
- Variety in learning
- Opportunities to work with other students as well as individually
- Safety from being embarrassed or cajoled into learning
- Understanding of strategies for learning and problem solving
- A "humanized" curriculum that connects their outside lives to what is being taught
- Clear rules and procedures and a classroom structure that makes the behavioral and learning expectations explicit
- Detailed and accurate feedback
- Willing extra assistance from teachers when necessary
- Minimized classroom competition
- Teachers with high but accurate expectations of their ability
- Equity in teachers' treatment of students

Not surprisingly, there are some interesting parallels between the Search Institute's list of 40 developmental assets and this list of students' wants and needs. The entire list draws a picture of a *caring school climate* and provides details of what it would take to facilitate *school engagement* and *bonding to school*. Bonding with peers grows out of *interpersonal competence* and skill in *peaceful conflict resolution*. Because this list is drawn from motivation literature, it makes sense that the items on this list would encourage and enhance *achievement motivation*. Making school an engaging place to learn and attending to both academic and affective needs would also foster resilience to stressful life events.

Further examination of this list reveals that it is a mixture of emotional needs such as trust and academic needs such as purposeful and challenging schoolwork. Students are apparently aware that school is about both affective and academic growth, thus creating a safe emotional space in which to practice the risky business of learning, and that ideal learning focuses on both academic and prosocial skills. Some administrators and teachers have been confused into thinking that the choice is between a "get tough" academic approach and a "soft touch" social approach (Ridley & Walther, 1995). Balance, the appropriate amount of both, is the key to creating a positive learning community.

The perception of school as an uncaring place can have deadly consequences. Indeed, Baker (1998) proposed that school violence arises from a failure of community in schools. She pointed out that children who have not experienced an attached and bonded relationship come to school at a disadvantage to enter into the web of relationships that is the school community. If schools take advantage of what Noddings (1988) called the rich opportunities for caring offered by school life, they can foster a school affiliation that mediates against violent behavior (Baker, 1998). This school affiliation is reminiscent of the school engagement asset proposed by the Search Institute (see Table 8.1). It would appear to be an important building block of healthy behavior.

Unfortunately, schools can also participate in the process of alienating children from the school community. Baker (1998) proposed that, in part, school violence occurs because of a poor fit between the academic and social expectations for students and their capacity. Goodness of fit grows out of a caring environment that accommodates and compensates for the needs of students. In such a supportive community, there is a sense of common ground, reciprocity, and respect. When schools focus on the curriculum and pay little or no attention to the abilities and needs of students, they violate their social contract to provide caring and support. They also violate that contract when they fail to offer opportunities to care and to be cared for to children who come to schools without that experience (Noddings, 1988).

There are a couple of caveats that need to be offered at this point. Are school personnel uncaring? No, the vast majority of the people who work in schools do so because they do care and because they want to make a difference in young people's lives. Sadly, the process and methods schools choose are failing too often to convey that caring attitude.

Should schools be shamed and blamed and held solely accountable for school violence? Again, no. Violent acts by children take place in the context of a culture in which many factors, such as the way violence is portrayed by the media and the influence of disruptive families and poor parenting, also carry some of this responsibility. It is simply that schools can choose to be a part of the solution by accepting their rightful part of the responsibility and changing their approach to a balance between expectations for achievement and caring attention to the needs and abilities of students.

How can school counselors function as a part of this solution? The caring relationships formed in individual and group counseling are a beginning. School counselors can also help to forge caring connections between the members of the school community through consultation. In their work as child advocates, they can work to keep the education process child centered. They can offer caring opportunities to students by establishing peer facilitation projects. Working with administrators, school counselors can help to provide balance to the caring process of education. Within my own community, there is a school that could function as a prototype for this balanced approach. This school of at-risk children has a husband-and-wife team at its core. The husband as principal provides structure, expectations, and consequences in a caring way, whereas the wife as counselor offers caring in a structured way. They have purposefully designed this school to be a caring and connected community of teachers, parents, and students. While not suggesting that counselors marry their administrators, I provide this as an example of a kind of cooperation to create a balanced approach in a supportive community that is both admirable and effective.

RESPONSIVE AND RESPONSIBLE SCHOOLS

I have spent some time talking about how demonstrating caring supports the development of community. Next, I focus on the other side of the parental coin: rules and consequences. I begin by looking at some traditional and familiar forms of discipline and the implicit messages these systems convey. The last part of this section examines an approach that encourages student responsibility and an internal locus of control.

In their discussion of assertive discipline, an approach used in many schools, Ridley and Walther (1995) pointed out that this approach does have some positive attributes. An assertive approach is a distinct improvement over being "reactive and aggressive or avoidant and passive" (Ridley & Walther, 1995, p. 70).

However, Ridley and Walther (1995) emphasized that an assertive approach has some of the same shortcomings shared by all traditional teacher-directed approaches. First, the necessity of functioning as the behavior cop can grow burdensome and take the joy out of the teaching experience. Second, although it may stop the misbehavior, it does not teach students the skills to manage their own behavior. Third, it is based on the notion that punishment motivates students to do better. Instead, in many cases, punishment instills the desire to resist, get even, or stop trying (Ridley & Walther, 1995).

By using adult-directed discipline methods, schools inadvertently give the message to students that teachers are in charge of controlling their behavior. Such an approach fosters an external locus of control, which is the reverse of what has been proposed to be an important factor in resilience. In fact, Dykeman et al. (1996) found an external locus of control to be one of three precursors to violent behavior.

Ridley and Walther (1995) described a student-directed approach that draws on work by Thomas Gordon, Rudolph Dreikurs, and William Glasser. This discipline plan has five levels of planning:

1. The first level asks three questions: "What are you doing?" "What's the rule?" "Can you do that?" A yes answer gets the response "Thank you!"
2. The second level asks, "Is there something you can do to make this right" or "What else can you do the next time this happens?"
3. The third level asks for a written plan that contains logical and natural consequences created at least in part by the student.
4. The fourth level requires this plan to be written in a planning room and approved by the planning room monitor or assistant principal. At this level, parents are also called.
5. The fifth level, not necessary in most cases, is a designated decision day. A plan is created by the principal, parents, and the student. The student may continue to attend school on a day-to-day basis but is sent home if any school rule is broken. At home, the student must write a new plan and convince both parents and principal of his or her sincerity and commitment to this plan before the student returns to school. (see Ridley & Walther, 1995, pp. 76–79)

This approach would seem to encourage the development of several of the assets suggested by the Search Institute (Leffert et al., 1998). This approach requires students to assume *responsibility* for their behavior, practice *interpersonal competence*, and *peacefully resolve conflicts*. The clear setting of *school boundaries* should also enhance *personal power* as well as feelings of *safety*.

This suggested student-directed discipline approach fulfills several of Baker's (1998) suggestions about approaches that prevent violence by building community. Within this system, students learn and practice proactive social skills, take personal responsibility of behavior, and use skilled moral decision making. Rules are set in a cooperative manner, and conflict resolution skills are taught and practiced.

Functioning as a system's consultant with an eye on what is best for students, a school counselor can advocate for a schoolwide discipline approach that is student-directed through in-services and presentations with school personnel. On a smaller scale, responsibility planning could be readily adapted for use in individual and group counseling sessions. In some instances, school counselors could facilitate, or cofacilitate, the classroom meetings recommended by Ridley and Walther (1995). In any case, this discipline approach is a systematic intervention that facilitates the development of many building blocks of resilience and represents a balance between caring and the setting of boundaries and consequences.

IMPLICATIONS FOR SCHOOL COUNSELORS

Previously in this chapter, I suggested that school counselors as well as others in the school setting change the focus from a problem-centered to a resilience perspective and work to help students accumulate as many protective factors as possible. School counselors can be a part of the return of caring to the manner in which the children are educated and can advocate for student-centered discipline approaches. In addition to the ways already suggested, school counselors can use specific counseling techniques and approaches that can help to tip the balance toward health and success.

Rak and Patterson (1996) pointed out that age-appropriate guidance groups are a good venue in which to teach and reinforce coping strategies. They suggested that solution-focused problem-solving approaches in individual sessions have a positive impact. Dykeman et al. (1996) cited research that supports some specific approaches for school counselors. In particular, three cognitive–behavioral techniques have proved successful in increasing impulse control: self-instruction, cognitive problem solving, and modeling. The authors encouraged empathy training and a rational emotive approach to help students develop an internal locus of control.

CONCLUSION

Several images come to mind when considering the issue of violence in schools. The first is a canary in a mine shaft: Something is seriously amiss, and danger is among us. The second image is that of the robot in that old television show, *Lost in Space*, as the robot waves his arms wildly saying, "Danger! Danger, Will Robinson!" In the third image, schools are reaping the harvest of the dragon's teeth that society has sown. Somehow, society has raised up children with little empathy, taught them violence is entertaining and revenge is cool, and given them access to "weapons of mass destruction." This chapter has proposed that schools take these incidents as fair warning that they need to do more than bemoan what children are like today. They need to change the systems by which the children are educated or risk another horrible harvest.

REFERENCES

Baker, J. (1998). Are we missing the forest for the trees? Considering the social context of school violence. *Journal of School Psychology, 36,* 29–44.

Dykeman, C., Daehlin, W., Doyle, S., & Flamer, H. S. (1996). Psychological predictors of school-based violence: Implications for school counselors. *The School Counselor, 44,* 35–47.

Franz, C. E., McClelland, D. C., & Weinberger, J. (1991). Childhood antecedents of conventional and social accomplishments in midlife adults. *Journal of Personality and Social Psychology, 60,* 586–595.

Garmezy, N. (1992). Resilience and vulnerability to adverse developmental outcomes associated with poverty. In T. Thompson & S. C. Hupp (Eds.), *Saving children at risk: Poverty and disabilities* (pp. 45–60). Newbury Park, CA: Sage.

Leffert, N., Benson, P. L., Scales, P. C., Sharma, A. R., Drake, D. R., & Blyth, D. A. (1998). Developmental assets: Measurement and prediction of risk behaviors among adolescents. *Applied Developmental Science, 2,* 209–230.

Noddings, N. (1984). *Caring, a feminine approach to ethics and moral education.* Berkeley: University of California Press.

Noddings, N. (1988). An ethic of caring and its implications for instructional arrangements. *American Journal of Education, 96,* 215–230.

Rak, C. F., & Patterson, L. E. (1996). Promoting resilience in at-risk children. *Journal of Counseling and Development, 74,* 368–373.

Ridley, D. S., & Walther, B. (1995). *Creating responsible learners: The role of a positive classroom environment.* Washington, DC: American Psychological Association.

Search Institute. (1998). *The asset approach: Giving kids what they need to succeed.* Minneapolis, MN: Author.

Werner, E. E. (1989). High-risk children in young adulthood: A longitudinal study from birth to 32 years. *American Journal of Orthopsychiatry, 59,* 72–81.

Werner, E. E. (1992). The children of Kauai: Resilience and recovery in adolescence and adulthood. *Journal of Adolescent Health, 13,* 262–268.

9 | Preventing Violence by Promoting Virtues

David N. Aspy

With all the work school counselors already have to do, it is understandable that they might resist the suggestion that they become involved in the prevention and reduction of school violence. However, a cogent case for such involvement was stated by Crespi (1999), a psychologist at the University of Hartford.

Using 1990 data, Males (1996) stated the case more generally by writing: "The U.S. teen murder rate was twelve times that of other major urbanized, industrialized societies. . . . The U.S. adult murder rate is likewise seven times higher than that of the other six nations" (p. 127).

These statements underscore the need for counselors to consider approaching the prevention of violence through almost any reasonable means, including the promotion of virtues. However, it is prudent to recommend that before counselors initiate those interventions, they should acquaint themselves with a solid body of knowledge that explores both violence and virtue as well as the relationship between the two.

UNDERLYING ISSUES

It is customary to consider violence and virtuousness as opposite ends of a spectrum of human traits. A rather common belief is that violent behavior is not virtuous and that virtuous behavior is not violent. This chapter examines that proposition and supports it.

According to Freud, everyone is born with a potential, even propensity, for violence. Perhaps, then, virtuous people are violent only when they are nonvirtuous. That is, violence erupts only during moments of weakness or sin. If so, then violence is either sinful or evil. Is that true?

The germane issue for this chapter is whether school counselors should be involved in the prevention of violence. The proposed answer is yes. It supports that response by contending that virtue promotion is a viable intervention strategy, and I describe four methods for that purpose.

153

DEFINING TERMS

Virtue is a word that has many definitions. Many writers draw from the works of the ancients when discussing virtues. Bennett (1993), the modern virtues guru, referred to virtue as "certain fundamental traits of character" (p. 12).

Pelligrino and Thomasma (1993) cited Aristotle's definition of virtue: "A state of character that brings into good condition the thing of which it is the excellence and makes the work of that thing to be done well" (p. 5). Durant (1966) stated that Aristotle defined virtue "not as an act but a habit of doing the right thing. At first it has to be enforced by discipline, since the young cannot judge wisely in these matters; in time that which was the result of compulsion becomes a habit, a second nature, and is almost as pleasant as desire" (p. 534). Adler (1978) wrote that Aristotle told us that moral virtue is "the habit of making right choices" (p. 101). Carter (1996) stated that Aristotle believed that humans learn the habits of virtues through repetition.

In the mid-1990s, Wolfe (1998) recognized a societal factor while commenting about middle-class American families: "As important as virtues are to middle-class Americans, it is just as important that we realize them modestly. It is important to pay homage to such classic virtues as courage, perseverance, honesty, loyalty, and compassion, but nothing should ever be taken to extremes" (p. 126). Thus, Wolfe suggested that tolerance has become the prime virtue of the 1990s American society. Dionne (1996) cited William Kristol as an advocate of the notion that the cultural influence on virtues should be recognized and that the task of liberty should be assigned to politics and the task of virtue left to society at large.

An instrumental or mechanical concept of virtues is gaining support as the Information Age emerges. To Pinker (1997), the issue is functionality. He wrote, "The human mind occasionally catches a glimmering of the brute fact that often adversaries can both come out ahead by dividing up the surplus created by their laying down of arms" (p. 519). Kurzweil (1999) made virtues technological by stating,

> Values and emotions represent goals that often conflict with each other and are an unavoidable by-product of the levels of abstraction that we deal with as human beings. As computers achieve a comparable—and greater—level of complexity . . . they too will necessarily utilize goals with implicit values and emotions. (p. 5)

Fukuyama (1999) referred to the social capital of virtuous practice, by which he meant that virtue has a commercial value. That is, businesses like to invest in virtuous communities.

In summary, the meaning of the term *virtue* has varied across history, but the persistent quality has been the notion that virtues are positive character traits in the sense that they tend toward goodness. Woodward (1994) moved toward clarity in this area when he stated a definition that seems appropriate and that diminishes some of the variability of the meaning. He wrote, "A virtue is a quality of character by which individuals habitually recognize and do the right thing" (p. 38). Of course, in this time of relativism, even this statement is challenged, but, as an initial guideline, Woodward's definition of virtue seems helpful.

SPECIFIC VIRTUES

One way to understand the general quality of virtues is to examine lists of specific ones compiled by various writers. Bennett (1993) is the author of the highest profile summary of virtues. The validity of Bennett's list is bolstered by the fact that it has not been seriously challenged. He offered 10 virtues: compassion, courage, faith, friendship, honesty, loyalty, perseverance, responsibility, self-discipline, and work.

Pelligrino and Thomasma (1993) compiled a list of eight virtues they recommended for physicians. These virtues were compassion, fortitude, integrity, justice, prudence, self-effacement, temperance, and trust.

Others have developed similar lists. Erikson (1964) listed care, competence, fidelity, hope, love, purpose, will, and wisdom. Unell and Wykoff (1995) listed the 20 teachable virtues as caring, cooperation, courage, courtesy, empathy, fairness, helpfulness, honesty, humor, loyalty, patience, peacemaking, resourcefulness, respect, responsibility, self-discipline, self-motivation, self-reliance, tolerance, and trustworthiness.

A HISTORY OF VIRTUES IN WESTERN CULTURE

In broad strokes, Western civilization's formal consideration of virtues proceeded in three major stages. First, they were birthed in ancient Greece. Second, they were integrated with Judeo-Christian virtues. And third, they were challenged by the notion of relativism. Today, virtues are on the absolutist side of the ongoing contention between relativism and absolutism.

VIOLENCE

Quite probably, violence is as old as virtues, perhaps older, at least in a formal sense. In fact, violence is traceable to the dawn of the human race. The Bible refers to the violence between two brothers, Cain and Abel, when Cain killed Abel over a matter of jealousy.

Violence, like virtue, is known to everyone. At least everyone has a notion of what violence is. But, it is a bit more difficult to define in terms that produce a consensus. Bok (1998) stated, "People surely do define violence in different ways, but if we waited to debate almost any complex issue until doubts and disagreements about definitions were resolved, we would have little left to discuss" (p. 6). Later, he stated that the meaning offered by the *Oxford English Dictionary*'s core definition was minimally acceptable: "the exercise of physical force so as to inflict injury or damage to persons or property" (p. 7).

Perhaps violence can be defined by historic examples. The explosions of atom bombs in Japan at Hiroshima and Nagasaki were violent. The Manson killings were violent. Dick Butkus was a violent linebacker. The French Revolution was violent, especially the executions of the royal family. The Nazi treatment of the Jews in concentration camps was violent. Rocky Graziano was a violent boxer. The murders at the St. Valentine's Day Massacre were violent. This list could go on ad infinitum.

What is the common characteristic of violence? It appears that it involves the exercise of power for the intent of harming something that could have been used for constructive purposes. But, there are discernible differences between the violence at Omaha Beach in the Second World War and the treatment of Jews that occurred in the concentration camps. Also, there is a difference between a beating administered to a child and a beating given by one professional boxer to another. This raises questions about the discrepancy of strength between the attacker and the victim and also about the role of the perpetrator and the recipient.

A much-used classification system lists four areas of human activity, and violence can occur in each of them: physical, intellectual, emotional, and spiritual. *Physical violence* is the most commonly cited form and often is easily recognized. The characteristic signs are bruises, cuts, scrapes, bleeding, and broken bones. Once inflicted, they are visual unless they are limited to internal structures. *Emotional violence* is more subtle than its physical counterpart. In many instances, its consequences are invisible particularly immediately after the violent act; that is, its observable impact is apt to be delayed such as happens in posttraumatic stress syndrome. Only recently is society beginning to recognize and to mete out punishment for the harm produced by violence such as sexual abuse, child abuse, and spouse abuse. These cases demonstrate that emotional violence often requires years for the victim to recognize the symptoms and to have the perspective necessary to prosecute the offender.

Intellectual violence is even more subtle than is emotional violence. Yet, there are signs that society is gaining insight into this category. Some schools are being called to task for not providing students with an adequate education. For example, many schools are staffed by unqualified teachers, and there is a growing body of data to support the contention that students placed in classes with unqualified teachers are being deprived of the opportunity for an adequate education. As that type of data accumulate and it is demonstrated that an education is essential to life in the Information Age, then more of the intellectual violence charges will appear in the legal system. That is, it will be increasingly possible to document the facts needed to validate the accusation that some students were intentionally deprived of their right to an adequate education.

Spiritual violence is the most subtle form of violence yet mentioned. Thus, it is the most difficult to define. Perhaps a suitable starting point is the Jonestown incident in Guyana, where more than 100 people committed mass suicide in the name of spiritual devotion. Assuming that the adults made mature decisions, the violence issue involves the matter of the "innocents" who were caught up in the circumstances. Was their spiritual trust abused? Were they the victims of spiritual violence? Certainly, a good case can be made for an affirmative answer to both questions.

Viewed from these various perspectives, violence is a complex phenomenon. Clearly, it is possible to do violence to a person even though one never "lays a glove on them." A proposition presented in this statement is that *violence is the intentional use of power to prevent people from fulfilling their positive potential. A corollary is that the stronger the restraint the more violent the act.*

VIRTUES AS ANTIDOTES FOR VIOLENCE

If counselors choose to counteract violence by promoting virtues, then they face a serious question: Can virtues serve as antidotes for violence? If the Aristotelian notion of virtues is used as a standard, the logical answer is yes. According to Pelligrino and Thomasma (1993), Aristotle asserted that virtues are "a habitual disposition to act well" (p. 5). Similarly, Boonin-vail (1994) stated that Thomas Hobbes "claimed that virtues are not just dispositions but dispositions that are so strengthened by habit that they beget actions with ease and with reason unresisting" (p. 194).

Additional rational support for the use of virtues as an antidote for violence comes from the writing of Gilligan (1996), who contended that violence is caused by a pathogen, namely, shame. He makes the case that shame is the primary cause of violence. He explained that when shame threatens to overwhelm the psyche, violence restores pride, which assuages the life-threatening pain.

Using Gilligan's (1996) model, the case for countering violence with virtues is that if a person pursues virtue (excellence) then pride is increased by generating a base of earned success, which is the most dependable platform for positive self-regard. That is, a person who achieves excellence of character (virtue) gains an internal locus for self-assessment and is less vulnerable to the judgment (real or imagined) of others. Through this process the individual can gain a sense of guilt (internal judgment), which Gilligan contended is antithetical to shame and, thus, to violence. In short, virtue reduces shame.

Thus, the proposition is that if the Aristotelian concept of virtues is used then virtues dispose people to behave well to the degree that "good" (constructive) behavior becomes almost reflexive. That is, phronesis or prudence dominates a virtuous person's behavior. Pelligrino and Thomasma (1993) stated, "Phronesis is the term Aristotle used for the virtue of practical wisdom, the capacity for moral insight, the capacity, in a given set of circumstances, to discern what moral choice or course of action is most conducive to the good of the agent or the activity in which the agent is engaged" (p. 84).

This notion also is in accord with Plato's stance that there is but one virtue, which means that people who attain mastery or excellence in one of the classical virtues will at the same time attain mastery of all of them. Thus, the task is to foster excellence in one virtue. Not incidentally, this concept is consistent with the teachings of both Buddhism and Confucianism.

The stance taken in this statement is that virtues (intentional use of resources to accomplish constructive ends) and violence (intentional use of resources to accomplish destructive ends) are antagonistic in that a person cannot be violent (destructive) while simultaneously being virtuous (constructive). Thus, the deterrent (antidote) to violent behavior is to transfer the negative energy of violence into the pursuit of mastery of a virtue. Figure 9.1 depicts the diametric relationship between virtues and violence.

FOUR MODELS FOR PROMOTING
VIRTUES AS ANTIDOTES TO VIOLENCE

Kohlberg's Model of Virtue Promotion

Kohlberg (1970) referred to the "bag-of-virtues" theory that dominated American education during the middle 1900s. Moral education based on this notion had four components: exhorting children to practice those

Figure 9.1 |

Violence	Virtue
The intentional use of resources to accomplish destructive ends.	*The intentional use of resources to accomplish constructive ends.*

virtues; telling the students that they would be rewarded by happiness, fortune, and good repute; adults modeling those virtues; and giving children a daily opportunity to practice virtues. However, Kohlberg concluded that the bag-of-virtues method did not work. Yet, some practitioners believe it is an effective mode of promoting virtues.

Kohlberg (1970) suggested that "the only constitutionally legitimate form of moral education in the schools is the teaching of justice (Plato's core virtue) and that the teaching of justice in the schools requires just schools" (p. 67). He explained that justice is a moral principle that is a universal mode of choosing. It is a reason for action that says, "Treat everyone's claim impartially." Kohlberg supported his position by citing Plato's principle that what makes a virtuous action virtuous is that it is guided by knowledge of the good.

Kohlberg (1970) suggested a three-step teaching method: First, use the Socratic method to create dissatisfaction in the students about their present knowledge of moral good; second, expose them to disagreement and argument about specific moral situations; and third, point the way to the next level of moral development.

Sizer's Model of Virtue Promotion

Sizer (1984) defined decency as "fairness, generosity, and tolerance, and [stated] that these sturdy virtues are at the heart of the American system" (p. 125). He gave this summary of his views: "The tone of a school—the extent of its own inherent decency—is the sum of its assembled human characters and not something that exists by fiat . . . at best it can be persuaded, and the decency [that the school] ultimately exhibits will come from within, from [its] own convictions" (p. 125). Thus, Sizer's method is one of encouraging the growth of the existing potential for virtue.

The Christian Model of Virtue Promotion

Just as Plato contended that virtue was a singular factor (justice), so Christianity poses a unitary virtue: love. Specifically, a New Testament passage states, "Now abideth faith, hope, love. But, the greatest of these is love" (I Corinthians 13:13). The crux of the Christian mission is the enhancement of love, that single characteristic. Indeed, it presents God as love incarnate (God is love; I John 4:8).

It is reasonable to conclude that practicing Christians would not become involved in violence. That is, they would abstain from the intentional use of resources to accomplish destructive ends. On the contrary, they would be enthusiastically engaged in the intentional use of resources to promote constructive ends.

It should be noted that other religious faiths have virtue-promoting programs that are similar to that of Christianity. The Christian model was presented here because, in the United States, it has the largest membership. Also, there is solid substantive support for the involvement of religion in the effort to reduce violence. Bennett, Dilulio, and Walters (1996) wrote, "There is the growing body of scientific evidence from a variety of academic disciplines which indicates that churches can help curtail or cure many severe social pathologies" (p. 207).

Lickona's Model of Virtue Promotion

Lickona (1991) has worked extensively in education and has compiled a comprehensive list of virtue-promoting activities that can be implemented in almost any educational setting. In that sense, his model can accommodate an infinite variety of circumstances. His overarching philosophy is highly optimistic in that it seems to be based on the notion that each setting offers some gateway through which virtue promotion can enter and all of them are useful. The critical challenge is to use those entry points and strategies creatively.

Summary of the Four Models

The operative question for counselors is how to promote virtues in their role of violence prevention. The foregoing four models—Kohlberg ("bag of virtues" and Socratic), Sizer, Christian, and Lickona—are suggestions that can serve as modifiable templates from which counselors can develop their own unique applications. Fortunately, Crespi (1999) suggested some specific areas in which counselors could initiate efforts in early intervention and school-based intervention programs. Also, he cited the laudatory efforts of the University of Wisconsin at Milwaukee, which cooperated with the state's Violence Prevention Program. Crespi wrote that the program had "yielded positive behavioral changes in reducing negative conflict and fostering anger management within schools through parent workshops, peer mediation, and violence groups" (p. 8).

An excellent source of information is a book titled *Promising Practices in Character Education* edited by Phillip Vincent (1996). It describes nine programs for character education conducted in various sites throughout the nation.

Pelligrino and Thomasma (1993) asserted, "To test for this outcome (improved character), we would have to observe our subjects in a variety of moral situations before and after our attempts to teach virtue. The methodological difficulties of such a study are obviously insurmountable" (p. 179).

A PROPOSED MODEL OF RESEARCH

In spite of the rather dismal research summary given by Pelligrino and Thomasma (1993) and Bronowski and Mazlish (1960) as well as others, some investigations of virtues are progressing. Aspy, Russell, and Wedel (1999) have approached the problem from the perspective that the emergence of the Information Age with its technological base makes it imperative that the virtues efforts develop a database that addresses the topic from a scientific orientation. They contend that there is a significant audience for whom science is the home language and that anyone who wishes to communicate with them must speak from that format. In short, communication is enhanced by using the native language.

To develop a virtues referent database, Aspy et al. (1999) converted several lists of definitions of virtues into 9-point scales such as shown in Figure 9.2. For example, Bennett (1993) defined courage as "the act of despising things that are terrible and standing our ground against them" (p. 441). This definition was placed on a 9-point scale ranging from 1 (*low*) to 9 (*high*).

Figure 9.2 |

Directions: Circle the rating you would give yourself for each item.

Courage: The act of despising things that are terrible and standing our ground against them.

1	2	3	4	5	6	7	8	9

| Almost | | | About 1/2 | | | | Almost | |
| never | | | the time | | | | always | |

Similarly, all 10 of Bennett's (1993) definitions for a virtue were translated into 9-point scales, and the resulting 10-item instrument was administered to several groups of respondents. Two of the group results are listed in Table 9.1.

Some bottom-line findings emerged from those explorations. First, the scales were usable by all subject populations. Second, the mean scores were consistent across groups. Indeed, there were no significant differences between the means of any of the groups. Third, the results served effectively as entry points for conversations about virtues.

Aspy et al. (1999) extended their investigations by converting other lists of virtue definitions into Likert-scale instruments. Those lists included definitions proposed by Pelligrino and Thomasma (1993), the Bible, and Erikson (1964). The first purpose was to investigate the possibility that the response patterns yielded by the first studies were an arti-

Table 9.1 | Mean Scores for the Virtues Scale Developed From Bennett's (1993) Definitions

Virtue	120 Graduate Students M	38 Prison Inmates M
Self-discipline	6.6	6.8
Compassion	6.3	6.9
Responsibility	7.7	7.4
Friendship	7.5	7.0
Work	7.7	7.8
Courage	6.9	7.2
Perseverance	7.6	7.3
Honesty	7.7	7.4
Loyalty	7.8	7.7
Faith	7.6	7.1

Note. Comparisons between the two groups revealed no statistically significant differences.

fact of Bennett's (1993) choice of virtues and definitions. A summary of two of the group responses is listed in Table 9.2.

The means of the responses clustered around the value 7. Again, there were no significant differences between the population means for identical virtues. These results supported the contention that among Americans there is a tendency to assess their virtues as above average but less than the optimum.

As interesting as the numerical results proved to be, the most exciting and usable finding was that the instruments were an effective means to initiate meaningful discussions about virtues. This effect was especially pronounced in small groups, in which members examined their results

Table 9.2 | Mean Scores for Virtues Scales Developed From Proposed Definitions

Patients' Perceptions of Physicians' Level of Virtue Using the Definitions of Pelligrino and Thomasma (1993)		60 Fundamentalist Christians' Self-Report Using Biblical Definitions of Virtues	
Virtue	M	Virtue	M
1. Trust	7.4	1. Faith	8.2
2. Compassion	6.0	2. Hope	8.1
3. Prudence	6.9	3. Love	7.1
4. Justice	7.4	4. Justice	7.8
5. Courage	7.5	5. Mercy	7.2
6. Temperance	7.5	6. Humility	6.3
7. Integrity	7.1	7. Joy	7.4
8. Self-effacement	7.0	8. Peace	7.2
		9. Meekness	6.8
		10. Temperance	6.9

together. As the individuals discussed their scores, there was an increased understanding of the more profound dimensions of the separate virtues and, in most instances, a lowering of the participants' estimate of their practice of the virtue in question.

For counselors who initiate virtue-promoting efforts, the virtues scales are instruments that can be used to evaluate clients' changes occurring during interventions. For example, if counselors used Kohlberg's (1970) strategies, they could derive pre- and postmeasures by using the virtues scales (Bennett's [1993], Pelligrino & Thomasma's [1993], or Biblical). This type of data contributes to the badly needed database in this area.

CONCLUSION

This chapter contends that virtues and violence are related negatively. As one increases, the other decreases. Thus, it proposes and supports the strategy of reducing violence by focusing on the enhancement of virtues. Basically, it grows from the age-old hypothesis that if people do more of what is constructive, then they will do less of what is destructive.

Given this premise, the task becomes how to promote virtues. Several models of virtue enhancement are offered. Kohlberg (1970) described two procedures. The first is a bag-of-virtues strategy composed of three steps: encourage children to practice virtues; promise them rewards if they practice virtues; and give children opportunities to practice them. The second is a modified Socratic method that has three steps: generate dissatisfaction with students' current level of moral knowledge; expose them to arguments about moral issues; and lead them to the next level of moral understanding.

Sizer (1984) advocated a climate-oriented strategy. He proposed that virtues would be promoted if a school (organization) generated a virtuous climate by practicing them, thus allowing the growth of either the innate or learned virtuousness of students. This position is consistent with Wilson's (1993) concept of an innate moral sense.

Lickona (1991) proposed a multifaceted model of virtue enhancement that featured flexibility. The basic assumption was that schools offer a limitless range of entry points for moral instruction. Therefore, the would-be interventionists must have a large repertoire of responses in order to use the opportunities available to them. In essence, all entry points can be effective if the virtues promoter is sufficiently creative.

Christians, indeed most religions, have well-developed virtue promotion programs that include three stages: informal instruction of children by parents or parent surrogates, formal instruction by professional church people, and opportunities for virtuous behavior. This program is recycled for adults who become parents or parent surrogates. This type of effort has extensive historical roots that have been challenged severely by the emergence of relativism during the 20th century.

This chapter also recognizes that the entire virtues effort suffers from a weak base of support from systematic investigations. This shortage is a marked handicap in the Information Age culture, which is dominated by technology and its scientific orientation. Some investigators are attempting to address this research gap. For instance, Aspy et al. (1999) have developed and used instruments based on definitions of virtues proposed by writers such as Bennett (1993), Pelligrino and Thomasma (1993), Erikson (1964), and the Bible. Their strategy has been to convert the definitions into 9-point scales arranged to determine how frequently a respondent practices the virtue defined in the items.

These investigations have yielded a database that supports the notion that Americans tend to rate themselves as above average for the practice virtues. The data also indicate that although Americans rate themselves as above average, they recognize that their practice is not perfect. Thus, there is room for improvement. This factor is key to the success of virtues promotion efforts, because it is at that point that there is room for counselor intervention.

A key concept of this chapter is that the promotion of virtues is the prepotent method for counteracting violence, because it places the interventionists in a positive rather than negative stance. Thus, the major issue becomes how to accomplish that goal. It offers four specific suggestions for virtue promotion with the understanding that there is room for creativity and that better methods are needed badly. Therefore, this statement is a launch pad that, it is hoped, others will use to develop and use improved models.

The main ideas developed in this chapter are as follows:

1. There is a need to reassess the role of counselors in violence prevention.
2. Violence is the intentional use of resources to accomplish destructive ends.
3. Virtue is the intentional use of resources to accomplish constructive ends.
4. Violence and virtue are antithetical.
5. The best method for reducing or preventing violence is to promote virtue.
6. Methods for promoting virtues have been developed but better ones are needed.
7. There is a virtual dearth of direct research evidence to support virtues promotion.

Virtues promotion is timely. Sandel (1996) contended that there is a recrudescence (revival) of virtues and that it is being supported by both the conservative and liberal communities. It appears to be an opportune moment for counselors to benefit from the momentum of the cultural zeitgeist.

REFERENCES

Adler, M. (1978). *Aristotle for everybody*. New York: MacMillan.

Aspy, D., Russell, G., & Wedel, M. (1999). *Toward the systematic investigation of virtues* (Monograph No. 2). Edmond, OK: Center for the Systematic Study of Values and Virtues.

Bennett, W. (1993). *The book of virtues*. New York: Simon & Schuster.

Bennett, W., Dilulio, J., & Walters, J. (1996). *Body count*. New York: Simon & Schuster.

Bok, S. (1998). *Mayhem*. Reading, MA: Perseus Books.

Boonin-vail, D. (1994). *Thomas Hobbes and the science of moral virtue*. New York: Cambridge University Press.

Bronowski, J., & Mazlish, B. (1960). *The Western intellectual tradition*. New York: Barnes & Noble.

Carter, S. (1996). *Integrity*. New York: Basic Books.

Crespi, T. (1999, May). Childhood violence: Considerations for counseling in the schools. *Counseling Today*, p. 8.

Dionne, E. (1996). *They only look dead*. New York: Simon & Schuster.

Durant, W. (1966). *The life of Greece*. New York: Fine Communications.

Erikson, E. (1964). *Insight and responsibility*. New York: Norton.

Fukuyama, F. (1999, May). The great disruption. *The Atlantic Monthly*, pp. 55–80.

Gilligan J. (1996). *Violence*. New York: Random House.

Kohlberg, L. (1970). *Moral education*. Cambridge, MA: Harvard University Press.

Kurzweil, R. (1999). *The age of spiritual machines*. New York: Viking.

Lickona, T. (1991). *Educating for character*. New York: Bantam.

Males, M. (1996). *The scapegoat generation*. Monroe, ME: Common Courage Press.

Pelligrino, E., & Thomasma, D. (1993). *The virtues in medical practice*. New York: Oxford University Press.

Pinker, S. (1997). *How the mind works*. New York: Norton.

Sandel, M. (1996). *Democracy's discontent*. Cambridge, MA: Harvard University Press.

Sizer, T. (1984). *Horace's compromise*. Boston: Houghton Mifflin.

Unell, B., & Wykoff, J. (1995). *20 teachable virtues*. New York: Berkeley Publishing.

Vincent, P. (Ed.). (1996). *Promising practices in character education*. Chapel Hill, NC: Character Development Project.

Wilson, J. (1993). *Moral sense*. New York: Free Press.

Wolfe, A. (1998). *One nation, after all*. New York: Viking.

Woodward, K. (1994, June 13). What is virtue? *Newsweek*, pp. 38–39.

10 | School Violence: An Ecological, Social, and Cultural Perspective

Farah A. Ibrahim and Peter Tran

This chapter focuses on ecological, social, cultural, and historical factors that lead to violence in U.S. society, and ultimately in U.S. schools. The chapter presents developmental stage information to aid in understanding how violence is interpreted by the young. Additionally, we address the need for and provide examples of how to educate school children and adolescents in antiviolence approaches to life. Our perspective incorporates ecological, social, cultural, and historical factors and psychological theory to present a comprehensive approach for responding to school violence.

SOCIAL–CULTURAL HISTORICAL FACTORS: VIOLENCE AND AGGRESSION IN U.S. SOCIETY

World history, sociology, and psychology tell us that aggression is inherent in human beings (Bandura, 1973). Religion and culture have for centuries tried to create brotherhood and sisterhood among people of the world and within nations. School violence is not a phenomenon that is unique to the United States; it has persisted in various societies for several centuries. In fact, school bullying was first researched in Scandinavia (Olweus, 1985, 1993). Ross (1996) maintained that school violence and harassment are not 20th-century phenomena, as exemplified in books by Dickens (*Oliver Twist*, 1838) and Hughes (*Tom Brown's Schooldays*, 1857) and other historical accounts of childhood as noted by authors such as Aries (1962), Rose (1991), and Walvin (1982). These books tell us that children were subjected to violence by their families, peers, teachers, and other nonrelated adults.

We contend that children learn caring or bullying, as well as guilt and shame tactics, from their primary home environment and their community, society, and larger nation, and then treat others the way they have been treated. Contrary to the popular belief that suffering makes a person more human, it tends to increase violence as evidenced by the research on spousal battering and child abuse (Ibrahim & Herr, 1987).

ETIOLOGY AND DYNAMICS

We propose an ecological, cultural, social, and historical approach to understand and respond to violence in U.S. schools. To understand violence in the schools, one needs to consider (a) the sociopolitical history of the United States, (b) the implications of the movements in psychology in the last two decades, and (c) the culture of the United States in general. This includes the sociopolitical history of the country. In the case of the United States, it is a country won through several wars with the indigenous people that resulted in great bloodshed and sacrifices on both sides. The social dynamic that operates in war and colonial situations is "might is right." The United States' involvement in the First and Second World Wars, the Korean War, the Vietnam War, Operation Desert Storm, and now the North Atlantic Treaty Organization initiative in the Balkans sends a very definite message to the American people that supports our contention.

The United States has one of the longest histories of devaluing human beings as slaves (Takaki, 1993). Slavery was justified and human beings were captured from another continent and brought here and used for economic gain by landowners. History tells us that there was adequate labor available in the United States. However, it was considered economically more viable that we enslave people instead of paying wages to Europeans who were willing to do the same jobs for a reasonable wage (Takaki, 1993). Another dimension that addresses the inherent violence in U.S. culture is evidenced by racism, sexism, homophobia, and negative attitudes toward children, the elderly, people with disabilities, people from lower social classes, and people with inadequate education (Takaki, 1993).

As Bandura (1973) appropriately noted, the minute one dehumanizes people, one can commit violence on them. This has been an integral component of U.S. society for over 370 years. Only since the civil rights movement and the resulting changes in laws have we seen a drop in the overt and socially sanctioned violence against those who are different. The implicit cultural message for the young is that it is okay to be violent when it suits your purpose; it is okay to be violent against an ostracized member of society or an out-group. This is evident from the situation in Columbine High School in Littleton, Colorado. The young men who wreaked so much havoc on their own community and peers were isolated and rejected and felt powerless in reaching important people in their world to recognize their worth, so they got the attention they were craving (Walsh, 1999).

In the last 20 years there have been significant shifts in American psychology, specifically regarding the needs of the young and how to shape their behavior in a socially appropriate direction. Since 1950, the focus has been on creating a specific stage called childhood. It has been accepted in psychology that childhood must be respected as a vulnerable stage, with specific developmental issues, and that children must be protected and nurtured accordingly. However, Seligman (1998), in reviewing the reasons for the current spate of horrific violence in U.S. schools, noted that some messages have been carried too far. He argued that psychologists and counselors have moved from a negative model of child behavior shaping that involved only criticism from parents and teachers to a model that only focused on what was right with each child. In using this model, we in the helping profession have overlooked our responsibility to help young people come to terms with their limits and develop positive coping strategies. Seligman (1998) maintained that when confronted with deficits in their behavior or coping strategies, children who grew up in the "focus on positive" era are enraged. According to Seligman, it is "the first time someone holds up the mirror to them" (p. 2). These children are unable to handle their limits and respond with rage.

In the last 40 years since the Industrial Revolution, a significant amount of the responsibility for raising children has fallen to a couple or a single parent. When the U.S. society moved from an agrarian to an industrial society, the concept of the family was redefined from an extended system to one that included a mom, a dad, and 2.5 kids. This could also be attributed to the ethos of the 1960s, when the needs of the individual became paramount, and the "I" became the celebrated centerpiece of American culture. This was a cultural assumption that was an ideal value in European and Protestant individualized systems. It is operationalized as the core of counseling theories in all three major movements: psychodymanic, existential–humanistic, and behavioral. However, when raising children, both Hillary Rodham Clinton (1996) and Pipher (1996) noted in their books that it is a ridiculous notion to expect one or two parents to be responsible to meet all the needs of children. It is the responsibility of the community, the schools, and the extended family to nurture and rear children appropriately as the future citizens and leaders of a society.

The narcissism of the 1950s, as noted by May (1981), has intensified through the gluttonous 1980s to complete self-centeredness and lack of care and civility in the 1990s (Peck, 1997). Parents, teachers, counselors, and psychologists have a moral imperative to recognize their responsibilities in nurturing and socializing the young and getting involved with the communities beyond their specific "job descriptions." Teaching, counseling, parenting, and mentoring never were just jobs; they have always had a social responsibility component.

Another factor operating in U.S. society is akin to what Rogers (1942) considered the disparity between the ideal and real self that results in a psychological breakdown. This dynamic is also evident at a systemic level in our society. Takaki (1993) noted that in creating an ideal society, the founding fathers had proposed a set of laws and assumptions that would make this a truly democratic society. However, the power hierarchies that were created by mainstream culture and the disparity in individual rights on the basis of race, class, ethnicity, and gender have contributed to the violence, drug and alcohol abuse, and other negative social behaviors in U.S. society. As a society, we must reduce the disparity between our ideal values and real way of being and create congruence and hope in the young and ourselves.

SOCIAL, CULTURAL, AND ECOLOGICAL SYSTEMS OF VIOLENCE: INFLUENCES ON THE YOUNG

The explosion of violence in U.S. schools may be a reflection of what children witness in their everyday life. Current literature suggests that children are becoming both victims and witnesses of aggression and violence in their homes and community, and therefore it is a natural process for them to act out violence in schools (Van Biema, 1999).

Media Violence

Mass media, in particular television and movies, have glorified and sanctioned violence as a form of socially acceptable behavior for children. A general consensus in research relating violence and television watching concluded that a small causal effect exists between aggression and viewing television violence and that exposure to violent programming increases the likelihood of aggressive behavior (Cole, 1995; Hughes & Hasbrouck, 1996).

Researchers have estimated that by the time a child leaves elementary school, he or she has witnessed at least 8,000 murders and more than 100,000 other acts of violence on television (Hughes & Hasbrouck, 1996). Bandura and associates (as cited in Hughes & Hasbrouck, 1996) reported that children who watch violent films will imitate similar aggressive behaviors in free-play situations. Children model what they see in life, which suggests the *notion* that violent and aggressive behaviors are not completely prewired, inevitable, or unchangeable (Pepler & Slaby, 1994).

Although we cannot separate what is nature and what is nurture, we do know that there are some children who are predisposed with an impulsive temperament to violent behavior. Television and other media outlets must take on the responsibility of not modeling such violent and aggressive behavior for our children. The media and entertainment industry must take an active role to censor themselves for the welfare of the children who spend more time on the Internet and watching TV instead of reading or playing. Parents must also take a more active monitoring role to ensure that their children are watching age-appropriate television shows and are on Internet sites that are developmentally appropriate (Okrent, 1999). Social and cultural mores communicated through television, movies, and the Internet have great impact on attitudes and behavior of the young (Pepler & Slaby, 1994).

Children as Witnesses of Violence

Pynoos and Eth (as cited in van Dalen & Glasserman, 1997) estimated that children witness between 10% and 20% of the nation's homicides. Current research indicates that chronic exposure to violence can have detrimental developmental effects on children, including "psychological disorders, grief and loss reactions, impaired intellectual development, school problems, truncated moral development, pathological adaptation to violence, and identification with the aggressor" (Friday, 1995, p. 404). These enduring patterns of violence and aggressive behaviors are learned, developed, and maintained through social experiences and personal involvement as either the aggressor, the victim, or a bystander (Pepler & Slaby, 1994). Children who view the world as hostile will react with the same anger and aggression that they experienced during their socialization (Pepler & Slaby, 1994).

Trends in Violence

Children are increasingly the primary victims of violence in the school, at home, and in their community. The Federal Bureau of Investigation (as cited in Fried, 1997) reported that the frequency of violence against youths has risen significantly. These researchers further reported that violence has become the second leading cause of injury-related deaths. In places like New York City, homicide has become the leading cause of death for adolescent males between the ages of 15 and 19. Experiences of inner-city children have been compared with children from war zones in Ireland and Israel (Shakoor & Chalmers, 1991).

A survey conducted in 1991 reported that 26% of high school students have carried weapons (i.e., knives and guns) onto school grounds for personal protection or to feel safe. Guns and firearms are considered the weapon of choice for homicide and suicide, regardless of gender or race. Injuries from firearms are the eighth leading cause of death for all persons and the second leading cause of death for those ages 10 to 34 (Friday, 1995).

Although inner-city children are primarily victims of crimes, researchers have identified them also as covictims of crimes because these children observe violence acted out on others. Shakoor and Chalmers (1991) reported that 70–75% of inner-city children have witnessed someone being shot, stabbed, robbed, or killed. These researchers posited that children who are covictimized will cognitively, emotionally, and behaviorally suffer during the critical developmental stages of childhood and adolescence and are candidates for posttraumatic stress disorder (Harper & Ibrahim, in press).

Current research indicates that the majority (75%) of the victims in school violence know their attacker by name. However, these attacks are reported to the police only about 30% of the time; thus, over 70% of the time these incidents of violence go unreported (Steinmetz, 1980). Harootunian (1984) noted that this can be attributed to the cultural belief and attitude that "boys-will-be-boys." The majority of youth homicides are committed by someone known to the victim (Cirillo et al., 1998). Researchers have concluded that of all the predictors of teen violence, a history of exposure to violence is the strongest of all predictors (Pepler & Slaby, 1994).

Teachers and Violence

Teachers are the safety net for children in the schools, and children look to them for protection from violence. This is still the case even when teachers are at risk for violence in the schools. Teachers are now taught self-protection given the rising tide of violence in the U.S. schools (Harper & Ibrahim, in press). Additionally, a growing number of teachers across America are being targeted for violence, not just in inner-city schools.

Pietrzak, Petersen, and Speaker (1998) surveyed over 600 school professionals and found that 24% of them were very concerned about verbal attacks and physical threats by both students and parents in schools. Once the teacher is attacked, the likelihood of being subjected to a higher degree of violence the next time is greatly increased (Steinmetz, 1980). Pietrzak et al. (1998) indicated that 62% of teachers had been verbally threatened or intimidated, 26% had been physically threatened or intimidated, 12% had been sexually threatened or intimidated, 66% had been verbally attacked, 11% had been physically attacked, and 0.6% had been sexually attacked.

School as Enabler

Schools can unintentionally perpetuate aggressive behaviors on children by alienating or rejecting them through social–cultural norms, and in turn these children will act the part of the alienated and rejected as they understand it. Children who are unable to share in the experiences of their peers at school will likely experience feelings of alienation and rejection leading to aggressive behavior toward the school, school personnel, or peers (Baker, 1998; Cloud, 1999). They will automatically be labeled troublemakers, losers, and failures. Such labeling and rejection create an atmosphere that is unwittingly promoted by the school. For some of these students, the self-fulfilling prophecy of failure will come to fruition, therefore granting teachers and school administrators the evidence they need to confirm the worthlessness of these children. For the unfortunate children cast in these roles, schools will always be perceived as hostile.

Lack of bonding to the school results in students' associating with delinquent peers or others that are labeled as "outside the mainstream" (Apter & Propper, 1984). After being marginalized, alienated children will seek out those in a similar social situation for support, encouragement, and companionship, both for psychological and social support. Marginalized children seek reinforcement for aggressive behavior from people who will accept them (Baker, 1998; Beauvais, Chavez, Oetting, Deffenbacher, & Cornell, 1996). Further alienation occurs when their peers reject them because of their disruptive behavior or their role as "problems" or "troublemakers." Children stay away from children who are labeled, because they do not want to be categorized in the same group as the rejected children. The school unknowingly sanctions this rejection (Cloud, 1999).

Ethnic Minority Status

Ethnic minority, inner-city African Americans, Hispanics, and Native Americans are at a higher risk for violence than their White counterparts. African American youths, for example, are reported to be four times at greater risk for homicide than White youths, followed by Hispanics and then Native Americans (Botvin & Scheier, 1997). In the African American community, homicide is the leading cause of death for both males and females between the ages of 15 and 24. Furthermore, more African American males in this age group die from homicide than from all natural causes combined (Friday, 1995). The high level of disproportionate violence associated with minority groups is due to risk factors that are historical in nature (exploitation, oppression, racism, and discrimination), combined with below-poverty economic conditions and poor social and psychological conditions (Hawkins, 1990; Hill, Soriano, Chen, & LaFromboise, 1994). Hill et al. (1994) stated that ethnicity or race is not the greatest predictor of violence, but rather poverty and inequality through social, psychological, economic, and environmental conditions that these groups have to endure.

Minority Gangs

Parents of ethnic minority youths are usually oppressed, exploited, and discriminated by social and economic conditions and circumstances, and this may lead to their inability to provide the needed stability for their children to cope with the outside world (Hill et al., 1994). This may be the reason why so many inner-city youths join gangs. Gangs offer a sense of stability, belonging, and structure, as well as a sense of strength in numbers and individual identity to deal with problems such as racism, oppression, discrimination, and marginality felt within the community (Hill et al., 1994). It is not surprising that research into gang demographics reveals that a large proportion of gangs and gang members are ethnic minority youths (Goldstein & Soriano, 1994). Goldstein and Soriano (1994) noted that ethnic minority youths (African American, Mexican American, and Asian American) who join gangs bring diverse and often culture-specific motivations, perceptions, behaviors, and beliefs that must be dealt with on a social–cultural basis when interventions are designed.

Although accurate data on the number of youths affiliated with gangs and delinquent groups are difficult to obtain, the United States faces a rising problem with youth gangs that stretches from the major cities to suburban and rural areas (Goldstein & Soriano, 1994; Larson & Busse, 1998). Gang formation occurs as a result of youths seeking kinship, status, power, tradition, alliance, support, peer relations, pride, family and community, excitement, identity, and self-esteem (Goldstein & Soriano, 1994; Molidor, 1996). The style and type of violence exhibited by gangs increase in tactics and degrees similar to mainstream society as gang members compete for territory and drugs (Goldstein & Soriano, 1994).

Dating Violence

Another growing trend in youth violence is the increase in physical and emotional dating violence (Follette & Alexander, 1992). Various researchers have reported that 9% to 57% of adolescents have experienced some sort of physical or emotional violence in their dating relationships (Cano, Avery-Leaf, Cascardi, & O'Leary, 1998). Roscoe and Benaske's cross-sectional study (as cited in Cano et al., 1998) reported that the pattern of physical abuse begins during mid-adolescence and continues on into marriage if undetected and left untreated.

Domestic Violence

Domestic violence is considered to be one of the most underreported crimes in America today. It is estimated that one in six couples, married and unmarried, will experience a violent incident in their relationship (Carlson, 1987). O'Leary et al. (1989) concluded in their study that if physical abuse occurred during courtship, it would persist into marriage for half of the newly married couples. Van Dalen and Glasserman (1997) reported that 20–25% of all women in the United States would experience violence from their male partners at least once. Crime statistics indicate that violence is the leading cause of injuries to women in the home and that between 2 and 4 million women are battered by their partners each year (Hughes & Hasbrouck, 1996). Steinmetz (1980) reported that men as well as women are victims of battering. However, the data indicated that whereas men are likely to be victims of lower levels of violence (e.g., hitting, slapping, pushing, and throwing things), women experience a greater degree in severity and frequency. Wives are more likely to experience severe forms of violence and to endure a greater degree of injury and are less likely to be able to leave the relationship.

Researchers have reported that an estimated 3.3 million children witness violence in their homes (Krajewski, Rybarik, Dosch, & Gilmore, 1996). Intrafamily violence often occurs as a result of multidimensional factors previously mentioned, and it appears that it is one of the most underreported crimes in the United States (Kratcoski, 1984). Krajewski et al. (1996) reported that boys who witness violence against their mothers will more than likely become abusers in their adult relationships. They also stated that girls who witness such violence will as adult women be more prone to depression and developmental problems. According to Kratcoski (1984), violence in the home is usually due to stress in a current situation and social learning from past experiences of violence. Violent behavior stems from coping with a stressful situation in life coupled with the learning from social situations, perpetuating an ongoing cycle of violence from one generation to the next.

Risk Factors

Researchers (Apter & Propper, 1984; Botvin & Scheier, 1997; Friday, 1995; also cited in Harootunian, 1984; Hill et al., 1994; Kratcoski, 1984; and Monahan, 1990) have found a number of predictors of violence for youths in the United States, including demographic characteristics (unemployment, high population density, poverty, ethnic minority group membership, gender, age, and living in the inner city), family (drug and alcohol use, family mobility, weak bonding, ineffective monitoring and supervision, exposure to violence in the home, poor impulse control, problem-solving skills of caretakers, and acquisition of expectations, attitudes, and beliefs of violence), media influence (modeling of violence such as rape, murders, armed robberies, and violent assault), and dispositional factors (antisocial personality, attention deficit disorder, and poor impulse control). Alcohol and drug use, as well as gang affiliations and delinquent peer groups, are also predictors of violence.

Brondolo, Baruch, Conway, and Marsh (1994) stated that aggressive behaviors are multidimensional in nature, consisting of biological factors (which increase irritability or decrease emotional control), psychological factors (which affect problem-solving competence), and social factors (which affect access to resources for emotional and instrumental support). Intervention and prevention strategies must encounter all these aspects in order to be effective. Formal institutions such as psychiatric settings, reform school, and community programs often fail in their attempts to address violent or antisocial behavior because they fail to encompass all three dimensions in the rehabilitation process. Rather, these institutions attempt to modify a singular behavioral problem and neglect social and cultural factors such as peers, dysfunctional home or community, the school system, or lack of economic means when they reintegrate back to the community (Apter & Propper, 1984).

INTERVENTION AND PREVENTION

Effective prevention and intervention strategies must be ecological in nature, must focus on social and cultural issues, and must take into consideration different stages of development among the youths. Different areas of psychology (i.e., social, cognitive, and developmental theorists) have theorized the nature of violence and aggression. For example, social learning theorists including Bandura (1973) stated that aggressive behaviors are acquired and sustained through observation, direct experiences, and self-regulation (Pepler & Slaby, 1994). But the exact nature of human aggression and violence is yet to be deciphered. These theories contribute to the development of intervention and prevention programs developed for combating violent crisis that have risen dramatically across the United States.

In recent years, professionals have started to explore prevention and intervention strategies to curb the growing violence faced by children in the United States. Larson and Busse (1998) surveyed 213 school psychology training programs and concluded that a substantial amount of intervention training is directed toward traditional behavioral concerns, such as attention deficit hyperactivity disorder. They further reported that training in school violence prevention (e.g., gang violence) is a lower priority for training programs. Larson (1994) proposed that such training should be encouraged and that prevention and intervention should be ecological in nature, consisting of efforts across settings, individuals, and developmental levels. Currently, the majority of programs address the problem of violence through school-based interventions that are skill building for both children and parents (Baker, 1998).

This type of intervention and prevention may prove even more ineffective because it is unimodal and does not deal with the influences of the neighborhood and community context (Aber, Jones, Brown, Chaudry, &

Samples, 1998), culture, mass media, or other social–cultural contexts that socialize the children. It is more effective to use a multidimensional model of intervention and prevention. Social–cognitive behavioral interventions (social skills training, cognitive restructuring, behavioral consequencing, mentoring, and problem-solving approaches) usually do not result in significant differences for violence avoidance for teens if they are limited to one specific intervention or prevention technique (Cirillo et al., 1998; Guerra, Tolan, & Hammond, 1994). Unfortunately, any significant difference found in research after an intervention fades within a period of 2 years (Krajewski et al., 1996), partly because of the failure of the program to connect to everyday life in the social–cultural context of the community or neighborhood in which these children live.

To negate further violence in U.S. schools and communities, one must recognize the importance of understanding social–cultural and ecological systems that are producing it. Within this paradigm, violence in the school system is merely a reflection of the violence in the nation, in the community, and in the homes. The violence that children exhibit is not a breakdown in morality of the children or the nation but rather a reflection of what is modeled for the children in their social environment (Cole, 1995; Pietrzak et al., 1998). If we model violence in the home, community, social situations, national platform, media, and entertainment, then we should not be surprised when the children model the same intentional violence in their own worlds.

Interventions and prevention must reflect a broader, holistic, and multidimensional ecological system (Apter & Propper, 1984; Harootunian, 1984). The intervention must be designed for children in the context of their developmental, social, and cultural environments. Children must be taught not to act out maladaptive behavioral patterns and that violent strategies are inappropriate in conflict resolution.

STRATEGIES FOR PREVENTION OF VIOLENCE IN THE SCHOOLS

School–Community–Home Venture

We recommend interventions that incorporate a school–community–family collaborative approach. Unless all stakeholders buy into a nonviolent philosophy and model appropriate behavior, it will be impossible to institute a program that truly creates a new philosophical base and teaches children a nonviolent way of life. The way families, community, and schools relate to violence must be examined, and a consistent set of values and beliefs must be established that can be modeled to the young with appropriate safeguards to protect them from inappropriate behavior.

After a community has agreed on the values they wish to model, training must be provided to all involved, that is, civic leaders, parents, and school staff from upper management to the janitorial staff.

Curriculum for Violence Reduction

The next level of intervention focuses on a comprehensive approach to restructuring the curriculum to focus the goals of education on literacy, knowledge, social and interpersonal skills, along with civility and specific conflict resolution skills. Ibrahim (1998) proposed a schoolwide primary prevention and secondary prevention approach to handling violence in the schools. The primary prevention aspect is much more critical because schools must reverse sociohistorical, cultural, and social assumptions regarding violence by proactively teaching appropriate modes for handling conflicts and difficulties among children, adolescents, teachers, and staff personnel. The educational component must be integral to the curriculum and should include a discussion about alternatives regarding how the violent human history of the United States has enacted itself. These discussions must be age appropriate and match the cognitive stages of children and adolescents.

A moral–ethical ideology must be developed from kindergarten to Grade 12 that focuses on nonviolent methods of conflict resolution, that addresses the sanctity of human life, and that recognizes that under no circumstances can one justify taking someone's life (Rosenberg, 1999). In addition, social perspective-taking skills, empathy, and communication skills must be taught (Whiteley, 1982; Whiteley & Associates, 1986). Civility as a cultural and national value must be incorporated into the school system as a value that is believed in and acted on, not just discussed as an ideal (Peck, 1997). One model that was successful in achieving all these ideals was the character development project at the University of Irvine, California, which was later successfully replicated with students at the University of Connecticut, Storrs and with high school students (Ibrahim, Fried, & Kahn, 1985; Kessler, Ibrahim, & Flynn, 1986; Whiteley, 1982; Whiteley & Associates, 1986).

Classrooms should display posters that advocate alternatives to violence, and class activities should include adequate discussion and process time (Ross, 1996). Teachers must be trained to run classes as groups instead of using only a didactic instructional model. Affective education strategies can help children and adolescents to openly discuss their beliefs, values, and assumptions; clarify their worldview; and test the validity of their moral assumptions in a group situation. Furthermore, each child must be encouraged to recognize the source of his or her values and then taught to choose values that support a nurturing and supportive society.

Formal education must include conflict resolution skills, clarification of cultural and gender identity and worldview, and respect for different worldviews and value systems as long as they are life and community enhancing and not exclusionary and hurtful to any segment of society. In addition, appropriate social perspective-taking skills and communication skills must be taught and modeled by school staff. An atmosphere of civility and care must be created in the schools that reflects our highest ideals and belief system as a nation. In addition, schools must emphasize community building and social support networks that encourage children and adolescents to create communities that care and eliminate exclusion and isolation among children.

Teachers and school personnel must be on the forefront to identify children who are at risk of isolation or exclusion and work actively to create an inclusive environment in the schools. Schools must empower young people with a positive sense of identity, both from a cultural and gender perspective, and a strong self-concept that is based on accurate knowledge of their strengths, assets, and limitations (Ibrahim, 1994).

Americans value the ideals of liberty, equality, and fraternity. However, daily in the schools, on the streets, and in their homes, children learn there is no liberty, equality, or fraternity, when society recognizes material gain over all other values and ideals. Additionally, when the young are taught that every child has the right to achieve his or her unique potential, then parents, teachers, and community members must demonstrate that they value all children equally.

Children are taught that the United States is a democracy. Yet the model used most in our schools, organizations, and businesses is one of control through fear and intimidation. With all the information available on shaping behavior positively, we continue to use punishments and emotional warfare against the young as the only preferred mode of control in our homes, schools, and communities. We need to share power and create an empowered environment for the children. Sharing power means that we teach children to recognize power and entitlement and to share power and resources appropriately.

Secondary prevention involves providing support and counseling for children and adolescents who are identified as "at risk" in the school. Support groups to address issues of exclusion, isolation, self-concept enhancement, and cultural and gender identity empowerment must be instituted. Additionally, individual counseling must be provided to children who have become casualties in the schools by being physically or emotionally attacked, excluded, or stigmatized. Simply having a conflict resolution session, as exemplified by current secondary intervention models (Ross, 1996), with the parties apologizing and moving on is not enough. Both parties should have follow-up counseling to address the issues they were dealing with that made them the perpetrator and/or the victims of violence. Appropriate coping strategies must be taught based on the needs that are identified for each child (Ibrahim, 1998).

CONCLUSION

In this chapter, we have reviewed violence in the schools from an ecological, social, cultural, and historical perspective. We recommended moving beyond limited approaches that focus only on schools when the problem of evidence is a societal issue that may have its roots in history. Additionally, we reviewed the current violent events that today's children and adolescents face and the stress they place on them. We proposed a model for eradicating school violence that involves the community, the school, and the home, using a psychoeducational approach to reshaping the beliefs and assumptions in a community that all commit to and model for the young. Additionally, we proposed a complete curriculum overhaul that focuses on truly educating the young to live principled lives with appropriate values and beliefs that enhance life and provides the skills to act on these beliefs.

REFERENCES

Aber, J. L., Jones, S. M., Brown, J. L., Chaudry, N., & Samples, F. (1998). Resolving conflict creatively: Evaluating the developmental effects of a school-based violence prevention program in neighborhood and classroom context. *Development and Psychopathology, 10*, 187–213.

Apter, S. J., & Propper, C. A. (1984). Ecological perspectives on youth violence. In S. J. Apter & A. P. Goldstein (Eds.), *Youth violence: Programs and prospects* (pp. 140–159). New York: Pergamon Press.

Aries, P. (1962). *Centuries of childhood: A social history of family life.* New York: Knopf.

Baker, J. A. (1998). Are we missing the forest for the trees? Considering the social context of school violence. *Journal of School Psychology, 36*(1), 29–44.

Bandura, A. (1973). *Aggression: A social learning analysis.* Englewood Cliffs, NJ: Prentice Hall.

Beauvais, F., Chavez, E. L., Oetting, E. R., Deffenbacher, J. L., & Cornell, G. R. (1996). Drug use, violence, and victimization among White American, Mexican American, and American Indian dropouts, students with academic problems, and students in good academic standing. *Journal of Counseling Psychology, 43*, 292–299.

Botvin, G. J., & Scheier, L. M. (1997). Preventing drug abuse and violence. In D. K. Wilson, J. R. Rodrigue, & W. C. Taylor (Eds.), *Health-promoting and health-compromising behaviors among minority adolescents* (pp. 55–86). Washington, DC: American Psychological Association.

Brondolo, E., Baruch, C., Conway, E., & Marsh, E. (1994). Aggression among inner-city minority youth: A biopsychosocial model for school-based evaluation and treatment. *Journal of Social Distress and the Homeless, 3*(1), 53–80.

Cano, A., Avery-Leaf, S., Cascardi, M., & O'Leary, K. D. (1998). Dating violence in two high school samples: Discriminating variables. *Journal of Primary Prevention, 18,* 431–446.

Carlson, B. E. (1987, January). Dating violence: A research review and comparison with spouse abuse. *Social Casework: The Journal of Contemporary Social Work,* 16–23.

Cirillo, K. J., Pruitt, B. E., Colwell, B., Kingery, P. M., Hurley, R. S., & Ballard, D. (1998). School violence: Prevalence and intervention strategies for at-risk adolescents. *Adolescent, 33*(130), 319–330.

Clinton, H. R. (1996). *It takes a village: And other lessons children teach us.* New York: Simon & Schuster.

Cloud, J. (1999, May 31). Just a routine school shooting. *Time,* pp. 34–43.

Cole, E. (1995). Responding to school violence: Understanding today or tomorrow. *Canadian Journal of School Psychology, 11,* 108–116.

Follette, V. M., & Alexander, P. C. (1992). Dating violence: Current and historical correlates. *Behavioral Assessment, 14,* 39–52.

Friday, J. C. (1995). The psychological impact of violence in underserved communities. *Journal of Health Care for the Poor and Underserved, 6,* 403–409.

Fried, S. (1997). Bullies and victims: Children abusing children. *American Journal of Dance Therapy, 19,* 127–133.

Goldstein, A. P., & Soriano, F. I. (1994). Juvenile gangs. In L. D. Eron, J. H. Gentry, & P. Schlegel (Eds.), *Reason to hope: A psychosocial perspective on violence and youth* (pp. 315–382). Washington, DC: American Psychological Association.

Guerra, N. G., Tolan, P. H., & Hammond, W. R. (1994). Prevention and treatment of adolescent violence. In L. D. Eron, J. H. Gentry, & P. Schlegel (Eds.), *Reason to hope: A psychosocial perspective on violence and youth* (pp. 383–403). Washington, DC: American Psychological Association.

Harootunian, B. (1984). School violence and vandalism. In S. J. Apter & A. P. Goldstein (Eds.), *Youth violence: Programs and prospects* (pp. 120–139). New York: Pergamon Press.

Harper, F., & Ibrahim, F. A. (in press). Violence in the schools in the USA: Implications for counseling. *International Journal for the Advancement of Counselling.*

Hawkins, D. (1990). Explaining the Black homicides rate. *Journal of Interpersonal Violence, 5,* 151–163.

Hill, H. M., Soriano, F. I., Chen, S. A., & LaFromboise, T. D. (1994). Sociocultural factors in the etiology and prevention of violence among ethnic minority youth. In L. D. Eron, J. H. Gentry, & P. Schlegel (Eds.), *Reason to hope: A psychosocial perspective on violence and youth* (pp. 59–97). Washington, DC: American Psychological Association.

Hughes, J. N., & Hasbrouck, J. E. (1996). Television violence: Implications for violence prevention. *School Psychology Review, 25,* 134–151.

Ibrahim, F. A. (1994). Diversity education: Identity development from a culture and gender perspective. *Dialog, 24,* 33–43.

Ibrahim, F. A. (1998). *Responding to violence in the schools: Lecture notes.* Unpublished manuscript, University of Connecticut, Storrs.

Ibrahim, F. A., Fried, J., & Kahn, H. (1985, April). Character development: East. In J. M. Whiteley (Chair), *Character development: East and west.* Symposium conducted at the annual meeting of the American College Student Personnel Association, Boston.

Ibrahim, F. A., & Herr, E. L. (1987). Battered women: A developmental life career counseling perspective. *Journal of Counseling and Development, 65,* 244–248.

Kessler, G. R., Ibrahim, F. A., & Flynn, J. (1986). Character development in high school students. *Adolescence, 21,* 1–9.

Krajewski, S. S., Rybarik, M. F., Dosch, M. F., & Gilmore, G. D. (1996). Results of a curriculum intervention with seventh graders regarding violence in relationships. *Journal of Family* Violence, *11,* 93–112.

Kratcoski, P. C. (1984). Perspective on intrafamily violence. *Human Relations, 37,* 443–454.

Larson, J. (1994). Violence prevention in the schools: A preview of selected programs and procedures. *School Psychology Review, 23,* 151–164.

Larson, J., & Busse, R. T. (1998). Specialist-level preparation in school violence and youth gang intervention. *Psychology in the School, 35,* 373–379.

May, R. (1981). *Freedom and destiny.* New York: Dell.

Molidor, C. E. (1996). Female gang members: A profile of aggression and victimization. *Social Work, 41,* 251–257.

Monahan, J. (1990). The clinical assessment of violence potential. In L. J. Hertzberg, G. F. Ostrum, & J. D. Field (Eds.), *Violent behavior* (Vol. 1, pp. 259–279). Great Neck, NY: PMA Publishing.

Okrent, D. (1999, May 10). Raising kids online: What can parents do? *Time,* pp. 38–43.

O'Leary, K. D., Barling, J., Arias, I., Rosenbaum, A., Maloe, J., & Tyree, A. (1989). Prevalence and stability of physical aggression between spouses: A longitudinal analysis. *Journal of Consulting and Clinical Psychology, 57,* 263–268.

Olweus, D. (1985). 80,000 pupils involved in bullying. *Norsk Skoleblad, 2,* 30–42.

Olweus, D. (1993). *Bullying at school: What we know and what we can do.* Cambridge, MA: Blackwell.

Peck, S. (1997). *A world waiting to be born.* New York: Simon & Schuster.

Pepler, D. J., & Slaby, R. G. (1994). Theoretical and developmental perspectives on youth and violence. In L. D. Eron, J. H. Gentry, & P. Schlegel (Eds.), *Reason to hope: A psychological perspective on violence and youth* (pp. 27–58). Washington, DC: American Psychological Association.

Pietrzak, D., Petersen, G. J., & Speaker, K. M. (1998). Perceptions of school violence by elementary and middle school personnel. *Professional School Counseling, 1*(4), 23–29.

Pipher, M. B. (1996). *The shelter of each other: Rebuilding our families.* New York: Putnam.

Rogers, C. (1942). *Counseling and psychotherapy.* Boston: Houghton-Mifflin.

Rose, P. L. (1991). *The erosion of childhood: Child oppression in Britain, 1860–1918.* London: Routledge.

Rosenberg, M. (1999). *Nonviolent communication: A language of compassion.* Del Mar, CA: Puddledancer Press.

Ross, D. M. (1996). *Childhood bullying and teasing: What school personnel, other professionals, and parents can do.* Alexandria, VA: American Counseling Association.

Seligman, L. (1998). President's column. *APA Monitor, 1,* p. 2.

Shakoor, B. H., & Chalmers, D. (1991). Co-victimization of African-American children who witness violence: Effects on cognitive, emotional, and behavioral development. *Journal of National Medical Association, 83,* 233–238.

Steinmetz, S. K. (1980). Confronting violence in the 1980s: In the streets, schools, and home. In L. J. Hertzberg, G. F. Ostrum, & J. R. Field (Eds.), *Violent behavior* (Vol. 1, pp. 125–180). Great Neck, NY: PMA Publishing.

Takaki, R. (1993). *A different mirror: A history of multicultural America.* Boston: Little, Brown.

Van Biema, D. (1999, May 31). A surge of teen spirit. *Time,* pp. 58–59.

van Dalen, A., & Glasserman, M. (1997). My father, Frankenstein: A child's view of battering parents. *Journal of American Child and Adolescent Psychiatry, 36,* 1005–1007.

Walsh, E. (1999, April 21). Calm year in schools is shattered. *The Washington Post,* p. A12.

Walvin, J. (1982). *A child's world: A social history of English childhood, 1800–1914.* Hammonsworth, England: Penguin.

Whiteley, J. (1982). *Character development in college students.* Irvine: University of California Press.

Whiteley, J., & Associates. (1986). *Curriculum for character development in college students.* Irvine: University of California Press.

11 | Creative and Underused Counseling Strategies for the Prevention of Violence in Schools

Frederick D. Harper and James P. Griffin, Jr.

This chapter discusses (a) the current status of violence among American school youths, (b) etiological explanations for violence in the schools, (c) the issue of school security, (d) current school programs and approaches to violence prevention, and (e) counseling strategies for the prevention of youth violence in the schools. After briefly explaining some of the dynamics and causes of school violence, we give most of our attention to addressing programs, activities, and strategies for the prevention of school violence.

News media presentations often lead the public to think that violence among youths has increased over the years to epidemic proportions. Nevertheless, empirical data, based on a national survey of schools, report no significant increases in the incidence of violence and victimization from violence for school youths over a 20-year period from 1976 to 1996 (National Center for Education Statistics [NCES], 1998a). Just the contrary, a recent report by the NCES suggests a national decline in serious violent incidents involving school youths (Lippman, Johnson, & Heck, 1999). Lippman et al.'s study for the NCES reports decreases in adolescent firearm mortality, juvenile perpetrators of violence, and adolescent victims of serious crime.

Therefore, the question may be raised, and legitimately so, "Why is there now all the interest in school violence?" Some may even argue that White-on-White serious school violence of the last 2 years or so is getting

Personal interviews were conducted for this chapter with the following persons: Robert Williams, assistant principal and director of the Peer Mediation Program at Chamblee High School in the Atlanta metropolitan area; Robert White, assistant principal, and Barbara Finney, crisis coordinator and director of the Mediation Program, T. C. Williams High School in Alexandria, Virginia.

more attention by the media and government as compared with the Black-on-Black, urban youth gang violence and drug-sale-related violence of the 1980s and early 1990s. Then, there are others who conjecture that it is not race but the flagrant and terrorist nature of school violence today that demands immediate attention before events get out of hand, considering what appears to be a copycat pattern of school violence. Although there may be some iota of truth in both contentions, the latter may be more of a reason for the great concern in school violence by the entire nation. The number of persons killed per incident in recent, serious violent school attacks, the terrorist methods of violent school attacks, and the copycat tendency by young people to imitate or to try and outdo other violent school events are all significant concerns for preventive action.

The peak event among a series of random, terrorist-type school shootings between 1997 and 1999 occurred on April 20, 1999, in what was probably the most serious incident of youth-on-youth school violence in the history of U.S. schools in terms of the modus operandi of the attack and the number of resulting mortalities and wounded. On that date, two teenage boys, ages 17 and 18, entered their high school in Littleton, Colorado, with guns and explosives and killed 15 persons (including 12 students, 1 teacher, and themselves) and wounded 21 others (Walsh, 1999). This total of 36 persons killed or wounded by the perpetrators became a head-shaking national concern and the a priori to an imperative for Congress and the whole nation to act toward preventing future violent incidents such as this one. Nevertheless, in a copycat fashion in neighboring Canada, a male student in Alberta struck with a gun a week later, killing one person and wounding another. Moreover, exactly a month after the Colorado incident, on May 20th in Conyers, Georgia, another male student struck with a gun, wounding six fellow students as they waited during early morning for the school to open for the day.

It is not known when or if another comparably flagrant and reprehensible violent school event will occur; nevertheless, the U.S. Congress, federal agencies, businesses, universities, communities, schools, and counselors are seeking strategies to minimize and prevent blatant youth violence in school environments. In doing so, theorists, researchers, behavioral scientists, and educational authorities are attempting to identify or predict the types of youths and the psychosocial conditions that may influence serious violence in schools.

ETIOLOGICAL INDICATORS, PREDICTORS, AND CORRELATES

On the basis of a literature review on violence and school youths, we have attempted to put together a representative list of predictors, indicators, and correlates of violent and aggressive behavior. The following list represents some of the identifying factors that are related to highly aggressive youths or youths who are likely to act out in serious violence:

1. Teenage boys are much more likely to commit gun violence in school as compared with teenage girls, high school youths are more likely to commit serious violence when compared with middle school and elementary school youths, and serious youth violence is more likely to occur away from school than on school grounds (NCES, 1998b, 1998c). With respect to violence and gender, Katz (1995) purported that violence by males is associated with their perceived socialized roles regarding manhood, masculinity, dominance over females, and competition among themselves as males.

2. Withdrawn, quiet, or bizarre youths who are frequently teased, disrespected, rejected, and bullied by classmates and schoolmates, and sometimes by a parent or parents, may act out violently with guns if pushed to a breaking point and often may speak of "getting even" or getting revenge as a warning sign. Also, youths who have lost a loved one to death or a lost relationship may feel a sense of hurt and pain that could drive them to hurt the one who hurt them, related others, or innocent bystanders (Colvin, Tobin, Beard, Hagan, & Sprague, 1998; Ross, 1996; Walsh, 1999).

3. Weapon-carrying behavior is associated with violence, that is, youths who may regularly carry a weapon in school for some reason, including protection, ego enhancement, or bullying. Also, easy accessibility of automatic weapons to youths has been a factor in recent school homicides, for example, taking a parent's gun or guns from home or simply buying guns on the streets or at gun shows (Kenworthy & Thompson, 1999; Kingery, 1998).

4. An increasing number of cinema movies, videos, and TV programs are glorifying violence, portraying violence as glamorous, and failing to show the negative consequences of violence or a sense of remorse by the perpetrators of violence (Murray, 1998; Potter, 1999).

5. Glasser (1998) posited that teenagers often get into destructive activity because they are attempting to meet needs for belonging, power, security, and fun; however, they often choose to satisfy these needs in inappropriate ways, such as through violent gangs, drug abuse, and risk-taking activities. Moreover, Glasser attributed ineffective parent–child and teacher–student relationships as contributing factors to self-destructive or violent behaviors of youths.

6. Use of specific drugs or chemicals can interact with environmental situations to influence a young person to act out violently. Some of the psychoactive substances associated with violent behavior

include alcohol, cocaine, anabolic steroids, and phencyclidine or PCP (Doweiko, 1996). There are also particular prescribed medications, taken daily by youths, that can cause irritability and aggressive behavior.

7. Through observational learning and imitation, some youths learn the use of violent reactions from family members and persons in their immediate culture as a means of expressing anger and resolving conflicts and problems (Hoffman, 1996; Ross, 1996).

8. Violence-prone or angry-prone youths tend to experience physical damage to self, others, and property; to report higher-than-average levels of anxiety and depression and lowered self-esteem; to be likely to use alcohol or other drugs; to have disrupted interpersonal relationships; and to cope ineffectively with stressful events and conditions (Deffenbacher, Lynch, Oetting, & Kemper, 1996; Duan & Hill, 1996; Orton, 1997).

9. Some youths may not be violent but may set themselves up for violent victimization by associating with aggressive and violent youths or accepting the role of scapegoat to teasing and bullying, by bragging and becoming the source of jealousy and hatred, by being trusted and then violating the trust of a gang or clique, or by simply being popular and liked by others and thus becoming a mirror for the inadequacies of those who perceive themselves as outcasts.

As a caveat, the above list represents only some of the personality traits, social conditions, and practices that may contribute to or be associated with serious school youth violence. School officials, nevertheless, must be careful not to overreact in unfairly suspecting, accusing, or disciplining any youth based on a profile, image, or action. School officials must first seek to identify youths with problems and help them; discipline should be a last resort.

SECURITY IN THE SCHOOLS

Owing to the advent of recent blatant youth shootings in schools, school officials around the United States are establishing security measures to prevent violence or minimize the opportunities for violence to occur. Metal detectors and school guards were instituted in a number of urban schools, primarily in the late 1980s and early 1990s, as a result of gangs and drug-related street violence. An increasing number of rural and suburban schools have begun to follow this trend of security because of a string of nationally publicized incidents of serious fatal violence in small rural towns and suburban cities.

In a survey of violence and discipline in 1,234 elementary schools, middle schools, and high schools in all 50 states and Washington, DC, it was found that 2% of schools had random metal detector checks plus a full-time security guard, and 11% had either a part-time or full-time security guard or some type of screening for nonschool visitors (NCES, 1998c). The data for this national survey were collected during the spring and summer of 1997; therefore, it appears that there has been an increase in school security measures since 1997, seemingly driven by the subsequent school shootings of 1998 and 1999, based on recent news reports of reactions by various schools (Schulte, 1999).

Students at a very large high school in Alexandria, Virginia (T. C. Williams High School) were asked their opinions about the possible installation of metal detectors. The great majority who gave feedback opposed metal detectors and indicated that they did not want to feel they are entering a prison-type building or secured camp. Therefore, this high school opted to use a number of unobtrusive, mainly female guards with color vests and two-way communication radios to manage entrance points and patrol hallways (B. Finney, personal communication, May 20, 1999).

On the basis of recent literature and our interviews with high school officials, other security measures used by schools include (a) video cameras to monitor entrances and hallways; (b) random searches of student lockers, book bags, or students themselves; and (c) an emergency telephone number made available to all students in the school for use in case of impending danger or school violations. Often schools publicize a phone number by posting it around the school and making business-size cards with an emergency number printed. Students are encouraged to report violations and impending violence as a matter for their own personal and school safety. In addition, some high schools work closely with local police to identify and monitor students in the schools who have a record of repeated crime and violent behavior and to work with these students to prevent further violent behavior (Hoffman, 1996; Schulte, 1999; R. White, personal communication, May 20, 1999; R. Williams, personal communication, December 8, 1998 and May 20, 1999).

CREATIVE PREVENTION
PROGRAMS IN THE SCHOOLS

There are numerous violence prevention programs and efforts designed for all educational levels: elementary school, middle school, and high school. Larson (1994) provided an excellent review of selected violence curricula that are appropriate for the various school levels. Furthermore, he discussed these prevention programs in the context of the three levels of prevention: primary prevention, secondary prevention, and tertiary prevention. Primary prevention programs are designed to prevent students' involvement in violence before they have the opportunity to manifest violent behavior. Secondary prevention is targeted toward youths who are at risk for violent activities or behaviors to prevent them from becoming involved in violent activity or to prevent them from escalating the level of involvement in violence or with violence-prone groups. Tertiary prevention involves treating violent students so that their behavior is arrested or the likelihood of their becoming involved in serious violent behavior in the future diminishes substantially. Regarding the educational levels, (a) primary prevention tends to be aimed at the elementary school level, (b) secondary prevention can involve elementary and middle school youths (and sometimes high school youths) who have shown signs of being at high risk for serious violence involvement, and (c) tertiary prevention often involves youths of any educational level who have chosen a violent lifestyle or an aggressive interpersonal style. There is no clear line of demarcation with regard to what level of prevention is appropriate for what educational level or age range of youths. It depends on how early a child may get involved in aggressive behaviors or identify with high-risk groups and violent activities.

Larson's (1994) review includes descriptions of a number of curricular materials, often designed for classroom activity or special workshop training with youths of particular educational and developmental levels or with parents. The foci or goals of the violence prevention curricula that were reviewed include skills, attitude, and knowledge education in the areas of anger management, assertive training, empathy training, impulse control, social skills, prosocial behavior, conflict resolution, and moral education. On the basis of the prevention curricula reviewed by Larson (1994), some of the educational materials and techniques involved in the violence prevention training of students included videotape presentations, handouts, behavioral rehearsal, cognitive–behavioral methods, moral reasoning skills training, role-playing, homework, home visits, and role modeling. The parent prevention training programs that were reviewed focused on effective parenting of children to prevent them from adopting a violent lifestyle.

The following are examples of specific programs in schools or school systems that address, in some ways, violence prevention.

Yale's School Development Program (The Comer Project)

One of the most successful programs for the prevention of violence and the fostering of quality education is the Yale Child Study Center's "School Development Program" (SDP), sometimes referred to as the Comer Project. This SDP was initiated by Professor James P. Comer of Yale University in 1968 and is now implemented in more than 82 school districts in 21 states and Washington, DC. The SDP focuses on creating a cooperative and collaborative network of students, parents, teachers, administrators, and community leaders, all aimed at the healthy development of youths, the prevention of violence in schools, and the improved academic performance of school youths (Comer, 1993; Haynes, 1996). The project has built on years of training, service, and empirical research, especially in urban schools across the United States. Moreover, it has forged lasting working relationships with schools and various groups and leaders of urban communities.

The BRAVE Program

Building Resiliency and Vocational Excellence (BRAVE) is a prevention program that uses violence and substance prevention from a vocational point of view. BRAVE is a grant project funded by the National Institute on Drug Abuse (NIDA) and administered by Emory University in collaboration with the Atlanta public schools. It serves African American adolescent males primarily but will also incorporate females in the same age groups during the full implementation of the program.

Students participate in biweekly and triweekly training sessions that focus on prosocial skills development and decision making in the areas of violence prevention and substance abuse. The program uses empirically validated curricula, such as life skills training developed by Botvin (1983) and violence prevention curricula developed by DeJong, Spiro, Wilson-Brewer, Vince-Whitman, and Prothrow-Stith (1988) and Hammond and Yung (1991). Other components of the program include vocational goal setting ("Success Planning"), mutual peer support, a vocational speaker's bureau, case management, and performance incentives. One of the more interesting aspects of the program is the inclusion of a manhood development-training element. The manhood development curriculum, "African American Manhood Development: Training for the Man of the Future," redefines the role of the African American male in his quest for full maturation and development (Griffin, Tutu-Gxashe, & Griffin, 1999). In the future, a comparable curriculum will be developed to train girls in terms of ways to foster their womanhood.

The curricula of the BRAVE program instill a sense of vocational purpose and define the process of becoming a complete African American man or woman as being inconsistent with the use of alcohol, tobacco, and other drugs and with participation in violent activities. The mentoring component of BRAVE involves matching community role models with participants in the intervention component of the project for 1 hour a week. Mentors undergo training that focuses on working with young people, and they also undergo a criminal background check. One of the primary roles for the mentors is to facilitate project goals and to allow for positive role modeling.

CREATIVE AND UNDERUSED
COUNSELING STRATEGIES

We are cognizant of the reality that today's school counselors are often overloaded with paperwork and are strained with a large students-to-counselor ratio. Therefore, we suggest that counselors select ideas, resources, and strategies from this section that may be relevant and appropriate for their school and the educational level of their students.

Counselor Consultation

Consultation by school counselors is a role that is often underestimated and underused. This role of the counselor is especially important for the elementary school level and primary prevention level with regard to counselors consulting with both teachers and parents on violence prevention. In consulting with elementary as well as middle school teachers and administrators, counselors can provide input on curriculum development and the choice of curricular materials for violence prevention (Larson, 1994). Counselors can also facilitate schoolwide violence education programs aimed at knowledge, prosocial skills, attitudinal change, and violence prevention strategies for all school youths. Also, successful community role models, local police experts, and relevant school personnel can be brought in to assist in this educational event. This mass educational prevention workshop or conference should be required for all students within a school and should involve school administrators and teachers. Because of variations in age groups, especially at the elementary school level, multiple sessions may have to be arranged that involve age-sensitive learning media, methods, content, and goals.

Consultation with parents should center on training parents in effective child rearing so as to prevent or minimize violent behavior by their children. Often the aggressive and violent styles of a parent, parents, guardians, or other family members can serve to influence violent acting out by a child from the same family situation. Dinkmeyer and McKay's (1989) parent handbook provides training topics with regard to helping parents learn how to listen to their children, build their children's self-worth, and discipline them through the development of habits in responsibility and awareness of logical consequences. The handbook also emphasizes how each parent can become aware of oneself and one's role as a parent or guardian.

For a review of resources for parent training in violence prevention, counselors may consult Larson's (1994) review of violence prevention curricular training materials or Capuzzi and Gross's (2000) edited prevention resource book on youths at risk, which is designed for both parents and the teachers of their children.

Counselors at all educational levels, kindergarten through Grade 12, should be flexible and creative in assessing how they can use consultation to impact all persons who can positively shape the lives of youths toward preventing behaviors that can lead to violent acting out. Some of the possible community consultees, in addition to parents and guardians, who can be consulted to impact school youths in positive ways include religious leaders, police, governmental leaders, business leaders, human rights workers, medical personnel, prison inmates or former inmates, professional athletes, and university professors, among others.

Readers of the chapter who may need basic information about stages of counselor consultation and areas of preventive consultation in elementary and middle schools should consult Schmidt's (1991) *A Survival Guide for the Elementary/Middle School Counselor* (especially pages 83 to 86 addressing the consulting process).

Counselors must keep in mind that they cannot do everything for and with their young clients, and, by functioning in the role of consultant, the counselor can do a lot to change the school environment and to positively impact those who influence youths from day to day.

Peer-Mediation Programs

Peer-mediation programs, sometimes referred to as conflict resolution programs, have been established in a number of schools to prevent or reduce interpersonal violence and intergroup violence (Powell, Muir-McClain, & Halasyamani, 1995). Increasing in popularity, these programs usually involve an advisory committee and a program coordinator who oversees the facilitation, assignments, timetable of mediation sessions, training of mediators, evaluation of the program, and supervision of the mediators. A counselor can establish and coordinate a peer-mediation program or recommend the establishment of a program that might be coordinated by a full-time program coordinator or existing school personnel such as the assistant principal, a social worker, a teacher, or a combination of any two persons among these, including the counselor. The program coordinator or coordinators oversee the operations of the peer-mediation group and the overall program but do not serve as a mediator. Peer mediation usually uses only trained students as peer mediators; however, this does not rule out the use of trained teachers who may be free to replace a student mediator in case two student mediators happen not to be available during a scheduled mediation meeting. To minimize problems wherein two student mediators are not available, schools often designate a specific period or periods of the day for peer-mediation sessions (Schrumpf, Crawford, & Usadel, 1991).

During the peer-mediation group process, two student mediators sit in to mediate a conflict resolution between two student disputants who are in conflict (e.g., because of a physical fight, verbal argument, threat by one disputant or both, accused theft, a disrespectful comment or action, financial disputes such as unpaid borrowed money, or a conflict between friends or a romantic couple). The rules of the mediation meeting are usually set forth at the beginning of the meeting, and they include the following:

- No one will be prejudged
- There should be no name calling
- Each person is required to be honest and to remain seated at all times
- Only one person will talk at a time
- Everything said is required to be kept confidential

After a statement of the rules, each disputant is allowed to make his or her case and to discuss or argue his or her side of the conflict. After disputants have sufficiently argued their viewpoints, one of the mediators asks if both disputants would like to agree to resolve the conflict in some way. If resolved, the disputants and the mediators sign a contract that states the conditions of the settlement. If a resolution cannot be reached, the two disputing students (or sometimes, two disputing small groups) are referred either to the school principal for resolution and possible disciplinary action, to appropriate training as necessary (e.g., anger management), or to a school counselor for help. In most cases of peer mediation, on the basis of our school interviews and available literature, student disputants resolve the conflict or issue, and at least one of the mediators or a staff member proceeds in following up the disputants after a period of time to make sure no problem has reoccurred (Harper & Ibrahim, in press; Powell et al., 1995; Schrumpf et al., 1991; B. Finney, personal communication, May 20, 1999; R. Williams, personal communication, May 20, 1999).

Group Strategies

Group strategies or techniques are often underused by school counselors; however, they can prove to be creatively effective modalities of violence prevention. Harper and Bruce-Sanford (1989) succinctly presented a variety of group techniques that would be appropriate for use in violence prevention. The following are several group techniques, their descriptions, and some ways in which they can be used in the prevention of violence or violence-related behaviors.

1. *Role reversal.* This is a role-playing technique wherein a person plays an opposite or reversed role to his or her natural behavior. For example, in a controlled group counseling setting, an aggres-

sive youth or bully may be asked to role-play the victim or sub-missive person in order to experience hurt and pain of the victim.

2. *Modeling*. The counselor reinforces or rewards appropriate behav-ior within the group or a desirable role model within the group to influence disruptive or violence-prone youths to imitate appropri-ate or nonviolent behavior of the reinforced live model. Counselors have to be careful with this technique so as not to evoke jealousy within the group.

3. *Fishbowl technique*. This group-within-a-group requires a small group of about three or four persons (the fishbowl) within a larger group (the observers). Only students in the fishbowl are allowed to talk. Students can move in and out of the fishbowl as they feel the need to get in on the discussion of a topic or remove themselves from discussion of a topic. At intervals or at the end of the group process, observers are allowed to give feedback on the overall process and content as well as provide feedback to participants who were in the fishbowl at any point. This strategy may be used to allow students to explore feelings and thoughts about a school suicide, a violent homicidal attack, death of a classmate or class-mates, or other violence-related themes or issues.

4. *Behavioral reversal*. This technique involves the use of role-playing to practice effective and appropriate behaviors. Behavioral reversal can be used to practice social skills, assertive responses, and con-flict resolution responses for the purpose of avoiding the escalation of hostile confrontations or actual violent acts. Moreover, students often need to rehearse how to say "I'm sorry," how to admit wrong, how to say "no," or how to assertively express accurate feelings of anger, pain, hurt, and loss in appropriately acceptable ways.

5. *Psychodrama and sociodrama*. The role-playing technique of psycho-drama can be used to assist several members in a group or a class to resolve a problem that could escalate to violence. Sociodrama is a role-playing technique that would help to clarify social influences on and dynamics of violent behaviors and action. Students can even be allowed to develop sociodrama skits that center on the theme of violence.

6. *Play group counseling*. Play group counseling or play therapy can be use to diagnose violent patterns in the play behavior of young chil-dren on the basis of toys chosen and aggressive action toward toys and other children. Play groups also provide a medium for the counselor to communicate with the child about violent versus non-violent attitudes, values, and behaviors. This type of group modal-ity is frequently used with very young children. For upper-level elementary school and middle school youths, activity–interview groups can be used, which allow children to play with games or

sports first and then settle down to discussion in a group. The activity facilitates readiness for counseling by allowing children to establish rapport and relax first with games and sports.

Artistic Strategies

Artistic counseling techniques such as essay writing (about life themes), art therapy, music therapy, or poetry therapy can serve as diagnostic media as well as therapeutic strategies for releasing anger, tension, and violent impulsive urges. For some children who have a natural artistic talent for drawing, painting, music, and writing, these techniques can be a means of enhancing their self-esteem and raising the level of respect among peers.

Artistic techniques are especially effective with children as violence prevention strategies. For example, the writing of prose and poetry can have a cathartic value for youths as well as value for cognitive restructuring of inappropriate, negative, and destructive thoughts. Students can create their own artistic writing or share prose and poems written by others.

Counselors can use therapeutic poems or poetry therapy to alter illogical thinking or violent impulses. The following short poem is one example of words and verse that can be used to alter cognition or the way young people think about their own anger and violent tendencies:

IF YOU ARE ANGRY

If you are angry,
Don't curse the empty spaces, or damage
Things or self, or hurt somebody;
Don't retaliate, or mayhem, or kill—
Just because you've been hurt.

If you are angry, don't pout, or blame,
Or resist understanding and clarification;
If you are angry, try not to be angry
In order to do right and just for you.

If you are angry, just close your eyes
And breathe deeply and slowly;
If you are angry, just try to cool down
And think straight.

(From *Poems on Love and Life*, by F. D. Harper,
1985, p. 84. Copyright 1985 by F. D. Harper.
Reprinted with permission.)

Because rap poetry is exceptionally popular with today's youths, counselors may also consider the use of positive rap or therapeutic rap as a means of changing behavior and cognitive thought patterns.

Counseling Approaches and Other Counseling Strategies

When it comes to theoretical approaches of counseling, we recommend cognitive approaches or cognitive–behavioral approaches. These approaches tend to address the irrational, illogical, and unrealistic thinking that leads young persons to plan and carry out serious violent acts or to retaliate spontaneously and violently during intense provocative situations.

Regarding interpersonal counseling techniques, we suggest the verbal techniques of encouragement and reassurance as being important for those violence-prone students who are losing hope or who have lost hope. Empathy is also important in the face of a client's anger. The counselor must be alert to empathize with the pain and hurt that underlies the client's anger rather than spontaneously react with anger and intolerance. The client's anger can often just be the surface emotion that covers up a hurtful reaction to being rejected, disrespected, embarrassed, excluded, or subjected to loss of a loved one. Orton (1997) recommended the following counselor strategies in dealing with the angry client:

1. Show interest, concern, and love.
2. Don't provoke anger.
3. Don't get angry yourself.
4. Avoid action that would lead to the client's physical punishment.
5. Disapprove hostile behavior without rejecting the client.
6. Encourage logical decision making on the part of the client to resolve an issue.

CONCLUSION

The content of this chapter has been limited to youth-on-youth school violence. It does not address violent conflict between any combination of youths, teachers, staff, and administrators. It would be too broad a scope for this chapter to address the total sphere of violence in school environments, for example, youths who assault teachers, teachers who physically discipline or assault youths, physical conflicts between teachers, parents who assault teachers and vice versa, estranged lovers or spouses who fatally assault teachers in the presence of students, and other violent confrontations and acts that have occurred and can occur in the school environment. Therefore, we want to be clear that we are not suggesting that school violence is limited to aggression by school youths.

Moreover, we must emphasize that a higher percentage of serious violent incidents involving youths occur when they are away from school as compared with when they are in a school environment (NCES, 1998b), and the percentage of serious incidents of school violence has declined over the last several years (Lippman et al., 1999), which is also true for the

United States as a whole (Federal Bureau of Investigation, 1998). Again, the dire concern of the nation and the counseling profession should be the gravity of multiple, fatal, and injurious serious violent incidents of the past 2 or 3 years, as well as the terrorist nature of attacks by school youths who have been involved in these incidents. We are talking about children and teenagers walking into schools with guns, and sometimes explosives, and indiscriminately as well as vindictively killing their peers and teachers. We are talking about teenagers who can be confused about reality, emotionally disturbed, too angry, and hurt to the point of planning to destroy others or put others in pain.

A special target group of concern in violence prevention is teenage girls. Although teenage boys are more likely than teenage girls to commit serious violence, there are indications that serious violence by teenage girls has increased in some schools and U.S. cities (Hoffman, 1996).

One significant method of positively influencing youths and preventing serious violent behavior by youths is through parent training in child rearing. However, we must caution counselors that training programs for parents must be sensitive to the fact that all youths do not come from a nuclear family that is characterized by a father and a mother in the home and one or both parents gainfully employed. Counselors must be aware that American families nowadays are much more diverse than those of a previous generation. Counselors must consider cultural values and other cultural factors as they go about the process of empowering parents with effective child-rearing practices and skills. Moreover, counseling professionals must be cognizant that there are homeless families, single-parent families, foster parents, grandparents as sole guardians, gay and lesbian parents, and extended families. Also, there are parents addicted to drugs, parents in prison, and parents of all social classes who either spend no quality time with their children or treat their children as if they hate them. Counselors must also be aware that it is not the structure of the family or the social class level that makes a healthy family, but rather the quality of relationships within that family or how well that family functions as a system (Terry-Leonard, 1999).

A number of American families lack the presence of a positive male role model or any type of male model. This is especially true of families in urban cities, which can often be single-parent, female-headed families. This lack of positive male role models in the families of youths is often exacerbated when youths enter elementary school, wherein at times a school may be likely to have a female principal and female teachers and only one or two male teachers. This gender imbalance presents a greater negative impact on boys, who, in these type of cases, are lacking positive male role modeling with regard to learning the appropriate roles, responsibilities, and expectations as boys who are becoming men. Therefore, these boys are very likely to embrace the negative role models that are often portrayed in cinema films, video movies, computer video games, and urban street life—fictitious or vicarious male models that can often communicate or display aggressiveness and violence toward women and toward each other.

REFERENCES

Botvin, G. J. (1983). Prevention of adolescent substance abuse through the development of personal and social competence. In T. J. Glynn, L. G. Leukefeld, & J. P. Lunford (Eds.), *Preventing adolescent drug abuse: Intervention strategies* (NIDA Research Monograph No. 47). Rockville, MD: National Institute on Drug Abuse.

Capuzzi, D., & Gross, D. (Eds.). (2000). *Youth at risk: A prevention resource for counselors, teachers, and parents* (3rd ed.). Alexandria, VA: American Counseling Association.

Colvin, G., Tobin, T., Beard, K., Hagan, S., & Sprague, J. (1998). The school bully: Assessing the problem, developing interventions and future research directions. *Journal of Behavioral Education, 8,* 293–319.

Comer, J. P. (1993). *School power: Implications of an intervention project.* New York: Simon & Schuster.

Deffenbacher, J. L., Lynch, R. S., Oetting, E. R., & Kemper, C. C. (1996). Anger reduction in early adolescents. *Journal of Counseling Psychology, 43,* 149–157.

DeJong, W., Spiro, A., Wilson-Brewer, R., Vince-Whitman, C., & Prothrow-Stith, D. (1988). *Evaluation summary: Violence prevention curriculum for adolescents.* Newton, MA: Education Development Center.

Dinkmeyer, D., & McKay, G. D. (1989). *The parent's handbook* (3rd ed.). Circle Pines, MN: American Guidance Service.

Doweiko, H. E. (1996). *Concepts of chemical dependency* (3rd ed.). Pacific Grove, CA: Brooks/Cole.

Duan, C., & Hill, C. E. (1996). The current state of empathy research. *Journal of Counseling Psychology, 43,* 261–274.

Federal Bureau of Investigation. (1998). *FBI uniform crime index, 1998.* Washington, DC: Author.

Glasser, W. (1998). *Choice theory: A new psychology of personal freedom.* New York: HarperCollins.

Griffin, J. P., Jr., Tutu-Gxashe, T., & Griffin, K. E. (1999). *African-American manhood development: Training for the man of the future.* Unpublished manuscript, Emory University, Rollins School of Public Health, Atlanta, GA.

Hammond, W. R., & Yung, B. R. (1991). Preventing violence in at-risk African-American youth. *Journal of Health Care for the Poor and Underserved, 2,* 358–372.

Harper, F. D. (1985). *Poems on love and life.* Alexandria, VA: Douglass.

Harper, F. D., & Bruce-Sanford, G. C. (1989). *Counseling techniques: An outline and overview.* Alexandria, VA: Douglass.

Harper, F. D., & Ibrahim, F. (in press). Violence and schools in the USA: Implications for counseling. *International Journal for the Advancement of Counselling.*

Haynes, N. M. (1996). Creating safe and caring school communities: Comer School Development Program schools. *Journal of Negro Education, 65,* 308–314.

Hoffman, A. M. (Ed.). (1996). *Schools, violence, and society.* Westport, CT: Praeger.

Katz, J. (1995). Reconstructing masculinity in the locker room: The Mentors in Violence Prevention Project. *Harvard Educatonal Review, 65,* 163–174.

Kenworthy, T., & Thompson, C. W. (1999, May 4). Colorado man linked to killers' handgun: Suspect faces charge of arming minors. *The Washington Post,* p. A6.

Kingery, P. M. (1998). The adolescent violence survey: A psychometric analysis. *School Psychology International, 19,* 43–59.

Larson, J. (1994). Violence prevention in the schools: A review of selected programs and procedures. *School Psychology Review, 23,* 151–164.

Lippman, L., Johnson, D., & Heck, K. (1999). *America's children: Key national indicators of well-being, 1999* (No. 1999019). Washington, DC: National Center for Education Statistics.

Murray, B. (1998, June). Study says TV violence still seen as heroic, glamorous. *APA Monitor,* p. 16.

National Center for Education Statistics. (1998a). *The condition of education, 1998.* Washington, DC: Author.

National Center for Education Statistics. (1998b). *Indicators of school crime and safety, 1998* (No. 98251). Washington, DC: Author.

National Center for Education Statistics. (1998c). *Violence and discipline problems in the U.S. public schools: 1996–97* (No. 98030). Washington, DC: Author.

Orton, G. L. (1997). *Strategies for counseling with children and their parents.* Pacific Grove, CA: Brooks/Cole.

Potter, W. J. (1999). *On media violence.* Thousand Oaks, CA: Sage.

Powell, K. E., Muir-McClain, L., & Halasyamani, L. (1995). A review of selected school-based conflict resolution and peer mediation projects. *Journal of School Health, 65,* 426–431.

Ross, D. M. (1996). *Childhood bullying and teasing: What school personnel, other professionals, and parents can do.* Alexandria, VA: American Counseling Association.

Schmidt, J. J. (1991). *A survival guide for the elementary/middle school counselor.* West Nyack, NY: Center for Applied Research in Education.

Schrumpf, F., Crawford, D., & Usadel, H. C. (1991). *Peer mediation: Conflict resolution in schools.* Champaign, IL: Research Press.

Schulte, B. (1999, July 12). After Littleton, Montgomery schools rethink safety. *The Washington Post,* pp. A1, A5.

Terry-Leonard, B. L. (1999). *The relationship of self-esteem, perceived parental nurturance, and family functioning across three family structures in a sample of nontraditional undergraduate students.* Unpublished doctoral dissertation, Howard University, Washington, DC.

Walsh, E. (1999, April 21). Calm year in schools is shattered. *The Washington Post,* p. A12.

12 Preventing School Violence: Training for School Counselors

Sue A. Stickel, Irene Mass Ametrano, and Yvonne L. Callaway

We begin this chapter by defining violence, followed by a consideration of service models for school counseling. Primary, secondary, and tertiary prevention provide the framework from which to conceptualize service delivery. The chapter concludes with a review of preservice and in-service training issues.

School counselors, both in training and in the field, need to conceptualize their roles in relation to school violence and to use their counseling, consulting, and organizing skills in violence prevention and intervention. Hayes (1994) asked what counselors can do to effect necessary change in a world that appears chaotic to professionals and clients alike. School counselors work in a challenging environment. Acting as change agents in this milieu requires a sophisticated process of thinking and acting, while simultaneously reflecting on the consequences. Teaching counseling students and practitioners to enhance and articulate complex skills and to become aware of their role as change agents is a critical task for counselor educators.

School counseling is at a crossroad. School counselors represent the largest single group of mental health professionals working in schools, and current conditions demand that they be prepared to provide a range of services that address school violence (Crespi, 1999). Expressions of violence take multiple forms in society. Simple solutions will fail to address quickly or adequately the complex interplay of personal and societal variables that result in acts of violence. Efforts to gain a foothold on the spiral of violence and community deterioration start with a more sophisticated appreciation for what makes some people hurt other people (Bloom & Reichert, 1998). When counselors begin by exploring how violence is defined in society, they can more readily identify how it is expressed in the school environment.

DEFINING VIOLENCE

School shootings bedeck the covers of magazines and are the subject of presidential pronouncements. School violence becomes a canvas on which politicians, educators, and citizens project their opinions about what is wrong with schools and society and what everyone needs to do to fix the problems. However, school violence is complex and not new. Furlong, Poland, Babinski, Munoz, and Boles (1996) found a diversity of opinion about what is labeled as school violence and recommended that training activities examine scientific definitions of violence in addition to personal definitions of violence. Basically, what do we mean when we talk about violence?

Violence tends to be defined either in terms of specific incidents or in terms of a broader construct that includes nonphysical forms of harm. Kelly and Pink (1982) characterized school violence as disrespect to teachers and administrators, theft, and physical assaults. The federal government defines violence as the most serious behaviors, including rape, robbery, and simple and aggravated assaults (Bastian & Taylor, 1991). Astor (1995) noted that the meaning of violence affects a school's response, and definitions have generally been reserved for violence resulting in bodily harm. Such acts are most prevalent during adolescence. Van Soest and Bryant (1995) conceptualized a model incorporating three levels of violence: (a) violence aimed at individual people or property, (b) violence brought about by the harmful actions of social institutions, and (c) the ideological roots that support and give impetus to both individual and institutional violence.

We contend that school counselors must understand the influences of systemic and societal factors on individual acts of violence. Hoff (1995) took the position that violence is predominantly a social phenomenon, a means of exerting power and control that has far-reaching effects on personal, family, and public health worldwide. In a broad definition, violence is any act, whether overt or covert, that coerces or causes physical hurt, material loss, or mental anguish; that degrades human beings; or that militates against human rights, dignity, and decency (Rajgopal, 1987). School counselors can help other school personnel place violence within such operational frameworks. These frameworks then guide levels of service delivery and interventions.

SERVICE MODEL

School counseling has historically lacked a consistent organizational pattern that defines where counselors fit in the organizational structure, how they are to spend their time, and what services to offer and to whom. Professional organizations, as well as many states, now recommend or mandate that contemporary school counselors move toward a programmatic approach to school counseling. A comprehensive program model emphasizes services for all students in kindergarten through 12th grade and deemphasizes administrative and clerical tasks, individual counseling only, and limited accountability (Gysbers & Henderson, 1997). A comprehensive school counseling program is developmental and systematic, sequential, clearly defined, and accountable. It is jointly grounded in developmental psychology, educational philosophy, and counseling methodology (American School Counselor Association, 1997).

Schwartz (1998) reported that the most effective school-based programs for reducing violence accurately assess the existence of violence and gang activity, use all community resources, incorporate family services, intervene early in a child's life, use positive experiences, create and communicate clearly defined and enforced behavior codes, and prepare for a long-term effort. School counselors also affect school policies by actively serving on school improvement committees and consulting with administrators and teachers. Although most school counselors are already coordinating programs and providing services that address school violence, they may not be doing this in a systematic way and may not be receiving recognition for their efforts.

In the current era of school reform and restructuring, school counselors, in concert with other educational professionals, are considering what counseling services are to be delivered, when, and in what ways. Student outcomes and procedures for demonstrating accountability to stakeholders are important. School counselors will need to identify the model under which they are operating and begin the transition to a standards-based programmatic structure. Specific school violence prevention strategies can then be identified and integrated into this program structure. Of particular importance is expanding services so that all grade levels and students are covered.

Schools are in an excellent position to conceptualize the delivery of counseling services in terms of three levels of prevention (Bloom & Reichert, 1998). More than 30 years ago, Caplan (1964) discussed the importance of identifying at-risk populations and offering services to prevent crisis and enhance growth through primary, secondary, and tertiary prevention. The three-level prevention framework provides school counselors with a model from which to identify needed services and the methods for delivery of those services within a programmatic structure.

PRIMARY PREVENTION

Primary prevention focuses on reducing the occurrence of mental disability in a community by promoting growth, development, and crisis resistance (Hoff, 1995). Efforts are directed at "healthy," well-functioning individuals whose current coping skills can be strengthened and new ones learned. In addition, individuals known to be at risk for developing problems may be targeted. One approach to primary prevention is to eliminate or modify hazardous situations (Hoff, 1995) or, as discussed by Capuzzi (1998), to change the system to eliminate barriers to success and to better meet the needs of those at risk. In schools, an example of a systemic intervention would be reducing school size to replicate a small-town environment in which people are more likely to help others because they know them (Guetzloe, 1992). Other strategies include flexible scheduling and making curricula more relevant to students' lives. Systemic interventions also include programs that create linkages between schools and the larger community, including parents, businesses, community groups, and so on (Capuzzi, 1998).

Increasing coping ability, and thus reducing vulnerability, is another way of thinking about primary prevention (Hoff, 1995). School counselors are already engaged in providing primary prevention programs that teach social (interpersonal communication) and cognitive skills (decision making and problem solving), behavior management strategies (alternatives to violent behavior), peer negotiation skills, and self-esteem enhancement. In many schools, youths are being taught to resist peer pressure, to manage stress, to mediate disagreements, and to communicate more effectively.

SECONDARY PREVENTION

Because primary prevention programs are not always successful or available, it is imperative that secondary prevention strategies are in place. The goal of secondary prevention is to minimize the harmful effects of hazardous situations and to shorten the duration of disabilities (Hoff, 1995). Secondary prevention is aimed at individuals who are already engaging in problematic behaviors or who are in crisis following stressful events. Lindemann (1944) was probably the first to discuss the importance of preventing long-term negative outcomes of crisis by recognizing crisis responses in individuals who had experienced a traumatic event and making immediate assistance available to them. In schools, this translates into the early identification of students in distress followed by immediate intervention. School counselors, along with other mental health professionals, play a role in the early detection of students with psychological disorders, particularly depression, and in the identification of students in crisis.

TERTIARY PREVENTION

Tertiary prevention aims to reduce the long-term disabling effects of a crisis reaction or mental disorder. Youths who have been in substance abuse treatment may benefit from weekly support groups to prevent relapse (Capuzzi, 1998). School counselors help in identifying and assisting students who need more intensive, long-term treatment. They can refer to outside agencies and serve as liaisons between schools and agencies.

TRAINING ISSUES

Preservice training for counselors focuses on developing a critical awareness about self and others, building a professional knowledge base, and experiencing guided skill practice. The first step involves an academic understanding of didactic models, the second involves identifying applications of those models, and the third is practicing or implementing the models under supervision. In addition to learning theoretical models, student counselors acquire tools for self-organization, which includes self-awareness, self-assessment, and self-evaluation. To learn from practice, entry-level professional school counselors need the competencies necessary to provide a particular service and must be prepared to evaluate outcomes and their own performance. Egan (1990), in practical terms, saw novice counselors as needing integrative models or frameworks that help them to borrow from available models and then to organize from what they borrow.

Counselors have an ethical obligation to continually upgrade their skills and knowledge throughout their careers. The purpose of in-service training is to facilitate synthesis. In-service training helps professionals use their unique practice contexts to initiate a search for synthesis between the theory that they studied in preservice and the reality of practice. In-service training provides counselors the skills and knowledge necessary to provide more specific and in-depth levels of service. For example, school counselors may learn about different constituencies and stakeholders during preservice; during in-service they would need to learn political strategies for aligning the stakeholders to support particular interventions or systemic programming.

Professional counselors in the field must simultaneously implement, evaluate, and restructure services on the basis of ongoing evaluation. Schon (1987) called this process "knowing-in-action." Using a repertoire of past experiences, recollections from specific readings and coursework, additional details about a situation, as well as other images, understandings, and instinctive reactions, the counselor reframes a situation and generates problem-solving actions. In-service training should help counselors to engage in such a synthesis. Specialized skills and interventions based on client needs and informed practice can then be developed. Discussions of complex questions of practice can be facilitated.

In-service training for addressing school violence concentrates on specialized skills and services. It builds on preservice training that is infused throughout the professional curriculum. The standards of the Council for the Accreditation of Counseling and Related Educational Programs (CACREP, 1994) require coursework in eight core areas: human growth and development, social and cultural foundations, helping relationships, group work, career and lifestyle development, appraisal, research and program evaluation, and professional orientation. In addition, there are standards for clinical instruction, as well as specialized curricular experiences for school counseling. The skills and knowledge needed by school counselors to adequately address violence fit into the core and specialized CACREP areas. The three levels of prevention provide another way to think about these skills and knowledge: for primary, secondary, and tertiary prevention. The relationships between the curriculum, levels of prevention, and preservice and in-service training are summarized in Table 12.1.

PRIMARY PREVENTION SKILLS

To adequately prepare school counselors to address violence in schools, training in interpersonal intervention models, which is typically the focus of counselor training, is not enough. School counselors must begin to address the culture of violence (Lee & Brydges, 1998). To address the culture of violence in both the school and the outside community, school counselors must begin to see themselves as social activists who promote public awareness about the origins and prevention of violence, who collaborate with other professionals in the school and in the larger community to challenge the climate of violence, and who work to influence public policy aimed at reducing violence. They need knowledge and skills in consultation and advocacy. Consultation with teachers, administrators, parents, community leaders, legislators, and so on requires knowledge that can be taught in any of the specialized school counseling courses that are required of all students. Because school counselors are often not the first to have contact with students in distress, they have a responsibility to train those who do: teachers, administrators, and other students. Specialized in-service opportunities, for example, learning to use train-the-trainer models, can help counselors increase their efficacy in providing training for other professionals.

Table 12.1 | Counselor Training Curriculum: Skills and Knowledge for School Violence Prevention

Program Curriculum	Primary Prevention	Secondary Prevention	Tertiary Prevention
Human Growth and Development	Knowledge of factors that promote safe/healthy learning communities	Knowledge about early signs of psychological disorders related to violence (self and others)	*Specialized knowledge about psychological disorders related to violence (self and others) to prevent relapse*
Social and Cultural Foundations	Knowledge of how the counselor serves as a social advocate	Skills and knowledge to evaluate students' cultural contexts and related worldviews	*Coordination or adaptation of service components that speak to ongoing cultural and contextual issues*
Helping Relationships	Advanced accurate empathy and cultural competency	Crisis intervention skills Referral skills	*Skills for follow-up with students with chronic problems who been treated elsewhere*
Group Work	Understanding the structure, dynamics, and processes of group development *Skills for planning and facilitating diverse specialized or topic-focused group interventions for students, parents, and staff*	Debriefing models Small-group counseling skills	*Skills for conducting support groups to prevent relapse*
Career and Lifestyle Development	Knowledge of the lifestyle factors that play a role in the etiology of violence	Models to assess the lifestyle opportunity structures and barriers and supports within the environment	*Knowledge of specialized career services for special populations and school-to-work transition*

continues

Table 12.1 | continued

Program Curriculum	Primary Prevention	Secondary Prevention	Tertiary Prevention
Appraisal	Skills and knowledge to conduct family and community assessment	Recognizing signs of psychological disorders and crisis reactions; lethality assessment (self and others)	*Specialized knowledge of the assessment of psychological disorders and the relationship of diagnosis to a treatment plan*
Research and Program Evaluation	Knowledge of primary research design and evaluation models	Knowledge of primary research design and evaluation models	Knowledge of primary research design and evaluation models
	Skills for evaluating program effectiveness	*Skills for evaluating program effectiveness and designing modifications for specialized needs*	*Skills for evaluating program effectiveness in an interdisciplinary and interagency context*
Professional Orientation	Knowledge of ethical standards and the counselor as a social advocate	Knowledge of ethical and legal issues related to working with dangerous (to self, others) clients	*Skill at coordinating the roles and services provided by mental health professionals*
	Developing professional leadership and mentoring skills		
Clinical Instruction	Practica and internship experience that includes practice in multicultural group work and consultation	Practica and internship experiences in intake interviewing, lethality assessment, and practice in small-group counseling	*Specialized therapeutic skills to support population needs and service initiatives*

School Specialty	Consultation skills and knowledge of how to deliver training to other educational staff	Skills in resource identification	*Developing joint program initiatives within school systems and the broader community*
	Knowledge of how to organize, administer, and evaluate comprehensive developmental programs	Knowledge of how to organize, administer, and evaluate comprehensive developmental programs	

Note. Preventions listed in roman relate to preservice issues; preventions listed in italics relate to in-service issues.

Counselors in training need the knowledge and skills to utilize consultation, discussion, task training, psychoeducation, or counseling group formats. Models for negotiating intergroup conflicts and problem-solving strategies will help school counselors to facilitate team development and training. The knowledge base and guided practice for school and community teaming and consultation are provided in beginning group coursework. This becomes the foundation for experimenting with the models and interventions during supervised clinical experiences. In-service training will then help practicing counselors to develop frameworks for conducting specialty groups related to prevention and intervention.

Counselors in training need to develop assessment competencies and strategies for facilitating groups in which they teach skills for safe and healthy social interaction. This includes instruction and practice in handling anger and frustration. If core training courses include the development of competencies for using multiple group modalities to address violence prevention and intervention, counselors in training will be better prepared to guide students, parents, and other school professionals in understanding and negotiating frustration and anger.

To increase the coping abilities of all students, group guidance activities must focus on training in social, decision-making, and problem-solving skills; alternatives to violent behavior; peer negotiation skills; and so on. Heterogeneous groupings for each developmental level can provide a format for discussion, education, and training. Homogeneous groupings may be based on the salient factors in a particular school or on factors that have been demonstrated to influence perceptions, experiences, and behaviors related to violence, such as socioeconomic status, minority identification, gender, and levels of poverty. Consideration of these variables will equip counselors to avoid poor risk combinations that are likely to diminish the influence of the group configuration. Counselors able to use the natural controversy in groups can create powerful here-and-now learning experiences for group members. Likewise, counselors trained to use their assessment skills to separate developmental or preventive concerns from intervention issues can screen and select group members to optimize the use of group controversy to actively model respect.

A challenging aspect of violence prevention and intervention will be connecting counseling services to the many environmental variables that influence perceptions and behaviors. Delva-Tauili'ili (1995) commented that interventions must target the different environments with which individuals interact and that addressing the racism found among school personnel requires a relentless commitment to social justice. Counselors in training need to become aware of their own cultural, racial, social, and gendered identities, along with their corresponding beliefs and biases. Combined with this self-awareness, knowledge for understanding the personal variables most likely to influence stratification and marginalization in the school will facilitate skill development.

Counselor educators have a responsibility to break the silence and facilitate the discussion of difficult issues. In-service training must follow by providing counselors with the skills to confront instances of racism, sexism, homophobia, and other tensions that impact the school environment.

SECONDARY PREVENTION SKILLS

For secondary prevention, school counselors need skills and knowledge to identify students who have begun to experience difficulties in coping and to provide interventions for those students. Although school counselors are not trained as experts in the diagnosis of mental disorders, it is critical that they be taught to recognize signs of psychological disorders, such as depression, and the risk factors and warning signs for suicidal behavior and violence toward others. Early recognition of warning signs is the first step in prevention and must occur before any intervention can take place. There seems to be reluctance in society to acknowledge that children and adolescents do suffer from psychological problems. This reluctance leads to a pattern of ignoring or minimizing the signs and symptoms.

In a review of research on violence risk assessment, Borum (1996) noted that "mental disorder may be a robust and significant factor for the occurrence of violence" (p. 946). One of the common threads found among the perpetrators of recent school shootings is the presence of a psychological disorder, usually clinical depression. Children and adolescents may become rebellious and act out aggressively because of an inability to cope with feelings of hopelessness and pessimism. Other factors such as impulsivity, low levels of empathy, and an external locus of control leading to feelings of powerlessness and frustration (Dykeman, Daehlin, Doyle, & Flamer, 1996) have been associated with school violence.

The recognition of warning signs for a variety of problems, including potential violence, can be addressed in a number of courses, but particularly in assessment and crisis intervention courses. Without attaching diagnostic labels to groups of symptoms, student counselors can be trained to recognize general signs of depression in children and adolescents, as well as indicators of suicidal or homicidal ideation. Although neither homicide nor suicide risk can be predicted in any absolute way, awareness of risk factors is the crucial first step in prevention. At the same time, school counselors need to be aware of the tendency, among mental health professionals, to overestimate the risk of violence among non-White clients and to underestimate the risk among female clients (Hoff, 1995).

McNiel (1998) classified risk factors for violence toward others into personal history variables, clinical variables, and situational variables. Personal history variables include the following: a history of violence, usually considered the best single predictor; gender, with males engaging in more severe forms of violence than females; extent of planning; being a victim of abuse; growing up in a violent home; or being involved in a culture of violence such as a gang. Clinical variables include psychological problems and substance-related disorders. Situational variables include things such as the availability of potential victims, the availability of weapons, and the pervasiveness of violence in daily life. The perpetrators in all the recent school shootings had easy access to high-powered guns. School counselors certainly will not have all this information about any given student; however, various professionals together are likely to have much of this information. Knowledge of these factors will make school counselors more sensitive to potential problems, and intervention may occur early enough to prevent violence.

Risk factors for suicide, including the symptoms of depression, are well documented throughout the literature. Sommers-Flanagan and Sommers-Flanagan (1995) offered an excellent overview of suicide risk factors as well as strategies for assessing risk. The factors to consider in assessing risk among children and adolescents do not differ significantly from those used in adult risk assessment and include factors such as the presence and specificity of a suicide plan, previous attempts, depression, hopelessness, substance abuse, recent loss, resources and communication with significant others, and family (parent) history of suicide (Fremouw, de Perczel, & Ellis, 1990). Signs of depression such as sleep and eating disturbances, withdrawal from usual social contacts and from responsibilities, difficulty concentrating, and anxiety/restlessness should become familiar to school counselors. School counselors should be aware that any abrupt changes in a student's usual behavior might be a signal that something is wrong.

Although the recognition of warning signs is a crucial first step in the prevention of school violence, school counselors must know how to intervene once these signs are noticed. Even the most obvious signs may be ignored because the person receiving the signals does not know what to do. Students in distress may come to the attention of the school counselor through the students themselves, their friends and acquaintances, teachers, administrators, and parents. At this point, the counselor needs knowledge and skills for planning and implementing individual and group interventions. These include the following:

1. Crisis intervention skills that equip counselors to provide immediate, short-term intervention after an event leaves students with diminished coping capacity. Counselors provide assistance with

clarifying immediate needs, identifying and exploring coping strategies to meet those needs, taking concrete action, and follow-up, which may include identifying outside resources and making referrals (Hoff, 1995).

2. Skills for identifying resources and coordinating referrals, including an ability to evaluate social resources and the student's cultural context. Counselors must consider whether friends and family are seen as potential sources of help or as liabilities, as well as which cultural or socioeconomic factors may contribute to the student's vulnerability.

3. Skills to incorporate nontraditional approaches such as play, art, and music therapy to facilitate the learning experience for less verbal students and to engage students more readily in the process.

4. Group skills to conduct classroom debriefings based on Mitchell's Critical Incident Stress Debriefing (Johnson, 1998). This is a structured model for group interventions when the entire group (class or school) has been affected by a traumatic event such as the death of a peer. The counselor needs to be skilled in managing the expression of intense affect in a developmentally appropriate way.

5. Skills to plan and facilitate specialized counseling groups for identified students who have difficulties handling a traumatic event, such as parental divorce.

6. Skills for using traditional group structures, processes, dynamics, and therapeutic factors to help students identify harmful and inappropriate behavioral norms, acceptable alternative behaviors, and contextually specific and relevant peer reinforcement strategies. For example, groups may be provided for boys or girls who repeatedly use bullying or high levels of aggressive behavior.

7. Planning skills for annexing, involving, informing, and educating parents, professionals, the school, and the community and closely aligning these with the group interventions.

Group training builds on the competencies developed in cross-cultural training and prepares students to cofacilitate specialized groups during the practicum and internship. Training in group work incorporates the students' knowledge of the organizational structures of the school and community.

TERTIARY PREVENTION SKILLS

School counselors play a smaller, but still significant, role in tertiary prevention. Much of the skill training used to prepare counselors for tertiary prevention lends itself to an in-service approach. Schools particularly need to provide follow-up services for students who have received treatment elsewhere for substance-related or diagnosed mental disorders. To help these students cope in the school setting, counselors need skills to consult with teachers and to serve as liaisons with other professionals inside and outside of the school. Alignment with school and community initiatives may include visits to high-risk homes, empowerment training for girls exposed to violence in childhood homes, or professional and community consultation and teaming. Maintaining these linkages is critical. Teachers will need information about how to integrate the student back into the classroom and to address any special needs the student may have. Counselors may consider offering support groups to help these students maintain gains they have made in their outside treatment around issues such as substance abuse, sexual abuse, or depression. These types of supportive services can do a great deal in helping to prevent relapse.

CONCLUSION

For several decades, social science research has documented the relationship of environmental experiences, socioeconomic status, minority identification, gender, and levels of poverty to violence. It is sad that violence has entered the schoolroom in tragic ways. Schools alone cannot solve the problems that result from the deep incongruities in society. However, the notion that schools can adopt broadly conceived and well-coordinated strategies to cultivate emotional and social skills and help students to practice democracy can go a long way toward promoting resiliency and the school as a therapeutic community (Bloom & Reichert, 1998; Lantieri & Patti, 1996). In the wake of various explanations for particular violent episodes and assignments of blame that range from violent media to a lack of morality, school counselors may need to be a first line of defense to help ensure that all students are treated with basic decency. Schools are, for the most part, safe places, yet some practices designed to ensure that safety may, in the end, be frightening and demoralizing to many students.

Only when school counselors have clear and specific knowledge of these relationships can they assist in intentionally building the social and cultural foundations that facilitate equity and quality in school violence prevention and intervention programs. School counselors will need to identify and develop understanding of multiple cultural paradigms and environmental factors that affect the definition, experience, and consequences of inappropriate aggression and violence in schools. The counselor who has been trained to recognize and appreciate a diversity of worldviews is better equipped to effectively address the prevention and reduction of violence in schools.

REFERENCES

American School Counselor Association. (1997). *The school counselor and comprehensive school counseling programs: The position statement of the American School Counselor Association*. Alexandria, VA: Author.

Astor, R. A. (1995). School violence: A blueprint for elementary school interventions. *Social Work in Education, 17*, 101–115.

Bastian, L. D., & Taylor, B. M. (1991). *School crime: A national crime victimization survey report*. Washington, DC: U.S. Government Printing Office.

Bloom, S. L., & Reichert, M. (1998). *Bearing witness: Violence and collective responsibility*. Binghamton, NY: Haworth Press.

Borum, R. (1996). Improving the clinical practice of violence risk assessment: Technology, guidelines, and training. *American Psychologist, 51*, 945–956.

Caplan, G. (1964). *Principles of preventive psychiatry*. New York: Basic Books.

Capuzzi, D. (1998). Addressing the needs of at-risk youth: Early prevention and systematic intervention. In C. C. Lee & G. R. Walz (Eds.), *Social action: A mandate for counselors* (pp. 99–116). Alexandria, VA: American Counseling Association.

Council for the Accreditation of Counseling and Related Educational Programs. (1994). *Standards and procedures manual*. Alexandria, VA: Author.

Crespi, T. D. (1999, May). Childhood violence: Considerations for counseling in the schools. *Counseling Today*, pp. 11, 18, 22.

Delva-Tauili'ili, J. (1995). Assessment and prevention of aggressive behavior among youths of color: Integrating cultural and social factors. *Social Work in Education, 17*, 83–91.

Dykeman, C., Daehlin, W., Doyle, S., & Flamer, H. S. (1996). Psychological predictors of school-based violence: Implications for school counselors. *The School Counselor, 44*, 35–47.

Egan, G. (1990). *The skilled helper: A systematic approach to effective helping* (4th ed.). Pacific Grove, CA: Brooks/Cole.

Fremouw, W. J., de Perczel, M., & Ellis, T. E. (1990). *Suicide risk: Assessment and response guidelines*. New York: Pergamon Press.

Furlong, M., Poland, S., Babinski, L., Munoz, J., & Boles, S. (1996). Factors associated with school psychologists' perceptions of campus violence. *Psychology in the Schools, 33*, 28–37.

Guetzloe, E. (1992). Violent, aggressive, and antisocial students: What are we going to do with them? *Preventing School Failure, 36*, 4–9.

Gysbers, N. C., & Henderson, P. (1997). *Comprehensive guidance programs that work–II*. Greensboro, NC: ERIC/CASS.

Hayes, R. L. (1994). Counseling in the postmodern world: Origins and implications of a constructivist developmental approach. *Counseling and Human Development, 26*(6), 1–12.

Hoff, L. A. (1995). *People in crisis: Understanding and helping* (4th ed.). San Francisco: Jossey-Bass.

Johnson, K. (1998). *Trauma in the lives of children: Crisis and stress management techniques for counselors, teachers, and other professionals* (2nd ed.). Alameda, CA: Hunter House.

Kelly, D. H., & Pink, W. T. (1982). School crime and individual responsibility: The perpetuation of a myth. *Urban Review, 14*, 47–63.

Lantieri, L., & Patti, J. (1996). *Waging peace in our schools*. Boston: Beacon Press.

Lee, C. C., & Brydges, J. L. (1998). Challenging interpersonal violence. In C. C. Lee & G. R. Walz (Eds.), *Social action: A mandate for counselors* (pp. 67–81). Alexandria, VA: American Counseling Association.

Lindemann, E. (1944). Symptomatology and management of acute grief. *American Journal of Psychiatry, 101*, 141–148.

McNiel, D. E. (1998). Empirically based clinical evaluation and management of the potentially violent patient. In P. M. Kleespies (Ed.), *Emergencies in mental health practice: Evaluation and management* (pp. 95–116). New York: Guilford Press.

Rajgopal, P. R. (1987). *Social change and violence: The Indian experience*. New Delhi, India: Uppal.

Schon, D. A. (1987). *Educating the reflective practitioner*. San Francisco: Jossey-Bass.

Schwartz, W. (1998). *An overview of strategies to reduce school violence*. New York: ERIC Clearinghouse on Urban Education.

Sommers-Flanagan, J., & Sommers-Flanagan, R. (1995). Intake interviewing with suicidal patients: A systematic approach. *Professional Psychology: Research and Practice, 26*, 41–47.

Van Soest, D., & Bryant, S. (1995). Violence reconceptualized for social work: The urban dilemma. *Social Work, 40*, 549–557.

13 | Anger Management for Youths: What Works and for Whom?

Douglas C. Smith, James D. Larson,
Barbara DeBaryshe, and Michael Salzman

Continuing concerns about youth violence, particularly school-related violence, have led to a proliferation of anger management programs aimed at children and youths (Feindler, 1995; Nelson, Hart, & Finch, 1993). Despite the high public profile and strong professional interest in such programs, there have been few systematic attempts to evaluate their utility.

The purpose of this chapter is to provide a comprehensive review of anger management programs for children and adolescents. Our intent is to provide school counselors with a sense of the types and content of anger management programs described in the professional literature. The review covers both school-based programs and those conducted within clinic, residential, and other treatment settings. The chapter provides a summary and analysis of studies including descriptions of (a) participant characteristics, treatment settings, program content, and efforts to enhance generalization; (b) target outcomes and treatment effectiveness; and (c) implications for school counselors.

INTRODUCTION

Individuals who experience chronically high levels of anger are at risk for a variety of social, psychological, and health-related concerns. Anger can be an exceedingly dangerous emotion when experienced frequently and to an intense degree (Diamond, 1982; Friedman, 1992; McKay, Rogers, & McKay, 1989; Williams & Williams, 1993). Angry students within school settings are often avoided and/or rejected by peers (Cantrell & Prinz, 1985; Grotpeter & Crick, 1996), are rated by teachers as exhibiting more negative behaviors and attitudes (Smith & Furlong, 1994), and are less likely to achieve academic success and more likely to experience frustration with regard to school (Smith, Adelman, Nelson, Taylor, & Phares, 1987). Furthermore, chronically high anger is a key indicator of violence potential at school (Dwyer, Osher, & Warger, 1998).

It is clear that anger is an emotion with far-reaching consequences both for the self and for others with whom one has contact. Given the likelihood that these patterns are established early in life (Tolan, Guerra, & Kendall, 1995), it is crucial that anger management intervention efforts begin early.

CONCEPTUAL MODELS OF ANGER

Both researchers and mental health practitioners have commented on the lack of conceptual clarity with regard to defining anger and anger-related processes (see, e.g., reviews by Furlong & Smith, 1994; Spielberger et al., 1985). Most conceptualizations of anger do, however, distinguish three related but essentially independent dimensions corresponding to affective, cognitive, and behavioral domains.

The *affective* or emotional component of anger refers to a range of aversive feelings experienced as a result of negative consequences, interference, provocation, or frustration. Physiological correlates of angry affect include increased heart rate and muscle tension, pupil dilation, shallow breathing, and higher blood pressure (Williams & Williams, 1993). The *cognitive* or affective component of anger refers to a set of beliefs or attitudes about life and the actions of others. Chronically angry and aggressive individuals have been described as maintaining a "negative world view" and depicting others as antagonistic, threatening, or harmful (Buss, 1961; Spielberger, Krasner, & Solomon, 1988). Cognitions also include such social information-processing skills as social awareness, causal attributions, empathy, and moral reasoning (Hudley, 1994; Shantz, 1983). Aggressive and angry children frequently misread social and situational cues or misinterpret the intentions of others (Dodge, Price, Bachorowski, & Newman, 1990; Lochman & Dodge, 1994). The third dimension of anger is the *behavioral* or expressive component. Individuals express anger in a variety of ways depending on both intraindividual and situational variables (Feindler, Adler, Brooks, & Bhumitra, 1993). Positive expressions of anger are usually associated with active coping responses or problem-solving strategies such as discussing one's feelings or reframing the situation or issue. Negative expressions include both physical and verbal aggression as well as passive–aggressive behaviors. One may also choose to repress or suppress angry feelings.

METHOD FOR SELECTING STUDIES FOR REVIEW

Studies reviewed in this chapter were obtained through a literature search using PsycINFO. Descriptive terms used in the search were (*anger management*) or (*anger reduction*) or (*anger regulation*) and (*children and adolescents*). A total of 194 article abstracts were obtained in this manner. The initial pool of abstracts was then reviewed and reduced according to the following criteria:

1. The study had to include an intervention effort; that is, it had to describe a program designed to increase the range of anger-coping strategies or reduce the incidence and/or intensity of negative consequences of anger.
2. Anger management, coping, or reduction had to be the *primary* focus of the intervention effort. A number of studies were eliminated because they focused more broadly on social skills, emotional regulation, stress reduction, or self-esteem. Anger management, in these programs, was secondary to a broader agenda.
3. Participants were children or adolescents at the elementary or secondary school level although interventions could be conducted in school or nonschool settings.
4. Articles reviewed were published from 1980 to the present.

A total of 44 studies met the above criteria. Seven articles were not available at our institutions or through interlibrary loan, yielding a final pool of 37 articles that were included in the present review.

DESCRIPTIVE REVIEW OF STUDIES

Participants and Service Delivery Systems

The 37 articles included in this review are noted by an asterisk in the References section. These studies included a total of 1,911 participants. From those studies that provided participant gender data, it is clear that anger management programs for youths are primarily targeted toward males. Males outnumbered females by more than 4:1 as recipients of treatment in these studies (1,075 and 242, respectively). Only 21 of the 37 studies provided any information with regard to participant ethnicity, but the majority of those (14 of 21) indicated that programs served clients from diverse ethnic backgrounds. Only 4 studies were conducted with exclusively Caucasian samples, and 3 studies focused exclusively on children from Hispanic or African American backgrounds. The majority of studies reviewed (22 of 37) targeted youths at the secondary school level. The overall age of participants in these programs ranged from 6 to 18 years, with a median age of approximately 12 years.

Anger management interventions took place primarily in school settings (21 of 36 studies; 1 study failed to note where the intervention occurred). Details were rarely given about who actually conducted the intervention, for example, school staff versus someone from outside the school. Additional sites where interventions took place included clinics, hospitals, residential treatment centers, delinquent facilities, group homes, correctional facilities, private or agency offices, and in the community. The actual number of intervention sessions conducted in these programs ranged from 3 to 50, with a median of approximately 10 sessions.

The vast majority of programs (31 of 37 studies) targeted students who were already experiencing some problems with anger regulation and control (secondary prevention) or who had well-established patterns of such problems (tertiary prevention). Sixteen of these studies targeted students with a psychiatric, educational, or legal classification or diagnosis. The most common diagnoses were disruptive behavior disorders (6 studies), emotionally impaired (5 studies), and juvenile delinquent (3 studies).

Intervention Type and Content

The intervention strategies used in the reviewed studies were classified as emotion-focused, cognitive, cognitive–behavioral, behavioral, psychoeducational, pharmacologic, or family-oriented. Emotion-focused strategies included specific techniques for arousal regulation and reduction, including systematic desensitization, relaxation, affective self-awareness, and developing empathy for others. Cognitive strategies included cognitive restructuring (e.g., altering belief systems), problem-solving skills, and the use of self-talk to enhance motivation. Cognitive–behavioral strategies included the same range of cognitive techniques applied in conjunction with modeling, role-plays, rehearsal, and self-monitoring. Behavioral strategies focused more specifically on developing behavioral forms of emotional expression as well as specific skills such as assertiveness and communication. Psychoeducational strategies were designed to educate participants about the sequence of anger arousal and expression; the link among cognition, affect, and behavioral expression; and the consequences of angry feelings and behaviors. Pharmacologic approaches used psychotropic medications in an effort to manage emotional reactivity and negative behaviors. Finally, family-oriented treatments included parents, siblings, and other family members in the intervention effort.

Given the complexity of the anger construct, it is reasonable to assume that most anger management programs would include multiple treatment modalities or a combined focus on changing affect, cognition, and behavior. The vast majority of studies (29 total, or 78%) incorporated two or more treatment approaches. Furthermore, the inclusion of cognitive–behavioral components was almost universal. Cognitive–behavioral interventions were administered alone (8 studies) or in combination with psychoeducation (5 studies), behavior management (4 studies), emotion focus (3 studies), or drug treatment (2 studies). Eight studies combined cognitive–behavioral approaches with two or more additional modalities (two of these multisystemic programs included family members in treatment sessions).

The cognitive–behavioral components were themselves comprehensive. Typical cognitive–behavioral intervention protocols included training in recognizing physiological cues associated with angry feelings, use of intermediate strategies such as cognitive reappraisal to reduce emotional arousal, enhancement of alternative and consequential thinking as a tool for problem solving or conflict resolution, and use of modeling or role-plays to demonstrate and solidify acquired skills.

Generalization and Maintenance

There is impressive research to demonstrate that skills trained in the treatment setting will neither maintain over time nor generalize—whether to the classroom, the playground, or the neighborhood—without specific maintenance and generalization programming built into the fabric of the intervention (Herring & Northrup, 1998; Kazdin, 1994; Meichenbaum & Biemiller, 1998). Pupil insight and skill mastery within the training setting is an essential prerequisite, but it is only a prerequisite. The most critical feature of intervention—indeed, the raison d'etre of the entire effort—is to facilitate the adaptive transfer of skills acquired in treatment sessions to more authentic environments such as the classroom, playground, and home.

The articles reviewed for this chapter were closely examined for their attempts to promote both generalization and maintenance. Programmed generalization elements may include features such as (a) contingent reinforcement programs in an authentic setting, (b) training in multiple environments, (c) training with a variety of individuals who may trigger anger responses, (d) homework or other independent training assignments distinct in setting and time from the training setting, or (e) the use of trainees as consultants who have to describe their own generalization strategies to others. Steps to increase treatment maintenance might include (a) programming for naturally occurring reinforcers, (b) gradually removing or fading structured contingencies, or (c) providing booster sessions.

Slightly more than half the studies reviewed (23) included elements designed to enhance generalization. The most frequently cited attempt to foster generalization outside the treatment environment was the use of some form of written homework (noted in 8 studies). This typically took the form of a self-monitoring "hassle log" (e.g., Feindler, Marriott, & Iwata, 1984; Larson, 1992) or a reflective diary of children's daily anger experiences (e.g., Miller, 1995; Stern, 1999). No data were provided concerning the qualitative composition of these assignments or completion rate by the trainees. Two studies (Ninness, Ellis, Miller, Baker, & Rutherford, 1995; Spirito, Finch, Smith, & Cooley, 1981) used training in multiple environments, whereas 9 studies reported using some form of authentic or real-life scenarios within the training setting (e.g., Bosworth, Espelage, & Dubay, 1998). Classroom teachers were involved in goal attainment monitoring for 2 studies (Lochman & Curry, 1986; Lochman, Lampron, Gemmer, Harris, & Wyckoff, 1989), and nontreatment staff provided training in 2 studies (Kellner & Tutin, 1995; Nugent, Champlin, & Wiinimaki, 1997).

The work of Lochman and his colleagues (Lochman, Burch, Curry, & Lampron, 1984; Lochman & Curry, 1986; Lochman et al., 1989; Lochman, Nelson, & Sims, 1981) deserves mention as one of the few investigative groups to systematically study a number of treatment components designed to enhance generalization. Along with the typical use of self-monitoring homework, these studies examined the addition of classroom goal setting (Lochman et al., 1984) and teacher classroom consultation (Lochman et al., 1989). Whereas classroom goal setting tended to show some positive effects, the addition of teacher consultation to the group treatment showed no effect on the measured variables.

The reviewed studies, for the most part, ignored the issue of systematically building in treatment maintenance procedures, though a few (6) noted that they engaged in some form of follow-up study to determine treatment effectiveness over time. Unquestionably, future research needs to more systematically examine the differential effects of a variety of generalization and maintenance conditions on anger regulation and control.

Design Characteristics and Dependent Variables

Twenty-two of the 37 studies reviewed used experimental or quasi-experimental research designs (11 of each). An additional 7 studies used single-subject or multiple baseline designs, and 1 study used a combination of correlational and multiple baseline methods. Seven studies were categorized as nonexperimental.

Choice of treatment outcomes and methods of evaluation were areas in which we expected considerable differences across studies. We categorized treatment outcomes by dependent variable content or domain. Each dependent variable (most studies had multiple outcome measures) was coded as follows: *anger, other emotions* (usually depression or anxiety), *cog-*

nitions (reasoning about emotions, self-statements, and self-perceptions), *positive behavior* (prosocial skills), *negative behavior* (disruption, aggression, and antisocial acts), and *other* (e.g., peer sociometric ratings).

Most studies (29 of 37) examined multiple treatment outcome domains in evaluating the utility of anger management interventions. By far the most common choice of dependent variable content was negative behavior, which appeared in 32 studies. This is interesting given the fact that most interventions are distinctly cognitive in content and presumably use behavioral rehearsal and other strategies to promote *positive* behavioral alternatives to aggressive behavior. Positive behavior outcomes were measured in about half (19) of the studies reviewed. Cognitive outcomes appeared in only 14 studies, which is again surprising given the cognitive emphasis of most intervention efforts. Likewise, there was relatively little interest in measuring affective outcomes as a result of anger management training. Such a focus appeared in only 13 studies.

Rating scales proved to be the measure of choice for the majority of studies reviewed (29 of 37). Of these, self-report was used in 19 studies. A total of 14 studies used teacher or staff ratings of behavior as a dependent variable, but only 2 studies included parent ratings and only 1 study used peer ratings. Observations of specific behaviors were included in only 15 studies, which is somewhat surprising given the emphasis on reduction of negative behavior as a treatment outcome. Standardized tests appeared as a dependent variable in 8 studies, whereas archival data were included in 3 studies. Analogues as an assessment technique were used in only 8 studies, which is again surprising given both the content of treatments and the general focus on behavioral outcomes.

On a positive note, it should be pointed out that the majority of researchers (24 of 37 studies) included multiple measures of treatment effectiveness. Most of these studies included perspectives from more than one informant or supplemented self- or other ratings with observations of targeted behaviors.

Evaluation of Outcomes

The purpose of this section is to provide an evaluation of anger management intervention efforts. We first consider whether the reviewed studies, as a group, had a positive and significant impact on children's emotions, cognitions, or behaviors. Then, we consider whether intervention programs selectively affected particular kinds of outcomes. Finally, we explore the extent to which treatment outcomes varied as a function of study characteristics such as intervention content and subject selection criteria. Rather than relying on a subjective review, what follows is a brief summary of findings based on a statistical technique (meta-analysis) that allowed us to combine outcome data across a number of studies. Of the studies reviewed, 19 provided sufficient data to allow us to compute effect sizes and to thus evaluate treatment effects for these interventions.

Overall, the studies showed a positive and moderate treatment effect. Collapsing across dependent variable types, treatment outcomes were 0.63 standard deviations better than control outcomes or pretest levels. Thus, it can be concluded that, as a group, anger management interventions with children and youths were effective.

The anger management interventions were not, however, equally effective for all outcomes measured across the studies. Anger management interventions appeared most useful in reducing angry *feelings* as opposed to angry *thoughts* or nonanger emotions such as anxiety or depression. Anger interventions also appeared effective in reducing impulsiveness and enhancing peer status. As a group, the interventions appeared moderately effective in reducing inappropriate *behavioral expression* of angry feelings.

Effect sizes also varied by dependent variable type. Large treatment effects were found for analogue and archival measures. A small treatment effect was found for other report, which included behavioral ratings provided by teachers, parents, and other adults. No treatment effects were found for standardized tests, direct observation, or self-report.

Design and quality of the intervention also appeared to be important factors in overall treatment efficacy. High-quality studies defined as those using random assignment, matched control groups, and a reasonable number of sessions demonstrated a moderate overall effect. This suggests that well-designed interventions do create desirable change. Moderate effects were also found for comprehensive interventions with three major treatment components. Small positive effects were seen for single-focus interventions and secondary interventions. No treatment effects were found for low-quality studies, within-subjects designs, primary and tertiary interventions, or interventions with either two or four major treatment components.

CONCLUSION

Our review of 37 anger management intervention studies with children and adolescents over the past 18 years suggests some interesting trends and directions for future efforts. First, it is clear that a wide range of treatment strategies fall under the anger management umbrella. Although most programs include multiple cognitive–behavioral components, there is wide variation in the specific content of these programs and in how the material is delivered. The extreme diversity in program content and delivery makes it difficult to adequately assess what does and does not work. More controlled studies are needed that compare specific treatment components in an effort to identify those components associated with positive outcomes.

Second, most anger management interventions both within and outside school settings are oriented toward students with well-established patterns of poor anger regulation and control. The majority of interventions reviewed here included secondary-level students, many of whom were already labeled as emotionally impaired, behavior disordered, or delinquent. Given the stability of aggressive and antisocial behavior throughout the life span, it seems imperative that programs for youths address these problems earlier and take a more preventative approach toward anger management.

Perhaps related to the above considerations, it is also clear that most anger management programs for youths target mainly boys. Of course, this may simply reflect the fact that more boys than girls are involved in anger-related incidents on or around school campuses or that aggressive behavior is systematically reinforced in boys. Of concern, however, is the possibility that girls may be overlooked in anger management intervention efforts, not because they do not experience anger to the same degree as boys, but because they have been socialized to suppress or indirectly express angry feelings. More studies are needed to understand girls' experiences and expressions of anger.

On a similar note, there is a lack of understanding of cultural and ethnic factors related to anger expression and control. To compile a more comprehensive database, it is imperative that studies at a minimum provide information on the ethnic identity of participants.

Do anger management interventions pass the acid test of improving real-life behavior outside of the therapy or testing situation? The good news with regard to this evaluation of programs is that anger management interventions do seem to work. The programs work best in reducing the intensity or frequency of the affective or emotional component of children's anger. With regard to observed behavior, however, the picture is less clear. There was no treatment effect for the nine comparisons involving direct observation of children's behavior. However, the archival outcomes had a large treatment effect. In the studies included for the meta-analytic review, archival outcomes were actually indirect measures of everyday behavior (e.g., teacher and staff records of behavioral infractions). In each of these studies, unit or school staff were unaware of participants' treatment condition. Only three studies used archival data, so interpretations must be tentative. However, the results suggest the intriguing possibility that anger management programs curtail the occurrence of the most severe and inappropriate negative behaviors in classroom and residential settings.

Anger management interventions also do quite well in improving children's peer social status. Because negative behavior and peer rejection are intimately related and the combination of the two is associated with the tendency to coalesce with antisocial peer groups in adolescence (Patterson, DeBaryshe, & Ramsey, 1989), it is possible that anger management interventions could contribute toward reducing the risk for later delinquency and criminal behavior.

Despite the current high profile of anger management issues, the state of the art of anger management program evaluation leaves much to be desired. As a whole, the number of evaluation studies is not large, nor are they of high quality. Cautions to consider include the following:

1. Given the goal of affecting widespread changes in children's anger management strategies, it is remarkable how little attention is paid in the literature to maintenance and generalization issues. Meichenbaum and Biemiller (1998) offered numerous suggestions aimed at generalizing academic skills that are readily applicable to behavioral skills including anger control.
2. Because only 19 studies had sufficient data to be useful for a meta-analysis, the results presented here must be seen as preliminary. As the body of literature grows, effect size estimates should become more stable and interpretable.
3. This review is based on published research articles. Because there is a bias against publishing nonsignificant results, the literature may overestimate the true impact of attempted treatments. (This phenomenon is widely known as the "file-drawer problem"—studies with null results fail to be disseminated.) Furthermore, research studies are often staffed by university personnel and delivered under conditions that may not be typical of most school counseling offices. Success in the field may be dependent on the extent to which school personnel can create the conditions followed in research settings.
4. More attention needs to be paid to the frequency, expression, setting conditions, and effective amelioration of anger in girls, minority students, and young students.
5. Almost no studies address anger management from the perspective of primary prevention.
6. There is a strong need for systematic tests of individual treatment components. Most programs offer a complex conglomerate of ingredients, so we cannot say at this time which treatment elements are necessary and/or sufficient for success.

What we can say to practitioners is that anger management interventions, as a whole, appear to be a worthwhile endeavor. This should provide welcome news to school counselors, not only those who are currently working with angry, aggressive students, but also those who are considering the prospect. Given the myriad and often overwhelming demands placed on the counselor's time, it is necessary to focus on only those programs that offer a reasonable chance of positive outcomes. Although evaluation research is in a nascent stage, what evidence there is suggests that these interventions result in statistically significant and clinically respectable gains. As more studies accumulate, analysis efforts such as this will be better able to answer the questions of which intervention approaches work, for whom, and how.

REFERENCES

*Denotes studies included in the review of anger management programs for youths.

*Bosworth, K., Espelage, D., & Dubay, T. (1998). A computer-based violence prevention intervention for young adolescents: Pilot study. *Adolescence, 33,* 785–795.

*Bosworth, K., Espelage, D., Dubay, T., Dahlberg, L. L., & Daytner, G. (1996). Using multimedia to teach conflict-resolution skills to young adolescents. *American Journal of Preventive Medicine, 12,* 65–74.

Buss, A. H. (1961). *The psychology of aggression.* New York: Wiley.

Cantrell, V. L., & Prinz, R. J. (1985). Multiple perspectives of rejected, neglected, and accepted children: Relation between sociometric status and behavioral characteristics. *Journal of Consulting and Clinical Psychology, 53,* 884–889.

*Dangel, R., Deschner, J., & Rasp, R. (1989). Anger control training for adolescents in residential treatment. *Behavioral Modification, 13,* 447–458.

*Deffenbacher, J. L., Lynch, R. S., Oetting, E. R., & Kemper, C. C. (1996). Anger reduction in early adolescents. *Journal of Counseling Psychology, 43,* 149–157.

Diamond, E. L. (1982). The role of anger and hostility in essential hypertension and coronary heart disease. *Psychological Bulletin, 92,* 410–433.

Dodge, K. A., Price, J., Bachorowski, J., & Newman, J. (1990). Hostile attributional biases in severely aggressive adolescents. *Journal of Abnormal Psychology, 99,* 385–392.

Dwyer, K., Osher, D., & Warger, C. (1998). *Early warning, timely response: A guide to safe schools.* Washington, DC: U.S. Department of Education.

*Feindler, E. L. (1995). Ideal treatment package for children and adolescents with anger disorders. *Issues in Comprehensive Pediatric Nursing, 18,* 233–260.

Feindler, E. L., Adler, N., Brooks, D., & Bhumitra, E. (1993). The development of the Children's Anger Response Checklist: CARC. In L. VanderCreek (Ed.), *Innovations in clinical practice* (Vol. 12, pp. 337–362). Sarasota, FL: Professional Resources Press.

*Feindler, E. L., Ecton, R. B., Kingsley, D., & Dubey, D. R. (1986). Group anger-control training for institutionalized psychiatric male adolescents. *Behavioral Therapy, 17,* 109–123.

*Feindler, E., Marriott, S. A., & Iwata, M. (1984). Group anger control training for junior high school delinquents. *Cognitive Therapy and Research, 8,* 299–311.

Friedman, H. S. (1992). *Hostility, coping, and health*. Washington, DC: American Psychological Association.

Furlong, M. J., & Smith, D. C. (Eds.). (1994). *Anger, hostility, and aggression: Assessment, prevention, and intervention strategies for youth*. New York: Wiley.

*Garrison, S. R., & Stolberg, A. L. (1983). Modification of anger in children by affective imagery training. *Journal of Abnormal Child Psychology, 11*, 115–130.

Grotpeter, J. K., & Crick, N. R. (1996). Relational aggression, overt aggression, and friendship. *Child Development, 67*, 2328–2338.

*Guerra, N. G., & Slaby, R. G. (1990). Cognitive mediators of aggression in adolescent offenders: 2. Intervention. *Developmental Psychology, 26*, 269–277.

*Hains, A. A. (1989). An anger-control intervention with aggressive-delinquent youths. *Behavioral Residential Treatment, 4*, 213–230.

*Hains, A. A. (1994). The effectiveness of a school-based, cognitive–behavioral stress management program with adolescents reporting high and low levels of emotional arousal. *School Counselor, 42*, 114–125.

*Hains, A. A., & Szjakowski, J. (1990). A cognitive stress-reduction intervention program for adolescents. *Journal of Counseling Psychology, 37*, 79–84.

Herring, M., & Northrup, J. (1998). The generalization of social skills for a child with behavior disorders in the school setting. *Child and Family Behavior Therapy, 20*, 51–66.

*Hinshaw, S. P., Buhrmester, D., & Heller, T. (1989). Anger control in response to verbal provocation: Effects of stimulant medication for boys with ADHD. *Journal of Abnormal Child Psychology, 17*, 393–407.

*Hinshaw, S. P., Hencker, B., & Whalen, C. K. (1984). Self control in hyperactive boys in anger inducing situations: Effects of cognitive training and of methylphenidate. *Journal of Abnormal Child Psychology, 12*, 55–77.

*Horton, A. (1996). Teaching anger management skills to primary age children. *Teaching and Change, 3*, 281–296.

Hudley, C. (1994). Perceptions of intentionality, feelings of anger, and reactive aggression. In M. J. Furlong & D. C. Smith (Eds.), *Anger, hostility, and aggression: Assessment, prevention, and intervention strategies for youth* (pp. 39–56). New York: Wiley.

*Hudley, C., Britsch, B., Wakefield, W. D., Smith, T., Demorat, M., & Cho, S.-J. (1998). An attribution retraining program to reduce aggression in elementary school students. *Psychology in the Schools, 35*, 271–282.

Kazdin, A. E. (1994). *Behavior modification in applied settings* (5th ed.). Pacific Grove, CA: Brooks/Cole.

*Kellner, M. H., & Tutin, J. (1995). A school-based anger management program for developmentally and emotionally disabled high school students. *Adolescence, 30*, 813–825.

*Larson, J. D. (1992). Anger and aggression management techniques utilizing the Think First curriculum. *Journal of Offender Rehabilitation, 18*, 101–117.

*LeCroy, C. W. (1988). Anger management or anger expression: Which is most effective? *Residential Treatment for Children and Youth, 5*, 29–39.

*Lochman, J. E. (1985). Effects of different treatment lengths in cognitive–behavioral interventions with aggressive boys. *Child Psychiatry and Human Development, 16*, 45–56.

*Lochman, J. E., Burch, P. R., Curry, J. F., & Lampron, L. B. (1984). Treatment and generalization effects of cognitive behavioral and goal setting interventions with aggressive boys. *Journal of Consulting and Clinical Psychology, 52,* 915–916.

*Lochman, J. E., & Curry, J. F. (1986). Effects of problem-solving training and self-instruction training with aggressive boys. *Journal of Clinical Child Psychology, 15,* 159–164.

Lochman, J. E., & Dodge, K. A. (1994). Social cognitive processes of severely violent, moderately aggressive, and nonaggressive boys. *Journal of Consulting and Clinical Psychology, 62,* 366–374.

*Lochman, J. E., Lampron, L. B., Burch, P. R., & Curry, J. F. (1985). Client characteristics associated with behavior change for treated and untreated aggressive boys. *Journal of Abnormal Psychology, 13,* 527–538.

*Lochman, J. E., Lampron, L. B., Gemmer, T. C., Harris, S. R., & Wyckoff, G. M. (1989). Teacher consultation and cognitive–behavioral interventions with aggressive boys. *Psychology in the Schools, 26,* 179–187.

*Lochman, J. E., Nelson, W. M., & Sims, J. P. (1981). A cognitive behavioral program for use with aggressive children. *Journal of Clinical Child Psychology, 3,* 146–148.

McKay, M., Rogers, P. D., & McKay, J. (1989). *When anger hurts.* Oakland, CA: New Harbinger.

Meichenbaum, D., & Biemiller, A. (1998). *Nurturing independent learners: Helping students take charge of their learning.* Cambridge, MA: Brookline.

*Miller, D. B. (1995). Treatment of adolescent interpersonal violence: A cognitive–behavioral group approach. *Journal of Child and Adolescent Group Therapy, 5,* 191–200.

Nelson, W. M., Hart, K. J., & Finch, A. J. (1993). Anger in children: A cognitive behavioral view of the assessment–therapy connection. *Journal of Rational–Emotive and Cognitive Behavior Therapy, 11,* 135–150.

*Ninness, H. A., Ellis, J., Miller, W. B., Baker, D., & Rutherford, R. (1995). The effects of a self-management training package on the transfer of aggression control procedures in the absence of supervision. *Behavior Modification, 19,* 464–490.

*Normand, D., & Roberts, M. (1990). Modeling of anger/hostility control with preadolescent Type A girls. *Child Study Journal, 20,* 237–262.

*Nugent, W. R., Champlin, D., & Wiinimaki, L. (1997). The effects of anger control training on adolescent antisocial behavior. *Research on Social Work Practice, 7,* 446–462.

*Omizo, M. M., Hershberger, J. M., & Omizo, S. A. (1988). Teaching children to cope with anger. *Elementary School Counseling and Guidance, 22,* 241–245.

Patterson, G. R., DeBaryshe, B. D., & Ramsey, E. R. (1989). A developmental perspective on antisocial behavior. *American Psychologist, 44,* 329–335.

*Rangaswaami, K. (1990). Anger management: A case report. *Indian Journal of Clinical Psychology, 17,* 49–51.

*Raynor, C. M. (1992). Managing angry feelings: Teaching troubled children to cope. *Perspectives in Psychiatric Care, 28,* 11–14.

*Saylor, C. F., Benson, B., & Einhaus, L. (1985). Evaluation of an anger management program for aggressive boys in inpatient treatment. *Journal of Child and Adolescent Psychotherapy, 2,* 5–15.

*Schlichter, K. J., & Horan, J. J. (1981). Effects of stress inoculation on the anger and aggression management skills of institutionalized juvenile delinquents. *Cognitive Therapy and Research, 5,* 359–365.

Shantz, C. (1983). Social cognition. In P. Mussen (Ed.), *Handbook of child psychology: Vol. 3. Cognitive development* (pp. 495–547). New York: Wiley.

Smith, D. C., Adelman, H. S., Nelson, P., Taylor, L., & Phares, V. (1987). Perceived control at school and problem behavior and attitudes. *Journal of School Psychology, 25,* 167–176.

Smith, D. C., & Furlong, M. E. (1994). Correlates of anger, hostility, and aggression in children and adolescents. In M. J. Furlong & D. C. Smith (Eds.), *Anger, hostility, and aggression: Assessment, prevention, and intervention strategies for youth* (pp. 15–38). New York: Wiley.

*Smith, S. W., Siegal, E. M., Conner, A. M., & Thomas, S. B. (1994). Effects of cognitive–behavioral training on angry behavior and aggression of three elementary aged students. *Behavioral Disorders, 19,* 126–135.

Spielberger, C. D., Johnson, E. H., Russell, S. E., Crane, R. J., Jacobs, G. A., & Worden, T. J. (1985). The experience and expression of anger: Construction and validation of an anger expression scale. In M. A. Chesney & R. H. Rosenman (Eds.), *Anger and hostility in cardiovascular and behavioral disorders* (pp. 5–29). New York: Hemisphere.

Spielberger, C. D., Krasner, S. S., & Solomon, E. P. (1988). The experience, expression, and control of anger. In M. P. Janisse (Ed.), *Health psychology: Individual differences and stress* (pp. 89–108). New York: Springer-Verlag.

*Spirito, A., Finch, J., Smith, T. L., & Cooley, W. H. (1981). Stress inoculation for anger and anxiety control: A case study with an emotionally disturbed boy. *Journal of Clinical Psychology,* 60–70.

*Stern, S. B. (1999). Anger management in parent–adolescent conflict. *American Journal of Family Therapy, 27,* 181–193.

Tolan, P. H., Guerra, N. G., & Kendall, P. C. (1995). A developmental–ecological perspective on antisocial behavior in children and adolescents: Toward a unified risk and intervention framework. *Journal of Consulting and Clinical Psychology, 63,* 579–584.

*Valliant, P. M., Hensen, B., & Raven-Brook, L. (1995). Brief cognitive behavioral therapy with male adolescent offenders in open custody or on probation: An evaluation of management of anger. *Psychological Reports, 76,* 1056–1058.

Williams, R., & Williams, V. (1993). *Anger kills.* New York: Time Books.

14 | Practical Solutions to Violence in American Schools

Andrew K. Tobias

It is thought that life is a contest between destruction and education. It is crucial in the democratic society of the United States that we ensure the victor is education. Most individuals assumed the destruction would be World War III or some nuclear eradication. It looks as if the destruction and devastation may be internal, possibly "homegrown" (Futrell & Powell, 1999).

Society's concern about school violence is revealed in media reports, Congressional hearings, educational summits, and a variety of reports and analyses that keenly accentuate the pervasiveness of the problem. The magnitude of the nation's concern is nowhere reflected more urgently than in Goal 7 of the "Goals 2000: Educate America Act," adopted by Congress and signed into law by President Bill Clinton in March 1994. This goal states that "by the year 2000, every school in America will be free of drugs and violence [and] will offer a disciplined environment conducive to learning." The subsequent report for this goal suggests that no child or youth needs to be afraid of traveling to school, attending school, or being coerced into making unsafe choices (Futrell & Powell, 1999).

It is difficult for students in violent-prone schools to complete assignments, accomplish goals and objectives, or remain in school. When administrators, teachers, parents, community members, and students are more concerned about their safety than about education, it makes teaching and learning nearly impossible.

This chapter explores some of the facts about school violence. It also focuses on the impact of school violence and provides a better understanding of this epidemic. In addition, this chapter looks at some of the pragmatic interventions to violence in American schools. The emphasis is on 9 logical interventions: administrative, teacher focused, curriculum, community based, legal solutions (state and federal), physical school and facility alterations, security personnel, student oriented, and parent oriented. Useful definitions of violence and discipline are assessed carefully, along with the current tenor of practice toward eradicating violence in American schools.

SOME FACTS ABOUT SCHOOL VIOLENCE

Violence continues to be the most perplexing problem facing American schools today. Every Gallup poll, except one since 1969, has indicated that school violence is the most significant concern facing public schools (Purris & Leonard, 1988). School officials persist on searching for solutions to the mounting enigma of violence. In-school suspensions and out-of-school suspensions are increasing, with 20.2% of students being suspended from public schools. Public schools throughout the nation are faced with the growing rate of violence. According to the U.S. Department of Education (1986a), 96% of all public schools suspend students for violent behaviors: 35% for selling illegal drugs, 82% for theft, and 72% for violation of laws that were reported to police by school officials. Many schools (33%) transfer violent students to special alternative schools.

School violence is like a medical epidemic. It is widespread and affects every segment of society. Schools are intimately connected with their local communities. Typically, schools are geographically nestled within the community, depend on economic and other community support, and often act as a measure of the community's quality. According to a recent statement by U.S. Education Secretary Richard W. Riley, all communities—urban, suburban, and rural—have reported increases in violence over the past 5 years.

School violence is preventable. However, no single program, person, or approach can prevent violence because no single factor is the sole cause of violence. Before interventions to school violence can be implemented, it is crucial to determine the root causes. Thus, it is important to know the purpose of the crime, the social malfunction, the goal, and the desire of the violent offenders.

Suggestions for violent-free school campuses are many. First, many schools are encouraged to involve students in sports, after-school clubs, and even weekend clubs. These activities are intended to keep the students busy and help them develop some social skills. A second idea involves inviting parents to participate in educational and social programs in school. This not only gives parents more visibility but may also provide some necessary skill building for them to use in their interactions at home with their children. Third, students are advised to avoid interaction with other students who may have negative influences on them. Peer pressure is still one of the most, if not the most, powerful influences in

American culture. Teaching students to develop proper friendships early may pave the way for successful friendships later. A fourth suggestion is to teach students how to dream and stay focused on their dreams. This is the power of positive thinking. This idea helps students stay achievement oriented. The goal is to help students develop priorities and move them toward accomplishing those priorities. Thus, the thought of behaving poorly rarely surfaces because their minds are focused on something positive. A fifth suggestion is to make students more aware of the consequences for violent behavior, such as suspensions, expulsions, imprisonment, and an adverse record. Oftentimes students behave badly because they are not fully aware of the consequences for their actions. If they are alerted about what repercussions their violent behavior could have on their careers, possibly they will think more clearly before acting.

Although these suggestions focus mainly on the parents and school, it is significant to recognize that violence is a public health issue. Families, schools, and communities must work together to resolve this issue. The message that violence is destructive and offers no advantage must be heard. Violence is one of the most destructive forces in U.S. society, and if not brought under control will destroy not only schools but families as well. Therefore, lifetime involvement by every part of society is crucial to solving school violence, which continues to eat away daily at the moral and social fiber of the nation.

VIOLENCE AND THE PUBLIC SCHOOL

Violence causes major disruptions in public schools in the United States on a daily basis. Communities, school personnel, and students are intimidated by violence in and around school. It also hampers social and moral development, student achievement, and learning. For instance, 900 teachers are threatened, and over 2,000 students and nearly 40 teachers are physically attacked on school grounds every hour of each school day each year. In addition, every day 100,000 youngsters carry guns to school, and 40 youngsters are injured or killed by guns. Incidents like these make it difficult for thousands of students to learn (Furlong & Morrison, 1994).

TEACHERS

Students are not the only victims of violence in schools. Even though most teachers believe that they will never become victims of violence in and around school, quite the opposite is true. The majority of teachers feel safe at school during the day, but after school many teachers, especially those in urban areas, feel unsafe. Younger, less experienced teachers and women are usually targets, but they are not the principal victims of violence among school staff. Teachers who hold high, austere academic and behavioral standards and who insist that students adhere to them are most at risk of being victimized. Thirty-eight percent of teachers and 57% of students rank strict teachers as more at risk of victimization than any other members of the teaching staff (The Metropolitan Life Survey of the American Teacher, 1993). This insight can have adverse effects on education reform and school restructuring.

If teachers continue to be targets of violence in schools, many may lessen their stance on strict academic and behavioral standards. This most certainly is true where teachers perceive that school administrators do not support them. It is crucial for morale that school administrators provide an environment that is safe to teach in as well as conducive for learning. In addition, teachers will be hesitant to intervene in student altercations if they do not believe that parents, the community, and school officials will support them. Also, teachers hesitate to intervene in fights or other acts of violence because of fear of being sued and accused of child abuse (U.S. Department of Education, 1986b).

STUDENTS

Students in the elementary grades are much more likely to be victims of violence than those in middle and high school. The Department of Justice reported that students whose families moved often and minority students within the schools were more likely to be assaulted. Also, students who wear expensive or trendy clothing or jewelry or who bring various electronic equipment to school are more likely to be victims of school violence. Student assaults on each other continue to be the leading type of violence in the public schools (U.S. Department of Education, 1990).

UNDERSTANDING SCHOOL VIOLENCE

How serious is this issue of school violence in the public schools? Whatever the source of the problem, it is one of the most perplexing issues facing the educators. Unless something is done, the number of incidents will increase (Ramsey, 1988). A distinct, thorough definition of school violence must be understood before there can be violence-free schools. Violence refers to a forceful and intense situation that results in injury to the psychological, social, or physical well-being of an individual or group. A more comprehensive definition ascertains that school violence is any deliberate act that harms or threatens to harm a student, teacher, or other school official and that substantially interferes with the goals of school.

Discipline Problems

Behavior by a person against another person that threatens, attempts, or completes intentional affliction of physical or psychological harm can be classified as a discipline problem. The following is a list of the most common discipline problems within schools: fighting/attacking, abusive language, failure to observe school rules and follow rules of school staff, skipping classes, excessive tardiness, bus misconduct, and classroom disruption. Students who engage in these behaviors inhibit their own learning in school. According to Walker (1990), these students exhibit behaviors that hinder or vigorously contend with learning. Some of these students learn slowly and might receive little individual attention from teachers or peers. Others are aggressive and can disturb the entire learning process in a classroom. These students are often suspended or even expelled from school.

There is a trend in schools toward increased frequency and severity of students' violent behavior. Violent behaviors pose a serious challenge for professional educators, mental health specialists, and school social workers. Thus, more effective strategies and techniques need to be developed and used in working with these students.

Longitudinal studies of students with discipline problems suggest that one out of three boys and one out of five girls display behavior problems. According to The Metropolitan Life Survey of the American Teacher (1994), 20.4% of students in Grades kindergarten through 12 are perceived by their teachers to exhibit behavior problems.

Discipline referrals reached 38%, or 16.5 million students out of an enrollment of 43.4 million students. Drug referrals reached 37%, or about 16.1 million students, whereas truancy referrals rose to 9%, or 3.9 million students. All of these numbers are projected to increase by the year 2000. With current trends and the belief that future numbers will increase, there is an increasing need for effective intervention strategies (The Metropolitan Life Survey of the American Teacher, 1994).

Many of the strategies and interventions that have been suggested to resolve this issue are not used in schools on a widespread basis (Walker, 1990). Teachers view many of the methods today as too impractical and time consuming. More effective and practical techniques and strategies need to be developed for managing problem-behavior students in the schools (Stradly & Aspinall, 1975). According to Miller (1994) and Alley (1990), the nature of school discipline problems has changed over the past few decades. In the 1950s, teachers thought that fighting, stealing, and disrespect toward authority were the most serious forms of student misbehavior. Today, however, violent assault on teachers and students, gang warfare, burglary, extortion, and destruction of school property are among the major discipline problems.

Impact of School Violence

Despite the fact that there is little information regarding the effects of persistent or ubiquitous exposure to school violence, other studies have discovered that inner-city school-age students exposed to extreme violence suffer negative developmental results, including decreases in academic achievement, less supportive interpersonal relationships, withdrawn and dissenting social behavior, and increased risk of future aggression. Exposure to excessive types of violence has a negative impact on the youths' coping mechanisms and overall social functioning. The impact may also result from less serious, but chronic, types of violent behavior. The presumption is that children who are the victims of multiple forms of school violence will also have similar negative impacts and will differ from nonvictims in terms of social relationships, perceptions of the school climate, school performance, and attitudes.

Although recent school shootings have elevated concerns about firearms, knives and razors are the weapons most likely carried by students in school. Approximately 100,000 to 135,000 guns are brought to school on a daily basis nationwide. Between 1992 and 1995, firearms accounted for 103 to 131 fatalities in schools. Although firearms pose a serious threat to children's safety, only about 1% of firearm-related deaths occur in school-age children on or around the school. A total of 22% of boys and 4% of girls report that they have brought weapons to school at some time. Why? Of the responses, 66% of students said to gain "acceptance" from peers and 44% cited "protection" as their reason. Twenty-two percent of students in Grades 9–12 have carried a weapon at least once during a 30-day survey period. Nearly one third of these students carried a gun (The Metropolitan Life Survey of the American Teacher, 1993).

Predicting School Violence

The interest in predicting school violence stems from a desire to prevent it rather than an attempt to control or limit it after it occurs. Ideally, if educators ascertain the conditions that breed violence, and the types of students most likely to engage in it, auspicious interventions could be initiated to prevent its occurrence. According to Larson (1994), school violence prevention is based on two predictor variables: personality and situational factors, and their interaction. One preeminent factor in prediction is that the probability of future school violence increases with every violent deed. Thus, it is predicted that students who are exposed to these events will more likely engage in school violence.

Crime and violence continue to reek havoc on U.S. public schools. For instance, during the 1996–1997 school year, more than half of U.S. public schools reported experiencing at least one crime, and 1 in 10 schools reported at least one serious violent crime during that school year (Futrell & Powell, 1999). Most public schools reported having zero-tolerance policies toward serious offenses. Many schools also used low-level security measures. In addition, most schools reported having formal school violence prevention programs (Stephens, 1994).

PERCEPTIONS OF SCHOOL VIOLENCE

Most teachers (77%) from elementary through high school feel safe in and around school. However, only 50% of students in elementary through high school feel very safe in and around school. Of students in Grades 3–12, 20% feel that threats and the use of weapons are major problems in their schools. Nearly one fourth, or 22%, of students in Grades 3–12 are concerned that they will be harmed while at school. Approximately 160,000 students miss class each school day because of fear of physical harm (The Metropolitan Life Survey of the American Teacher, 1994).

Almost one half (43%) of the public believes that there is more crime in their neighborhoods. Only 17% feel there is less crime in their neighborhoods. Juveniles account for 12.8% of all crime. The majority of the public (80%) is in favor of putting more police on the streets and paying higher taxes to do it. A total of 82% of the public want to make it harder to parole violent inmates, and 79% want tougher sentences for all crimes (The Metropolitan Life Survey of the American Teacher, 1993).

PRACTICAL INTERVENTIONS
TO SCHOOL VIOLENCE

Although schools usually provide a safe environment for learning, violence is an increasing concern for public schools nationwide. Most teachers, counselors, and administrators have received many in-service programs and workshops to learn how to better manage violent students. However, student-to-staff ratios often make it difficult to implement new approaches. The existence of violence in schools is a reflection of violence that occurs in communities and societies. Because of the intricate nature of violent issues, school-based violence prevention programs should be thorough and exhaustive to provide a safe and conducive environment for spiritual, physical, and psychological growth. According to Goldstein (1994), there are nine categories of potential solutions to school violence. I discuss the nine categories in the following sections: administrative, teacher focused, curriculum, community based, legal solutions (state and federal), physical school and facility alterations, security personnel, student oriented, and parent oriented.

Administrative-Oriented Interventions

The implementation of these interventions can help deter violence in the schools. Administrators are the key figures in preventing the spread of violence in the schools. Once a school has hired an administrator to manage discipline problems, it is important that teachers and parents understand these procedures. These practices and procedures should be openly discussed within the faculty, and also by parents and students.

Principal Availability and Visibility
The single most important factor in establishing an environment conducive to learning is having a principal who is observable and accessible.

Enhancement of Communication Skills by Administrators
In working with students today, it is crucial that administrators are skilled in verbal and especially nonverbal communication with students.

School-Procedures Manual
The development of a manual for handling discipline problems is one of the most important steps for a school. Many schools have developed lengthy and almost meaningless codes of conduct, which are printed in students' handbooks but have little or no meaning to the student body. There are some basic principles, which should be adhered to, for developing an effective procedural manual, such as (a) recognition and identification of student misbehavior, (b) specific remedial and preventive actions to be taken at each level, and (c) identification of specific personnel to be involved at each step of the disciplinary process. Once these aspects are identified and delineated, it would be relatively easy for the school staff to incorporate other essential operational details.

Clear Lines of Responsibility and Authority Among Administrators
Teachers and students should know which administrators to turn to for specific concerns at school.

School Safety Committee
Safety committees should involve representatives of those groups that will be directly affected by the rules and procedures developed by these committees—teachers, students, administrators, parents, and members of the community. Other administrative-oriented interventions include (a) school administration and police coordination, (b) aggression management training for administrators, (c) use of skilled conflict negotiators, (d) democratized school governance, (e) relaxation of arbitrary rules, (f) effective intelligence networking, (g) human relations courses, (h) written codes of rights and responsibilities, and (i) increased knowledge by administrators of students with behavior problems.

Teacher-Focused Interventions

Just as in curriculum design and implementation, the teacher must assume the responsibility for playing an important ongoing role in behavior management. That means that he or she must become involved as a designer and initiator of effective behavioral actions and activities. Teacher emphasis must be concerned with the fact that student behavior is directly affected by classroom instruction, expectations of students, and the frequency of students' performance success. Teacher-oriented interventions include the following: (a) individualized teaching strategies, (b) firm, fair, consistent teacher discipline, (c) increased teacher–parent interaction, (d) enhanced teacher knowledge of problem-behavior students, (e) low teacher–pupil ratio, (f) increased teacher– student nonclass contact, (g) aggression-management training for teachers, (h) teacher–student–administrator group discussion, (i) robbery, rape, hostage-taking survival training, (j) instructions on dangerous settings, and (k) self-defense training.

Curriculum-Oriented Interventions

Because there is a direct relationship between classroom demands and potential student frustrations, and consequent discipline problems, it is imperative that each staff member devotes time to the selection of curriculum material that gives each student the best opportunity to succeed. Learning activities must be selected with the student's skills, functioning level, and knowledge base in mind. The following list of interventions can prove helpful in preventing violence in the schools: (a) developing schools within schools, (b) career preparation courses and activities, (c) law courses, (d) police courses, (e) continuation centers (street academies, evening high schools), (f) more art and music courses, (g) apprenticeship programs, (h) courses dealing with practical aspects of adult life, (i) prescriptively tailored course sequences, (j) work-study programs, (k) equivalency diplomas, (l) learning centers (magnet schools, education parks), (m) minischools, (n) self-paced instruction, and (o) idiographic grading.

Community-Oriented Interventions

If community assistance is to be effective, there must be clearly delineated guidelines for community involvement in the daily operations of the school. These guidelines must be written and structured so that both staff and members of the community can function within them. This encompasses understanding of roles, functions, and responsibilities, as well as the operational structure for each individual. More and more schools are using a communitywide parent structure as a means of preventing and resolving violence in the schools. The following interventions can be effective in combating violence: (a) adopt-a-school programs, (b) open schools to community use after hours, (c) improved school–juvenile court liaison, (d) neighborhood day, (e) community education programs, (f) more effective programs and training for disruptive students, (g) school–community resource coordinator, (h) helping-hands programs, (i) restitution programs, (j) vandalism-prevention education, (k) mass-media publication of cost of vandalism, (l) family back-to-school week, (m) vandalism watch on or near school grounds via mobile homes, and (n) encourage reporting of vandalism by those who observe it.

Legal Interventions (State and Federal)

One method of prevention that has proved effective is having students and parents be held legally responsible for students' behavior. Putting the burden on the shoulders of parents and students can teach both that there are specific consequences to pay for certain behavior. There have been mixed results on the success of this method; nevertheless, it is widely used in many schools. Some of the legal interventions that can help stem the tide of violence in schools include the following: (a) establish a uniform violence and vandalism reporting system, (b) establish a state anti-violence advisory committee, (c) enhance national and moral leadership, (d) have better coordination of relevant federal, state, and community agencies, (e) implement stronger gun-control legislation, (f) enforce stronger antitrespass legislation, (g) introduce more prosocial child-labor laws, (h) teach law courses, and (i) hold parents legally responsible for their child's behavior.

Physical School Interventions (Alterations)

Schools nationwide spend millions of dollars each year for the destruction to facilities. Many educators would be shocked to know the degree of destruction of school property and equipment that takes place in the public schools today. Many school boards and districts have authorized experts to research this problem so that school personnel, students, parents, and community members can be aware of the cost in terms of lost time learning, down time of equipment, and money. The interventions delineated in Table 14.1 can help to offset this problem.

Security Personnel Interventions

A police officer working with students at the elementary, middle, and high school levels can be effective in reducing violence. The officer's role becomes more of a teacher than a police officer. This offers the students and the officer an opportunity to get to know and understand each other

Table 14.1 | Physical School Interventions

New Interventions	Repair/Replace Existing Interventions
Reduce school size	Use extensive lighting program
Reduce class size	Close off isolated areas
Sponsor clean-up, pick-up, fix-up days	Increase staff supervision
Employ personal alarm system	Remove tempting vandalism targets
Implement rapid repair of vandalism targets	Recess fixtures where possible
	Paint lockers bright colors
Use electronic monitoring for weapons detection	Use ceramic-type, hard-surface paints
	Pave or asphalt graveled parking areas
Have safety corridors (school to street)	Mark all school property for identification
Instill graffiti boards	Have preventive custodial maintenance
Encourage student-drawn murals	Alter isolated areas to attract people traffic
Use Plexiglas or polycarbon windows	Deploy alarm systems
Design open and observable school buildings	
Use intruder detectors (microwave, ultrasonic, infrared, mechanical)	

better. Most schools, especially inner-city schools, have police officers assigned to their schools full time. These officers are known as resource officers. They have two basic functions: (a) to spend time in the halls so that they are available for students between classes for brief dialogue or to arrange time to see the students later and (b) to engage in discussions with small groups of students who have permission to leave class for this purpose. Both schools and police personnel view these programs as successful. The following are security personnel interventions that could be useful in deterring violence in the schools: (a) use of police K-9 patrol units, (b) use of security personnel for crowd control, (c) use of security personnel for record keeping, (d) use of security personnel for teaching (e.g., law courses, self-defense training), (e) police helicopter surveillance, (f) use of security personnel for intelligence gathering, (g) use of police officers as resources within the school, and (h) use of police officers as faculty members.

Student-Oriented Interventions

In addition to individual student frustration and anger incidents, many school discipline problems stem from some kind of dissenting student leadership, either through direct overt behavior from the leadership group or by the environment created as a result of the actions of this group. Often these negative groups have more influence over some students than do teachers. Every school should have some type of program to assist students in adjusting to a world of challenge. Students who are involved in fights and aggressive acts against others in school are expressing symptoms of deeper problems, which usually lead them toward bullying and/or gangs. The student-oriented interventions outlined in Table 14.2 can help prevent violence in school.

Parent-Oriented Interventions

Parents must accept equal responsibility in resolving their children's discipline problems. However, many parents are too emotionally involved with their children to function positively when consistent and firm discipline is required, or they lack the skills to know what to do to help discipline their children. It is not uncommon to find parents who have given up in regard to discipline with their children, respect, and other socialization skills. Therefore, effective parental strategies must include some help for training parents. The following parental interventions can help diminish violence in the schools: (a) telephone campaigns to encourage PTA attendance, (b) parental-skills training, (c) parents as guest speakers, (d) increased parent legal responsibility for their children's behavior, (e) family education centers, (f) parent–student nonviolent contracts, (g) antitruancy committee (parent, counselor, student), (h) parents as apprenticeship resources, (i) parents as work-study contacts, and (j) involve, don't just invite, parents in school (give them specific responsibilities, such as room mom or dad, activity coordinator, or community liaison).

There are alternatives to violence in schools. A variety of school-based interventions are being implemented to address school violence and to educate students, school personnel, parents, and community members about alternatives to violence. As mentioned in the nine types of interventions to school violence, promising programs require a comprehensive

Table 14.2 | Student-Oriented Interventions

Counseling Interventions	Training Interventions	Structural Interventions
Group counseling	Problem solving	School transfer
Individual counseling	Interpersonal skills	Student advisory
Peer facilitation programs	Moral education	committees
Behavior modification	Aggression replacement	Attainable rewards
Peer mediation programs	Values clarification	Identification cards
Self-esteem enhancement	Conflict resolution	Grievance process
Academic support	Stress inoculation	School safety committees
Diagnostic evaluation		Security advisory counsel
Occupational counseling		Interracial student
Student governing boards		patrols
Financial counseling		Clear students' codes of
		conduct

approach, an early start and long-term commitment, strong school leadership and disciplinary policies, staff development, parental involvement, community links and partnerships, and a culturally sensitive and developmental approach.

Students can come away from a violent school thinking that violence is an easy solution to everyday problems or a keen, efficient manner to handle troublesome people. Educators need to pursue programs that focus on conflict resolution and problem solving. The educators' role in reducing violence should not be limited to the school but extended to parents, the media, and the community. Educators should strive to make America a less violent, more humane society.

SUGGESTIONS FOR SCHOOL COUNSELORS

The most important suggestion for counselors is to not try and resolve issues of violence alone. The counselor's role should be one of encourager, supporter, and teacher/coach when appropriate. In each of the nine potential solution areas, school counselors can provide assistance to teachers, parents, administrators, security personnel, and community members in implementing strategies and plans.

According to Myrick (1997), school counselors can provide effective interventions by having a reliable, comprehensive developmental counseling program in place. Through this program, counselors can provide assistance through six counselor interventions.

1. *Individual counseling.* This involves personal communication between the counselor and a student as they work together on a problem or an issue of concern or interest.
2. *Small-group counseling.* Small-group counseling involves a counselor working with two or more students simultaneously. In the schools, this means working with four to six students.
3. *Large-group guidance.* Large-group guidance consists of meeting 15 or more students in a group. Counselors can work with a class (20–30 students) or an entire grade (150 or more students).
4. *Peer facilitator training and projects.* Students helping students is a concept that has been around since the one-room schoolhouse. Peer facilitators function in four basic roles: (a) student assistants to counselors and teachers, (b) tutors, (c) special friends, and (d) small-group leaders. Students learn how to assist others and participate in supervised projects.
5. *Consultation.* This is probably the most valuable role for counselors to play in preventing violence in the schools. Counselors can consult with teachers, parents, students, administrators, security per-

sonnel, and community leaders in those issues directly related to school violence.

6. *Coordination of counseling services.* The counselor's role as coordinator involves a variety of activities from testing and scheduling to routine paperwork. Counselors also help coordinate the educational placement of students, which could be very helpful in preventing adjustment problems.

RECOMMENDATIONS

The final recommendations for school counselors in helping to develop a violence-free school are threefold:

1. Get on your principal's agenda and find out what his or her priorities are for the school. Previous ideas and plans are useless until you know your principal's goals.
2. Develop a comprehensive developmental counseling plan to address the needs you and your principal agree are central to having a quality school. Use the six counselor interventions to help address issues and problems before they reach the violent stage.
3. Involve as many teachers, students, parents, community members, and especially administrators as possible in developing a guidance committee that will help you establish a program to meet the needs of the students, parents, and community members at your school.

CONCLUSION

It is essential that administrators, teachers, parents, and community members work together to use successful solutions for preventing violence in the schools. Schools and communities have spent millions of dollars on security measures, but they must realize that these measures in and of themselves will not eradicate violence from schools nor make students, teachers, parents, and administrators feel safe.

We can no longer afford to overlook or underestimate the enormity of violence in American schools and the impact this has on society. Nor can we afford to continue just to suspend and expel these students, place them in detention centers, and eventually house them in jail. It is imperative that schools institute interventions that are practical and invest in the lives of youths. These students are the future of the country. They will be expected to provide the nation's social, economic, political, individual, and moral structure. Successful investments in their lives now may mean a less violent-prone society later.

REFERENCES

Alley, R. (1990). Student misbehaviors: Which ones really trouble teachers? *Teacher Education Quarterly, 17,* 63–70.

Furlong, M. J., & Morrison, G. M. (1994). Introduction to mini-series: School violence and safety in perspective. *School Psychology Review, 23,* 139–150.

Futrell, M. H., & Powell, L. E. (1999). Preventing violence in schools [On-line]. Available: http://www.ericweb.tc.columbia.edu/monographs/uds//preventing_longterm.html.

Goldstein, A. P. (1994). School violence: II. Potential solutions. *The School Psychologist: Division of School Psychology, 48,* 10–11.

The Metropolitan Life Survey of the American Teacher. (1993). *Violence in America's public schools.* New York: Louis Harris & Associates.

The Metropolitan Life Survey of the American Teacher. (1994). *Violence in America's public schools: The family perspective.* New York: Louis Harris & Associates.

Miller, G. (1994). School violence mini-series: Impressions and implications. *School Psychology Review, 23,* 257–262.

Myrick, R. D. (1997). *Developmental guidance and counseling: A practical approach.* Minneapolis, MN: Educational Media Corporation.

Purris, J. R., & Leonard, R. (1988). Student handbooks: An analysis of contents. *NASSP Bulletin, 72,* 93–96.

Ramsey, E. (1988). Family management correlates of antisocial behavior among middle school boys. *Behavioral Disorders, 13,* 187–201.

Stephens, R. D. (1994). Planning for safer and better schools: School violence prevention and intervention strategies. *School Psychology Review, 23,* 204–215.

Stradly, W. E., & Aspinall, R. D. (1975). *Discipline in the junior high/middle school: A handbook for teachers, counselors, and administrators.* New York: Center for Applied Research in Education.

U.S. Department of Education. (1986a). *Discipline in the public schools.* Washington, DC: Author.

U.S. Department of Education. (1986b). *Public school teacher perspective on school discipline.* Washington, DC: Author.

U.S. Department of Education. (1990). Opinions on education. *Phi Delta Kappan, 1,* 9–11.

Walker, H. M. (1990). Middle school behavior profiles of antisocial and at-risk control boys: Descriptive and predictive outcomes. *Exceptionality: A Research Journal, 1,* 61–77.

15 | School-Based Violence Prevention Programs: What Works

Mary K. Lawler

Schools throughout the United States are being challenged to develop and implement effective school-based violence prevention programs to reduce aggressive and violent behavior. Even though less than 1% of all violent deaths of children occur on school grounds, schools and communities have discovered through the events of the past few years that no school is immune from violence (Arnette & Walsleben, 1998; Dwyer, Osher, & Warger, 1998). This chapter describes the current state of violence prevention programming, characteristics of programs that work or have the potential to be successful, programs that do not work and why, the challenges school districts face in selecting programs that will work for their system, and a compendium of programs that have been found to be effective.

STATE OF VIOLENCE PREVENTION PROGRAMMING

The public health prevention model forms the basis for most violence prevention programs. This model includes prevention efforts at the primary, secondary, and tertiary levels. Primary prevention efforts consist of programs directed at large heterogeneous groups of people to prevent the emergence of a problem. Primary prevention programs identify behavioral or environmental risk factors associated with a problem and take steps to educate the community about, or protect it from, these risks. Secondary prevention programs focus on vulnerable or at-risk populations to reduce the risk of and vulnerability to aggressive and violent behavior. Tertiary prevention programs focus on preventing recurrence of violent behavior or further deterioration of those who have been violent (Hamburg, 1998; Haugen, 1998).

The public health model emphasizes the prevention of violence before it occurs. Many school-based prevention programs are primary prevention programs presented to the total population of students in a classroom, grade, and/or school site. The uniform nature of the intervention is not tailored to specific situations. Finally, the public health model integrates efforts of diverse communities, organizations, and scientific disciplines (Powell et al., 1996; Prothrow-Stith, 1995).

Most school-based violence prevention programs contain multiple strategies (Schwartz, 1996) and include an instructional component and a component aimed at altering classroom management strategies. These strategies often are combined with programs to teach students new ways of thinking about and managing potential problems. These multicomponent strategies are realistic because student behavior is influenced by peers, classroom environment, and school environment. Prevention programs are often organized by developmental level rather than by program type to focus on the key developmental tasks for that age group (Samples & Aber, 1998). Prevention programs, thus, should consider the interconnections among prevention components and the interdependence of different contexts (Consortium on the School-Based Promotion of Social Competence, 1996).

CHARACTERISTICS OF PROGRAMS THAT WORK

Programs that work provide individual attention to students and multiple activities that involve parents, teachers, community leaders, and neighboring residents (Haugen, 1998). More specifically, experts have identified nine critical elements of promising violence prevention programs (Safe Schools, Safe Students, 1998):

1. Clear and specific norms of behavior.
2. Skills training strongly based on theory.
3. A comprehensive, multifaceted approach.
4. Coordination across programs.
5. Physical and administrative changes.
6. At least 10 to 20 sessions.
7. Training for the total school staff.
8. Multiple teaching methods.
9. Cultural sensitivity.

First, schools must establish clear and specific norms of behavior, and these norms must be reflected in school policies that respect students. Both students and faculty need to understand that violence is not the norm and cannot be accepted within the school environment. Positive reinforcement seems to be more effective than punitive measures.

Skills training based on a strong theoretical foundation is a second critical content element. Whatever the content, it should be derived from a theoretical perspective that has demonstrated a relationship to the desired behavior change. Violence prevention programs should teach skills in anger management, social perspective taking, social problem solving, peer negotiation, conflict management, peer resistance, and active listening and effective communication. Students need to learn that when conflict occurs, everyone present plays a role in either escalating or reducing the risk of violence.

Third, a successful program will also include a comprehensive, multifaceted approach that includes peer, family, community, and media. General strategies to reduce violent behaviors of all students should be integrated with targeted programs for students with problems controlling anger or aggression. Comprehensive programming faces several challenges, including coordination among different community-based organizations, successful navigation of politics in the community and school, and a lack of parental involvement in the school.

Fourth, coordination of the diverse prevention programs offered at each school and in the school system is essential. Programs on violence prevention, drug prevention, and social competency have many common elements that can be reinforced across programs and in different settings. Identification of these core elements and similarities and differences in curricula will help teachers reinforce learning across programs. Because of the close association of alcohol use, drug use, and violence, coordination within these programs will also enable teachers to identify and refer at-risk students.

Physical and administrative changes that promote a positive school climate is the fifth essential element for successful violence prevention programs. Physical changes might include additional lighting in dark corridors or other areas of the school, school renovations to increase visibility and security, and clearing debris and excess shrubbery from the school campus. Staggering class periods for the higher grades will reduce hallway congestion and will separate age groups that often have altercations. Scheduling lunch hours by grades may also reduce opportunities for conflict.

Sixth, programs that are successful offer at least 10–20 sessions during the first year of implementation, followed by 5–10 booster sessions in the next 2 years. Comprehensive programs focused on a range of social competency skills should be delivered over a long period of time to continually reinforce skills. Schools with higher turnover in their student population may need to consider offering the complete program on a yearly basis. Schools may consider implementing these programs in early fall to help set the stage for a successful school year.

Seventh, training the total school staff will distribute the burden of implementation across subject areas and grades. The more teachers involved in teaching the curriculum, the greater the impact on students and teachers. The concepts presented in the program need to be embedded in the total academic experience for all students. Continuity and consistency in program intervention from kindergarten through 12th grade will enhance the impact of the program. Programs teaching normative education and the development of social skills should begin in the elementary grades.

Eighth, students appear to respond more positively to interactive teaching methods. Intervention programs should include a variety of teaching methods, including group work, cooperative learning, role-play, discussion, and practice of new social skills. Didactic techniques such as lectures and passive reading of materials tend to minimize learning.

And finally, ninth, prevention programs should be culturally sensitive and include various racial, ethnic, and demographic materials to fit the diversity of the student population. Additional guidance should be provided to teachers to enable them to adapt materials for particular student groups. For example, material on dating relationships may require revision when offered to certain cultural groups so that the student is not placed in conflict with family customs.

PROGRAMS THAT DON'T WORK AND WHY

Many violence prevention and intervention programs don't work because of a variety of reasons. Most commonly, the problem is the lack of adequate evaluation tools to truly measure the impact of the program. Even when adequate evaluation strategies are implemented, the complexity of the intervention and the student population may result in change of such a small magnitude that it is not statistically significant or directly attributable to the intervention.

Several types of intervention strategies have failed to reduce risk factors for crime or to prevent crime (Sherman et al., 1998). Programs that offer counseling and peer counseling of students in schools were not effective. Drug prevention classes that focus on fear and other emotional appeals, including self-esteem, also were not effective. Scare tactics that show videos and pictures containing violent scenes may encourage students susceptible to violence. The adolescent attitude that "it won't happen to me" often reduces the impact of scare tactics (Safe Schools, Safe Students, 1998). School-based leisure-time enrichment programs in the absence of other prevention programming also did not reduce crime.

Grouping antisocial or aggressive students together can be counterproductive because it establishes a negative peer group. Instructional programs that are too brief have also been ineffective. Programs not supported positively by school administration have also been unsuccessful. Self-esteem programs have consistently been ineffective. Adolescents involved in gang behavior may have very high self-esteem but still engage in violent behaviors. Providing didactic information without helping students develop the skills needed to avoid or handle conflict is ineffective.

CHALLENGES SCHOOLS FACE IN SELECTING APPROPRIATE PREVENTION PROGRAMS

Most likely, the primary concern facing most school districts is the question of resources, both financial and human. The cost of prevention programs can range from being free to the school to several thousand dollars when teacher training is included. Freeing up teacher time for training is also a cost to the district.

Conducting a needs assessment will help to identify both strengths and problem areas of the school and community. This requires an extensive amount of work by administrators, teachers, students, parents, and other community stakeholders to identify problems and goals. The needs assessment should address five areas: (a) policies and procedures; (b) architecture, landscaping, and environment as they relate to safety and contribute to a positive learning environment; (c) violence prevention curricula and programs; (d) intervention strategies for handling crises; and (e) response for dealing with crisis aftermath, including counseling. Once the needs assessment is completed, the committee can identify clear program goals and interventions to address specified problems. The process of change will take time and require periodic review of progress toward identified goals. The school needs to establish a partnership with community stakeholders. This is a long-term investment for the school and community. Many schools in urban settings may lack the organizational infrastructure needed to successfully implement an intervention program (Sherman, 1997).

Yet another challenge for schools is the need to match the theoretical orientations of the violence prevention program with the problem the school is trying to address. Gottfredson (1997) noted the prevention focus on risk and protective factors is popular among practitioners and has moved prevention practices toward plausible strategies. Some risk-based strategies reduce aggressive behavior and school conduct problems but have less effect on other measures of criminal activity.

Programs delivered by researchers are usually more effective than those delivered by practitioners because researchers attend more to issues of strength and integrity of program implementation. Researchers need to examine how programs deemed effective as research models can be transferred to real-world settings.

PROGRAMS THAT HAVE
BEEN FOUND TO BE EFFECTIVE

Even though many intervention programs are clearly grounded in a theoretical model, it is still difficult to determine their efficacy. Several extensive reviews of violence prevention programs published in the past several years have noted that few violence prevention programs have been adequately scientifically evaluated to determine their effectiveness on both process and outcome indicators (Annual Report on School Safety, 1998; Center for the Study and Prevention of Violence, 1999; Gottfredson, 1997; Haugen, 1998; Powell & Hawkins, 1996; Safe Schools, Safe Students, 1998; Tolan & Guerra, 1994; Wahler, Fetsch, & Silliman, 1997). Working with a congressional mandate to examine the effects of programs on risk and protective factors for youth violence and drug abuse, researchers from the University of Maryland reviewed and reported on 149 crime prevention programs designed to prevent a variety of problem behaviors, including violence. Most of these programs measured risk or protective factors directly targeted by the program but were found to be ineffective or to lack adequate information to determine effectiveness (Gottfredson, 1997).

Wahler et al. (1997) reviewed over 380 programs for violence prevention found in several summary compilations of violence prevention materials to identify 23 programs that are research-based and empirically effective. The Annual Report on School Safety written by the U.S. Departments of Education and Justice (1998) evaluated 24 effective school-based violence prevention programs. Safe Schools, Safe Students (1998) provided evaluation information on 84 programs, 11 of which met some of the evaluation criteria described above. The Center for the Study and Prevention of Violence at the University of Colorado has identified three effective school-based Blueprints Model Programs (1999) from a review of over 450 violence prevention programs.

Programs listed in this section have been identified as research-based effective programs because they included a strong research design consisting of random assignment to control and intervention groups and low attrition, evidence of significant prevention or deterrent effects, replication at multiple sites with similar results, and/or demonstration of both short-term effects and sustained effects (Center for the Study and Prevention of Violence, 1999). The programs selected as demonstrated programs may not have met all criteria but have come close as a group to meeting the criteria set for selection (Annual Report on School Safety, 1998; Center for the Study and Prevention of Violence, 1999; Gottfredson, 1997; Safe Schools, Safe Students, 1998; Wahler et al., 1997).

Twenty programs distilled from these reports are presented in Tables 15.1 and 15.2 by developmental age, following Wahler et al.'s (1997) format. Programs identified with an asterisk were identified in at least two of the review documents. Information not provided in the program review was marked "not available" but may be accessible from the developer or source of the program. Table 15.1 contains the programs identified for elementary school-age children, and Table 15.2 contains programs for middle and high school age youths.

Table 15.1 | Programs for Elementary School-Age Children

Title	Second Step: A Violence Prevention Curriculum, Grades Pre-K–K; Grades 1–3; Grades 4–5*	Promoting Alternative Thinking Strategies (PATHS)*
Source	Kathy Beland Committee for Children 2203 Airport Way, S. Suite 500 Seattle, WA 98134 (800) 634-4449	Developmental Research and Programs (800) 736-2630 Mark Greenberg, PhD (814) 235-3053 E-mail: mxg47@psu.edu
Website		www.drp.org/paths.html
Suggested Audience	Pre-K–5th grades	K–5; has also been tested with special needs students
Program Goal	To reduce impulsive and aggressive behavior by teaching students skills in empathy, impulse control, problem solving, and anger management	To promote emotional competence through expression, understanding, and regulation of emotions. To develop cognitive problem-solving skills
Key Teaching Strategies	Story starter/discussions, teacher modeling behaviors and skills, activities/role-playing	Didactic instruction, role-playing, modeling by teachers and peers, social and self-reinforcement
Type of Materials	11 × 17 photo lesson cards, teacher guide, posters, videos, puppets, song tape	Curriculum with worksheets and posters
Length of Instruction	Variable depending on grade and student needs	60 lessons sequenced on increasing difficulty
Cost	$245 pre-K, $255 Grades 1–3, $235 Grades 4–5	Not available
Teacher Training	Recommended; provided by Committee for Children; either 1-day staff training or 3-day training of trainers model; available through Prevention First, (800) 252-8951	3-day workshop with weekly consultation and observation from project staff to enhance quality of implementation through modeling and feedback

continues

Table 15.1 | continued

Title	PeaceBuilders: A Schoolwide, Communitywide, and Mass Media Approach to Foster Resiliency and Prevent Violence	Bullying Prevention Program Center for the Study and Prevention of Violence University of Colorado, Boulder Institute of Behavioral Science
Source	Heartsprings, Inc. P. O. Box 12158 Tucson, AZ 85732 (520) 299-6770	Campus Box 442 Boulder, CO 80309-0442 (303) 492-8465 FAX: (303) 443-3297
Website		http://www.colorado.edu/cspv
Suggested Audience	K–Grade 6+, families, schools, community media	Elementary grades
Program Goal	Decrease violence by promoting cognitive, social, and emotional competencies	Reduction and prevention of bully/victim problems
Key Teaching Strategies	Live story modeling; recognition and praise; environmental cues and alterations; peer/self-monitoring; threat reduction; Socratic questioning; response cost and generalization tools	School conferences to discuss problem; formation of Bullying Prevention Coordinating Committee; enforcement of class rules; regular class meetings; interventions with individual students
Type of Materials	Teacher's manual, students, families, mass media, community; English and Spanish	Not available
Length of Instruction	"It is a way of everyday living, learning and working"	Not available
Cost	Range of $10.00–$14.00 per student, depending on options; $255–$360 per year for class of 30 students	Not available
Teacher Training	4-hour basic, plus planning, optional site visits, and institutes	Not available

continues

Table 15.1 | continued

Title	Resolving Conflicts Creatively (RCCP)*	I Can Problem Solve: An Interpersonal Cognitive Problem-Solving Program
Source	RCCP National Center 163 Third Avenue #103 New York, NY 10003 (212) 509-0022 FAX: (212) 509-1095 E-mail: esrrc@aol.co	Myma B. Shure Research Press P. O. Box 9177, Dept. 170 Champaign, IL 61826 (217) 352-3273
Suggested Audience	K–12th grades	Pre-K–6th grades
Program Goal	To prepare educators to provide high-quality instruction and effective school programs in conflict resolution and intergroup relations; to transform the culture of participating schools so that they model values and principles of creative nonviolent conflict resolution	Teaches thinking skills to help children resolve interpersonal problems and prevent antisocial behavior
Key Teaching Strategies	Role-play, interviews, group dialogue, brainstorming, and other affective experiential learning strategies	Direct instruction via lesson plans, classroom interaction, and integration into the curriculum
Type of Materials	Curricula K–12, videos, resource materials	3 program guides
Length of Instruction	15–20 lessons, then infused into all curriculum areas	Varies by grade level
Cost	$33.00 per pupil	$39.95 each volume
Teacher Training	Required	Provided by Mental Health Association in Illinois (312) 368-9070

Table 15.2 | Programs for Middle and High School Youths

Title	Aggressors, Victims and Bystanders: Thinking and Acting to Prevent Violence*	Dealing With Anger: Givin It, Takin It, Workin It Out. A Violence Prevention Program for African American Youth (Female or Male Version)
Source	Christine Blaber Education Development Center 55 Chapel St., Suite 25 Newton, MA 02458 (800) 255-4276, ext. 2364 E-mail: Cblaber@edc.org To order: Education Development Center, Inc., P. O. Box 1020 Sewickley, PA 15143-1020 (800) 793-5076 FAX: (412) 741-0609	Research Press 2612 North Mattis Avenue Champaign, IL 61821 (217) 352-3273
Suggested Audience	6th–9th grades	African American youths 6th–12th grades (each video set is specific for females or males)
Program Goal	Build skills in solving social problems nonviolently and critically evaluate beliefs that support violence	Teaches ways to express angry feelings (Givin It), accept criticism (Takin It), and negotiate (Workin It Out)
Key Teaching Strategies	Full class and small-group discussions, games, role-playing, skill-building exercises	Discussion stimulated by videos and role-playing
Type of Materials	Teacher's guide, handouts	Video and discussion guide
Length of Instruction	12 sessions, 45 minutes each	Variable: 3 lessons per video set
Cost	$45.00 plus $4.50 for shipping and handling	$405.00/each set of videos, or $740.00 both sets
Teacher Training	Area trainers available, teacher training encouraged	Includes footage of trainers working with adolescent groups

continues

Table 15.2 | continued

Title	PACT–Positive Adolescent Choices Training: A Model for Violence Prevention Groups With African American Youth	The Prepare Curriculum: Teaching Prosocial Competencies
Source	W. R. Hammond & B. R. Yung Research Press 2612 N. Mattis Avenue Champaign, IL 61821 (800) 519-2707	Arnold P. Goldstein Research Press 2612 N. Mattis Avenue Champaign, IL 61821 (217) 352-3273
Suggested Audience	6th–12th grades African American adolescents	6th–12th grades
Program Goal	To reduce youth violence by teaching violence-risk education, anger management, and prosocial skills	To teach problem solving, interpersonal skills, situational perception, anger control, and moral reasoning
Key Teaching Strategies	Instruction, behavioral modeling, role-playing, group discussion, and homework assignments	Instruction, behavioral modeling, role-playing, feedback, group discussion, and homework assignments
Type of Materials	30-minute videotape and 142-page program guide	Book
Length of Instruction	Minimum of 10 sessions of 60–90 minutes	10 (1-hour) weekly sessions or open-ended
Cost	$250.00	$29.95
Teacher Training	Provides detailed staff training information. For consulting or in-service training, contact Dr. W. Rodney Hammond at (513) 873-4300	For consulting or in-service training, contact Dr. Arnold P. Goldstein at (315) 443-9641

continues

Table 15.2 | continued

	Second Step: A Violence Prevention Curriculum Grades 6–8* (see Elementary Version)	Viewpoints: A Guide to Conflict Resolution and Decision Making for Adolescents*
Title		
Source	Kathy Beland Committee for Children 172 20th Ave. Seattle, WA 98122 (206) 322-5050	N. Guerra, A. Moore, R. Slaby Research Press P. O. Box 9177, Dept. 204 Champaign, IL 61821 (217) 352-3273
Suggested Audience	6th–8th grades	6th–12th grades
Program Goal	To reduce impulsive and aggressive behavior by teaching students skills in empathy, impulse control, problem solving, and anger management	To teach social problem-solving skills, increase impulse control, promote empathy, and develop prosocial attitudes
Key Teaching Strategies	Lessons, discussion, role-playing, and various activities	Instruction, reading, and writing exercises; role-playing; and group discussion
Type of Materials	3-ring binder containing Teacher's Guide, detailed lesson plans, overhead transparencies; action video	Book
Length of Instruction	15 lessons over a variable amount of time	Minimum of 12 (1-hour) group sessions
Cost	$285.00/binder and video	$13.95/book (10+ $12.55/each); $8.95/Teacher's Guide
Teacher Training	Recommended; provided by Committee for Children either a 1-day staff training or 3-day training of trainers model; training available through Prevention First (800) 252-8951	The Teacher's Guide provides helpful guidelines for implementing a successful training program

continues

Table 15.2 | continued

Title	Aggression Replacement Training: A Comprehensive Intervention for Aggressive Youth	The Anger Coping Program*
Source	Arnold P. Goldstein and Barry Glick Research Press 2612 N. Mattis Ave Champaign, IL 61821 (217) 352-3273	John E. Lochman Psychology Dept. Box 870348 University of Alabama Tuscaloosa, AL 35487 (205) 348-5083 FAX (205) 348-8648
E-mail		jlochman@GP.AS.UA.EDU
Suggested Audience	Adolescents in schools or residential/juvenile centers	Middle school male students
Program Goal	To replace aggression and antisocial behaviors with positive alternatives; focuses on teaching prosocial skills, anger management, and moral reasoning	To teach self-management, self-monitoring, perspective taking, and social problem-solving skills for aggressive male students
Key Teaching Strategies	Instruction, behavioral modeling, role-playing, performance feedback, group discussion, and homework	Operant conditioning techniques and small-group discussion sessions
Type of Materials	Book	Not available
Length of Instruction	Three 1-hour weekly sessions for 10 weeks	18 weekly small group sessions, each 45 minutes to an hour in length
Cost	$19.95	Not available
Teacher Training	Dr. Arnold P. Goldstein Division of Special Education Syracuse University 805 S. Crouse Syracuse NY 13244 (315) 443-9641	Not available

continues

Table 15.2 | continued

Title	BASIS*	Responding in Peaceful and Positive Ways (RIPP)*
Source	Denise Gottfredson Department of Criminology Lefrak Hall, Room 2220 University of Maryland College Park, MD 20742 (301) 405-4717 FAX: (301) 405-4733	Aleta Lynn Meyer Life Skills Center Virginia Commonwealth University P. O. Box 842018 Richmond, VA 23284-2018 (888) 572-1572 FAX: (804) 828-0239
E-mail	dgottfredson@bss2.umd.edu	
Suggested Audience	Middle school	6th–7th grades
Program Goal	To increase discipline, by enforcing school rules, improving classroom management and organization, tracking student behaviors (good and bad), reinforcing positive behaviors, and increasing frequency of communication with parents about student behavior	Reduce fights and incidents of being threatened with a weapon by teaching students to stop, calm down, identify the problem and feelings about it, decide among nonviolent options (resolve, avoid, ignore, or defuse), do it, look back, and evaluate; tested in ethnically mixed populations
Key Teaching Strategies	Not available	Small groups targeting clarifying values, prejudice, and how to resolve conflicts
Type of Materials	Not available	Not available
Length of Instruction	Not available	25 sessions
Cost	Not available	$75 for class of 30 students
Teacher Training	Not available	Strongly recommended

continues

Table 15.2 | continued

Title	Safe Dates*	Life Skills Training (LST)*
Source	Vangee Foshee Health Behavior & Health Ed. School of Public Health UNCCH, Box 7400 Chapel Hill, NC 27599 (919) 966-6616 or 966-6353	Gilbert J. Botvin Institute for Prevention Research Cornell University Medical Center 411 East 69th St., Rm. KB201 New York, NY 10021 (212) 746-1270
Website E-mail	vfoshee@sph.unc.edu	www.lifeskillstraining.com ipr@mail.med.cornell.edu
Suggested Audience	8th and 9th grades	7th–9th grades
Program Goal	Changing norms for dating violence, gender stereotyping, conflict management skills, belief in need for help, awareness of services, and help seeking	Teaching personal self-management skills, general social skills, drug resistance skills, adaptive coping strategies, assertiveness, and decision-making skills
Key Teaching Strategies	Classroom curriculum, play, poster contest; community component includes training for service providers, a crisis line, and a support group for teen victims	Class sessions in each grade taught by either adults or peer leaders
Type of Materials	Not available	Not available
Length of Instruction	10-session curriculum, play	Number of sessions range by grade, approximately 45 minutes; sessions can be given weekly or as an intensive minicourse
Cost	Free	Not available
Teacher Training	Not available	Not available

continues

Table 15.2 | continued

Title	Project ALERT*	Reconnecting Youth*
	Project ALERT 725 South Figueroa Street Suite 1615 Los Angeles, CA 90017-5416 (800) 253-7810	Derek Richey National Education Service P. O. Box 8 Bloomington, IN 47402-0008 (800) 733-6786
Website E-mail	www.projectalert.best.org alertplus@aol.com	www.nes.org
Suggested Audience	6th–8th grades	9th–12th grades
Program Goal	Teach social resistance skills for ethnically mixed students and build repertoire of skills to resist pro-drug pressures	Truancy/dropout prevention; students at risk for drug use, depression, aggression
Key Teaching Strategies	Class lessons and home learning involvement with parents	Didactic instruction and social activities to promote school bonding
Type of Materials	Not available	Not available
Length of Instruction	11 weekly lessons in 6th or 7th grade; 3 booster lessons in 7th or 8th grade	5-month program taught daily in small group sessions
Cost	Not available	Approximately $139 for class of 30 students
Teacher Training	Not available	Offered

Note. Resolving Conflict Creatively Program (RCCP)*, Bullying Prevention Program, and Teaching Students to Be Peacemakers are multilevel programs that were described in the previous section but are also appropriate for middle and high school youths.

CONCLUSION

The selection of which program or programs to implement probably is not as critical as the process the school system and each school site should go through to get to the point where the selection is well-grounded on information collected about the unique strengths and weaknesses, or risks and protective factors, for the school and the students. It might be productive to network with similar school systems in the region to identify what strategies they have used or are using that appear to be working. This may assist in the decision on which prevention program or programs to implement. Having similar programs implemented regionally would provide resources for consultation, for training, and for evaluation of the intervention. Resources listed in the Appendix will provide additional information to assist in the selection, development, and successful implementation of a school-based violence prevention program.

REFERENCES

Annual Report on School Safety. (1998, October). [On-line]. Available: http://www.ed.gov/pubs/AnnSchoolRept98.html.

Arnette, J. L., & Walsleben, J. C. (1998). Combating fear and restoring safety in schools. *Office of Juvenile Justice and Delinquency Prevention Juvenile Justice Bulletin* [On-line]. Available: http://www.ncjrs.org/pdffiles/167888.pdf.

Blueprints Model Programs. (1999). Boulder: University of Colorado, Institute of Behavioral Science, Center for the Study and Prevention of Violence [On-line]. Available: http://www.colorado.edu/cspv/blueprints/model/navigate.htm.

Center for the Study and Prevention of Violence. (1999). [On-line]. Boulder: University of Colorado, Institute of Behavioral Science. Available: http://www.colorado.edu/cspv/blueprints.

Consortium on the School-Based Promotion of Social Competence. (1996). The school-based promotion of social competence: Theory, practice, and policy. In R. J. Haggerty, N. Garmezy, M. Rutter, & L. Sherrod (Eds.), *Risk and resilience in children and adolescents: Processes, mechanisms, and interventions* (pp. 268–316). New York: Cambridge University Press.

Dwyer, K., Osher, D., & Warger, C. (1998). *Early warning, timely response; a guide to safe schools* [On-line]. Washington, DC: U.S. Department of Education. Available: http://www.ed.gov/offices/OSERS/OSEP/earlywrn.html.

Gottfredson, D. C. (1997). School-based crime prevention. In L. W. Sherman, D. Gottfredson, D. MacKenzie, J. Eck, P. Reuter, & S. Bushway (Eds.), *Preventing crime: What works, what doesn't, what's promising* [On-line]. Available: http://www.ncjrs.org/works/chapter5.htm.

Hamburg, M. A. (1998). Youth violence is a public health concern. In D. H. Elliot, B. Hamburg, & K. R. Williams (Eds.), *Violence in American schools: A new perspective* (pp. 31–54). New York: Cambridge University Press.

Haugen, H. L. (1998). *Prevention of youth violence: A resource guide for youth development and family life professionals and volunteers.* Ithaca, NY: Cornell Cooperative Extension.

Powell, K. E., Dahlberg, L. L., Friday, J., Mercy, J. A., Thornton, T., & Crawford, S. (1996). Prevention of youth violence: Rationale and characteristics of 15 evaluation projects. *American Journal of Preventive Medicine, 12*(Suppl.), 3–11.

Powell, K. E., & Hawkins, D. F. (Eds.). (1996). Youth violence prevention: Descriptions and baseline data from 13 evaluation projects. *American Journal of Preventive Medicine, 12*(Suppl.), 3–12.

Prothrow-Stith, D. B. (1995). The epidemic of youth violence in America: Using public health prevention strategies to prevent violence. *Journal of Health Care for the Poor and Underserved, 6,* 95–101.

Safe Schools, Safe Students. (1998). (Available from Drug Strategies, 2445 M Street, NW, #480, Washington, DC 20037)

Samples, R., & Aber, L. (1998). Evaluations of school-based violence prevention programs. In D. H. Elliot, B. Hamburg, & K. R. Williams (Eds.), *Violence in American schools: A new perspective* (pp. 217–252). New York: Cambridge University Press.

Schwartz, W. (1996). An overview of strategies to reduce school violence. *ERIC Digest: Clearinghouse on Urban Education* [On-line]. Available: http://ericweb.tc.columbia.edu/digests/dig115.html.

Sherman, L. W. (1997). The effectiveness of local crime prevention funding. In L. W. Sherman, D. Gottfredson, D. MacKenzie, J. Eck, P. Reuter, & S. Bushway (Eds.), *Preventing crime: What works, what doesn't, what's promising* [On-line]. Available: http://www.ncjrs.org/works/chapte10.htm.

Sherman, L. W., Gottfredson, D. C., MacKenzie, D. L., Eck, J., Reuter, P., & Bushway, S. D. (1998). Preventing crime: What works, what doesn't, what's promising. *National Institute of Justice Research in Brief* [On-line]. Available: http://www.ojp.usdoj.gov/nij.

Tolan, P., & Guerra, N. (1994). *What works in reducing adolescent violence: An empirical review of the field.* Boulder: University of Colorado at Boulder, Center for the Study and Prevention of Violence.

U.S. Departments of Education and Justice. (1998). Annual report on school safety [On-line]. Available: http://www.ed.gov/pubs/AnnSchoolRept98.

Wahler, J. J., Fetsch, R. J., & Silliman, B. (1997). *Research-based, empirically-effective violence prevention curricula: A review of resources* [On-line]. Available: http://www.nnfr.org/violence/yvplitrev.html.

APPENDIX

1. Department of Education, Safe and Drug Free Schools Program, Portals Building, 600 Independence Avenue, SW, Washington, DC 20202, 1-800-USA-LEARN, website: www.ed.gov/offices/OESE/SDFS.
   - *Creating Safe and Drug-Free Schools: An Action Guide* (September, 1996) available at http://www.ed.gov/offices/OESE/SDFS/actguid/index.htmlor. 800-624-0100.
   - *Early Warning, Timely Response: A Guide to Safe Schools* (August, 1998) available at http://www.ed.gov/offices/OSERS/OSEP/earlywrn.html.
   - *Annual Report on School Safety* (October, 1998) available at http://www.ed.gov/pubs/AnnSchoolRept98.html.
   - *Preventing Youth Hate Crime: A Manual for Schools and Communities*, available at http://www.ed.gov/pubs/HateCrime/start. html.
2. U.S. Department of Justice, Office of Juvenile Justice and Delinquency Prevention, 950 Pennsylvania Avenue, NW, Washington, DC 20530-0001 800-638-8736, website: http://www.ojjdp.ncjrs.org.
   - *Combating Fear and Restoring Safety in Schools* by J. L. Arnette and J. C. Walsleben (April, 1998). Available at http://www.ojjdp.ncjrs.org/pdf-files/167888.pdf.

- Website: http://www.usdoj.gov/kidspage/ is a website for children and youth on crime prevention, staying safe, and volunteer and community service.
- Centers for Disease Control and Prevention , National Center for Injury Prevention and Control, Mailstop K60, 4770 Buford Highway, Atlanta, GA 30341-3724, 770-488-4362, website: http://www.cdc.gov
- *The Prevention of Youth Violence: A Framework for Community Action* by M. A. Fenley, J. L. Gaiter, M. Hammett, L. C. Liburd, J. A. Mercy, P. W. O'Carroll, C. Onwuachi-Saunders, K. E. Powell, & T. N. Thornton. (1993). (Order # 099-4109). Atlanta, GA: Centers for Disease Control and Prevention, National Center for Injury Prevention and Control.
- Facts About Violence Among Youth and Violence in Schools (Fact Sheet, 1999), available at http://www.cdc.gov/ncipc/dvp/schoolvi/htm.
- Youth Violence in the United States (Fact Sheet, 1999), available at http://www.cdc.gov/ncipc/dvp/yvfacts.htm.
3. Violence Prevention Programs, Harvard School of Public Health Website: http://www.hsph.harvard.edu/organizations/php/violence.htm.
   - School-Based Crime Prevention by D. C. Gottfredson, in *Preventing Crime: What Works, What Doesn't, What's Promising* by L. W. Sherman, D. Gottfredson, D. Mackenzie, J. Eck, P. Reuter, and S. Bushway (1997), available at http://www.preventingcrime.org. This is a large document, so download chapter 5 in sections.
4. National Parent–Teachers Association (PTA), 330 N. Wabash Avenue, Suite 2100, Chicago, IL 60611-3690, (800) 307-4PTA, website: http://pta.org.
   - *Community Violence Prevention Kit* available at http://www.pta.org/events/violprev/violprev.pdf.
5. Federal Resources for Educational Excellence (FREE), website: http://www.ed.gov/free.
6. Regional Education Laboratories, website: http://www.nwrel.org/national/index.html.
   This provides a map of links to all 10 laboratories supported by the U.S. Department of Education to provide technical assistance to educators.
7. National Association of School Psychologists, 4340 East West Highway, Suite 402, Bethesda, MD 20814, (301) 657-0270, website: http://www.naspweb.org/center/safe_schools/safeschools_disteach.html.
8. Center for the Study and Prevention of Violence, Institute of Behavioral Science, University of Colorado at Boulder, 900 28th Street, Suite 107, Campus Box 442, Boulder, CO 80309, (303) 492-1032, Fax (303) 443-3297, website: http://www.colorado.edu/cspv/blueprints, E-mail: Blueprints@colorado.edu
9. National Network for Family Resiliency, website: http://www. nnfr.org.
   - *Research-based, empirically-effective violence prevention curricula: A review of resources* by J. J. Wahler, R. J. Fetsch, & B. Silliman (1997), available at http://www.nnfr.org/violence/yvplitrev.html.

10. Safe Schools, Safe Students (1998), available from Drug Strategies, 2445 M Street, NW, #480, Washington, DC 20037, Fax (202) 663-6110 at cost of $12.95 plus shipping.
National School Safety Center, 4165 Thousand Oaks Boulevard, Suite 290, Westlake Village, CA 91362, website: http://www.nccs1.org/.

11. National Network of Violence Prevention Practitioners, website: http://www.edc.org/HHD/NNVPP/product.html. This website provides a list of materials including some of the programs identified in this chapter that are available for purchase from the Education Development Center, supported by the Carnegie Foundation.

VIOLENCE IN
SPECIAL POPULATIONS

INTRODUCTION

He was different. How hard that word sounds even now, *different*. When did "different" become a bad thing? He was tall, brilliant, and had an engaging smile. The fight with a peer began over an imagined insult that had not been intended. The Swiss Army knife (with its multiple tools) buried in a pocket became a weapon by definition later in the principal's office, and suspension was automatic. That was the rule. He didn't understand. Alternative school introduced him to a new group; they were isolated and unhappy. Drugs became their solace. One bad decision followed another. Spiraling out of control, he traded the chaos for institutionalization and stability. But these drugs took away his edge, his personality, and he traded them for those on the street. He was lost and he couldn't find his way back. Hopeless, he planned his exit. And under the cover of darkness, he executed his plan. Where before, success had been denied, at last he found culmination. A life that offered such promise ended in despair, and we are all the less for it.

This story is neither unique nor uncommon. For adolescents today, it is a "hard knock life." What could have been done to change this story? Perhaps nothing. And then, perhaps a great deal. Schools must be attentive to the emotional world of students as well as the intellectual.

This section addresses three special situations that influence the emotional lives of students: adolescents with depression, gay men and lesbians, and the targets of hate crimes and the violence of discrimination. Jeannine R. Studer begins the section in chapter 16 with a discussion of adolescent suicide as violence turned inward. In chapter 17, Mark Pope elucidates the essentials in preventing violence directed toward gay, lesbian, bisexual, and transgendered youths. Finally in chapter 18, David N. Aspy and Cheryl B. Aspy describe the problem of hate crimes and the role of violence in schools when racial/ethnic prejudice is not eliminated.

School violence is often a response to the marginality created by discrimination and isolation. Whether turned inward or projected onto those who are identified as tormentors, violence reduces options and leaves in its wake broken lives and physical and emotional trauma. For individuals or groups who are identified as "different," the risk of violence increases, and the dominant culture must stand trial for the intolerance that breeds violence.

16 | Adolescent Suicide: Aggression Turned Inward

Jeannine R. Studer

Approximately 5,000 teens commit suicide each year, averaging approximately 14 completions with approximately 65 suicide attempts each day (Tisher, McHenry, & Morgan, 1982, as cited in Henry, Stephenson, Hanson, & Hargett, 1993). Although these rates are alarming and invite public attention, this is not a new problem. The first symposium surrounding the issue of adolescent suicide was held in 1910 under the chair of Sigmund Freud.

Today, within the adolescent population, suicide is ranked as a leading cause of death, ranking below accidents as the primary cause of death and equal to or just after homicides. Because suicide is underreported by approximately 24% (Ladely & Puskar, 1994, as cited in Aquilera, 1998), it is possible that suicide may be the leading cause of death among adolescents; it is difficult to prove whether an unexpected death was an accident or an actual suicide. Teenage boys complete suicide more than teenage girls (Alen, 1987, as cited in Henry et al., 1993; Marttunen, Aro, & Lonnqvist, 1993). Five out of six suicide completions are made by teenage boys (Garrison et al., 1993, as cited in Wagner, Cole, & Schwartzman, 1995). Girls represent the majority of ideators and attempters (Kienhorst, deWilde, Diekstra, & Wolters, 1992; Reinherz et al., 1995) in comparison with their male peers. This difference is due to boys using more lethal means such as guns and knives, compared with girls (Allison, Pearce, Martin, Miller, & Long, 1995).

SUICIDAL RISK FACTORS OF YOUTHS

Researchers report numerous affective, cognitive, behavioral, and situational factors associated with adolescent suicide. Parenting and family issues, poor problem-solving strategies, psychopathological considerations, and hopelessness are linked to this public concern. Running away from home, experiencing multiple stressors, and knowing a suicide attempter or completer are also characteristics of a suicidal adolescent. Finally, the adolescent's gender, identity issues, learning concerns such as giftedness or learning disabilities, and either a real or perceived loss may also be responsible for this self-destructive act.

Parenting and Family Issues

When family life is repeatedly disrupted by parental discord, parental separation, caretaker changes, and physical or sexual abuse, suicidal behavior may be evident (Allison et al., 1995; Granboulan, Zivi, & Basquin, 1997; Wagner et al., 1995). In a study by Goldney (1985, as cited in Allison et al., 1995), girls with suicidal behaviors reported parents as being less caring and overly protective. The link between family discord and suicide was substantiated by Tishler et al. (1981, as cited in Henry et al., 1993). Arguments with family members, particularly parents, tended to be a precipitating factor in adolescent suicide: 52% of adolescent suicide attempters revealed problems with their parents and 15% communicated ineffectively with siblings.

Family structure also appears to be a predictor of suicidal ideation. Reinherz et al. (1995) stated that youth suicide attempts were reported by 10.5% of teens from intact families, 16.3% from stepparent families, 16.8% from mother-only families, and 22.6% from father-only families. Additionally, 42.6% of youths from families in which neither biological parent lived with the adolescent reported suicide attempts, and adolescents living without either parent were more than three times more likely to attempt suicide than adolescents with depression, and more than six times more likely than a comparison group of suicidal adolescents.

Researchers emphasize that support from family and friends is the most powerful predictor of later healthy development (Clark & Olissold, 1982, as cited in Morano, Cisler, & Lemerond, 1993). Because individuals experiencing a crisis are often difficult to be around (Aquilera, 1998), the real or imagined distance created between the suicidal individual and significant others may result in greater isolation, loneliness, and loss of a support system.

Problem Solving

Maladaptive coping skills (Wagner et al., 1995) and poor problem-solving skills may restrict the adolescent's ability to generate solutions to a problem; suicide may appear to be the sole option (McBride & Siegel, 1997). Suicidal youths experience a greater number of stressful events compared with their nonsuicidal peers (Cole, Protinsky, & Cross, 1992). One negative event by itself may create coping difficulties, but when this stressor is compounded by other negative events, problem-solving difficulties are intensified. Self-esteem is associated with adaptive skills. When a number of stressful events provide an opportunity for successful personal growth, the adolescent may acknowledge a sense of competence contributing to a higher self-concept (Rak & Patterson, 1996).

Negron, Piacentini, Graae, Davies, and Shaffer (1997) reported that only a small minority of both suicide ideators and attempters were able to generate feasible solutions to cope with the suicidal stressor. The persistence of suicidal thoughts by attempters was more markedly pronounced than by the ideators. Ideators, however, reported greater dissociation and anger during the suicidal episode than did the attempters. It is possible that this coping skill may serve as an adaptive mechanism to protect the individual from attempting suicide (Negron et al., 1997).

Other researchers have substantiated these findings (L. K. Brown, Overholser, Spirito, & Fritz, 1991; Kienhorst et al., 1992). Suicide attempters, in comparison with depressed adolescents, have a cognitive style that attaches more negativity and paranoia to a situation.

Psychopathological Symptoms

Wagner et al. (1995) and Kienhorst et al. (1992) reported that adolescent suicide attempters and ideators are more likely than nonattempters to have a depressive disorder. However, this symptom is complex because not all depressed adolescents consider suicide, and many suicide ideators and attempters are not always diagnosed as depressed (Morano et al., 1993).

A vast majority of suicidal adolescents were reported to have mental disorders, particularly affective disorders and substance abuse problems (Shafii et al., 1988, as cited in Marttunen et al., 1993). This conclusion was further substantiated in a longitudinal study by Reinherz et al. (1995). Male and female teens with psychiatric disorders diagnosed at an early age had significantly more lifetime suicide attempts in comparison with their peers without an affective disorder diagnosis. The early onset of a psychiatric disorder, in particular, phobias, drug abuse, and/or alcohol abuse, significantly increased the risk for male suicidal ideation during mid-adolescence. For girls, major depression, alcohol abuse, and a diagnosed affective disorder by age 14 significantly increased the risk for suicidal ideation. Compared with nonsuicidal peers, ideators reported significantly more overall emotional and behavior problems as well as lower self-esteem, which contributed to suicidal gestures by age 18.

Hopelessness

Hopelessness is one aspect of depression. Depression may be construed as symptomatic of suicidal ideation. Yet, because adolescents do not manifest signs of depression in the same way as adults, hopelessness is a better indicator of suicidal ideation than is depression (Cole et al., 1992).

The cognitive dimension of hopelessness is pessimism (Beck, 1967, as cited in Allison et al., 1995). Beck emphasized the central role of negative thinking to suicidal behavior, as well as related loss and rejection to negativity. Hopelessness prior to and following adolescent suicide attempts was studied by Negron et al. (1997), who found that attempters, compared with ideators, reported significantly more hopelessness prior to the suicidal event. Both groups, however, had similar rates of hopelessness after the suicide precipitant. These researchers also concluded that adolescent attempters, compared with ideators, had more persistent suicidal thoughts.

Running Away From Home

Physically removing oneself from daily stressors is another characteristic of teen suicidal behaviors. Wagner et al. (1995) concluded that suicide attempters were more likely to have run away from home in comparison with their nonsuicidal peers. Based on responses of adolescents in Grades 7–12, this trend was higher among junior high students than senior high school students. It was revealed that leaving home was greater for those adolescents reporting a suicide attempt than depressed/ideator adolescents or a comparison group of adolescents. These findings suggest that running away may be a stronger risk factor for younger adolescents than older teens.

Stressors Influencing Suicidal Adolescents

Myriad negative life events are characteristically experienced by adolescents with suicidal behaviors (Reinherz et al., 1995). These pressures are likely to overburden the adolescents' coping skills because of inexperience with life situations (Wagner et al., 1995).

Suicidal youths display a pattern of problems that can be identified as early as age 5 by mothers and teachers, according to Reinherz et al. (1995). For example, male teens with suicidal ideation at age 15 were reported by their mothers as being more dependent at age 5 than nonideators. When these same boys reached the age of 9, mothers reported more severe behavioral problems, including anxiety and dependency. Teachers revealed poor social–emotional adjustment and poor peer relationships at this same age.

Suicidal female teens also reveal a history of early risk factors. Female ideators at age 15 were rated by their mothers as having more behavioral problems at age 5, and at age 6 these same female ideators were viewed by kindergarten teachers as more hyperactive and aggressive than their nonsuicidal peers (Wagner et al., 1995).

Wagner et al. (1995) also compared adolescent suicide attempters with depressed, nonattempting adolescents and adolescents who were neither depressed nor suicidal. The suicide attempters reported higher degrees of family stress, concerns with sexuality, and a lack of supportive adults. Sexual abuse within families and physical violence during adolescence were also identified as possible predictors of suicidal behaviors in adolescent girls (Hawton, 1986, as cited in L. K. Brown et al., 1991). Furthermore, children who have disabilities are particularly vulnerable to sexual and physical abuse, a traumatization associated with suicidal behaviors and thoughts ("Child abuse," 1981, as cited in Guetzloe, 1989).

Adolescent suicide ideation is associated with a lower income and greater responsibilities (Cosand et al., 1982, and Smith, 1981, as cited in Henry et al., 1993). For example, married adolescents have a greater suicide rate than do single adolescents; this trend is reversed for adults. Married adults have a lower suicide rate, whereas single adults have higher rates of suicide attempts. Married adolescent males have a suicide rate approximately 1.5 times greater than single adolescent males. In comparison, married female teens have a suicide rate 1.7 times greater than unmarried female teens. Additionally, pregnancy and abortion also appear to be factors predisposing teens to suicidal behavior (Henry et al., 1993). It is not surprising, then, that pregnant adolescent females and new mothers, and those who recently had an abortion, are at a higher risk for self-destructive behaviors (McHenry, 1980, as cited in Henry et al., 1993).

Knowing a Suicide Attempter/Completer

A history of family suicide attempts is prevalent among suicidal adolescents (Allen, 1987, as cited in L. K. Brown et al., 1991). In a study by Shaffer (1988, as cited in Marttunen et al., 1993), 41% of male and 33% of female suicide victims had a close relative who made a suicide attempt or completion. This behavioral trend may occur because of (a) an acceptable form of problem solving or (b) a more permissive attitude toward suicidal behavior as a result of knowing significant others who attempted or committed suicide (Kienhorst et al., 1992).

Identity Issues

Gender identity issues are predictive of suicide attempts. Identity, the developmental task of adolescents, includes moving away from one's home of origin and developing a sense of self. This process is frustrating enough for adolescents, but for homosexual teenagers, the anxiety is increased dramatically. As teens move from home, identification with a peer group promotes self-identification, yet, for homosexual teens, social ostracism may make this supportive peer group nonexistent (Borhek, 1988, as cited in Teague, 1992). Negative societal attitudes, poor self-esteem, verbal and physical abuse from family members, and substance abuse are negative factors faced by homosexual youths (McFarland, 1998).

Gay and lesbian adolescents are two to three times more likely than their heterosexual peers to attempt suicide (McWhirter, McWhirter, McWhirter, & McWhirter, 1998). This report was substantiated in a study by Ramafedi, Farrow, and Deisher (1991), who reported that nearly one third of homosexual adolescents made an attempt at suicide, with many of these teens reporting repeated attempts. Suicide attempts were linked with significant developmental events such as "coming out" to family and friends (McWhirter et al., 1998). Individuals who recognized their homosexual orientation earlier and had an initial sexual experience at an earlier age were more likely to attempt suicide in comparison with individuals who acknowledged their orientation at an older age (Ramafedi et al., 1991). These self-destructive behaviors at an earlier age may be a result of fewer life opportunities providing a chance to learn adaptive skills.

Learning Styles

Little has been written regarding the association of adolescent suicidal behaviors and learning differences. According to McBride and Siegel (1997), psychiatric disorders that are similar to suicidal behaviors (e.g., impulse control, a low frustration level) are sometimes found in individuals with learning disabilities. In addition, these individuals often have poor problem-solving skills and a negative peer group (Wagner et al., 1995), leading to greater social isolation and suicidal behaviors.

Another group that has been overlooked in the literature is the cognitively gifted population. In a 1988 survey of students listed in Who's Who Among High School Students, 30% of the respondents stated that they considered suicide as a problem-solving technique. Often times, gifted children have not had much experience with failure, and a crisis results when they do not meet the usual high expectations placed on them. Peer relationships are another concern of gifted students, as gifted students often see things only in black or white, and they express impatience with peers who see things in shades of gray (L. L. Brown, 1993).

Gifted teens often show traits associated with suicidal tendencies, such as perfectionism and lack of humor, and they often believe that academics are equated with self-worth (Delisle, 1990, as cited in Popenhagen & Qualley, 1998). Therefore, the higher the grade average, the greater the personal value. Conversely, inferior grades are associated with lower self-esteem.

Loss

Loss is associated with suicidal behaviors. In a study by Morano et al. (1993), half of adolescent suicide attempters reported losing a significant other prior to their suicide attempt. Separation, divorce, and death are events associated with loss and linked with adolescent suicidal behavior. In each case, these external life-changing events are often beyond the adolescent's control and frequently leave the adolescent with feelings of helplessness.

There is no single predictor of suicide, but rather multiple characteristics are associated with adolescent suicidal behavior. The mental health worker has a legal and ethical obligation to intervene with a suicidal client. Although commercial suicide assessment instruments exist, they often give faulty results in the form of a false positive or a false negative. In other words, a suicidal individual may appear not suicidal on paper and a nonsuicidal person may be identified as at risk. The most reliable method of assessing suicide is to directly ask the adolescent, "Are you thinking of harming yourself?" (McWhirter et al., 1998; Peters, 1985).

ASSESSMENT

Adolescents often feel uncomfortable about revealing their self-destructive thoughts, particularly if they feel this disclosure will be met with ridicule or scorn. Normalizing the situation by conveying to the teen that his or her feelings are a normal reaction to a life-threatening event (Shreve & Kunkel, 1991) will facilitate the therapeutic relationship. When the mental health worker asks the adolescent if he or she is thinking of harming him- or herself, an honest assessment may ensue. To assist with this assessment, the Suicide Assessment Checklist may be used (see the Appendix). This assessment includes the acronym STRESS as a concrete tool to assist in the evaluation process.

Specifics of the plan. The more specific the plan, the greater the risk for suicide. An adolescent with vague, uncertain plans with few details as to how the suicide will be carried out is at a lower risk for suicide. A higher risk adolescent has a well thought-out method with a clear idea of when it will occur, how it will be carried out, and where the attempt will take place.

Timing of the last suicide attempt. A previous suicide attempt is one of the greatest danger variables the practitioner should consider because it is one of the greatest predictors of suicide. In a study by Levensohn, Rohde, and Seeley (1994, as cited in McWhirter et al., 1998), adolescents who made prior attempts were approximately 18 times more likely to attempt suicide compared with adolescents in a control group. The more recent the attempt, the greater the danger for future attempts.

Ambivalence is often displayed in suicidal individuals. These individuals do not want to die, but they do want to escape from the pain of living. The majority of suicidal clients display warning signs (Gilliland &

James, 1997). Yet, as individuals begin to improve in affect, behavior, and cognition, the next 90 days are crucial because the ambivalence may now be replaced with action in the form of a suicide attempt or completion (Wyman, 1982, as cited in Kanel, 1999). A decision has now been reached, affect has improved, and a surge of energy emerges, giving the adolescent strength to complete the plan.

Rescue available. The practitioner should consider whether or not the adolescent accounted for discovery time in a previous suicide attempt or in the present plan. Leaving an opportunity for discovery may have been a factor in a previous attempt, probably indicating that death is not the desired outcome. If no prior attempt was indicated, the practitioner should determine whether the adolescent is considering rescue time in the present plan.

External locus of control. Suicidal individuals perceive a sense of help-lessness. Negative life events such as a death or a change in schools are viewed as situations that are beyond the adolescents' personal control and power to change. Loss is paramount to this issue (Morano et al., 1993). A possible change of homes and the move to an unfamiliar neigh-borhood as the result of a divorce or parental death may be beyond the individual's coping ability.

The appearance of an unwanted stepparent or the unavailability of a previously accessible mother who now has to work may exacerbate the precipitating event. Taking one's life may be the only event the adolescent can control.

Skill deficits. Poor social skills, negative interpersonal relationships, maladaptive problem-solving solutions, and higher levels of anger are linked to suicidal individuals (McBride & Siegel, 1997). Greater stress may bring about insufficient problem-solving strategies, and as the individual becomes more desperate for a crisis resolution, suicide often appears to be the only solution. Training in interpersonal conflict resolution may improve the affective state of the depressed and suicidal adolescent (McFarland, 1998) and the personal growth of the individual.

Support system. The greater the availability of caring, concerned indi-viduals in the suicidal adolescent's life, the lower the risk factors for these suicidal adolescents. It could be that the mental health person may be the only available individual to provide assistance and emotional support (Aquilera, 1998).

INTERVENTION AND PREVENTION

It is difficult to distinguish between intervention and prevention, because an intervention with a suicidal adolescent may actually serve to prevent a possible suicide attempt. At the same time, preventive measures such as education may serve as an intervention.

Controversy exists regarding modes of working with suicidal adolescents. According to the Harvard Medical School Mental Health Newsletter (1989), because only a small percentage of teens (1 in 10,000) commit suicide, preventive efforts directed at the adolescent population is considered a waste of time. Also, adolescents using crisis services such as hotlines (usually female teens) show a reluctance to follow the given advice, such as making an appointment with a mental health worker. Other researchers feel that suicide education programs may be appropriate only for the at-risk individuals (Gilliland & James, 1997).

Popenhagen and Qualley (1998) suggested that school-based suicide prevention programs do not produce the anticipated positive results because of (a) a lack of controlled studies, (b) programming that does not acknowledge the current factors contributing to suicidal ideation, and (c) the failure to introduce the topic of depression (Clark, 1993; Ryland & Kruesi, 1993). Additionally, the setting in which the program is delivered, the time allotted to education, the materials presented, and the instructors' credentials have been contributing factors for the program success or failure (Guetzloe, 1989). It has also been suggested that talking about suicide may actually plant the idea in the teen's mind, thus making the act much more probable (Guetzloe, 1989).

Adolescents are more likely to seek assistance from peers before seeking the help of an adult. Therefore, researchers suggest that peers need to be educated about the warning signs of adolescent suicide as well as the proper procedures to follow if someone displays signs of suicide (Gilliland & James, 1997).

One common intervention used with low-risk adolescents is the "no-suicide" contract. This agreement is a short-term (usually 2–3 days) agreement in which the teen at risk signs a contract with the mental health worker (Kanel, 1999). A written contract appears to be more binding and serious than a verbal contract (McWhirter et al., 1998). The contract may be a few simple statements, such as:

I, _____, agree to:
    (adolescent's signature)
eat appropriately, sleep eight hours each night, and exercise in
moderation. When my thoughts of suicide become too strong to control,
I will call _____ at _____.
       (counselor)   (phone number)
If I am unable to contact my counselor, I promise to call the community
crisis center at _____.
     (phone number)

Signed _____ _____
       (client)   (date)

      _____ _____
     (counselor)   (date)

Other proven techniques with suicidal adolescents include cognitive therapy to reframe negative thoughts, social skill management, and family therapy.

Cognitive Therapy

Negative thought patterns may lead to suicidal ideation. Decatastrophizing, or identifying the consequences of the worst possible scenario, is one technique used to change these thought patterns. For example, the therapist may ask, "What's the worst thing that can possibly happen to you in this situation?" The answer to this question may provide the client with insight that the situation may be problematic but not necessarily disastrous (Spirito, 1997).

A direct approach that involves the active participation of the teen may help the teen recognize other options to resolve the crisis besides suicide. For example, the teen could be encouraged to concretely identify the problem and to list all the possible actions that may be taken in response to the difficult situation. Following this exercise, the teen could be encouraged to rank the options from the easiest action plan to the most difficult strategy to implement (Spirito, 1997).

Social Skill Management

Because suicidal adolescents have difficulty with social interactions, education about and practice in social skills are recommended, particularly skills that may be generalized to life situations. Role-playing exercises to develop communication skills and practicing conflict resolution strategies to improve impaired relationships may also assist teens in resolving problems at home or at school (Rak & Patterson, 1996).

Because depression and anger are common emotions found in suicidal adolescents (Wagner et al., 1995), mental health experts may assist in identifying, mediating, or altering these traits. Teaching assertiveness, active listening, and relaxation are all skills for the mental health expert to consider in mediating these emotions (Spirito, 1997).

Assertiveness

Assertiveness is one method in which individuals can do something about their problems rather than to just talk about them. Yet, there is much confusion as to the differences between aggressiveness, passive responses, and assertiveness. According to Baer (1976), aggressiveness enhances the aggressor and violates the rights of the other individual. Humiliation and domination are the intentions behind this behavior. Passive responses disregard the individual's own right, but at the same time the other individual's needs are met. Assertive behavior provides a win–win solution for both individuals.

Alberti (1986) proposed a four-step model to assist clients in recognizing and practicing assertiveness:

Step 1: "When . . ." (The speaker concretely describes the other individual's behavior.)

Step 2. "The effects are . . ." (The speaker describes how the other individual's actions have influenced his or her life.)

Step 3: "I feel . . . " (The speaker accurately describes his or her feelings.)

Step 4: "I prefer . . ." (The speaker suggests what he or she would like to happen.)

Active Listening

Listening and reflecting is another suggested method for assisting suicidal individuals. According to Young (1998), individuals need to recognize statements of affect, content, and the desired goal. Three steps are involved in this process. One, feelings need to be identified and stated. Two, the content of the message should be reflected. Three, the desired outcome should be described. This process may be summarized as follows:

Step 1: You're feeling _____ (affect).

Step 2: You're feeling _____ because (content).

Step 3: You're feeling _____ because (content) and you want (desired outcome).

This communication strategy may be used with the adolescent, family members, or both as a method to learn and practice appropriate communication.

Relaxation

An adolescent experiencing anxiety or stress may benefit from relaxation techniques. Relaxation is especially significant for adolescents who have difficulty recognizing times they are stressed. Teaching adolescents about deep breathing, body awareness, and progressive muscle relaxation are recommended techniques (Moursund, 1993; Young, 1998). The relaxation instructions should be developmentally appropriate and taught in the mental health practitioner's office so the youth may learn and practice these exercises at home (Morris & Kratochwill, 1998).

Family Intervention

No suicide intervention program can work without parental involvement. Intervention programs need specific components that will focus on changing negative family interactions to positive communication patterns to treat the family risk factors associated with adolescent suicide. The mental health practitioner may provide succor to families who are struggling emotionally, financially, or physically by referring them to social service agencies. Additionally, appropriate strategies may include teaching parenting skills and educating parents that disruption in the family leads to an impaired ability to function (Rak & Patterson, 1996), because the entire family is in crisis when a family member is suicidal (McWhirter et al., 1998).

CONCLUSION

As a society, we cannot ignore the rise in adolescent suicide. Numerous factors contribute to this concern, such as psychosocial factors evident at an early age, problems with parents, family structure, and age-inappropriate responsibilities.

To provide assistance to the suicidal adolescent, mental health professionals need to be aware of assessment variables. Inquiries about the specifics of the plan, the timing of the last suicide attempt, whether this last attempt accounted for rescue, the adolescent's locus of control, possible skill deficits, and support system availability are all major assessment considerations.

Professionals have debated about the effectiveness of intervention and prevention models. Some researchers have argued that such programs are not beneficial, whereas others have argued that these programs are effective when depression and negative factors contributing to suicidal ideation are discussed. Professionals can promote positive growth through developmentally appropriate strategies that encourage productive problem solving, social skill management, and effective family communication.

REFERENCES

Alberti, R. E. (Speaker). (1986). *Making yourself heard: A guide to assertive relationships* (Cassette Recording No. 29532). New York: BMA Audio Cassettes.

Allison, S., Pearce, C., Martin, G., Miller, K., & Long, R. (1995). Parental influence, pessimism, and adolescent suicidality. *Archives of Suicide Research, 1,* 229–242.

Aquilera, D. (1998). *Crisis intervention: Theory and methodology.* St. Louis, MO: Mosby Press.

Baer, J. (1976). *How to be an assertive (not aggressive) woman in life, in love, and on the job: A total guide to self-assertiveness.* New York: New American Library.

Brown, L. K., Overholser, J., Spirito, A., & Fritz, G. K. (1991). The correlates of planning in adolescent suicide attempts. *Journal of American Academy of Child and Adolescent Psychiatry, 30,* 95–99.

Brown, L. L. (1993). Special considerations in counseling gifted students. *The School Counselor, 40,* 184–189.

Clark, D. (1993). Suicidal behavior in childhood and adolescence: Recent studies and clinical implications. *Psychiatric Annals, 23,* 271–283.

Cole, D. E., Protinsky, H. O., & Cross, L. H. (1992). An empirical investigation of adolescent suicidal ideation. *Adolescence, 27,* 813–817.

Gilliland, B. E., & James, R. K. (1997). *Crisis intervention strategies.* Pacific Grove, CA: Brooks/Cole.

Granboulan, V., Zivi, A., & Basquin, M. (1997). Double suicide attempt among adolescents. *Journal of Adolescent Health, 21,* 128–130.

Guetzloe, E. C. (1989). *Youth suicide: What the educator should know* (Office of Educational Research and Improvement Report No. ED 316963). Reston, VA: ERIC Clearinghouse.

Harvard Medical School Mental Health Letter. (1989). [On-line serial]. http://www.mentalhealth.com/mag1/p5h-5014.html.

Henry, C. S., Stephenson, A. L., Hanson, M. F., & Hargett, W. (1993). Adolescent suicide and families: An ecological approach. *Adolescence, 28,* 291–308.

Kanel, K. (1999). *A guide to crisis intervention.* Pactific Grove, CA: Brooks/Cole.

Kienhorst, C. W. M., deWilde, E. J., Diekstra, R. F. W, & Wolters, W. J. G. (1992). Differences between adolescent suicide attempters and depressed adolescents. *Acta Psychiatric Scandinavian, 85,* 222–228.

Marttunen, M. J., Aro, H. M., & Lonnqvist, J. K. (1993). Adolescence and suicide: A review of psychological autopsy studies. *European Child and Adolescent Psychiatry, 2,* 10–18.

McBride, H. E. A., & Siegel, L. S. (1997). Learning disabilities and adolescent suicide. *Journal of Learning Disabilities, 30,* 652–658.

McFarland, W. P. (1998). Gay, lesbian and bisexual student suicide. *Professional School Counseling, 1,* 26–29.

McWhirter, J. J., McWhirter, B. T., McWhirter, A. L., & McWhirtler, E. H. (1998). *At-risk youth: A comprehensive response* (2nd ed.). Pacific Grove, CA: Brooks/Cole.

Morano, C. D., Cisler, R. A., & Lemerond, J. (1993). Risk factors for adolescent suicidal behavior: Loss, insufficient familial support, and hopelessness. *Adolescence, 28,* 851–863.

Morris, R. J., & Kratochwill, T. R. (1998). *The practice of child therapy* (3rd ed.). Boston: Allyn & Bacon.

Moursund, J. (1993). *The process of counseling and therapy* (3rd ed.). Englewood Cliffs, NJ: Prentice Hall.

Negron, R., Piacentini, J., Graae, F., Davies, M., & Shaffer, D. (1997). Microanalysis of adolescent suicide attempters and ideators during the acute suicidal episode. *Journal of American Academy of Child and Adolescent Psychiatry, 36,* 1512–1519.

Peters, L. J. (1985). *Suicide: Theory, identification, and counseling strategies* (Report No. BBB 02305). Ann Arbor, MI: ERIC Clearinghouse on Counseling and Personnel Services. (ERIC Document Reproduction Service No. ED 265 464)

Popenhagen, M. P., & Qualley, R. M. (1998). Adolescent suicide: Detection, intervention, and prevention. *Professional School Counselor, 1,* 30–35.

Rak, C. F., & Patterson, L. E. (1996). Promoting resilience in at-risk children. *Journal of Counseling and Development, 74,* 368–373.

Ramafedi, G., Farrow., J. A., & Deisher, R. W. (1991). Risk factors for attempted suicide in gay and bisexual youth. *Pediatrics, 87,* 869–875.

Reinherz, H. Z., Giaconia, R. M., Silverman, A. B., Friedman, A., Bilge, P., Frost, A. K., & Cohen, E. (1995). Early psychosocial risks for adolescent suicidal ideation and attempts. *Journal of American Academy of Child and Adolescent Psychiatry, 34*, 599–607.

Ryland, D. H., & Kruesi, M. J. P. (1993). Erratum: Suicide among adolescents. *International Review of Psychiatry, 5*, 119.

Shreve, B. W., & Kunkel, M. A. (1991). Self-psychology, shame, and adolescent suicide: Theoretical and practical consideration. *Journal of Counseling and Development, 69*, 305–311.

Spirito, A. (1997). Individual therapy techniques with adolescent suicide attempters. *Crisis, 18*, 62–64.

Teague, J. B. (1992). Issues relating to the treatment of adolescent lesbians and homosexuals. *Journal of Mental Health Counseling, 14*, 422–439.

Wagner, B. M., Cole, R. E., & Schwartzman, P. (1995). Psychosocial correlates of suicide attempts among junior and senior high school youth. *Suicide and Life-Threatening Behavior, 25*, 358–372.

Young, M. (1998). *Learning the art of helping: Building blocks and techniques.* Upper Saddle River, NY: Prentice Hall.

APPENDIX

Suicide Assessment Checklist

Directions: Check all that apply.

I.   Lethality of Plan
     high risk plan _____   low risk plan   _____

II.   Family Functionality
     a. communication problems   _____
     b. problems with siblings   _____
     c. family structure (e.g., divorce, stepparent)   _____
     d. support system unavailable   _____

III. Problem Solving
     a. unable to generate solutions   _____
     b. dissociation   _____
     c. pessimistic outlook   _____

IV.   Psychopathological Symptoms
     a. hopelessness   _____
     b. substance abuse evident   _____
     c. low self-esteem   _____

V.   Behaviors
     a. running away from home   _____
     b. early pattern of behavior problems   _____

VI.   Other Stressors Influencing the Adolescent
     a. sexually abused or violent home life   _____
     b. married adolescent   _____
     c. pregnancy and/or abortion   _____

VII. Knowledge of a Suicide Attempter/Completer
     a. history of family suicide attempts   _____

VIII. Identity Issues
     a. gay/lesbian orientation   _____

IX.   Learning Styles
     a. learning disabilities   _____
     b. giftedness   _____

X.   Loss
     a. experience of external events (e.g. as divorce, death)   _____

S̲ (Specifics of Plan)   _____ (very detailed)
                                                _____ (not detailed)
T̲ (Timing of Last Attempt)   _____ (recently, within past year)
R̲ (Rescue)   _____ (room for discovery)
E̲ (External Locus of Control)   _____ (does not feel in control)
S̲ (Skill)   _____ (poor)
                                                _____ (good)
S̲ (Support System)   _____ (available)
                                                _____ (nonexistent)

Assessment:
Low risk _____   Medium risk _____   High risk _____

17 | Preventing School Violence Aimed at Gay, Lesbian, Bisexual, and Transgender Youths

Mark Pope

Pearl, Mississippi. Jonesboro, Arkansas. Paducah, Kentucky. Springfield, Oregon. Littleton, Colorado. These small towns will forever live in the history of the United States at the end of the 20th century. Angry and hurting, and believing that there was only one way to handle these feelings, adolescent boys did what their fathers, culture, and society told them to do. Hurt those who are hurting you. Get revenge. Take a gun and blow them away so they can never hurt you again, ever.

"Fag." "Dweeb." "Dyke." "Geek." "Wuss." "Queer." "Lezzie." Different words having the same meaning. "You're different and that is bad." "You're different and not a member of our group," at a time when an adolescent so desperately wants and needs to belong. "Why are you crying? You must be a faggot!" said by a seventh-grade boy to his classmate. Words are powerful.

Every one of the boys involved in school shootings during 1998–1999 were called "faggot," "wuss," and "queer," and they were physically as well as verbally harassed (CNN Morning Live, 1999; Sullivan, 1998; Wilkinson & Hendrickson, 1999). "Jocks pushed them against lockers, [and] they yelled 'faggot' and 'loser' at them while they ate lunch in the cafeteria" (Wilkinson & Hendrickson, 1999, p. 50). This is the lexicon of adolescence in America. This verbal and physical harassment is designed to elicit conformity from those so targeted and security for the deliverer, "No matter how bad my life is, at least I'm not one of THEM." To be a boy or girl who is "different" from one's peers' notions of what a male or female is supposed to do or be is to become the object of derisive comments challenging one's sexual orientation. In the United States, if a teen is a sensitive boy who cries at movies or an athletic girl who wears jeans and no makeup, he or she is subject to whispers or catcalls from peers. To be different during a time when conformity to a peer group is the norm is to be a target for verbal and physical harassment from that same group, especially about sexuality (Allport, 1958).

In this chapter, the following issues are addressed: the extent of the violence against gay, lesbian, bisexual, and transgender (GLBT) youths; effects of this violence, including stunted psychosocial development; and what can be done to stop this violence, including such interventions as role of the parents and schools, separation (e.g., separate schools for GLBT youths) or culture change, deliberate psychoaffective education, valuing differences, and the power of subtle symbols.

EXTENT OF VIOLENCE AGAINST GLBT YOUTHS

Schools are social molds where rigid expectations of conduct and behavior are reinforced. Conformity is tyrannical. The wrong clothes or the wrong comment can result in ostracism. Sexual conformity is enforced most rigidly. Those that do not conform are open to the physical, verbal, and mental bullying of the majority. Reports from lesbian and gay teens range from putdowns and "rude comments and jokes" through "profanities written on my locker" and threats to actual violence and physical abuse. The overall result is loneliness, fear, and self-loathing. (Owens, 1998, pp. 95–96)

Lesbian, gay, and bisexual youths face stigmatization and a significant number of stressors in the school environment, including ostracism, physical violence, and verbal harassment (Allport, 1958; Gustavsson & MacEachron, 1998; Jordan, Vaughan, & Woodworth, 1997). The search for one's sexual identity (male or female) is an important part of adolescence (Sexuality Information and Education Council of the United States [SIECUS], 1995), but when that is intertwined with minority status— either race or sexual orientation—it is even more complex.

There is great fear and loathing of gay and lesbian people in general in the United States. Ilnytzky (1999) reported that all antigay attacks in the entire United States dropped 4% in 1998, but the assaults were more violent and led to more hospitalizations. The number of attacks dropped from 2,665 in 1997 to 2,552 in 1998; however, the number of victims requiring inpatient hospitalization more than doubled, from 53 in 1997 to 110 in 1998. There also was a 71% rise in assaults and attempted assaults with guns. Incidents in which bats, clubs, and other blunt objects were used increased by 47%.

There is great fear and loathing of gay and lesbian adolescents in particular. In fact, gay and lesbian high school students face more prejudice in school than African American teen students do, according to a 1999 CBS News poll that surveyed the attitudes of the high school senior class of the year 2000. The findings included the following: (a) A third of students know that gay or lesbian students were made fun of, verbally or physically abused, and threatened; (b) 28% of students polled have made antigay remarks themselves; (c) nearly a third of those polled have a family member or close friend who is gay or lesbian; (d) among those making antigay remarks, boys are more than twice as likely than girls to have done so; and (e) those who report their parents make antigay remarks are more than twice as likely to do so themselves (CBS News, 1999). A survey conducted in 14 U.S. cities found over 46% of gay youths who disclosed their homosexual orientation ("came out") to friends lost at least one of them as a friend (Ryan & Futterman, 1997). In a national survey of young people who were 15 to 19 years of age, Marsiglio (1993) found only 12% would feel "comfortable" having a lesbian or gay male friend. Male youths in particular were more likely to hold negative stereotypes regarding lesbian and gay youths, as 89% of the male adolescents in this study reported that they felt sex between two men was "disgusting." In a study of 27 self-identified lesbians and bisexual girls from ages 15–21 years, Malinsky (1997) found that only 2 of her participants reported no first-hand knowledge of harassment, with abuse sometimes directed at those who even associated with these young lesbians or bisexuals.

These feelings are compounded by the indifference of school workers to these issues. Derogatory remarks by fellow students directed to GLBT students are many times not challenged by teachers, administrators, or counselors, whereas a similar racist statement would more likely prompt a reprimand (Krivascka, Savin-Williams, & Slater, 1992; O'Conor, 1994). The dynamics, when such comments are made in full view of a GLBT school worker, are complicated when GLBT workers are trying to hide their sexual orientation and to distance themselves from GLBT youths (Jordan et al., 1997). Reluctant or unable to support sexual minority youth, these GLBT teachers, counselors, administrators, or other school staff fail to provide the role modeling or safety that other cultural minority school workers (e.g., African American, Asian American, Native American, or Hispanic American) provide for students from their own specific culture.

Rofes (1989) wrote eloquently about the violence against GLBT youths and pointed out its effects.

> Many young people—especially those who were cross-dressers, or young men who were effeminate, or young women who were "too butch" (tough, independent, and "masculine")—found their peers hostile, often to the point of violence. For gay youth who could "pass" and remain undetected in the school system, advocates found the hiding process robbed students of much of their energy and vitality. Whether lesbian and gay youth were open about their identities or were closeted, societal prejudice took its toll; young gay people were often anti-social, alcohol- and drug-abusing, and/or depressed to the point of suicide. (p. 449)

Anthony Gomez, a 14-year-old student at Hayward, California, tells it like this:

> A lot of people pick on me at school and pick fights with me. At school, I've had fag spray-painted on my locker, gay porn pinned to my locker, and death threats on my locker too. I had three boys suspended the other day for harassing me, saying they're trying to pick fights with me, calling me a faggot, a queer, and all that stuff. (Gray, 1999, p. 81)

Finally, the Associated Press, in an article dated June 2, 1999, reported that two college preparatory school students, one with an appointment to the Naval Academy in Greenwood, Massachusetts, were charged with a hate crime for carving an antigay slur into another student's back because he liked to listen to the British rock band Queen. Jonathan Shapiro, 18, and Matthew Rogers, 20, used a pocketknife to cut "HOMO" into the back of a 17-year-old student at the school. "There was apparently a disagreement over the style of music he liked," said Police Chief David Hastings. "Rogers called it a gay band." Hastings described the wounds as "deep enough to draw blood. When I saw them, they were three days old and they were still very visible. The letters were 4- to 5-inches high and ran all the way across his back." The victim, a junior, did not require hospitalization and initially kept quiet about the May 27 incident. He has since left school and returned to his family. Shapiro, of Keene, New Hampshire, and Rogers, of Franklin, Tennessee, pleaded innocent to charges of assault and battery with a dangerous weapon, assault with intent to maim, and assault with intent to intimidate resulting in bodily harm. The third charge made the incident a hate crime, which would require the suspects to undergo counseling and diversity training if convicted. Each suspect faced a maximum sentence of 25 years in prison if convicted. Rogers had accepted an appointment to the U.S. Naval Academy. "Once we are able to verify the charges we will have to reconsider the appointment," said Karen Myers, an academy spokeswoman.

Concerned Students of Des Moines reported that the average high school student hears approximately 25 antigay remarks in a typical school day (The Advocate, 1997).

EFFECTS OF VIOLENCE
AGAINST GLBT STUDENTS

Adolescents who are different face a variety of barriers to healthy psychological development, most delivered by their peers, family, culture, and society. Besner and Spungin (1997) reported consequences for lesbian and gay adolescents, such as high incidence of acting out in school;

rebelling against authority; abusing alcohol and other substances; feeling depressed, isolated, and confused; engaging in prostitution; and attempting suicide, many times succeeding. In a study of 34 GLBT high school students, Jordan et al. (1997) reported a clear relationship between derogatory language directed against GLBT students by their peers and adults in the school setting and self-harmful behavior, such as attempted suicide, suicidal ideation, running away, bad grades, and truancy. Considering the stress of adolescence and the additional "cultural minority stress" of being a gay youth, it is particularly disheartening to discover that a survey found that less than one in five lesbian and gay adolescent students could identify someone who was very supportive of them (Telljohann & Price, 1993).

Delayed Psychosexual Identity Development

"Coming out to self," or accepting one's own same-sex feelings, attraction, and orientation, is an important and necessary developmental task for anyone who is gay or lesbian but is especially important for the gay or lesbian adolescent (Morrow, 1997; Pope, 1995). Males tend to define themselves as gay in the context of same-sex erotic contact, but females experience lesbian feelings as insinuations of romantic love and emotional attachment (Troiden, 1979). Coleman, Butcher, and Carson (1984) gave a good explanation of general developmental stages and the tasks associated with each stage.

> If developmental tasks are not mastered at the appropriate stage, the individual suffers from immaturities and incompetencies and is placed at a serious disadvantage in adjusting at later developmental levels—that is, the individual becomes increasingly vulnerable through accumulated failures to master psychosocial requirements. . . . Some developmental tasks are set by the individual's own needs, some by the physical and social environment. Members of different socioeconomic and sociocultural groups face somewhat different developmental tasks. (p. 111)

Pope (1995) stated that this developmental task of discovery and acceptance of who one is and how one functions sexually plays an important role especially in adolescence. This is, however, also the time for many gay male and lesbian teens when there is the most denial of differences with their peer group. Unfortunately, if the developmental tasks of sexual orientation identification are not accomplished during this critical time and are denied and delayed, then other tasks are also delayed, causing a developmental "chain reaction" and thereby delaying other tasks such as relationship formation. It is common to hear gay men who came out when they were substantially past adolescence have all the problems associated with those of teenagers who have just begun dating. It is important to note that, once the critical period has passed in the developmental task, it may be very difficult or impossible to correct the psychological difficulties that have occurred as a result of this.

Adolescence is not an easy time in anyone's life because of the required psychosexual identity development, but it is even more difficult if, when a teen is called a "faggot," the teen is or thinks he or she might actually be one. This verbal and physical harassment is designed to elicit conformity from those so targeted and security for the deliverer, who thinks, "No matter how bad my life is, at least I'm not one of THEM." A large study of Minnesota junior and senior high school students found that about 11% were still unsure about their sexual orientation (Remafedi, Resnick, Blum, & Harris, 1992). Twenty percent of self-identified gay and bisexual men surveyed on college campuses knew about their sexual orientation in high school, and another 17% knew as far back as grade school they were gay. The figures are 6% and 11%, respectively, for lesbians (Elliott & Brantley, 1997).

Gay and Lesbian Psychosexual Identity Formation Process

Coming to terms with one's gayness during the teen years makes forming a sexual identity a greater challenge (D'Augelli, 1992). This is because youths are socialized in the home and school, in the media, and throughout most of life to appreciate falling in love with members of the other gender (Rotheram-Borus & Fernandez, 1995). Though there is wide variation in sexual identity formation in adolescence, some common themes emerge for many gay teens: feeling different, experiencing confusion, and finally expressing acceptance (Mannino, 1999).

Gay men and lesbians often report feeling different from others during childhood. Many of these differences are in gender nonconformity, that is, play and sport interests are more in line with the other gender (Mondimore, 1996). Boys may find they are quieter, less active, and more sensitive than other boys.

Some gay youths cope with their confusion by concretizing their gay identity very quickly. This is sometimes initiated by puberty, during which time feeling different now takes on a more clear and precise feeling of sexual attraction. Herdt and Boxer (1996), in a study of 200 ethnically diverse lesbian, gay, and bisexual youths, found that awareness of same-sex attraction occurred between ages 11 and 12 on average. Other gay teens try to deny their same-sex feelings and become superheterosexual, trying to "retrain" themselves; still others become bewildered, guilt ridden, lonely, and escape into substance abuse, depression, and suicidal ideation.

Not all gay and lesbian teenagers accept themselves, and this is understandable given the constant battering from some cultures and religions as well as from their peers, family, and society (Mannino, 1999). Eventually, however, the majority of gay youths who do accept their sexuality begin to feel a need to disclose their sexual orientation to others. There are many strategies to such disclosure, but close friends are usually told first, with parents being told later. The fear of rejection, isolation, and parental sanctions tends to be ever present, so some gay teens decide to not disclose at all, especially if they are still in high school (Newman & Muzzonigro, 1993). Guidelines for coming out to parents are posted at http://www.umsl.edu/~pope.

Savin-Williams (1990) reported in a study of gay and lesbian youths that most of those who had successfully come out to self could be described as follows:

1. They were politically and socially involved with other gay men and lesbians, had numerous homosexual encounters, regularly frequented bars, and described an early onset of homosexual feelings that were beyond their control.
2. They felt acceptance by family members and friends and felt they had more friends.
3. They felt they were accomplished and self-sufficient, but did not feel competitive and forceful or affectionate and compassionate.
4. They were generally older and well-educated, coming from wealthy urban families.
5. Possessions and good looks were not important to their sense of well-being; they measured their self-esteem by their friends, career, and academic achievements.
6. They were politically liberal and supportive of the feminist movement.

GLBT Youths Attempt Suicide

Remafedi (1987) found, through a series of studies of self-identified gay male adolescents, that they were at high risk for physical and psychosocial dysfunction as a result of experiencing strong negative attitudes from parents and peers. Following up those studies, Remafedi, Farrow, and Deisher (1991), in a study of 137 gay and bisexual male youths, found that 30% had attempted suicide once and 13% had made multiple attempts. The mean age of those attempting suicide was 15.5 years. Three quarters (75%) of first attempts came after the teenagers had labeled themselves as homosexual. Risk factors that increase the potential for suicide in GLBT youths are posted at http://www.umsl.edu/~pope.

According to Gibson (1989), suicide is the leading cause of death among gay youths. They are three to five times more likely to attempt suicide than their heterosexual peers (Bailey & Phariss, 1996; Brown, 1991;

Gibson, 1989; Hafen & Frandsen, 1986; Mondimore, 1996). Gibson also found that gay male adolescents are six times more likely to attempt suicide compared with their heterosexual counterparts.

Currently, there is much discussion among researchers about these statistics based on the skewed demographics of the populations sampled (Saulnier, 1998). The results of many of these studies have been criticized for the retrospective nature of the reports, the involvement of many of the youths in social service systems, and the recruitment of study participants from bars, which might inflate the actual numbers. It is quite difficult to gather generalizable data on this population because of the difficulty of operationalizing sexual orientation and the previously cited issues.

WHAT CAN BE DONE TO STOP THIS VIOLENCE

To prevent violence against GLBT students, schools must take an active role in eliminating such harassment. In this section, the role of parents and school workers is explored, along with specific issues dealing with separation (e.g., separate schools for GLBT youths) or culture change, deliberate psychological education, valuing differences, and the power of subtle signs.

Role of Parents and School Workers

Parents and school workers often teach homophobic attitudes in subtle, and sometimes not so subtle, ways (Besner & Spungin, 1995; Fontaine, 1997). Some adults do this quite consciously because they feel that this is the best way to negatively reinforce such behavior, that it will somehow persuade the child through their disapproval to not be gay or lesbian. For other adults, it is not a conscious process, only one that is ingrained and reinforced through others in their environment. They do not even think that they are emotionally victimizing the gay or lesbian child; however, when people the child trusts are joking about him or her, it is emotionally injuring.

Through persistent derogatory jokes, behavioral admonitions ("don't be a sissy" or "don't hold your hand that way, that's too gay" or "girls don't sit like that"), and overheard homophobic conversations, gay and lesbian children absorb these attitudes, becoming victims of the adults they trust and who profess love for them. How do these gay and lesbian children deal with this incongruity?

> Some respond by denying their sexual orientation and dating and engaging in sexual activities with members of the opposite sex, trying to pass as heterosexual. Others respond by developing a strong contempt for those gays

and lesbians who are more open and obvious. They may take out their own sexual frustrations through varying degrees of aggression toward gay and lesbian members of the community. Other gay and lesbian teenagers respond by withdrawing from society and becoming shy and isolated. They are reluctant to join in social activities with friends and family and live in a world all their own. Some of these teenagers are so filled with self-hatred they cannot find anything acceptable or positive to say about themselves. Some seek out groups that believe their homosexual orientation can be changed. These individuals will go to great extremes and will be highly motivated to do whatever it takes to be straight. (Besner & Spungin, 1995, p. 47)

In Savin-Williams's (1990) study predicting self-esteem among lesbian and gay youths, the teenagers with the highest levels of self-esteem felt accepted by their mothers, male and female friends, and their academic advisors. Lesbian youths who had positive parental relationships felt comfortable with their sexual orientation. Satisfying parental relationships, maternal knowledge of their homosexuality, and having relatively little contact with fathers predicted positive self-esteem for gay men. Mothers are important for self-esteem for both gay men and lesbians as they are viewed as considerably more supportive, warm, and compassionate than fathers. Early parent–child interactions, physical affection, childhood rearing practices, and family religious teachings are considered good predictors of the state of comfort with children's sexual orientation.

Messages that parents give to their children are important in the children's developing self-esteem. Phrases such as "Be who you are and never be afraid to express your feelings" or "I love you for you" or "It's okay to talk about anything with me, even if I do not like what you have to say, I will always love you" convey a message of unconditional positive acceptance no matter what the situation is. Unfortunately, parental words spoken in haste and anger can destroy years of positive communication. It is always important for parents to weigh the impact of their words before speaking them to their children. Never should a parent say to the child, "You are so stupid" or similar phrases even in joking, as these negative phrases are powerful and are rarely forgotten.

When a student comes out to school personnel, this is a major event in the student's life and deserves to be treated in a sensitive and caring way by the school worker. Some guidelines to help school personnel respond to students when they disclose their sexuality are posted at http://www.umsl.edu/~pope.

Separation or Culture Change

During the 1980s and 1990s, between the political far-right's attempts to take control of school boards and the unionization of school workers, the schools became the battleground on which was played many of the tough political questions of the day. During this time, the issue of what to do with GLBT students also came to the top of the school agenda.

Different schools had different responses. In the New York City schools, the Harvey Milk School was established in 1985 for gay and lesbian students who were not succeeding. In Dallas, Texas, a private school for lesbian and gay youths opened in 1997 (Williams, 1997). In the Los Angeles Unified School District, Dr. Virginia Uribe established "Project 10," a dropout prevention program offering emotional support, information, and resources to young people who identify themselves as lesbian, gay, or bisexual or who want information about sexual orientation (Uribe & Harbeck, 1992). The San Francisco Unified School District under the leadership of Kevin Gogan began a similar program called Project 21 shortly thereafter (Gustavsson & MacEachron, 1998). Most other school districts have established programs like Project 10 and have not chosen to go with the separate school, which seems to isolate gay and lesbian students from the mainstream.

Changing the school culture is imperative in this process of stopping school violence against GLBT youths. Each school worker has a role in solving this problem, including administrators, teachers, counselors, and cafeteria, maintenance, and transportation workers. School workers need tools to combat this violence, which will enable them to at least promote an environment of tolerance or preferably to promote an environment of appreciating and valuing of the sexual minority youths. Just being a sympathetic teacher is not enough, as a self-report study found that over 62% of health and education professionals said they very much needed newer and more knowledge and skills to discuss and teach about homosexuality and bisexuality (Kerr et al., 1989).

As reported in the February 10, 1999, issue of the *St. Louis Post-Dispatch*:

> A school newspaper survey in the Kirkwood Call last year showed 61% of the students who had answered said they insult people every day using such words as "gay." [Kirkwood, Missouri High School Principal Franklin] McCallie equated his student's use of "gay" or "fag" as a putdown to a racial or ethnic slur. . . . In November, his teachers took a "Teaching Respect for All" workshop [created by the Gay, Lesbian, Straight Educators Network and Parents and Friends of Lesbians and Gays]. . . . "I just felt that it is so obvious that a principal and a staff of a high school ought to be on the side of safety for all students, that it really shouldn't be a monumental step whatsoever," he said. "I'm not telling you that everyone agrees on the subject of homosexuality. I think that we are in agreement that everyone be safe in the schools." (Schremp, 1999, p. B4)

The "Teaching Respect for All" workshop was created by the Gay, Lesbian, Straight Educators Network (GLSEN) and Parents and Friends of

Lesbians and Gays (PFLAG) and is an important resource in combating the violence against GLBT students and changing the school culture that tolerates such violence. As Principal McCallie said in the newspaper article, "You do not have to accept homosexuality as equal to heterosexuality, but you do have to accept that everyone should be safe in the schools" (Schremp, 1999, p. B4).

Deliberate Psychoaffective Education

What connects the recent shootings in the schools with antigay violence is reported in the May 3, 1999, article and cover story ("Why? There Were Plenty of Warnings") in *U.S. News & World Report*: "Surely it is a rare and complicated convergence of factors. Still, experts see some common threads in the spate of shootings: These adolescent boys can't manage their emotions. They feel rejected, enraged, jealous" (p. 19). They were boys who never learned how to identify, accept, and cope with their feelings.

Boys are not taught how to handle feelings, not by their fathers or by the schools (Pollack, 1998). Pope (1998) stated that elementary and secondary schools in the United States do an acceptable job of cognitive education, excellent on information, and okay on critical thinking, but most schools get an "F" when it comes to "affective" education. This is not what is being termed "moral education" or "character education"; it is *affective education, psychological education,* or *psychoaffective education.* Teaching these important affective skills, such as interpersonal, social, and psychological skills, is rarely included in any school curriculum even though such pioneers as Sprinthall (1984) have written about "deliberate psychological education" for many years.

The deliberate psychoaffective education of American children must become a priority or we will continue to see even more school killings by young people who feel they have no hope, no place to turn, no one to talk with, no one who listens, and no perspective on life (Pope, 1998). These youths feel that any little personal rejection or emotional hurt they have is a tragedy from which they can "never" recover. Only in touch with feelings of hurt and emotional pain and having no other interpersonal skills to cope with these overwhelming feelings, they blast away, killing some whom they feel have caused them that pain and many times innocent bystanders, but it is directed at the institution they know best. Their parents take their rage to their workplace as that is their primary institutional focus; their children take their rage to their schools.

For example, in the Jonesboro, Arkansas, massacre of 10 students and a teacher by an 11-year-old boy and a 13-year-old boy with semiautomatic weapons, shooting their victims as they exited school during a fire alarm, many of their classmates now tell how the boys had talked about doing this for a while. What caused this? According to news reports, one of the boys was "enraged" over having been "dumped by his girlfriend."

Pope (1998) reported that many people and the U.S. school systems undervalue psychoaffective education. Although the schools cannot cure all the ills of society, education is more than information and even more than critical thinking. It is also about who we are and who we love during a time in our lives (school age) when we have many questions about those issues. Not enough attention to these issues is given in the schools. Schools must educate the whole child, not just the cognitive part. What we are seeing is the effect of that omission.

School counselors are important to the total care and education of students, from elementary school through high school (Pope, 1998). The following three types of school counselor activities are examples of deliberate psychoaffective education in the school: school counselors providing mental health counseling, providing career counseling, and providing a safe place to openly discuss sex. The more homosexuality is treated as a taboo subject and not discussed openly, the greater the risk of homophobia and misinformation, and the greater the risk of violence to GLBT youths.

Valuing Differences

Respecting, appreciating, and valuing differences are essential to stopping the violence against GLBT students.

> Teachers, counselors, administrators, and parents need to be more outspoken in their desire to teach their children about developing positive self-esteem and greater acceptance of differences. Although most individuals would agree with this on a case-by-case basis, everyone seems to have his or her area of difficulty in the acceptance of diversity. (Besner & Spungin, 1995, p. 36)

Because of this difficulty, inclusive diversity training workshops have been developed. *Inclusive* is used here to mean that "diversity" is inclusive of ethnic and racial minorities as well as sexual minorities (Pope, 1995). An excellent tool in teaching individuals to appreciate and value human differences is the Myers-Briggs Type Indicator (MBTI), a Jungian personality inventory. One of the most important outcomes of using the MBTI is to teach the importance of the individual's opposite personality traits. For example, although one's personality preference may be for extraversion whereas others' may be for introversion, there is no inherent hierarchy in which one is better than the other; in fact, both are required for successful functioning in the world (Myers & McCaulley, 1985).

Other tools are available for teaching multicultural and diversity lessons, including GLSEN's "Teaching Respect for All" and Besner and

Spungin's (1995) model workshop for educators on homophobia in their Appendix B (pp. 133–153). The National Coalition Building Institute, B'nai B'rith, and the American Friends Service Committee all offer excellent workshops on these topics and more (Owens, 1998).

In terms of the school curriculum, it is important to integrate and infuse gay and lesbian examples into all courses when appropriate. For example, when discussing U.S. history and the role of Native Americans, it would be appropriate to mention the revered position of "winktes" and "berdaches" (Native American terms for GLBT persons) in the spiritual life of American Indians as the shaman or medicine person of the tribe as well as the many examples of female warriors (Katz, 1976). After reading "The Picnic," a story by African American author James Baldwin, teachers can discuss Baldwin's gay orientation and the results of having a double oppression (being gay and African American).

Finally, school workers who are themselves GLBT should be encouraged to disclose their sexual orientation and be offered support and employment protection. One openly gay or lesbian teacher can affect the atmosphere of the entire school in a positive way. The importance of GLBT role models cannot be overstressed, and openly GLBT school workers challenge the myths and stereotypes for all students, not just the GLBT ones (Owens, 1998).

The Power of Subtle Signs

There are also many ways of letting GLBT and questioning students know that you, as a counselor, teacher, administrator, or other school worker, are supportive of their struggle. If, because of the school district, you are unable to be as overtly supportive as you would like to be, there remain some other ways in which you can still relay the message of your support for GLBT students.

Here are a few of the more obvious ones:

1. Have a "safe zone" sticker at the entrance to your office or classroom (available from the Bridges Project of the National Youth Advocacy Coalition).
2. Stock your school guidance office and library with literature on gay and lesbian concerns (see http://www.umsl.edu/~pope).
3. Post on-line resources for GLBT students, such as International Lesbian and Gay Youth Association (http://www.ilgya.org); Parents and Friends of Lesbians and Gays (http://www.pflag); Gay, Lesbian, and Straight Educators Network (http://www.glsen.org); Gay and Lesbian Teen Pen Pals (http://www.chanton.com/gayteens.html); National Resources for GLBT Youth (http://www.yale.edu/glb/youth.html); Oasis (teen magazine) (http://www.

oasismag.com); Outright (http://www.outright.com); Out Proud, National Coalition for GLBT Youth (http://www.cybrespaces.com/outproud); The Cool Page for Queer Teens (http://www.pe.net/~bidstrup/cool.html); and National Gay and Lesbian Task Force (http://www.ngltf.org).

4. Offer free family counseling services on campus to deal with the issues of homosexuality.
5. Use gay and lesbian positive examples in your teaching or counseling.
6. Use inclusive, stigma-free language in the classroom and in all communication, such as "partners" instead of "husbands and wives."
7. Post pictures of famous GLBT people (see http://www.umsl.edu/~pope).

By demonstrating an accepting attitude, school workers can send a strong message to students and create a tolerant environment within the entire school. The issues of tolerance, acceptance, and value can be explored under the umbrella of diversity.

CONCLUSION

The relationship is clear between derogatory language directed against GLBT students by their peers and adults in the school setting and self-harmful behavior, such as attempted suicide, suicidal ideation, running away, bad grades, and truancy (Jordan et al., 1997).

Furthermore, GLBT students are more likely to come out to their counselors than any other school worker, according to a survey of 262 men and women who were lesbian, gay, or bisexual (Harris & Bliss, 1997). Friends were rated first, counselors second, teachers third, and principals last. Counselors must be prepared to deal with GLBT youths when they do present themselves for counseling (Brown, 1991).

Indeed changes are occurring for gay teens. On January 21, 1999, *CBS This Morning* reported a story titled "Gay Teen Teaches Tolerance," about Sam Hanser, a 16-year-old high school student in Newtown, Massachusetts. Hanser told of assaults at the hands of his classmates: "A lot of people called me faggot and spat on me and did a lot of annoying things," said Hansen. But as Massachusetts was the first state to pass a law making harassment of lesbian and gay students a crime, Sam has been empowered and taken on a role of leadership. He runs a hotline for lesbian, gay, bisexual, transgender, and questioning youths, and speaks publicly about GLBT youth issues. He closed by saying, "I think that seeing diversity starts the whole process of being comfortable and acceptance of different people."

In 1998, a jury in Louisville, Kentucky, awarded $220,000 to a 17-year-old girl because the school she attended acted with "deliberate indifference" by permitting other students to call her "lezzie," assault her, and attempt to rape her. In 1996, a Wisconsin high school student was awarded $900,000 in punitive damages from a school district because it did not adequately protect him from antigay harassment (Herscher, 1998). Other lawsuits are working their ways through the courts, including the 12-year-old boy who is suing his Pacifica, California, school district for refusing to intervene in his years of harassment, and the gay teen who was brutally attacked by eight other students who secured the American Civil Liberties Union to aid his lawsuit against the Kent, Washington, school district (Owens, 1998).

A national organization called the Gay, Lesbian, and Straight Educators Network rated 42 of the nation's largest public school districts on their policies and programs designed to serve GLBT students and school workers. Only 4 districts got an "A": Los Angeles, San Diego, Philadelphia, and Dade County, Florida. Twenty major school districts received a grade of "D." According to spokesperson Kate Frankfurt, "that means nearly 2 million students go to school in districts that fail" in basic gay human rights (Herscher, 1998).

Clearly the momentum is turning toward the protection of GLBT teens in schools. In 1993, Massachusetts became the first state to ban antigay discrimination in its schools and create a statewide "safe schools" program. The U.S. Department of Education issued guidelines in March 1997 spelling out that gay teens are covered by federal prohibitions against sexual harassment.

Attitudes on sexuality are indeed changing, and this should bode well for gay teens, and ultimately the entire GLBT community. Although the message is not as strong as many of us would like, it is becoming clear that people can have their own private hatreds; however, when this becomes public as physical or verbal harassment or written into policy, it will not be allowed. The harassment of sexual minority students and teachers should not be tolerated.

Heterosexism, which according to Lorde (1984) is defined as a "belief in the inherent superiority of one pattern of loving and thereby its right to dominance" (p. 45), and homophobia, which is the fear of being gay and hatred of gays and lesbians (Herr, 1997), must be exposed just as racism and sexism have been.

The Massachusetts Governor's Commission on Lesbian and Gay Youth issued a report in 1993 that summarized succinctly a blueprint for ending violence in the schools against gay and lesbian youths. The recommendations included the following:

1. School policies that protect gay and lesbian students by (a) antidiscrimination policies that include sexual orientation for students and teachers, including teacher contracts; (b) policies that guarantee equal access to education and school activities; (c) antiharass-

ment policies and guidelines that deal with handling incidents of antigay language, harassment, or violence; and (d) multicultural and diversity policies.

2. Training teachers in suicide prevention and violence prevention as well as changing teacher certification requirements and school accreditation to include this training.
3. School-based support groups for gay and straight students.
4. Curriculum that includes gay and lesbian issues.
5. Information in school libraries for gay and lesbian adolescents.

As a consequence of this report, the Massachusetts Board of Education unanimously adopted the nation's first state educational policy prohibiting discrimination against lesbian and gay elementary and secondary school students and teachers (Besner & Spungin, 1995). Many cities in the United States have adopted similar policies in their schools.

The lives of GLBT students in the schools are getting better, and the sad picture painted by many may not apply to all GLBT youths. However, it is important not to minimize the detrimental effects of verbal and physical violence and harassment on GLBT students' academic performance and social development. What counselors, teachers, administrators, and other school workers must focus on are the recommendations in this chapter for improving the school environment and the quality of life for GLBT students. It just makes it better for all students.

REFERENCES

The Advocate. (1997, April 15). *Agenda.*

Allport, G. W. (1958). *The nature of prejudice.* Garden City, NY: Doubleday Anchor Books.

The Associated Press. (1999, June 2). *Anti-gay slur carved on student.*

Bailey, N. J., & Phariss, T. (1996, January). Breaking through the wall of silence: Gay, lesbian, and bisexual issues for middle level educators. *Middle School Journal,* 38–46.

Besner, H. F., & Spungin, C. I. (1997). *Gay and lesbian students: Understanding their needs.* Washington, DC: Taylor & Francis.

Brown, S. (1991). *Counseling victims of violence.* Alexandria, VA: American Counseling Association.

CBS News. (1999, January 21). *CBS poll: Gay intolerance.* New York: Author. Available: http://www.cbs.com.

CNN Morning Live. (1999, April 22). *Columbine High School female student interviewed on the two shooters in Littleton, Colorado.*

Coleman, J. C., Butcher, J. N., & Carson, R. C. (1984). *Abnormal psychology and modern life* (7th ed.). Glenview, IL: Scott, Foresman.

D'Augelli, A. R. (1992). Teaching lesbian/gay development: From oppression to exceptionality. In K. Harbeck (Ed.), *Coming out of the classroom closet* (pp. 213–227). New York: Harrington Park Press.

Elliott, L., & Brantley, C. (1997). *Sex on campus: The naked truth about the real sex lives of college students.* New York: Random House.

Fontaine, J. H. (1997). The sound of silence: Public school response to the needs of gay and lesbian youth. In M. B. Harris (Ed.), *School experiences of gay and lesbian youth* (pp. 101–109). New York: Harrington Park Press.

Gibson, P. (1989). Gay male and lesbian youth suicide. In M. R. Feinleib (Ed.), *Report of the Secretary's task force on youth suicide. Vol. 3: Preventions and interventions in youth suicide* (pp. 110–142; U.S. Department of Health and Human Services Publication No. ADM89-1623). Washington, DC: U.S. Government Printing Office.

Gray, M. L. (Ed.). (1999). *In your face: Stories from the lives of queer youth.* New York: Harrington Park Press.

Gustavsson, N. S., & MacEachron, A. E. (1998). Violence and lesbian and gay youth. In L. M. Sloan & N. S. Gustavsson (Eds.), *Violence and social injustice against lesbian, gay and bisexual people* (pp. 41–50). New York: Harrington Park Press.

Hafen, B. Q., & Frandsen, K. J. (1986). *Youth suicide: Depression and loneliness.* Evergreen, CO: Cordilerra Press.

Harris, M. B., & Bliss, G. K. (1997). Coming out in a school setting: Former students' experiences and opinions about disclosure. In M. B. Harris (Ed.), *School experiences of gay and lesbian youth* (pp. 85–100). New York: Harrington Park Press.

Herdt, G., & Boxer, A. (1996). *Children of horizons: How gay and lesbian teens are leading a new way out of the closet* (2nd ed.). New York: Beacon Press.

Herr, K. (1997). Learning lessons from school: Homophobia, heterosexism, and the construction of failure. In M. B. Harris (Ed.), *School experiences of gay and lesbian youth* (pp. 51–64). New York: Harrington Park Press.

Herscher, E. (1998, September 10). S.F. schools get A from gay group—But Oakland gets C in safety rating. *San Francisco Chronicle,* p. A20.

Ilnytzky, U. (1999, April 7). Anti-gay attacks said more violent. *The Associated Press.*

Jordan, K. M., Vaughan, J. S., & Woodworth, K. J. (1997). I will survive: Lesbian, gay, and bisexual youths' experience of high school. In M. B. Harris (Ed.), *School experiences of gay and lesbian youth* (pp. 17–34). New York: Harrington Park Press.

Katz, J. (1976). *Gay American history.* New York: Thomas Y. Crowell.

Krivascka, J. J., Savin-Williams, R. C., & Slater, B. R. (1992). *Background paper for the resolution on lesbian, gay, and bisexual youths in schools* [The American Psychological Association Council of Representatives Agenda, February 26–28, 1993, pp. 454–489]. (Available from the American Psychological Association, 750 First Street, NE, Washington, DC 20002)

Lorde, A. (1984). *Sister outsider.* Freedom, CA: Crossing Press.

Malinsky, K. P. (1997). Learning to be invisible: Female sexual minority students in America's public high schools. In M. B. Harris (Ed.), *School experiences of gay and lesbian youth* (pp. 35–50). New York: Harrington Park Press.

Mannino, J. D. (1999). Coming out under fire: Gay teens. In J. D. Mannino (Ed.), *Sexual themes and variations: The new millennium* (Feature box, p. 185). New York: McGraw-Hill.

Marsiglio, W. (1993). Attitudes toward homosexual activity and gays as friends: A national survey of heterosexual 15- to 19-year-old males. *Journal of Sex Research, 30*(1), 12.

Mondimore, F. M. (1996). *A natural history of homosexuality*. Baltimore: Johns Hopkins University Press.

Morrow, S. (1997). Career development of lesbian and gay youth: Effects of sexual orientation, coming out, and homophobia. In M. B. Harris (Ed.), *School experiences of gay and lesbian youth* (pp. 1–15). New York: Harrington Park Press.

Myers, I. B., & McCaulley, M. (1985). *Manual to the development of the Myers-Briggs Type Indicator*. Palo Alto, CA: Consulting Psychologists Press.

Newman, B. S., & Muzzonigro, P. G. (1993). The effects of traditional family values on the coming out process of gay male adolescents. *Adolescence, 28*, 213–226.

O'Conor, A. (1994). Who gets called queer in school? Lesbian, gay and bisexual teenagers, homophobia, and high school. *The High School Journal, 77*, 7–12.

Owens, R. E. (1998). *Queer kids: The challenges and promise for lesbian, gay, and bisexual youth*. New York: Harrington Park Press.

Pollack, W. (1998). *Real boys: Rescuing our sons from the myths of boyhood*. New York: Random House.

Pope, M. (1995). The "salad bowl" is big enough for us all: An argument for the inclusion of lesbians and gays in any definition of multiculturalism. *Journal of Counseling and Development, 73*, 301–304.

Pope, M. (1998, March 25). School counselors and whole person education [Online listserv]. *The Education Forum*.

Remafedi, G. J. (1987). Adolescent homosexuality: Psychosocial and medical implications. *Pediatrics, 79*, 331–337.

Remafedi, G. J., Farrow, J., & Deisher, R. (1991). Risk factors for attempted suicide in gay and bisexual youth. *Pediatrics, 87*, 869–875.

Remafedi, G. J., Resnick, M., Blum, R., & Harris, L. (1992). Demography of sexual orientation in adolescents. *Pediatrics, 89*, 714–721.

Rofes, E. (1989). Opening up the classroom closet: Responding to the educational needs of gay and lesbian youth. *Harvard Educational Review, 59*, 443–453.

Rotheram-Borus, M. J., & Fernandez, I. (1995). Sexual orientation and developmental challenges experienced by gay and lesbian youths. *Suicide and Life Threatening Behavior, 25*, 26–34.

Ryan, C., & Futterman, D. (1997). Lesbian and gay youth: Care and counseling. *Adolescent Medicine—State of the Art Reviews, 8*, 221.

Saulnier, C. F. (1998). Prevalence of suicide attempts and suicidal ideation among lesbian and gay youth. In L. M. Sloan & N. S. Gustavsson (Eds.), *Violence and social injustice against lesbian, gay and bisexual people* (pp. 51–68). New York: Harrington Park Press.

Savin-Williams, R. C. (1990). *Gay and lesbian youth: Expressions of identity*. Washington, DC: Hemisphere.

Schremp, V. (1999, February 10). Kirkwood High fosters a culture of openness. *St. Louis Post-Dispatch*, p. B4.

Sexuality Information and Education Council of the United States (SIECUS). (1995). *Facts about sexual health for America's adolescents*. New York: Author.

Sprinthall, N. A. (1984). Primary prevention: A road paved with a plethora of promises and procrastinations. *Personnel and Guidance Journal, 62*, 491–495.

Sullivan, R. (1998, September 17). A boy's life: Death in the schoolyard (Part 1). *Rolling Stone*, pp. 76–85, 106–107.

Telljohann, S. K., & Price, J. H. (1993). A qualitative examination of adolescent homosexuals' life experiences: Ramifications for secondary school personnel. *Journal of Homosexuality, 26*(1), 48.

Troiden, R. R. (1979). The formation of homosexual identities. *Journal of Homosexuality, 17*(1–2), 362–373.

Uribe, V., & Harbeck, K. (1992). Addressing the needs of lesbian, gay, and bisexual youth: The origins of Project 10 and school-based intervention. In K. Harbeck (Ed.), *Coming out of the classroom closet* (pp. 9–28). New York: Harrington Park Press.

Why? There were plenty of warnings, but no one stopped two twisted teens. (1999, May 3). *U.S. News & World Report*, p. 19.

Wilkinson, P., & Hendrickson, M. (1999, June 10). Humiliation and revenge: The story of Reb and VoDkA. *Rolling Stone*, pp. 49–54, 140–141.

Williams, M. (1997, September 21). Nation's first private school for gays opens in Dallas, education: Facility is run by two teachers as a haven from the harassment that occurs on traditional campuses. So far, enrollment totals seven. *The Los Angeles Times*, p. 35.

18 | Hate Crimes: What They Are, Why They Happen, and Counselors' Roles in Preventing Them

David N. Aspy and Cheryl Blalock Aspy

At first glance, the term *hate crime* might appear to be redundant in that it is difficult to imagine a crime without some degree of hate. It seems that no one commits a crime in the name of love for either the victim or someone else. Fortunately, the Bureau of Justice Assistance (1997) has generated a definition of hate crimes that delineates them sharply enough to permit a reasonable discussion of the topic. Their definition addresses both the content and motivation for the crime: "Hate crimes, or bias-motivated crimes, are defined as offenses, motivated by hatred against a victim based on his or her race, religion, sexual orientation, handicap, ethnicity, or national origin" (p. ix).

Hate crimes are not a recent phenomenon. Historical examples include the Romans' persecution of the Christians, the Nazis' "final solution" for the Jews, ethnic cleansing in Bosnia, and genocide in Rwanda (Bureau of Justice Assistance, 1997). During the 16th and 17th centuries, Native Americans were the targets of bias-motivated intimidation and violence by the Europeans. Further examples include the lynchings of African Americans, cross burnings to drive Black families from predominantly White neighborhoods, assaults on homosexual men and women, and the painting of swastikas on Jewish synagogues. One might argue cogently that history is replete with hate crimes.

Hate crimes are relatively rare when compared with other crimes. In 1993, only 11 of the 24,526 murders reported in the United States were classified as hate crimes, as were 13 of the 104,806 reported rapes (Bureau of Justice Assistance, 1997, p. x). An additional significance of hate crimes is based on the notion that they have a ripple effect in the sense that they impact an entire class of people. So, it is not just a matter of harming one person but rather of "sending a message" to a whole group, especially a vulnerable one. In biblical terms, it is similar to the concept expressed in the verse, "In as much as ye have done it unto the least of these of these my brethren you have done it unto me" (Matthew 25:40). In psychological parlance, it is akin to a generalization factor or stereotyping.

The intellectualization of hate crimes tends to diffuse their emotional content and, thus, disguise the force of the human agony associated with them. Therefore, descriptions of two recent hate crimes at two different sites are offered as vivid examples of the phenomenon: Jasper, Texas and Laramie, Wyoming.

ABCNEWS.com (1999) gave the following report of the testimony of a pathologist at the trial of John William King, a White man accused of the murder of James Byrd, an African American man in Jasper, Texas:

> The 24-year-old is charged in last June's killing of James Byrd, Jr., a black man, who was chained at the ankles and dragged to death behind a pickup truck. . . . The jury of 11 whites and one black today heard graphic testimony from a pathologist who said he thought Byrd was alive and trying to save himself as he was dragged along a bumpy three-mile road.
>
> "It's my opinion, while being dragged, Mr. Byrd was conscious and was attempting to relieve the pain and injuries he was receiving," Dr. Brown said after a lengthy description of the horrible wounds suffered by the 49 year-old victim. "He was alive when the head, shoulder and right arm were separated."
>
> Brown told of how Byrd, severely wounded, tried to ease the pain to his torso and elbows by lifting his body as flesh was torn away on the bumpy asphalt road, eventually exposing many of his limbs to the bone. (p. 1)

Kennedy (1999) reported about a hate crime committed in Laramie, Wyoming, in *The Dallas Morning News* of November 5, 1999. He wrote that in Golden, Colorado, Aaron McKinney was sentenced to two life sentences for the felonious murder of Matthew Shepard, a gay University of Wyoming student. The article gave a vivid description of the death situation:

> It was 13 months ago that Mr. McKinney and an accomplice (Russell Henderson) posed as gays and lured Matthew Shepard from a bar, drove him to the outskirts of Laramie, tied him to a fence, savagely pistol-whipped him and left him to die. (p. A3)

In his discussion of the same hate crime, Miller reported in the December 21, 1998, edition of *Newsweek* that, "On October 7, Shepard—comatose and savagely beaten—was found tied to a fence on the outskirts of Laramie, and died five days later" (p. 30). Miller commented that "[Shepard's] death prompted outrage and renewed the debate over hate crimes against gays" (p. 30).

In the November 8, 1999, edition of *The Dallas Morning News*, Hoppe reported that, "In November 1993, Nicholas R. West, 23, was abducted by three men from a Tyler park and taken to a gravel pit outside of town. He was forced to strip, placed on his knees and shot nine times" (p. A6). Hoppe added that David Aldrich, who was convicted of capital murder for the crime, stated that, "He chose to victimize gay men because 'they don't want people to know they're gay and they're not going to report it to police'" (p. A6).

In the same article, Hoppe (1999) described a second hate crime. She wrote:

> In November 1997, Angelo Farrer, a 26-year-old white man was convicted in Dallas of aggravated assault in a racial attack. Mr. Farrer was driving a pickup when it nearly collided on Loop 12 with a car driven by Melvin Scruggs, a black man.
> He followed Mr. Scruggs' car for several miles, ultimately pulling alongside. A witness testified that Mr. Farrer hurled racial slurs and made an obscene gesture. His passenger, Michael Boyd, then shot Mr. Scruggs, paralyzing him from the neck down. (p. A6)

There is an understandable propensity toward muting reports of hate crimes by omitting their unseemly details, but this approach only serves to soften their real-world severity. Apparently, hate crimes are unusually tortuous and, as such, demand that others view their full-fledged horror in order that they might be appropriately energized to initiate countermeasures. Surely, this would be especially true for counselors whose interventions are, in many respects, a "final barrier" against the murderous release of fury upon victims.

WHY ARE HATE CRIMES COMMITTED?

It is appropriate to begin the discussion of this topic with an exploration of what hate is. Gilligan (1996), former mental health director of the Massachusetts prison system, offered a vivid explanation of hate among convicted criminals. He wrote:

> Without love (by which I mean love for oneself), the self collapses, the soul dies, the psyche goes to hell. Men will quickly and ferociously attack others, even kill them, if they think it will prevent their own souls from being murdered. . . . The kind of man I am describing protects himself from the risk of being deprived of love by emptying his soul of love for others to an unimaginable degree. . . . For the only way a man can stop himself from what he experiences as the danger of loving others is by hating them instead. . . . When I speak of murderers as feeling engulfed by hate, and the world as entirely hateful, I am quoting what these men have told me. (Gilligan, 1996, p. 53)

In Gilligan's (1996) framework, hate is an adjustment to love depriva-tion. It develops when people believe that being deprived of love threat-ens to destroy their very essence. Thus, hate is a survival strategy. But Gilligan (1996) commented, "What they [violent murderers] immediately discover when they commit a violent act, however, is that the strategy is self-defeating. And this is why so many murderers finally decide to end their own lives as well" (p. 53). Certainly, this diagnosis fits the sequence of tragic events at Columbine High School in Colorado.

May (1953) discussed hate by stating, "Hating or resenting is often the person's only way to keep from committing psychological or spiritual sui-cide. It has the function of preserving some dignity, some feeling of his own identity, as though the person—or persons, in the case of nations—were to be saying silently to their conquerors, 'You have conquered me, but I reserve the right to hate you'" (p. 149).

May (1953) offered an explanation of the relationship between hate and scapegoating by contending, "Another proof of the fact that if people sur-render their freedom they must hate is seen in the fact that totalitarian governments must provide for their people some object for the hatred which is generated by the government's having taken away their free-dom. The Jews were made the scapegoat in Hitler's Germany, along with the 'enemy nations'" (p. 150). Certainly, individuals also can serve as scapegoats.

May (1953) concluded that hatred and resentment are destructive emo-tions unless the maturing process converts them into constructive ones. He summarized by writing, "The fact that the human being will destroy something—generally in the long run himself—rather than surrender his freedom proves how important freedom is to him" (p. 151).

Allport (1954) described hatred as deep-rooted and desiring the extinc-tion of the object of hate. He distinguished between rational hate and character-conditioned hate. Rational hate serves certain biological func-tions that prevent the violation of one's fundamental natural rights. Character-conditioned hate is a continuing readiness to hate that is the product of a series of bitter disappointments and has little relation to real-ity. Allport contended that hate is a secondary response to a frustrated affiliative desire and a related humiliation to one's self-esteem or values.

Allport (1954) explained the relationship between hatred and "sense-less" crimes. His position was as follows:

The person carries a vague, temperamental sense of wrong which he wishes to polarize. He must hate something. The real roots of the hatred may baf-fle him, but he thinks up some convenient victim and some good reason. The Jews are conspiring against me, or the politicians are set on making things worse. Thwarted lives have the most character-conditioned hate. (Allport, 1954, p. 364)

West (1993) used the terms "rootless" and "dangling" to describe people who have little connection with their families, friends, and school. He stated,

> The result is lives of what we call "random nows", of fortuitous and fleeting moments preoccupied with "getting over"—with acquiring pleasure, property, and power by any means necessary. . . . Sexual violence against women and homicidal assaults by young black men on one another are only the most obvious signs of this empty quest for pleasure, property and power. (p. 5)

West's (1993) brand of violence might be seen as a step above the type described by Gilligan (1996) in that West saw violence as a grasp for sources of power, whereas Gilligan presented a category that destroys the perceived holder of power without transferring it to the attacker. That is, when such hate culminates, everyone is left powerless as if power is the real enemy.

In his discussion of emotions, Damasio (1999) contended that they are "part of the bioregulatory devices with which we come equipped to survive" (p. 53). He further held that they are the result of a long history of evolutionary fine-tuning. Damasio described the role of emotions in human behavior:

> Emotions are part of homeostatic regulation and are poised to avoid the loss of integrity that is a harbinger of death or death itself, as well as to endorse a source of energy, shelter or sex. And as a result of powerful learning mechanisms such as conditioning, emotions of all shades eventually help connect homeostatic regulation and survival "values" to numerous events and objects in our autobiographical experience. Emotions are inseparable from the idea of reward and punishment, of pleasure or pain, of approach or withdrawal, of personal advantage and disadvantage. Inevitably, emotions are inseparable from the idea of good and evil. (pp. 54–55)

In short, emotions, including hate, are primal reactions to events that are perceived as critically important.

Ashbrook and Albright (1997) stated that the limbic system generates emotional signals that serve as guides to action. The autonomic nervous system alerts the body when rapid actions are necessary. Therefore, a case can be made for the notion that hate triggers an overwhelming physiological response that negates the usual cognitive, emotional, and physiological controls. Often, this state is referred to as "losing it."

Combs, Richards, and Richards (1988) supported the notion that all emotions arouse similar physiological responses, which they cited as (a) sweating of the palms of the hands; (b) increased activity of certain glands, particularly the adrenals, which make it possible for the blood to coagulate more rapidly; (c) the release of blood sugar, which provides large stores of quick energy; and (d) the increase in heart rate and breathing, which makes great excretion possible should it be necessary. Combs et al. further contended that people assign various meanings to those symptoms according to their interpretation of the situation.

Given that line of reasoning, hate can be defined as an arousal state that an individual interprets as so threatening that it requires an action directed toward the destruction of the invading person, place, or thing. It is commonly said that drastic situations require drastic measures.

Faludi, author of *Stiffed* (1999b), addressed the increasing susceptibility of males to hate during the Information Age. When referring to Mark O. Barton, who gunned down a score of people in two brokerage firms, she wrote, "Like so many men in this telemarketed, outsourced economy, Barton's earning power came from enterprises far removed from him" (Faludi, 1999a, p. 31). She contended that in that anonymous circumstance Barton acted out his rage by discharging it onto people close to him because he felt unneeded by his family and isolated from his peers.

Two common threads run through these various discussions of hate. First, hate is a profound response to situations that are perceived as deeply endangering the individual's freedom. Second, there appear to be two types of hate, one with rational roots under at least some conscious control and another that is a free-floating hostility without conscious control. Whatever its etiology, hate can serve as a trigger mechanism for actions that inflict harm on its object. When it does or when it threatens to do so, it is a cause for counselor concern.

COMMUNITY INTERVENTIONS

Hate crimes occur when a hating person enters a climate that encourages the discharge of hate-driven violence on certain targets (Bureau of Justice Assistance, 1997). One incident, such as the Rodney King affair in Los Angeles, can incite a wave of hate crimes. In short, hate crimes are contagious because they serve as the "straw that breaks the camel's back" for many persons whose hate is near threshold levels. In that sense, one hate crime endangers untold numbers of potential victims.

Carrier (1999) identified 10 ways that communities can fight hate. He suggested that communities must be committed to changing the climate that allows hate to exist and target specific groups. His list of 10 includes the following:

1. Act—do something because apathy is interpreted as acceptance.
2. Unite—organize a group of allies.
3. Support the victims—they are especially vulnerable.

4. Do your homework—determine if a hate group is involved.
5. Create an alternative—hold a unity rally instead of a hate rally.
6. Speak up—hate must be exposed and denounced.
7. Lobby leaders—to take a stand against hate.
8. Look long range—hold annual events to celebrate diversity.
9. Teach tolerance—bias is learned early.
10. Dig deeper—explore issues that divide people.

For some communities, the necessity of organizing against hate is often ignored until a hate crime occurs. East Peoria, Illinois recognized that responsibility after a former World Church member went on a killing rampage against Jews, African Americans, and Asian Americans (Thomas, 1999). As a response, the mayor of the city set up a Human Relations Commission to direct the city's efforts in combating hate and teaching tolerance.

HOW DO COUNSELORS RESPOND TO CLIENTS WHO HATE?

The Multidimensional Model of Prejudice Prevention and Reduction (MMPPR) as proposed by Sandhu and Aspy (1997) and Aspy and Sandhu (1999) is consistent with the explanation of hate posited by the Bureau of Justice Assistance (1997). According to this model, prejudices (or hate crimes) occur in a multidimensional life space, which means that counselor activities must likewise be based on a range of factors. Predisposing factors to prejudice include the individual, social, and political. The individual factors include (a) unresolved personality conflicts, (b) negative racial/ethnic identity, (c) negative self-concept, (d) low-order interpersonal skills, and (e) low-order cognitive skills. Social predisposing factors include (a) traditional group superiority, (b) traditions of group inferiority, (c) negative child-rearing practices, (d) traditions of ignorance of others, and (e) traditions of paranoia. The political predisposing factors are (a) disputes with other nations over military power, (b) disputes over financial power, (c) disputes over legal power, (d) disputes over information control, and (e) disputes over disease control.

Drawing on an awareness of the factors that predispose individuals toward hatred and thus hate crimes, counselors can use the Multidimensional Prejudice Predisposition Scale (MPPS) to identify the clients who might benefit most fully from a counseling intervention. The MPPS is presented in Figure 18.1 (Sandhu & Aspy, 1997, p. 157).

A total score for the MPPS consists of the sum of the scores for all 15 items. Subscores can be computed for each of the three components by adding the item scores for each section. Subscores range from −25 to +25.

Figure 18.1 | Multidimensional Prejudice Predisposition Scale (MPPS)

Directions: Circle the appropriate number for each item.
Section I: The individual has:

	Internalized	Factor	Externalized
1.	−5 −4 −3 −2 −1	Unresolved personality conflicts	+1 +2 +3 +4 +5
2.	−5 −4 −3 −2 −1	Negative racial/ethnic identity	+1 +2 +3 +4 +5
3.	−5 −4 −3 −2 −1	Negative self concept	+1 +2 +3 +4 +5
4.	−5 −4 −3 −2 −1	Low order empathy	+1 +2 +3 +4 +5
5.	−5 −4 −3 −2 −1	An inclination toward categorical thinking	+1 +2 +3 +4 +5

Section II: The person's native society has traditions of:

6.	−5 −4 −3 −2 −1	Group superiority	+1 +2 +3 +4 +5
7.	−5 −4 −3 −2 −1	Group inferiority	+1 +2 +3 +4 +5
8.	−5 −4 −3 −2 −1	Exclusion	+1 +2 +3 +4 +5
9.	−5 −4 −3 −2 −1	Ignorance about others	+1 +2 +3 +4 +5
10.	−5 −4 −3 −2 −1	Traditions of paranoia	+1 +2 +3 +4 +5

Section III: The person's native society has disputes with other nations over:

11.	−5 −4 −3 −2 −1	Military power	+1 +2 +3 +4 +5
12.	−5 −4 −3 −2 −1	Financial power	+1 +2 +3 +4 +5
13.	−5 −4 −3 −2 −1	Legal power	+1 +2 +3 +4 +5
14.	−5 −4 −3 −2 −1	Information control	+1 +2 +3 +4 +5
15.	−5 −4 −3 −2 −1	Disease control	+1 +2 +3 +4 +5

Note. Scoring scale ranges from 1 = *trait present but weak* to 3 = *trait present and moderate* to 5 = *trait present and strong.* Plus sign (+) indicates that the emotion of the trait is directed outwardly; minus sign (−) indicates that the emotion of the trait is directed inwardly. From *Counseling for Prejudice Prevention and Reduction,* by D. Sandhu and C. Aspy, 1997, p. 157. Copyright 1997 by the American Counseling Association. Reprinted with permission.

Positive scores indicate that a person has a predisposition toward prejudicial behavior, whereas negative scores indicate that an individual is more likely to be a victim of prejudice. The higher the score despite its positive or negative status, the greater the risk of prejudice either as a perpetrator or a victim.

Selecting Clients

After counselors have determined their clients' MPPS scores, they are equipped to identify those individuals or groups who are most likely to benefit from counseling as well as the behaviors they wish to target for change. Counselors have answers to two questions: (a) With whom should they work? and (b) What behavioral traits should they attempt to modify? Three dimensions offer important information about client selection: (a) How predisposed to prejudicial behavior is the potential client? (b) How aware is the client of the predisposition? and (c) How willing is the client to discuss the predisposition?

Assuming that the MPPS can be used to identify the amount of predisposition of prospective clients, the data related to awareness and willingness to discuss may be gathered during a clarification of the results of the MPPS when clients explore their past discussions of their predisposition toward prejudiced behavior. The number and depth of those previous discussions as well as the clients' inclination to having more of them are both behavioral indicators of the clients' awareness of their predisposition and their motivation to discuss them. Of course, direct questioning is always available. The counselor can simply ask the client if he or she is aware of his or her predisposition to prejudicial behavior and how motivated he or she is to discuss his or her predisposition to prejudicial behavior. Both responses yield behavioral indexes, and historically, direct questioning has been used extensively and successfully to select counseling clients.

Treatment of Clients

Treatment of clients for prejudicial predispositions using the MMPPR proceeds through five phases (Aspy & Sandhu, 1999; Sandhu & Aspy, 1997). Phase 1 involves screening with the MPPS to determine whether the individual is likely to be a perpetrator or victim of prejudice and the strength of the predisposition. Phase 2 involves a client-centered approach to present the results of the screening and to determine the client's awareness of the problem and willingness to discuss these issues.

Phase 3 also involves a client-centered approach and focuses on exploring the dimensions that constitute the individual factors that contribute to prejudice. Phase 4 continues with the counselor providing insight into and interpretation of the client's behavior using psychodynamic models. Additionally, the client and counselor identify behaviors that can be targeted for change. In Phase 5, these behaviors are translated into tasks and step-by-step activities that can be implemented to ensure prejudice reduction using behavioral techniques.

A CASE STUDY

Raymond was an 18-year-old White male who had returned to high school after having dropped out for 1 year. Following his return, he earned Cs in most of his classes. He was physically large, which was the principal reason he was attracted back to school, where he could participate in football, which he did with a good deal of success.

As part of her routine counseling procedure, Raymond's counselor administered the MPPS to Raymond's psychology class of 25 regular students (moderate achievers). Raymond scored +20 for each of the subscales of the MPPS and a total score of +60, which indicated his high predisposition toward prejudiced behavior, which generally is regarded as a precursor to hate. The counselor consulted with Raymond's teachers, who concurred that Raymond was aware of his predisposition toward prejudice and was open to counseling related to that topic. After reviewing Raymond's levels of predisposition for prejudice, willingness to discuss, and level of awareness, the counselor selected Raymond as one of her counselees.

The counselor (identified in the dialogue as "Co") initiated her contact with Raymond by inviting him to her office to discuss the results of the MPPS. At that time, she reviewed the scores and asked Raymond what those results meant to him. The following exchange occurred:

Co: What do you think about those scores?

Ray: I'm not surprised. Everybody I know hates niggers. I guess I'm supposed to call them Blacks now.

Co: You feel trapped in the same views your friends have.

Ray: Yeah, we all are. You can't live with people for 18 years and not get to be like them. They aren't bad. They just never went to school. They don't know any better.

Co: You're sorry they didn't go to school.

Ray: Yeah, my old man is smart as the devil. He could have made a fortune in the garage business. Instead, he's a broken down mechanic.

Co: You're afraid you might get caught in the same situation.

Ray: Sure, I'm heading that way. I'm just trying school. If I flunk out it's back to fixing tires. [Raymond laughs.]

Co: You're not sure you can be different from your dad but you have a glimmer of hope.

Ray: Yeah, I'm tougher and stronger than he is. I'm also a little smarter. If I can get a break I think I can do a little better. Then I won't have to run around all day with the Blacks.

Co: So, doing better means separating yourself from Black people.

Ray: Not all of them but some of them. They're the bottom feeders, like carp or crawfish, just scavengers. I don't want that. Of course, some Blacks are OK. Some of the Black guys on the team are a lot of fun. But, I can't take 'em home. My folks would kill me.

Co: Some Blacks are OK but others are bad?

Ray: Yeah, I don't want to be like those ghetto dwellers. I want something better than that.

Co: Let me see, right now you are afraid that, like your dad, you will get caught up in some Black people's situation and you want to be able to achieve something more than your father did.

Ray: Yeah, I really don't hate Blacks but they scare me to death when I think of living like some of them do in those government boxes.

Co: So the best way for you to get to your goal is to focus on doing well enough in school to get more training. That way you can overcome the threat of being poor like some of the Blacks you know.

Ray: Yeah, if I focus on doing my stuff I won't have to worry about those Black folks. The coaches keep telling me that if I do my job the team will do OK. They say, "Don't worry about others. Just do your job and things will work out fine."

The counselor and Raymond looked at his transcript and plotted the credits he needed for graduation. The counselor asked Raymond to join a counseling group of people who were not certain about their vocational plans. The weekly 1-hour sessions in the counselor's office helped Raymond see that he had the ability to attend college where he believed he might play football and study to become a coach.

At subsequent sessions, Raymond didn't mention Blacks, and the counselor observed that in the cafeteria he sat with some Black students. As a check on Raymond's progress, the counselor asked him to retake the MPPS. Raymond answered, "Naw, I'm past that jazz. Like they said, 'Take care of my stuff and other things would take care of themselves.'"

CONCLUSION

This chapter has discussed hate crimes by presenting three aspects of the problem: what hate crimes are, why hate crimes are committed, and methods counselors can use to intervene to prevent them. Hate crimes are defined as those offenses that are motivated by hatred of individuals or groups on the basis of their race, religion, sexual orientation, disability, ethnicity, or national origin. Hate crimes are doubly perplexing because they tend to incite groups to even more violence because they target essential characteristics of group identity and affiliation.

Hatred may originate as a self-protective mechanism in order to protect oneself from the risk of loving others and being vulnerable to them. It has also been described as an adjustment to love deprivation. Because of its intensity, hatred may trigger an overwhelming physiologic response that negates cognitive control.

Counselors have many tools for de-escalating the physiologic response of hatred. Anger management is one alternative and was covered in Chapter 13. Another model, the MMPPR developed by Sandhu and Aspy (1997; Aspy & Sandhu, 1999) is a potent tool for counselors to use because it recognizes that hatred and prejudice are ecological and that all aspects of the person and environment that create the problem must be considered in the solution to the problem.

Hate crimes are not new and will continue as long as societies allow them. While legislation will be helpful in the battle, it will also require the efforts of individuals and communities to speak out against hate and hate groups. Silence in the face of aggression is interpreted as acceptance.

REFERENCES

ABCNEWS.com. (1999, February 22). Testimony over in Jasper murder trial [Online]. Available: http://abcnews.go.com/sections/us/DailyNews/jasper990222_final.html.

Allport, G. (1954). *The nature of prejudice*. Reading, MA: Addison-Wesley.

Ashbrook, J., & Albright, C. (1997). *The humanizing brain*. Cleveland, OH: Pilgrim Press.

Aspy, C. B., & Sandhu, D. S. (1999). *Empowering women for equity: A counseling approach*. Alexandria, VA: American Counseling Association.

Bureau of Justice Assistance. (1997). *A policymaker's guide to hate crimes*. Washington, DC: U.S. Department of Justice.

Carrier, J. (1999). *Ten ways to fight hate*. Montgomery, AL: Southern Poverty Law Center.

Combs, A., Richards, A., & Richards, F. (1988). *Perceptual psychology: A humanistic approach to the study of persons*. New York: University Press of America.

Damasio, A. (1999). *A feeling of what happens*. New York: Harcourt Brace.

Faludi, S. (1999a, August 16). Rage of the American male. *Newsweek*, p. 31.

Faludi, S. (1999b). *Stiffed*. New York: Morrow.

Gilligan, J. (1996). *Violence*. New York: Vantage.

Hoppe, C. (1999, November 8). Hate crimes experts say statistics don't tell story. *The Dallas Morning News*, pp. A1, A6–A7.

Kennedy, T. (1999, November 5). Man convicted of beating gay student sentenced to life. *The Dallas Morning News*, p. A3.

May, R. (1953). *Man's search for himself*. New York: Delta.

Miller, M. (1998, December 21). The final days and nights of a gay martyr. *Newsweek*, pp. 30–31.

Sandhu, D., & Aspy, C. (1997). *Counseling for prejudice prevention and reduction*. Alexandria, VA: American Counseling Association.

Thomas, J. (1999, September 21). A city takes a stand against hate. *The New York Times*, p. A12.

West, C. (1993). *Race matters*. Boston: Beacon Press.

VIOLENCE INTERVENTION STRATEGIES: INDIVIDUAL, FAMILY, SCHOOL, AND COUNSELOR TRAINING PROGRAMS

INTRODUCTION

He stood with his back against the wall, the broken bottle in his hand, his eyes flashing with fear and anger. "Don't come near me!" he yelled. The principal turned toward the crowd that had assembled around the incident. "Clear the halls," he said firmly. "Everyone has a place to be. Now!" The students dispersed, chattering in their high-pitched voices, revealing the strain of fear. When the hall had cleared, the principal turned his attention to Kyle, a 17-year-old junior who had erupted in chemistry class, grabbed a beaker, broke it, and threatened his teacher and fellow students as he ran from the room.

"OK, Kyle. Want to tell me about it?" the principal ventured. At the same time, members of the police S.W.A.T. officers arrived and, seeing Kyle isolated in the hall, ran toward him with guns drawn. Kyle sank to the floor and covered his head. The officers grabbed his hands, retrieved the broken beaker, and handcuffed him in one smooth motion. Kyle began to sob as he was picked up and hustled out to the waiting van. Counselors and teachers spent the remainder of the day talking with students who had witnessed Kyle's outburst. No one knew what had gotten into him. Nobody really knew him. He'd always been so quiet—never said very much to anybody. He'd only been in this school a few weeks.

The story that emerged over the next few weeks was a sad one of family violence, alcohol abuse, juvenile crime, and abandonment. Kyle's secret life was not a pretty one. The event that had set him off that morning was really a trivial one in the eyes of most people. The chemistry teacher had returned a test, and Kyle's lab partner saw that Kyle's score was a C and had made one of the not uncommon comments often heard in high schools that suggested Kyle was stupid. On that day, on top of everything else, Kyle was in no mood to be teased about anything by anyone. He had intended only to intimidate the other student, but the teacher had yelled at him to put the beaker down and when he did, it broke. That was the last straw, and Kyle lost control. Kyle was lucky. A youth diversion program linked him with the interventions that he needed. He was assigned to a community service site that teamed him with a vocational arts teacher from another high school. As they worked together repairing playground equipment, Kyle discovered a mentor and friend. A foster home placement removed Kyle from the chaos of his family of origin and placed him in the school where his mentor taught. Kyle continued with counseling over the next 2 years and graduated in the top 25% of his class.

For Kyle and others who commit acts of violence, a positive intervention can make the difference between a life that is directed toward crime and one that can make a healthy contribution to the community. Schools can play a major role in rehabilitating youths. This section is dedicated to interventions for individuals, families, and schools, as well as recommendations for counselor training.

Gerald A. Juhnke and Robin Guill Liles begin in chapter 19 by addressing the problem of adolescents who are violent and addicted to alcohol or other drugs. They recommend a behavioral family therapy model and provide a case example of a successful intervention using this model.

In chapter 20, Gary G. Gintner provides a comprehensive review of the issues related to selecting the appropriate diagnosis and treatment strategies for children and adolescents presenting with conduct disorder and violent behavior. Treatments described from an evidence-based perspective include medications, social problem-solving skills training, anger management, family-based treatments, school-based interventions, and peer-based interventions.

In chapter 21, Joanne M. Tortorici Luna advocates leadership roles for counselors when schools experience violence crises. She maintains that counselors have the best knowledge of the school's resources and personnel, as well as the training to intervene. She also provides a comprehensive critical incident stress management guide book that can be adapted for any school.

In chapter 22, the final chapter of this section, M. Sylvia Fernandez provides recommendations for counselor training programs to address the skills that school counselors should have. Her recommendations bridge preservice as well as in-service training to prepare counselors to manage crisis response. The recent spate of school violence tragedies are, in her words, "a wake-up call and it is time to reevaluate the type, amount, and level of crisis response preparation provided in school counselor training programs" (pp. 371–372).

19 Treating Adolescents Presenting With Comorbid Violent and Addictive Behaviors: A Behavioral Family Therapy Model

Gerald A. Juhnke and Robin Guill Liles

A robust correlation exists between adolescent violence and alcohol and other drug (AOD) abuse (Hawkins, Catalano, & Miller, 1992). This correlation is predominant and reoccurring within existing professional research literature (Beck, Kline, & Greenfeld, 1988; Dembo, Williams, Fagan, & Schmeidler, 1994; Johnston, O'Malley, & Bachman, 1995; McCutcheon & Thomas, 1995; National Institute of Justice, 1994; Snyder & Sickmund, 1995). It is clear the number of adolescents engaging in violent behaviors is increasing at an alarming rate and has evolved into a primary public health crisis (Koop & Lundberg, 1992). For example, juvenile arrest rates for violent behaviors (e.g., homicide, aggravated assault, and rape) increased 47% between 1988 and 1992 (Office of National Drug Control Policy, 1999). Concomitantly, firearm homicide rates for youths ages 15 to 19 increased 155% between 1987 and 1994 (Centers for Disease Control and Prevention/National Center for Injury Prevention and Control, 1996), and homicide arrest rates for youths ages 14 to 17 increased 41% between 1989 and 1994 (Fox, 1996). The most recent Violent Offense Arrests Reports published by the U.S. Federal Bureau of Investigation indicated that 34,323 children ages 14 and under and 86,130 adolescents ages 15 to 17 were arrested in 1997 for committing severe acts of violence (U.S. Bureau of Justice, 1999).

Trends related to adolescent AOD abuse are less well defined. However, it quickly becomes apparent when surveying existing literature that AOD abuse among adolescents has increased within recent years and that adolescents' attitudes regarding the inherent dangers associated with AOD abuse are deteriorating. One example of research reflecting such adolescent AOD abuse and attitudinal deterioration is a longitudinal study conducted by University of Michigan's Institute for Social Research. The research began in 1975 and is funded by the National Institute on Drug Abuse (NIDA). This research surveys nationally representative samples of 8th-, 10th-, and 12th-grade classes and annually includes nearly 50,000 students from more than 400 public and private secondary schools. Survey results report that (a) 54% of the participants had used an illicit drug by the time they reached their senior year in high school, (b) the annual use of any illicit drug among seniors increased from 27% in 1992 to 42% in 1997, and (c) the percentage of seniors who had used an illicit drug within 30 days prior to survey participation increased from 14% in 1992 to 26% in 1997 (NIDA, 1997).

FAMILY THERAPY'S EFFICACY IN TREATING VIOLENT AND AOD-ABUSING BEHAVIORS

Treating Violent Adolescents

Behavioral family therapy is a recommended treatment for violent adolescents (Ollendick, 1996). It is believed that maladaptive familial patterns reinforce adolescents' aggressive and violent behaviors (Ollendick, 1996). Behavioral family therapy moderates such negative familial patterns, thereby reducing violent behaviors. Family therapy has also been identified as helpful with offending adolescents (adolescents arrested or incarcerated because of illegal violent [e.g., homicide, aggravated assault] and nonviolent [e.g., property destruction, prostitution] behaviors). Henggeler, Melton, and Smith (1992) reported that offending adolescents who participated in family therapy designed to mitigate their families' organizational problems experienced significantly (a) lower recidivism rates (e.g., fewer repeat arrests), (b) improved academic performance, and (c) enhanced family functioning.

Another comparison study treated violent adolescents by means of either outpatient family or individual therapy. Immediately following treatment, adolescents from both groups demonstrated improved conduct. However, 1 year following treatment, adolescents who had participated in family therapy exhibited fewer violent behaviors (Bank, Marlowe, Reid, Patterson, & Weinrott, 1991).

Treating AOD-Abusing Adolescents

Family therapy is also an appropriate treatment for general AOD-related symptomatology. Adolescents specifically appear to benefit from its use. For example, O'Farrell (1999) noted behavioral family therapy's efficacy in promoting AOD abstinence. Hedberg and Campbell (1974) found behavioral family therapy significantly contributed to their chemically dependent clients' 80% abstinence rate. And Szapocznik et al. (1988) found adolescents' postfamily therapy AOD abstinence rates dramatically increased from 7% to 80%.

Concomitantly, family therapy was noted as efficacious in one of the most comprehensive reviews of AOD-controlled outcome research to date (Liddle & Dakof, 1995). Moreover, no empirical research was found that either alluded to or indicated that family therapy was ineffective in treating AOD-abusing adolescents. This controlled treatment literature analysis appears to compellingly support family therapy's use when treating AOD-abusing adolescents.

Our Clinical Experiences With Violent, AOD-Abusing Adolescents

Our clinical experiences with adolescents reflect the above-noted correlation between violent behaviors and AOD abuse. Specifically, our violent adolescents typically report that as they decrease their AOD abuse, they experience a reduction in both the frequency and severity of their violent behaviors. This seems supported by family members' perceptions. Additionally, like the treatment researchers noted above, we have found behavioral family therapy helpful to adolescent clients as they strive for abstinence from both violent and AOD-abusing behaviors. Given such favorable results, the intent of this chapter is to (a) provide a practitioner-relevant behavioral family therapy overview, (b) describe how we use behavioral family therapy with adolescents presenting with violent and AOD-abusing behaviors, and (c) illustrate this model with a case presentation.

BEHAVIORAL FAMILY THERAPY: A PRACTITIONER-RELEVANT OVERVIEW

What Is Behavioral Family Therapy?

Behavioral family therapy began in the early 1960s (Jacobson, 1981). Most behavioral family therapy researchers were employed in university or governmental settings where research activities were required. Thus, substantial research was accumulated generally supporting behavioral family therapy's use and efficacy (Jacobson, 1981).

Behavioral family therapists increasingly realized social exchange theory's value (Nichols, 1984). This theory suggests that "people strive to maximize 'rewards' and minimize 'costs'" (Nichols, 1984, p. 303). Thus, satisfied family members engage in activities that maximize rewards and minimize costs. The opposite is noted with "dissatisfied" family members, who tend to concentrate on minimizing costs and expect little reward from their family involvement.

In general, behavioral family therapists believe problems result from ineffective reinforcement patterns between family members and focus treatment on observable behaviors. Concomitantly, behavioral family therapists place little importance on history, except to identify (a) the family's current dysfunctional patterns, (b) common pattern precipitators, and (c) rewards and sanctions commonly affiliated with these dysfunctional patterns and their precipitators. Thus, the treatment model stays in the present and focuses on immediate family behaviors. The primary goal, then, is to restructure family interactions by means of behavioral changes (Levant, 1980). Restructuring is accomplished by increasing perceived rewards for desired behaviors while increasing sanctions for undesired behaviors (Gurman & Knudson, 1978; Jacobson, 1981).

Behavioral Family Therapy Constructs

A number of basic social learning constructs are continued within present-day behavioral family therapy and warrant review. Behavioral family therapy's central construct is operant conditioning (Nichols, 1984). As likely remembered from undergraduate psychology courses, operant conditioning (Skinner, 1953) differs from classical conditioning (Pavlov, 1934) in that the organism's response is voluntary in the former rather than involuntary. Thus, unlike Pavlov's dog, which involuntarily salivated when conditioned to respond to the sound of a bell (conditioned - response), operant conditioning is a voluntary response. Operant conditioning suggests persons choose to respond according to perceived consequences. Therefore, an adolescent may be verbally abusive and physically violent, believing such behaviors will be rewarded. Here, the reward may be that parents distance themselves from the adolescent, thereby providing greater freedom from adult supervision while concomitantly providing the adolescent with verbal encouragement to replicate violent behaviors.

Positive reinforcement, punishment, and intermittent reinforcement constructs are equally important. Positive reinforcement indicates that as one perceives positive benefits for a specific behavior, the behavior will likely continue. Here, for example, an adolescent who is verbally praised by respected peers for violent behaviors is likely to continue or increase those violent behaviors. Conversely, punishment suggests that consistent noxious responses to a specific behavior will lead to truncation and the behavior's eventual extinguishment.

It should be noted that punishment can take two forms (Nichols, 1984). Punishment can be an aversive stimulus, such as corporal discipline. Or, it can take the form of removing a positively perceived privilege (e.g., television). Thus, an adolescent behaving violently and being verbally reprimanded by respected peers would likely discontinue these violent behaviors.

Finally, intermittent reinforcement leads to behaviors that are the most resistant to change. Intermittent reinforcement indicates indiscriminate rewards for the replication of specific behaviors. Therefore, on certain occasions the behavior will receive immediate reward. At other times, the behavior will continue over an extended time period before being rewarded. Therefore, an adolescent receiving indiscriminate rewards by respected peers for his or her violent behaviors will likely continue being violent and the behaviors will be difficult to extinguish.

Commonly Used Behavioral Family Therapy Interventions

Baseline and Functional Analysis

Behavioral family therapists counseling violent and AOD-abusing adolescents collect baseline target frequency data and complete a functional analysis at treatment onset. The adolescent and parents record the frequency and duration of the adolescent's violent and AOD-abusing behaviors.[1] Frequently, family therapists provide a list of conduct disorder and general substance abuse and substance dependency criteria to the adolescent and parents. The adolescent and parents then record how many times each day the adolescent's behaviors matched the criteria (e.g., bullying).

It is helpful to understand (a) when the violent behaviors most frequently occur, (b) who is typically present (or absent),[2] (c) location of the violent incident (e.g., school, convenience store), (d) the client's beliefs as to the precipitating trigger (e.g., break up with girlfriend), and (e) the parents' beliefs as to the precipitating triggers. The baseline and responses to the above questions will later be compared with functional analysis results.

Immediately following the behavioral baseline, clients describe how they could have responded differently. Thus, if they were violent, they list

---

[1]Under certain instances, we have also asked teachers, significant family members who regularly interact with the client (e.g., grandparents, aunts), and even respected peers to help collect this baseline data with the adolescent.

[2]Especially noteworthy are the persons commonly present when these violent and AOD-abusing behaviors occur. Once identified, interactions with these persons should be eliminated.

nonviolent behaviors that could have been used. Then they describe how they could have initiated these nonviolent behaviors.

Additionally, a "reverse behavioral baseline" is used. This process is similar to the baseline process described above. Only this time, clients and their families identify times when the adolescent was nonviolent and non-AOD-abusing. Although insight is not a prerequisite for behavioral change, the reverse behavioral baseline often promotes useful insight and accompanies nonviolent behaviors. One client who completed the assignment reported that he finally understood "the guys I've been hanging [around] with act like my friends, but they keep getting me in trouble." Although he had a more difficult time achieving abstinence, he found changing peers played a significant role in eliminating his violent behaviors.

The functional analysis notes stimuli that precipitate violent or AOD-abusing behaviors and records behavioral consequences. For example, we might note that Johnny is teased by classmates. He responds by consuming alcohol. As the alcohol's effects increase, he becomes impulsive, belligerent, and verbally threatening toward those who teased him. The events culminate when Johnny assaults a student. This increases Johnny's notoriety among his peers and recognition by his alcohol-dependent father, who lauds Johnny for "proving you're not a wimp." Thus, the functional analysis notes the reinforcement contingencies that positively reward Johnny's violent and AOD-abusing behaviors. Once the triggers and reinforcement contingencies are noted, the behavioral family therapist can begin treatment.

Behavioral Family Therapy Interventions

Contingency Contracting. A number of behavioral family therapy interventions are especially helpful. One of the most effective is contingency contracting (Rinn, 1978). Here, parents and adolescents jointly establish a clearly worded contract that describes acceptable and unacceptable behaviors. The contract also indicates how the adolescent will be rewarded for contracted behavior compliance.

One contingency contracting experience that we have used with our violent and AOD-abusing adolescents is the Nonviolence/Sobriety Contract Calendar. Parents and adolescents identify a time each day when all can meet for approximately 15 minutes. During these meetings, adolescents verbally commit to remaining violence free and AOD abstinent. Furthermore, they commit to their relationships with their parents, siblings, and themselves. Here, an adolescent might say, "Mom, I am committed to staying violence and drug free. I will not be violent or use drugs today. I love you mom, and am committed to staying free from violence and drugs for you, my little brother Sean, who may try to emulate my behaviors, and for myself." Parents can voice any specific concerns about upcoming events that may incite a violent or AOD relapse. Adolescents verbally indicate how they will respond to noted parental concerns. Once adolescents indicate how they will respond, parents are not allowed to ask further questions. Adolescents, then, in their parents' presence, take any prescribed medications for presenting violent or AOD-abusing symptomatology (e.g., Antabuse), and the parents place an "X" on the contract calendar. The intent is to ritualize this daily experience and encourage parents and adolescents to direct their violent and AOD-abusing abstinence.

Cost–Benefit Analysis. In addition to the expected request to describe costs associated with the targeted behaviors, we require adolescents to describe current behavior benefits and anticipated costs for extinguishing them. Often our violent adolescents experience significant reinforcements (e.g., increased freedom from parental supervision) that encourage continued violence. Concomitantly, many adolescents incur unexpected costs when establishing more functional nonviolent behaviors. Such costs clearly warrant client discussion. For example, friends frequently disappear when our clients discontinue their violent and AOD-abusing behaviors. Given the importance of peers, we would be foolish to expect immediate compliance with suggested behavioral changes if the client believes these changes will cost important friendships.

Heartening to adolescents is our requirement that parents describe benefits associated with their adolescents' violent and AOD-abusing behaviors. Parents usually are surprised by our request. However, upon closer examination, the parents report that these negative behaviors frequently reduce their feelings of responsibility. One parent stated, "I can't stop him from drinking and fighting. . . . He won't listen to me anyhow." Such fatalistic perceptions echo this parent's frustration and inadvertently suggest the parent's diminished responsibility. Thus, we may state, "Parenting is difficult and thankless. Adolescents demand attention. They may never fully appreciate our investment of time, love and energy. This is the time to get effective, not frustrated. What do you need right now to overcome your frustration and demonstrate to your child and yourself that you are not giving up?"

Building Communication Skills. Another intervention we use builds communication skills. We find this intervention helpful in a number of ways. First, it trains adolescents and parents to effectively communicate family rules. Second, it helps individual family members learn how to present their needs in a healthy, nonthreatening manner. Third, we have noticed that an improvement in adolescents' family communication skills frequently overlaps into general, nonfamilial interactions as well. Thus, adolescents who have gained communication skills can settle conflicts verbally without the need to become violent. They also seem to request help more often and make their concerns known before the situation escalates into violence.

1. "Family As A Business" Communications: We begin communication skills training by explaining how families are similar to businesses. We state successful businesses use communications to unify disparate departments, cogently present concerns without emotional overtones, establish clear charges, and work toward common goals. Then we ask members to rate their family's current success in each of the noted areas. This is done using a 10-point scale, 1 indicating *limited success* and 10 indicating *significant success*. Then, we ask what behaviors would need to be initiated to begin making these communication areas more successful. Next, we practice these identified initiating behaviors.

2. "I" Statements. During treatment sessions, we encourage families to use "I" statements (e.g., "I believe. . ."). The use of "I" statements allows persons to own feelings and beliefs. Additionally, it helps clients move away from "you" statements, which often condemn and suggest others have external control over the adolescents' violent behaviors (e.g., "You make me violent").

3. Behavioral Descriptors. Next we use behavioral descriptors. Often parents tell adolescents to "grow up" or "behave." Adolescents, too, use phrases devoid of behavioral descriptors. We once saw a skit with a comedian and a young boy. The boy's charge was to tell the comedian how to smoke a cigarette. Nearly all the boy's instructions were taken literally. When the boy said "put the cigarette in your mouth," the comedian placed the entire cigarette in his mouth. When the boy instructed the comedian to "light the cigarette," the comedian lighted the filtered end. We discuss skit details to demonstrate how instructions devoid of behavioral descriptors often create frustration and error. We then practice using behavioral descriptors in session. The intervention goal is to break desired behaviors into simple, small, observable, concretely stated, understandable language.

4. Globalizations. The last communication area we practice relates to globalizations, such as "You always do that" or "Can't you do anything right?" The intent is to reduce globalizations and increase specific language. Therefore, we encourage clients to use the words *frequently* and *often* rather than *always*. An example would be "You often yell at me." This suggests yelling doesn't always happen. In many cases, the violent and AOD-abusing behaviors do not happen as frequently as our clients' language suggests. Practicing such simple communication skills benefits our clients and their families. It certainly should be noted that cultural and English-as-a-second-language distinctions should be considered when providing such training. However, the benefits can be significant and promote positive familial verbal communications.

Catch Your Kids/Parents/Siblings Doing Something Positive. Our clients and their parents are often angry, frustrated, and hurt. Their family interactions frequently focus on the identification of others' pathology. Therefore, we use an assignment in which a roll of pennies is given to each family member. The assignment is to give away all pennies. Each time family members notice another doing something positive, they respond by giving a penny.

At the beginning of the next session, the family identifies the member who gave away the most pennies. Jointly, the family determines a way to honor this person. Such honoring experiences are often novel for the family and the "honored" family member. This intervention encourages families to interact differently and helps them focus on the positive ongoing behaviors vis-à-vis dysfunctional and caustic behaviors.

Appreciation Days. As progress is noted, we use an intervention similar to Stuart's (1980) "caring days." Unlike Stuart's intervention, which was dyadic and devised for couples experiencing marital distress, our intervention is systemically oriented and used with the entire family system. Furthermore, we advise parents that adolescents are developmentally like children—often egocentric and unable to demonstrate significant "adult" behaviors. We make this announcement within session. Given that our violent clients tend to be males, we often up the ante by suggesting that the adolescent likely wishes to be a man and demonstrate his manliness, but he is still an immature boy, unable to demonstrate appreciation toward others as "real men do."

Next we ask the adolescents what "appreciation behaviors" they demonstrate within their home. Interestingly enough, many adolescents indicate that they do participate in appreciation behaviors. So, we ask them to describe the claimed appreciation behaviors. If a number of behaviors are presented, we ask parents how they reward these behaviors. Then, we ask parents how they will thank their adolescents in the future for such behaviors. Should the adolescents fail to describe appreciation behaviors, we ask parents to describe behaviors that would be most appreciated and, again, describe how they will acknowledge such future behaviors.

Finally, we encourage family members to identify a day in the upcoming week when they will demonstrate at least one "appreciation behavior" per hour at home. This "appreciation day" is to be a secret. No one should share their intended appreciation day. Family members then write on separate sheets of paper which day they choose to make into an appreciation day. The clinician records the noted appreciation days. At the next family session, each member identifies the appreciation behaviors they witnessed and indicates others' appreciation days. In other words, family members attempt to identify the secret appreciation days. Many times we have had families indicate that they could not identify which days were the appreciation days because of the increased number of positive behaviors occurring within the home.

BEHAVIORAL FAMILY
THERAPY CASE PRESENTATION

The Referral

A 16-year-old, Richard, was referred by a local hospital emergency room social worker and Richard's child protective services (CPS) case manager. Two times within the preceding 14 days, Richard had intentionally burned himself with lighter fluid. This resulted in second- and third-degree burns to his hands, face, neck, and chest. Although the burns were painful, they were not life threatening, and Richard was ambulatory.

The Initial Intake Session and Brief Psychosocial History

Richard was accompanied to his initial intake session by his only sibling, 22-year-old, custodial sister, Amber. Richard and Amber reported that their father had abandoned the family when they were quite young. Their mother suffered from advanced Alzheimer's disease and had been placed in a nursing home approximately 1 year earlier. Richard originally attempted to live independently after his mother's nursing home placement. However, Richard was arrested on assault charges, and CPS became involved upon his release. A juvenile magistrate gave Richard the choice between juvenile detention center incarceration and living with his sister. Richard chose to move in with Amber and her 27-year-old partner, Andy.

Assessment results suggested Richard qualified for conduct disorder and was phencyclidine (PCP) dependent. It was noted that Richard (a) perceived significant familial discord, (b) had authority problems, (c) was hypersensitive to criticism, and (d) had conduct problems. Amber indicated Richard had initiated physical fights with her and her live-in partner within the preceding 3 weeks.

Initial Behavioral Family Interventions

Using a flip chart and markers, Richard and Amber helped develop a violent, AOD-abusing, and self-injurious (targeted) behavior baseline. The baseline reviewed the previous 14 days. This was the same period in which Richard twice had received emergency medical services. Both Richard and Amber indicated Richard's targeted behaviors occurred primarily on Friday and Saturday evenings. Typically, Amber and Andy's friends were partying at the trailer, and alcohol consumption by all but Richard was noted. Richard would become violent when others were intoxicated and the party was about to come to a close. It was at these times Richard would use PCP. Amber believed Richard's PCP use caused his violent behaviors. Richard denied PCP use as the precipitator and indicated he became violent when intoxicated guests insulted him.

Directly below this behavioral baseline, we developed a reverse behavioral baseline. It was noted that Richard had not demonstrated targeted behaviors (a) when Amber and Andy were not consuming alcohol, (b) during weekdays and weekday evenings, (c) when Richard was not using PCP, and (d) when Richard and Amber were alone. Information provided by both baselines enabled us to identify behaviors to be included in the contingency contract.

Richard and Amber jointly created a contingency contract. This contract indicated Richard would be required to (a) clean his room on Mondays and Thursdays before 5 p.m., (b) be home no later than 11 p.m., (c) remain PCP and AOD abstinent, (d) attend a young people's 12-Step meeting on Friday and Saturday evenings, (e) be verbally pleasant and nonabusive toward Amber and Andy, (f) walk away from insulting behaviors, (g) not fight, and (h) not be self-injurious. In return, Amber and Andy would allow Richard the privilege of staying in their trailer, which included specifically outlined television and food privileges. Furthermore, Amber indicated she would file a police report and have Richard removed from the trailer on any noted infraction.

Nonviolence/Sobriety Contract Calendar and Cost–Benefit Analysis Interventions

Richard, Amber, and Andy arrived the next day as scheduled and were informed that Richard's juvenile probation officer and CPS case manager were present and wished to join the session. The session began once the necessary releases were signed. We started by thanking Andy for his attendance and recognizing Richard's contingency contract compliance. We then asked Richard's probation officer and case manager to summarize Richard's option related to drug screens and housing.[3] The option was clear: Richard could participate in random weekly drug screens, counseling two times per week, and daily young people's 12-Step meetings (except Sundays) or be housed in a county foster care facility. Noncompliance would result in immediate removal from Amber's trailer.

---

[3]Richard had significant CPS and juvenile justice court histories, which included housing and drug screen agreements.

Once Richard understood the consequence for noncompliance, he verbalized his full participation.

After Richard's probation officer and case manager left, we discussed the contract benefits. Andy stated, "This is Richard's problem," and was unwilling to enter into the contracting procedure. Amber, however, agreed to try the contract for 30 days. Both she and Richard identified 8 a.m. as their meeting time.

Next we introduced the cost–benefit analysis and asked Richard to identify violent, AOD-abusing, and self-injurious behavior benefits. The benefits stated were (a) Amber, Andy, and their friends' attention, (b) escape from boredom, (c) Amber and Andy's nurturing behaviors, (d) release from responsibilities, and (e) respect for acting violently. Richard admitted a number of target behavior costs. These included others' verbalized feelings of anger and disappointment, loss of friends, mandated counseling, pending detention time, and required community service.

Costs associated with eliminating his targeted behaviors were also discussed. Richard reported that he was concerned if he wasn't physically intimidating and aggressive that he would be perceived as "weak." Specifically, he was concerned that others would lose "respect" for him. Additionally, he reported costs related to losing peer relationships. Furthermore, he stated few costs associated with giving up his self-injurious behaviors. When pressed, he reported that he might lose Amber's support and be held more accountable by his probation officer for violent and AOD-abusing behaviors. The foremost reported benefit for changing his targeted behaviors was "staying free." Here, Richard noted that he didn't want to leave Amber and Andy's trailer, because "it's one easy life." Other noted benefits for change included Amber and Andy's support and a "more adult lifestyle."

Amber and Andy reported the costs associated with Richard's targeted behaviors were primarily related to others' perceptions that Amber and Andy were "self-sacrificing" and "willing to give up our lives for Richard." Andy noted another potential cost of Richard's improvement would be Amber's fear of losing Richard and "her last family contact." Although this was quickly denied by Amber, she later stated concern that if Richard improved she would have little to do except focus on Andy and visit her infirmed mother. Andy further indicated that as long as Richard was experiencing problems and asking Amber for help, Amber would delay Andy's marriage proposal. Amber and Andy noted that the primary benefits associated with Richard's new nonviolent, non-AOD-abusing, and non-self-injurious behaviors included time between Amber and Andy and reduced arguing, which was typically associated with "the parenting of Richard."

At the session's conclusion, we discussed in detail the perceived costs and benefits associated with Richard's current behaviors, as well as potentially changed behaviors. Additionally, we identified ways in which Richard, Amber, and Andy could reward each other and increase their satisfaction without resorting back to Richard's targeted behaviors. The "penny game" was described, and all agreed to participate. Each person received one roll of 50 pennies and a baseline tracking table on which they were to record Richard's targeted behaviors. They also were to note who was present during targeted behaviors, where the behaviors occurred, and the perceived triggering events.

Continued Sessions

The following sessions primarily revolved around communication-building exercises and reviewed rewarding behaviors experienced by Richard related to his new nonviolent, non-AOD-abusing, and non-self-injurious behaviors. As Richard's contingency contract compliance was affirmed and he was consistently rewarded for improvements in the three target areas, new, healthier behaviors became established. Here, for example, Richard began working at a local automotive supply store and purchased a dirt bike.

CONCLUSION

We have found behavioral family therapy to be helpful to many of our adolescent clients presenting with comorbid violent and AOD-abusing behaviors. Existing literature appears to support behavioral family therapy's use—especially with this population. Certainly, behavioral family therapy is not the answer for every violent adolescent. As with all intervention models, it is critical to match the intervention to the individual client and the client's specific needs. However, we believe clinicians working with violent and AOD-abusing adolescents will find behavioral family therapy to be an efficacious treatment model.

REFERENCES

Bank, L., Marlowe, J. H., Reid, J. B., Patterson, G. R., & Weinrott, M. R. (1991). A comparative evaluation of parent training interventions for families of chronic delinquents. *Journal of Abnormal Child Psychology, 19*, 15–33.

Beck, A. J., Kline, S. A., & Greenfeld, L. A. (1988). *Survey of youth in custody, 1987.* Washington, DC: U.S. Department of Justice.

Centers for Disease Control and Prevention/National Center for Injury Prevention and Control. (1996). *National summary of injury mortality data, 1987–1994.* Atlanta, GA: Author.

Dembo, R., Williams, L., Fagan, J., & Schmeidler, J. (1994). Development and assessment of a classification of high risk youths. *Journal of Drug Issues, 24,* 25–53.

Fox, J. A. (1996). *Trends in juvenile violence: A report to the United States Attorney General on current and future rates of juvenile offending.* Washington, DC: U.S. Department of Justice, Bureau of Justice Statistics.

Gurman, A. S., & Knudson, R. M. (1978). Behavioral marriage therapy: A psychodynamic–systems analysis and critique. *Family Process, 17,* 121–138.

Hawkins, J. D., Catalano, R. F., & Miller, J. Y. (1992). Risk and protective factors for alcohol and other drug problems in adolescence and early adulthood: Implications for substance abuse prevention. *Psychological Bulletin, 112,* 64–105.

Hedberg, A. G., & Campbell, L. (1974). A comparison of four behavioral treatments of alcoholism. *Journal of Behavioral Therapy and Experimental Psychiatry, 5,* 251–256.

Henggeler, S. W., Melton, G. B., & Smith, L. A. (1992). Family preservation using multisystemic therapy—An effective alternative to incarcerating serious juvenile offenders. *Journal of Consulting and Clinical Psychology, 60,* 953–961.

Jacobson, N. S. (1981). Behavioral marital therapy. In A. Gurman & D. Kniskern (Eds.), *Handbook of family therapy* (pp. 556–591). New York: Brunner/Mazel.

Johnston, L. D., O'Malley, P. M., & Bachman, J. G. (1995). *National survey results on drug use from the Monitoring the Future Study, 1975–1995: Vol. I. Eighth, tenth, and twelfth graders.* Washington, DC: National Institute on Drug Abuse.

Koop, C. E., & Lundberg, G. D. (1992). Violence in America: A public health emergency: Time to bite the bullet back. *Journal of the American Medical Association, 267,* 3075–3076.

Levant, R. F. (1980). A classification of the field of family therapy: A review of prior attempts and a new paradigmatic model. *American Journal of Family Therapy, 8,* 3–16.

Liddle, H. A., & Dakof, G. A. (1995). Efficacy of family therapy for drug abuse: Promising but not definitive. *Journal of Marital and Family Therapy, 21,* 511–543.

McCutcheon, A. L., & Thomas, G. (1995). Patterns of drug use among White institutionalized delinquents in Georgia: Evidence from a latent class analysis. *Journal of Drug Education, 25*(1), 61–71.

National Institute of Justice. (1994). *Drug use forecasting—1993 annual report on adult arrestees: Drugs and crime in America's cities.* Washington, DC: U.S. Department of Justice.

National Institute on Drug Abuse. (1997). High school and youth trends: Monitoring the Future Study [On-line]. Available: http://www.nida.nih.gov/Infofax/HSYouthtrends.html.

Nichols, M. P. (1984). *Family therapy concepts and methods.* New York: Gardner Press.

O'Farrell, T. J. (1999, April/May). Systems therapy key to prevention and treatment: BCT offers good outcomes, study shows. *Family Therapy News,* p. 1.

Office of National Drug Control Policy. (1999). Juvenile drug use, crime, and violence [On-line]. Available: http://www.whitehousedrugpolicy.gov/drugfact/juvenile.html.

Ollendick, T. H. (1996). Violence in youth: Where do we go from here? Behavior therapy's response. *Behavior Therapy, 27,* 485–514.

Pavlov, I. P. (1934). An attempt at a physiological interpretation of obsessional neurosis and paranoia. *Journal of Mental Science, 80,* 187–197.

Rinn, R. C. (1978). Children with behavior disorders. In M. Hersen & A. Bellack (Eds.), *Behavior therapy in the psychiatric setting* (pp. 25–53). Baltimore: Williams & Wilkins.

Skinner, B. F. (1953). *Science and human behavior.* New York: Macmillan.

Snyder, H. N., & Sickmund, M. (1995). *Juvenile offenders and victims: A national report.* Washington, DC: Office of Juvenile Justice and Delinquency Prevention.

Stuart, R. B. (1980). *Helping couples change: A social learning approach for marital therapy.* New York: Guilford Press.

Szapocznik, J., Perez-Vidal, A., Brickman, A. L., Foote, F. H., Santisteban, D., Hervis, O., & Kurtines, W. (1988). Engaging adolescent drug abusers and their families in treatment: A strategic structural systems approach. *Journal of Consulting and Clinical Psychology, 56,* 552–557.

U.S. Bureau of Justice. (1999). Report on violence offense arrests by age, 1970–97 [On-line]. Available: http://www.ojp.usdoj.gov/bjs/crimoff.htm#dat.

20 | Conduct Disorder and Chronic Violent Offending: Issues in Diagnosis and Treatment Selection

Gary G. Gintner

In the past 15 years youth violence has escalated to such a degree that it is considered among the top public health problems (Centers for Disease Control, 1991; Howell, Krisberg, & Jones, 1995). A first step in stemming this epidemic of youth violence is identifying high-risk perpetrators. Although the violent activities of most youthful offenders persist for only a year or less, about 15% show a chronic pattern that lasts for years (Howell et al., 1995). These chronic offenders account for nearly three quarters of all violent juvenile crime (Thornberry, Huizinga, & Loeber, 1995). Diagnostically, most of them will meet criteria for conduct disorder (Loeber, Green, Keenan, & Lahey, 1995; Moffitt, 1993). According to the *Diagnostic and Statistical Manual of Mental Disorders* (4th ed. [*DSM–IV*]; American Psychiatric Association [APA], 1994), the cardinal feature of conduct disorder is a chronic pattern of behavior in which the rights of others are violated (e.g., fighting, armed robbery) or age-appropriate norms or rules are transgressed (e.g., truancy).

The importance of accurate identification is highlighted by the fact that standard interventions to curb disruptive or antisocial behavior are not effective for those with conduct disorder (American Academy of Child and Adolescent Psychiatry [AACAP], 1997; Kazdin, 1997). For example, school-based interventions such as individual or group counseling, in-school suspension, and alternative schools have not been found to reduce recidivism (Short & Shapiro, 1993). Similarly, there is no good evidence for the long-term positive effects of individual outpatient therapy, residential treatment, group homes, training schools, and wilderness programs for those with conduct disorder (AACAP, 1997; Kazdin, 1997). Not only are these programs ineffective for these youths, but their presence in these programs can adversely affect the treatment gains of less antisocial participants who do have the potential to benefit from the programs (Kazdin, 1997).

The purpose of this chapter is to address two major questions. First, how can individuals with chronic violent forms of conduct disorder be differentiated from those with a more benign and transitory course? In addressing this question, the next section discusses issues in diagnosing conduct disorder and its subtypes. The second major question examines which treatments are effective for conduct-disordered youths, especially those who show a more chronic and violent history.

DIAGNOSTIC ISSUES

Conduct disorder is characterized by antisocial behaviors that occur in a variety of settings, such as the home, school, and neighborhood. The *DSM-IV* (APA, 1994) field trials indicated that the optimal number of symptoms to accurately identify those with conduct disorder was three in the past year, with at least one of these present in the past 6 months (Lahey et al., 1994). A key concept is that this pattern of symptomatic behavior is indicative of dysfunction within the individual and not simply due to cultural or situational (e.g., homelessness) factors (APA, 1994; Sommers-Flanagan & Sommers-Flanagan, 1998). Next, the symptoms and subtypes of conduct disorder are examined with particular attention paid to their developmental appearance and progression.

DSM–IV Symptoms of Conduct Disorder

Types of Antisocial Symptoms
DSM–IV arranges symptoms into four groups: (a) aggression to people and animals, (b) destruction of property, (c) deceitfulness or theft, and (d) serious violation of the rules. In this section, each group is examined more closely in terms of its diagnostic significance.

The symptoms included under aggression to people and animals consist of behaviors that involve direct confrontation of the victim, such as bullying, fighting, sexual assault, using a weapon, animal mutilation, and robbery. Of the symptoms in this group, the appearance of chronic fighting, especially where the victim is seriously harmed, is one of the best predictors of subsequent full-blown conduct disorder (Loeber et al., 1995). In terms of the developmental progression of these aggressive symptoms, minor aggressive behaviors such as bullying appear in preschool and early elementary school (Loeber & Stouthamer-Loeber, 1998). Physical fighting is the next symptom to emerge and tends to persist into adolescence. In more serious cases, this may be accompanied by animal mutilation. By mid-adolescence, these youths engage in more violent attacks on others, including rape and serious battery (Thornberry et al., 1995). Symptoms from the aggressive group are the best predictors of chronic violent offending that persists into adulthood (AACAP, 1997; Moffitt, 1993; Thornberry et al., 1995).

Destruction of property (e.g., vandalism, fire-setting) or deceitfulness and theft (e.g., lying to con, shoplifting, burglary) do not involve direct confrontation of the victim (Loeber & Stouthamer-Loeber, 1998). Fire-setting is particularly pathonomic as a marker for violence. Developmentally, frequent lying and shoplifting may appear in elementary school. These behaviors then escalate into other covert crimes such as vandalism and even fire-setting. By mid-adolescence, burglary, car theft, and fraud may enter the clinical picture.

Serious violations of rules include symptoms such as truancy, running away, and staying out late despite parental prohibition. DSM–IV (APA, 1994) added age of onset before age 13 to both truancy and staying out late to more clearly differentiate these behaviors from normal adolescent acting-out. In the preschool years, there is the appearance of stubborn behavior that later develops into defiance and chronic disobedience (Loeber & Stouthamer-Loeber, 1998). Later, more serious authority-avoidant behaviors emerge, such as truancy and running away.

Subtypes of Conduct Disorder

DSM–IV (APA, 1994) classifies conduct disorder into either the childhood-onset type (i.e., symptoms start before age 10) or the adolescent-onset type (i.e., no symptoms before age 10). The main reason for this subtyping was the finding that antisocial behavior that began in childhood was associated with a more chronic course than antisocial behavior that arose in adolescence (APA, 1994; Moffitt, 1993).

Childhood-onset type. Of those who will later become chronic violent offenders, most will have had conduct disorder with a childhood onset (AACAP, 1997; APA, 1994; Lahey et al., 1994). In fact, the childhood-onset type is roughly seven to nine times more likely to exhibit aggressive behaviors in comparison with the adolescent-onset type (Lahey et al., 1998). The aggression is also very likely to become a chronic feature in the youth's behavior.

Data from longitudinal studies suggest that the development of the childhood-onset type is the result of interacting child and environmental factors (Brestan & Eyberg, 1998; Loeber et al., 1995; Thornberry et al., 1995). Child factors include physiological, cognitive, and social variables. In terms of physiological factors, genetic predisposition may account for a sizable proportion of the variance of the conduct disturbance (AACAP, 1997). Another reported physiological factor is reduced levels of serotonin, a neurotransmitter known to aid in the modulation of aggressive behavior (AACAP, 1997). Reduced autonomic arousal has also been found and may be related to the trait of fearlessness (AACAP, 1997). A repeated finding in especially aggressive children is the presence of neuropsychological anomalies, such as language, reading, and writing impairments (Moffitt, 1993). These physiological factors may predispose the child to acting-out, risk taking, and academic difficulties (Moffitt, 1993).

Youths with the childhood-onset type disorder frequently exhibit attributional biases and deficits in social problem solving. The attributional biases entail interpreting ambiguous social situations (e.g., a bump in the hallway at school) as intentionally hostile (Lochman & Dodge, 1994). Deficits in social problem solving are manifested in a restricted repertoire of responses to conflict situations in other than aggressive means (Dodge, 1993). As a result, these children tend to interpret situations as provocative and respond in ways that escalate conflict (Dodge, 1993).

Risk factors that lie in the child's environment can be found in the family, school, and community (AACAP, 1997; Thornberry et al., 1995). For the childhood-onset type, family factors include parental antisocial behavior or substance use (Kazdin, 1997; Loeber et al., 1995), low parental socioeconomic status (Loeber et al., 1995), punitive and inconsistent discipline (Short & Shapiro, 1993), and minimal attention to positive behavior. The result is a home atmosphere in which there is a predominance of negative interactions and little positive warmth expressed. The stress of poverty, high-crime neighborhoods, and unemployment, which many of these families endure, only exacerbates these negative interactions (Kazdin, 1997).

In terms of school factors, Kamps and Tankersley (1996) reviewed research indicating that inconsistent and punitive classroom discipline as well as less attention to and reinforcement of appropriate behavior can contribute to the onset and maintenance of conduct disorder. Also, if teachers are not familiar with dealing with aggressive youths, they may respond to hostile behavior with a hostile disciplinary response. Thus, child and school risk factors can interact to make the school atmosphere much like that of the home.

Peer relationship patterns have also been found to contribute to the development of childhood-onset conduct disorder. The social and cognitive deficits noted above result in peer rejection by prosocial peers (Dodge, 1993). In fact, Coie and Kupersmidt (1983) found that in newly forming groups, nonproblem children began to label antisocial children as disliked within 2 or 3 hours of contact. As a result, the conduct-disordered child can be restricted to a small group of children with similar problems. As conduct symptoms persist into adolescence, delinquent peer affiliation has been shown to exacerbate and widen the antisocial repertoire (AACAP, 1997; Moffitt, 1993).

Adolescent-onset type. The adolescent-onset type of conduct disorder is markedly different from the childhood-onset type with regards to course, antisocial behaviors, and risk factor profile. Although the delinquent ranks swell from 5% of boys prior to age 10 to almost 30% of boys by age 15 (Farrington, 1986), these newcomers have short-lived antisocial careers (Moffitt, 1993). By age 17, there is a sharp decline in delinquency, and by their mid-20s, most have desisted from any type of antisocial involvement (Farrington, 1986).

Although both types of conduct disorder may manifest comparable impairment in adolescence (Lahey et al., 1998), the adolescent-onset type is much more likely to engage in more covert antisocial behavior, such as skipping school, burglary, and vandalism (APA, 1994; Moffitt, 1993). Additionally, the risk profile of the adolescent-onset type does not show the pervasive difficulties noted with the childhood-onset type. There is more attachment to parents, interest in close relationships, and intact academic and social skills (Clarizio, 1997). The major risk factor for onset and persistence of symptoms is deviant peer affiliation (Moffitt, 1993).

What accounts for the marked discrepancy in severity and chronicity between these subtypes of conduct disorder? Moffitt (1993) proposed that the physiological, cognitive, and social impairments evident in the childhood-onset type set the stage for school failure and alienation from prosocial attachments. The adolescent-onset type, on the other hand, emerges in response to adolescent strivings for parental independence and adultlike status. Delinquent behavior meets this need by providing a way of looking and acting older (e.g., smoking, drinking, and sex). The best models for this type of behavior are delinquent youths who are already engaging in them. However, by late adolescence, more legitimate adult roles become attainable (e.g., work, college, getting an apartment). Unlike the childhood-onset type, these individuals have the academic and social skills that make prosocial options viable.

Common Comorbid Disorders

The most common comorbid conditions are attention-deficit hyperactivity disorder (ADHD), oppositional defiant disorder (ODD), depression, and substance use disorders (APA, 1994). During the childhood years, the conduct-disordered child frequently has co-occurring ODD and ADHD (Loeber & Keenan, 1994). Typically, ADHD appears first during the early preschool years. Then ODD, which is characterized by negativistic and defiant behavior toward authority figures, emerges around age 5. Although many children grow out of ODD, a subgroup worsens and develops conduct disorder (Loeber & Keenan, 1994). In early adolescence, depression and substance use become common comorbid conditions.

Comorbidity has significant implications as far as course and persistence of conduct disorder. The presence of early onset ADHD, in comparison with its absence, has been shown to predict earlier onset of conduct disorder (Loeber et al., 1995) and more severe chronic violent offending (Loeber & Stouthamer-Loeber, 1998; Moffitt, 1993). Adolescents with conduct disorder and depression have three times the suicide risk as adolescents with just depression (Loeber & Keenan, 1994). Substance use has been implicated in the commission of more violent crimes (Loeber & Keenan, 1994). These types of findings highlight the importance of accurate assessment and treatment of these comorbid conditions.

Assessment Issues

The diagnosis of conduct disorder can be complicated because of limitations in the *DSM–IV* diagnostic system and because of core features of the disorder itself. Clinicians should be sensitive to the fact that the *DSM–IV* criteria best represent conduct problems of adolescents who engage in aggressive behaviors (Clarizio, 1997). Although it may be especially sensitive for the chronic violent offender, it may be less exact at identifying preschool and early elementary-age children. Furthermore, the emphasis on aggressive behaviors may result in the underdiagnosis of preadolescent girls who engage in more rule violations and covert behaviors (Loeber & Keenan, 1994; Loeber & Stouthamer-Loeber, 1998).

A second assessment consideration is obtaining accurate information. Self-report information may be difficult to obtain because of common characteristics of the disorder itself, deceitfulness, and the tendency to blame others (Sommers-Flanagan & Sommers-Flanagan, 1998). Compounding this self-report problem is the fact that symptoms may be present in some settings but not in others (Loeber & Stouthamer-Loeber, 1998). Because of these problems, assessment should include multiple raters (e.g., parents, teachers, and probation officer) who can report on functioning in the school, home, and community settings (AACAP, 1997; Sommers-Flanagan & Sommers-Flanagan, 1998).

TREATMENTS FOR CONDUCT DISORDER

As etiological factors have become clearer, treatments have been developed to address these factors (Kazdin, 1997). These efforts can be conceptualized as addressing different aspects of the child–environment equation that initiates and maintains conduct disorder. In this section, I review treatments that have targeted primarily child factors, environmental factors, or multiple factors simultaneously.

Treatments That Target Child Factors

Medications

A number of psychotropic medications have been examined with respect to reducing violent behavior, impulsivity, and antisocial acts in children and adolescents (AACAP, 1997; Karper & Krystal, 1997). Mood stabilizers (e.g., lithium, anticonvulsants, and serotonin reuptake inhibitors such as Prozac and Zoloft) have been shown to reduce aggressive acting-out. However, findings are mixed and may not generalize to severe conduct disorder (Karper & Krystal, 1997). A major problem for many of these medications is their significant side-effect profile, which can include increases in aggression. The best indications for their use are in the presence of a comorbid mood disorder such as depression or bipolar disorder (AACAP, 1997).

Because stimulants such as methylphenidate (e.g., Ritalin) have been shown to reduce aggression in children with ADHD, they have also been tested for those with conduct disorder (Karper & Krystal, 1997). Although there is some limited evidence that stimulants can reduce aggression in those with conduct disorder, a major contraindication is the potential for abuse (Karper & Krystal, 1997). Stimulants are most indicated if ADHD is also present, but their use needs to be carefully monitored (AACAP, 1997). In summary, the role of medications appears limited and is most indicated in the treatment of comorbid disorders.

Social Problem-Solving Skills Training

Social problem-solving skills training (SPSST) attempts to modify attributional biases and deficits in generating prosocial alternatives. In session, training entails generating alternatives, weighing options, and selecting and evaluating prosocial alternatives to provocative interpersonal situations (Kazdin, 1997; Lochman & Dodge, 1994). Treatment is typically individually oriented and, when conducted on an outpatient basis, requires about 25 sessions.

SPSST has been rigorously tested with inpatient and outpatient samples of 7- to 13-year-olds. Kazdin, Bass, Siegel, and Thomas (1989) found outpatient SPSST was superior to a relationship therapy in reducing externalizing behaviors, antisocial behavior, daily misbehavior, and aggressive school behavior. In another outpatient study, Kazdin, Siegel, and Bass (1992) found that SPSST significantly increased prosocial competence (e.g., adaptive assertiveness, following rules, and peer sociability) and significantly decreased measures of aggression, antisocial behavior, and delinquency. At 1-year follow-up, those receiving SPSST scored in the nonclinical range on measures of deviance. With inpatient samples, SPSST has also been shown to increase prosocial behavior and to decrease aggression and other externalizing behaviors (Kazdin, Esveldt-Dawson, French, & Unis, 1987).

SPSST appears to be a promising treatment for conduct disorder (Brestan & Eyberg, 1998; Kazdin, 1997). However, some caveats are in order. Treatments with a strong cognitive emphasis may be less effective in children younger than 10 (Brestan & Eyberg, 1998). For younger children (e.g., 4–8 years of age), more practice activities that use puppets and videotape modeling have been shown to improve problem-solving and conflict management skills (Webster-Stratton & Hammond, 1997). It is also unclear if SPSST would be as effective for those with the adolescent-onset type of conduct disorder who may have intact skills.

Anger Management

A number of studies have specifically targeted anger and aggression problems using variations of SPSST in combination with other interventions. These programs typically provide education about the anger response, which then sets the stage for training in relaxation (Feindler, Marriott, & Iwata, 1984), self-talk (e.g., Lochman, Lampron, Gemmer, Harris, & Wyckoff, 1989), and alternative coping behaviors such as assertion (Feindler et al., 1984). These programs have been shown to be effective in reducing anger problems among multisuspended delinquents (Feindler et al., 1984) and aggressive 9- to 13-year-olds (Lochman et al., 1989). Because diagnostic work-ups were not included in these studies, it is not clear whether these results would generalize to a conduct-disordered population.

Treatments That Target Environmental Factors

Family, school, and peer factors have all been implicated in the development and maintenance of antisocial behavior (AACAP, 1997; Moffitt, 1993). In this section, I review treatments that have attempted to ameliorate each of these areas.

Family-Based Treatments

Two general approaches to address family problems have been discussed in the clinical literature: enhancing parenting skills (e.g., Kazdin et al., 1992; Webster-Stratton & Hammond, 1997) and modifying dysfunctional family interaction patterns using family therapy (e.g., Alexander & Parsons, 1982; Minuchin, 1974).

Parent training (PT) is the most extensively studied treatment for conduct disorder (Brestan & Eyberg, 1998; Kazdin, 1997). Based on social learning theory, PT provides training in the use of reinforcement to increase prosocial behavior and mild punishment (e.g., loss of privileges, time-out) to decrease disruptive or antisocial behavior (for treatment protocols, see Kazdin et al., 1992; Webster-Stratton, 1990). Training typically involves 10 to 24 sessions and can either involve the parents primarily or require a parent and the child to attend each session.

PT has been found to be superior to a variety of other treatments with this population. PT has shown better overall outcome on measures of conduct problems in comparison with client-centered therapy (Bernal, Klinnert, & Schultz, 1980) and various control conditions (Kazdin et al., 1992). Populations that have been tested have ranged from 3 to 16 years of age and have included youths with severe conduct disorder and aggression problems (Bernal et al., 1980; Kazdin et al., 1992). Changes are evident in not only the parent's and the child's home behaviors but also among other siblings and in the school setting (for review, see Kazdin, 1997). Webster-Stratton (1990) tested a videotaped version of PT in which parents met in a weekly group and found that it was as effective as standard PT.

In parent interaction therapy, the parent and the problem child are seen together. In each session, the parent practices a particular parental skill (e.g., positive attending) with the child in some play activity. The counselor provides coaching to the parent during this activity using a bug-in-the-ear. In comparison with control conditions, parent interaction therapy has been shown to significantly reduce conduct problems and aggression in the home and school setting (Brestan & Eyberg, 1998; Peed, Roberts, & Forhand, 1977).

Family therapy approaches, in contrast to PT, involve all relevant family members in each session. The assumption is that antisocial behavior serves an interpersonal function in the family, such as maintaining distance between disengaged parents (Minuchin, 1974). Treatment is designed to improve overall family interaction and communication so that the antisocial behavior is no longer necessary. In a nonexperimental study of delinquent boys, Minuchin (1974) found that participants in systems family therapy were significantly improved 6 to 12 months after treatment. However, in the only comparison of systems family therapy and PT (Wells & Egan, 1988), PT was found to be more effective.

Functional family therapy combines aspects of systems family therapy (Minuchin, 1974) and social learning theory (Alexander & Parsons, 1982). In session, the counselor attempts to shape more adaptive interactions by praising comments that specify the problem, offer solutions, or provide feedback. Most studies of functional family therapy have focused on the families of adolescents with significant delinquency problems. Findings indicate that functional family therapy is more effective than client-centered or psychodynamic therapy and results in half the recidivism as comparison conditions (Alexander, Holtzworth-Monroe, & Jameson, 1994).

Despite these positive findings, several limitations of PT and family therapy should be noted. First, these treatments have attrition rates of almost 30% (Kazdin, 1997). Providing parents with brief supportive counseling during a portion of the session (e.g., as little as 10 minutes) has been shown to significantly reduce attrition (Prinz & Miller, 1994). Second, the data are mixed relating to whether treatment effects generalize to other settings (e.g., Kazdin, 1997). Third, the role of PT remains unclear for children with an adolescent-onset type conduct disorder whose parents may have intact parenting skills. Family therapy approaches versus PT per se may be more indicated with this population.

School-Based Interventions

These programs attempt to ameliorate risk factors such as academic failure, low commitment to school, school conflict, and antisocial school behavior (Brewer, Hawkins, Catalano, & Neckerman, 1995; Kamps & Tankersley, 1996). Three major types of interventions have been studied: (a) in-school therapy, (b) peer counseling and peer mediation, and (c) school organization and classroom instructional strategies. In terms of in-school therapy, Brestan and Eyberg (1998) reported that 43% of the outcome studies reviewed for conduct disorder were conducted in the school setting. These treatments are typically administered by an outside mental health professional using many of the treatments discussed above, including SPSST, anger management, and social skills training. Results indicate that these treatments reduce aggression and disruptive behavior in the school and home setting (see Brestan & Eyberg, 1998). These favorable findings may be due to the fact that treatment is accessible and more reliably monitored.

Peer counseling and peer mediation have been examined as vehicles for developing conflict resolution skills (see Brewer et al., 1995, for review). Peer counseling groups combine a number of high-risk students with one or more prosocial students with the goal of discussing more positive approaches to conflict situations. Available data, however, suggest that it is not effective with high-risk youths and may even result in the exacerbation of antisocial behavior (Brewer et al., 1995). In peer mediation, on the other hand, students who are involved in a conflict meet with a trained fellow student who helps them to resolve the problem (Brewer et al., 1995). Although this approach has yielded positive findings as far as changes in attitude and knowledge about conflict management, most studies have not shown concomitant changes in behavior and have not included conduct-disordered youths (Brewer et al., 1995).

A number of interventions have targeted school behavior and academic performance per se. Behavioral consultants who help the teacher devise behavioral management plans may help to increase on-task behavior and reduce antisocial school behavior (see Brewer et al., 1995, for review). Structured activities outside of the classroom, during and after school, appear to decrease antisocial behavior and aggression in particular. Attendance and academic performance have been shown to improve by consistent monitoring and reinforcement of class attendance. Thus, structured activities appear to be helpful with particularly disruptive and violent youths.

Classroom instructional style also seems to be important in promoting academic success with conduct-disordered youths (Brewer et al., 1995). Teachers who are more successful with behavior-disordered students provide a structured learning environment, predictable routines, high levels of praise, and an instructional style that promotes student participation and success (Wehby, Symons, Canale, & Go, 1998). Independent solitary learning activities are replaced by interactional and group activities, which encourage positive exchanges among students (Brewer et al., 1995).

In summary, school-based programs have demonstrated reductions in antisocial behavior, as well as gains in academic achievement. However, many of the studies in this area lack random assignment or long-term follow-up. Programs with either negative or mixed findings include peer counseling and peer mediation.

Reducing Deviant Peer Influence

Peer influence is one of the most robust risk factors for antisocial behavior in both children and adolescents (Moffitt, 1993). Two general approaches have been tested with delinquent and violent youths. First, community activity and recreational programs attempt to curtail unstructured time with antisocial peers by providing programs in sports, music, dance, and practical skills. Available data indicate that these programs do significantly reduce delinquency while the youth is involved (Jones & Offord, 1989). Importantly, however, Feldman, Caplinger, and Woduski (1983) found that groups composed of only delinquents resulted in poorer outcome in comparison with groups composed of prosocial and delinquent adolescents. These findings suggest that, to be successful, activity programs need to include prosocial peers and encourage sustained participation.

A second approach has been to increase parental monitoring of peer affiliations. Studies show that increased parental monitoring of the child's free time and peer affiliations predicts lower rates of antisocial activity across a variety of racial and ethnic groups (Reid & Eddy, 1997). Additionally, parents can encourage and support involvement with prosocial peers by taking their child to after-school and recreational programs. It is interesting to note that despite the important role of deviant peer affiliation, treatments in this area have not been extensively studied.

Multicomponent Interventions

The interventions discussed so far target a particular domain of risk factors, such as the home, school, or peers. Although some studies have shown transfer of effects to other domains (Kazdin et al., 1992; Peed et al.,

1977), most have not shown any lasting generalization (Kazdin, 1997). In recent years, investigators have tested two approaches that simultaneously target multiple domains: (a) combining interventions that have been shown to be effective individually and (b) providing a comprehensive program that targets relevant individual, family, school, and peer factors.

Combined Treatment Packages

The most common combined treatments have been PT with either SPSST or social skills training (Kazdin et al., 1992; Webster-Stratton & Hammond, 1997). In a population of 4- to 7-year-olds with significant conduct problems, Webster-Stratton and Hammond (1997) found that the combination of the child's treatment (i.e., videotaped modeling and social skills training) and the parent's treatment (i.e., videotaped PT) produced a broader range of improvements than either treatment alone. In an older population of 7- to 13-year-olds with conduct disorder, Kazdin et al. (1992) found that the combination of PT and SPSST was superior to either treatment alone in reducing antisocial behavior, parental stress, depression, and overall symptomatology. At 1-year follow-up, the combined treatment showed further improvement and had more participants in the nonclinical range. The results of both of these studies are encouraging, considering that many of these adolescents had the childhood-onset type of conduct disorder. However, there was no evidence that these changes generalized to the school and peer domains.

Multisystemic Therapy

In an effort to address the multiple determinants of serious adolescent antisocial behavior (i.e., individual, family, peer, and school risk factors), Borduin and Henggeler (1990) developed multisystemic therapy (MST). The cornerstone of this treatment package is family therapy, which is designed to improve family atmosphere and discipline. School interventions target academic achievement, discipline, and involvement in prosocial school activities by involving interested school personnel (e.g., teachers, school counselor). Regular meetings between school personnel and the parents ensure that there is consistency and cooperation between the home and school. Peer interventions include parental monitoring of peers and involvement in prosocial recreational activities. If individual work is indicated, interventions might include cognitive restructuring and social skills training (Borduin & Henggeler, 1990). A unique aspect of MST is that interventions are designed to improve functioning both within and between domains.

Empirical tests of MST have focused primarily on violent and chronically delinquent adolescents (Borduin & Henggeler, 1990; Borduin et al., 1995; Henggeler, Melton, & Smith, 1992). Studies typically compare MST with standard care, which might be individual outpatient therapy or juvenile justice services (e.g., curfews, strict probation). Results to date have shown that MST is superior to these standard treatments on measures of violent crime, delinquency, days incarcerated, family cohesion, nondeviant peer affiliation, and parental stress (Borduin & Henggeler, 1990; Borduin et al., 1995; Henggeler et al., 1992). The differences are not only large but also quite durable. For example, at 4-year follow-up the rearrest percentage was 71% for standard care versus 26% for MST (Borduin et al., 1995). At 1-year follow-up, Henggeler et al. (1992) found that the incarceration rate was 68% for standard care but only 20% for MST. These data indicate that MST is a particularly effective approach with chronic offenders with a history of violent behavior. Furthermore, gender, racial, and ethnic factors have not been shown to compromise treatment outcome (Borduin et al., 1995; Henggeler et al., 1992).

Despite these encouraging findings, MST is not without its limitations. Considering the caseloads of most clinicians, it may be unrealistic in day-to-day clinical practice. Instead, it may be useful for the clinician to use the MST model conceptually but to develop community liaisons with schools and other agencies to carry out various aspects of the plan. Second, MST has primarily been tested with serious adolescent delinquent offenders. Whether this approach is useful for younger clients is unknown.

CONCLUSION

A number of effective treatments have been identified for children and adolescents with conduct disorder (Brestan & Eyberg, 1998; Kazdin, 1997). Effective treatments for preschool and early elementary-age children and their parents include videotaped modeling, rehearsal of social and parenting skills (e.g., Webster-Stratton & Hammond, 1997), and parent interaction therapy (Brestan & Eyberg, 1998). Later elementary and middle school age children appear to profit from PT (e.g., Bernal et al., 1980; Kazdin et al., 1992) and more cognitively based treatments such as SPSST (e.g., Kazdin et al., 1992). MST, functional family therapy, and anger management show promise with adolescent populations (e.g., Borduin et al., 1995; Feindler et al., 1984). School-based interventions that can be helpful include in-school therapy, behavioral consultation to the teacher, a positive instructional style, and a more structured school routine behavior (e.g., Brewer et al., 1995). Peer interventions include recreational activity programs with nondeviant peers and parental monitoring of peer affiliations. There is some evidence that multicomponent programs such as MST and combinations of PT with SPSST or social skills training are superior to single-focus interventions (e.g., Kazdin et al., 1992).

Although these findings appear straightforward, there are unanswered issues. First, the risk factor literature makes clear distinctions between the childhood-onset type and the adolescent-onset type of conduct disorder (Lahey et al., 1998; Loeber et al., 1995). Despite these differences, no study to date has examined whether treatments are differentially effective for either type. Clinically, it would seem that the childhood-onset type would profit most from an array of treatments, including PT, SPSST, academic assistance, and careful peer monitoring. Multicomponent programs such as MST seem to be ideally suited for this purpose. However, the youth with adolescent-onset type conduct disorder typically has intact social and academic skills, and there is a history of adequate family functioning. Consequently, peer interventions and family therapy that improves communication and boundaries may be more indicated.

Second, the treatment of comorbid conditions in the context of conduct disorder has received scant attention in the literature (Kazdin, 1997). Studies either ignore comorbid conditions or make them exclusion criteria for participation in the study. This is ironic because comorbidity is more the rule than the exception with conduct disorder (Lahey et al., 1998; Loeber & Keenan, 1994). At this point, the best guidelines are to always assess for comorbid disorders and to take steps to provide for their treatment.

Although violent forms of conduct disorder can have a particularly insidious course, there are treatments that not only can significantly reduce antisocial behavior but also can help these youths to function in the nonclinical range (e.g., Kazdin et al., 1992). On the other hand, many of the popular approaches to dealing with these youths (e.g., unstructured group therapy, boot camps, alternative school programs that congregate delinquent youths) may actually exacerbate antisocial tendencies (AACAP, 1997; Kazdin, 1997). In the final analysis, it will be critical for clinicians to not only be proficient with more empirically validated treatments for conduct disorder (Brestan & Eyberg, 1998) but also be advocates for change in the ways that schools and other institutions deal with these youths.

REFERENCES

Alexander, J. F., Holtzworth-Monroe, A., & Jameson, P. B. (1994). The process and outcome of marital and family therapy research: Review and evaluation. In S. L. Garfield (Ed.), *Handbook of psychotherapy and behavior change* (4th ed., pp. 560–595). New York: Wiley.

Alexander, J. P., & Parsons, B. V. (1982). *Functional family therapy*. Monterey, CA: Brooks/Cole.

American Academy of Child and Adolescent Psychiatry. (1997). Practice parameters for the assessment and treatment of children and adolescents with conduct disorder. *Journal of the American Academy of Child and Adolescent Psychiatry, 36*(Suppl.), 122S–139S.

American Psychiatric Association. (1994). *Diagnostic and statistical manual of mental disorders* (4th ed.). Washington, DC: Author.

Bernal, M. E., Klinnert, M. D., & Schultz, L. A. (1980). Outcome evaluation of behavioral parent training and client-centered parent counseling for children with conduct problems. *Journal of Applied Behavior Analysis, 13,* 677–691.

Borduin, C. M., & Henggeler, S. W. (1990). A multisystemic approach to the treatment of serious delinquent behavior. In R. J. McMahon & R. De V. Peters (Eds.), *Behavior disorders of adolescence* (pp. 63–80). New York: Plenum Press.

Borduin, C. M., Mann, B. J., Cone, L. T., Henggeler, S. W., Fucci, B. R., Blaske, D. M., & Williams, R. A. (1995). Multisystemic treatment of serious juvenile offenders: Long-term prevention of criminality and violence. *Journal of Consulting and Clinical Psychology, 63,* 569–578.

Brestan, E. V., & Eyberg, S. M. (1998). Effective psychosocial treatments of conduct-disordered children and adolescents: 29 years, 82 studies, and 5,272 kids. *Journal of Clinical Child Psychology, 27,* 180–189.

Brewer, D. D., Hawkins, J. D., Catalano, R. F., & Neckerman, H. J. (1995). Preventing serious, violent, and chronic juvenile offending. In J. C. Howell, B. Krisberg, J. D. Hawkins, & J. J. Wilson (Eds.), *A sourcebook: Serious, violent, and chronic juvenile offenders* (pp. 61–141). Thousand Oaks, CA: Sage.

Centers for Disease Control. (1991). Weapon-carrying among high school students: United States, 1990. *Morbidity and Mortality Weekly Report, 44,* 681–684.

Clarizio, H. (1997). Conduct disorder: Developmental considerations. *Psychology in the Schools, 34,* 253–263.

Coie, J. D., & Kupersmidt, J. B. (1983). A behavioral analysis of emerging social status in boys'groups. *Child Development, 54,* 1400–1416.

Dodge, K. (1993). Social–cognitive mechanisms in the development of conduct disorder and depression. *Annual Review of Psychology, 44,* 559–584.

Farrington, D. P. (1986). Age and crime. In N. Tonry & N. Morris (Eds.), *Crime and justice: An annual review of research* (Vol. 7, pp. 189–250). Chicago: University of Chicago Press.

Feindler, E. L., Marriott, S. A., & Iwata, M. (1984). Group anger control training for junior high school delinquents. *Cognitive Therapy and Research, 8,* 299–311.

Feldman, R. A., Caplinger, T. E., & Woduski, O. S. (1983). *St. Louis conundrum: The effective treatment of antisocial youth.* Englewood Cliffs, NJ: Prentice Hall.

Henggeler, S. W., Melton, G. B., & Smith, L. A. (1992). Family preservation using multisystemic therapy: An effective alternative to incarcerating serious juvenile offenders. *Journal of Consulting and Clinical Psychology, 60,* 953–961.

Howell, J. C., Krisberg, B., & Jones, M. (1995). Trends in juvenile crime and youth violence. In J. C. Howell, B. Krisberg, J. D. Hawkins, & J. J. Wilson (Eds.), *A sourcebook: Serious, violent, and chronic juvenile offenders* (pp. 1–35). Thousand Oaks, CA: Sage.

Jones, M. B., & Offord, D. R. (1989). Reduction of antisocial behavior in poor children by non-social skill development. *Journal on Child Psychology and Psychiatry and Allied Disciplines, 30,* 737–750.

Kamps, D. M., & Tankersley, M. (1996). Prevention of behavioral conduct disorders: Trends and research issues. *Behavioral Disorders, 22,* 41–48.

Karper, L. P., & Krystal, J. H. (1997). Pharmacotherapy of violent behavior. In D. M. Stoff, J. Breiling, & J. D. Maser (Eds.), *The handbook of antisocial behavior* (pp. 436–444). New York: Wiley.

Kazdin, A. E. (1997). Practitioner review: Psychosocial treatments for conduct disorder in children. *Journal of Child Psychology and Psychiatry, 38*, 161–178.

Kazdin, A. E., Bass, D., Siegal, T., & Thomas, C. (1989). Cognitive–behavioral therapy and relationship therapy in the treatment of children referred for antisocial behavior. *Journal of Consulting and Clinical Psychology, 57*, 522–538.

Kazdin, A. E., Esveldt-Dawson, K., French, N. H., & Unis, A. S. (1987). Problem-solving skills training and relationship therapy in the treatment of antisocial child behavior. *Journal of Consulting and Clinical Psychology, 55*, 76–85.

Kazdin, A. E., Siegel, T. C., & Bass, D. (1992). Cognitive problem-solving skills training and parent management training in the treatment of antisocial behavior in children. *Journal of Consulting and Clinical Psychology, 60*, 733–747.

Lahey, B. B., Applegate, B., Barkley, R. A., Garfinkel, B., McBurnett, K., Kerdyk, L., Greenhill, L., Hynd, G. W., Frick, P. J., Newcorn, J., Biederman, J., Ollendick, T., Hart, E. L., Perez, D., Waldman, I., & Shaffer, D. (1994). DSM–IV field trials for oppositional defiant disorder and conduct disorder in children and adolescents. *Journal of American Psychiatry, 151*, 1163–1171.

Lahey, B. B., Loeber, R., Quay, H. C., Applegate, B., Shaffer, D., Waldman, I., Hart, E. L., McBurnett, K., Frick, P. J., Jensen, P. S., Dulcan, M. K., Canino, G., & Bird, H. (1998). Validity of DSM–IV subtypes of conduct disorder based on age of onset. *Journal of the American Academy of Child and Adolescent Psychiatry, 37*, 435–442.

Lochman, J. E., & Dodge, K. A. (1994). Social–cognitive processes of severely violent, moderately aggressive, and nonaggressive boys. *Journal of Consulting and Clinical Psychology, 62*, 366–374.

Lochman, J. E., Lampron, L. B., Gemmer, T. C., Harris, S. R., & Wyckoff, G. M. (1989). Teacher consultation and cognitive–behavioral interventions with aggressive boys. *Psychology in the Schools, 26*, 179–188.

Loeber, R., Green, S. M., Keenan, K., & Lahey, B. B. (1995). Which boys will fare worse? Early predictors of the onset of conduct disorder in a six-year longitudinal study. *Journal of the American Academy of Child and Adolescent Psychiatry, 34*, 499–509.

Loeber, R., & Keenan, K. (1994). Interaction between conduct disorder and its comorbid conditions: Effects of age and gender. *Clinical Psychology Review, 14*, 497–523.

Loeber, R., & Stouthamer-Loeber, M. (1998). Development of juvenile aggression and violence: Some common misconceptions and controversies. *American Psychologist, 53*, 242–259.

Minuchin, S. (1974). *Families and family therapy.* Cambridge, MA: Harvard University Press.

Moffitt, T. (1993). Adolescence-limited and life-course-persistent antisocial behavior: A developmental taxonomy. *Psychological Review, 100*, 674–701.

Peed, S., Roberts, M., & Forhand, R. (1977). Evaluation of the effectiveness of a standardized parent training program in altering the interaction of mothers and their noncompliant children. *Behavior Modification, 1*, 323–350.

Prinz, R. J., & Miller, G. E. (1994). Family-based treatment for childhood antisocial behavior: Experimental influences on dropout and engagement. *Journal of Consulting and Clinical Psychology, 62,* 645–650.

Reid, J. B., & Eddy, J. M. (1997). The prevention of antisocial behavior: Some considerations in the search for effective intervention. In D. M. Stoff, J. Breiling, & J. D. Maser (Eds.), *The handbook of antisocial behavior* (pp. 343–356). New York: Wiley.

Short, R. J., & Shapiro, S. K. (1993). Conduct disorders: A framework for understanding and intervening in schools and communities. *School Psychology Review, 22,* 362–375.

Sommers-Flanagan, J., & Sommers-Flanagan, R. (1998). Assessment and diagnosis of conduct disorder. *Journal of Counseling and Development, 76,* 189–197.

Thornberry, T. P., Huizinga, D., & Loeber, R. (1995). The prevention of serious delinquency and violence: Implications from the program of research on the causes and correlates of delinquency. In J. C. Howell, B. Krisberg, J. D. Hawkins, & J. J. Wilson (Eds.), *A sourcebook: Serious, violent, and chronic juvenile offenders* (pp. 213–237). Thousand Oaks, CA: Sage.

Webster-Stratton, C. (1990). Enhancing the effectiveness of self-administered videotape parent training for families with conduct-problem children. *Journal of Abnormal Child Psychology, 18,* 479–492.

Webster-Stratton, C., & Hammond, M. (1997). Treating children with early-onset conduct problems: A comparison of child and parent training interventions. *Journal of Consulting and Clinical Psychology, 65,* 93–109.

Wehby, J. H., Symons, F. J., Canale, J. A., & Go, F. G. (1998). Teaching practices in classrooms for students with emotional and behavioral disorders: Discrepancies between recommendations and observations. *Behavioral Disorders, 24,* 51–56.

Wells, K. C., & Egan, J. (1988). Social learning theory and systems family therapy for childhood oppositional disorder: Comparative treatment outcome. *Comprehensive Psychiatry, 29,* 138–146.

21 | The Counselor as Leader: Critical Incident Stress Management in the Long Beach Schools

Joanne M. Tortorici Luna

Despite the much-heralded declining crime rates, young people in Long Beach, California, continue to be jarred by neighborhood violence at the same time that schools are reported to be relatively safe (U.S. Departments of Education and Justice, 1999). Berthold (1998) reported that students in some Long Beach neighborhoods live in ongoing warlike conditions. Their emotional reactions are similar to, and as extreme as, those of U.S. combat war veterans who returned from Vietnam. It is notable that the student group studied was not a clinical population, and that a very small number of the people studied had actually sought psychological services. Not surprisingly, the students who were most severely affected emotionally showed the worst academic outcomes. Teachers with students from the most violent areas of Long Beach reported that children showed a preoccupation with death in their written and artistic work. Lifton (1974) noted a similar "death imprint" among children who have early, massive, or continuous exposure to violence. Embry (1996) noted the devastating impact violence has on learning and behavior.

Males (1999) reported that White adults over the age of 30 still account for most of California's violent crime and that federal agencies estimate three of four young murder victims are killed by adults, not by juveniles (Males, 1998). After the Fall 1998 semester, more than 15 youths, 7 of them Long Beach Unified School District (LBUSD) students, had been murdered (Kabar, 1999). Males (1996) also described the direct relationship between the number of violent youths and the explosion of teen poverty.

The purpose of this chapter is to describe the LBUSD's school violence reduction efforts as a process model for other schools. The chapter includes a brief history of violence response efforts, a case example of a response to a school crisis, and a detailed manual for Critical Incident Stress Management that can be adapted for any school.

COUNSELING REFORM AND CRITICAL INCIDENT STRESS MANAGEMENT

Morrison, Furlong, and Morrison (1994) noted the need for educators to consider school violence as an educational problem rather than a criminal justice problem, and the California Commission on Teacher Credentialing Task Force has recommended that violence prevention be included in educators' preservice training. Keys, Bemak, and Lockhart (1998) recognized that the school counselor is often the only mental health resource available to identify and address students' personal and social needs. Yet, once on the job, many counselors find that administrators do not include them in the preparation and organization of crisis plans, nor do they typically think of counselors as school leaders during critical incidents, despite evidence that the most highly effective school counseling programs are those in which the counselors spend most of their time providing direct services (Sexton, Whiston, Bleuer, & Walz, 1997). Furthermore, a recent review of school counseling outcome research (Whiston & Sexton, 1998) indicated that most studies focused on remedial rather than preventive interventions, perhaps also indicating an orientation in practice.

The American School Counselors Association recommends 250:1 as an appropriate student-to-counselor ratio; unfortunately, the current California ratio is 1,056:1 (Hatch, 1999), and 42% of California school districts have no school counselors at all. In the elementary schools that do have counselors, the ratio of students to counselor is 2,381:1 (Hatch, 1999). Even though the U.S. Departments of Education and Justice (1999) have advocated for all-student access to school psychologists or counselors, these counselor caseloads do not provide such access for all students.

To extend violence prevention efforts, the LBUSD established a Violence Prevention Team, which is a counselor–police partnership that serves on-site personnel and provides in-service training, ongoing needs assessment, and program development. One team partner is a counseling psychologist and school counselor with extensive local and international experience in school and community violence reduction. The other partner is a Long Beach Police Department officer and chaplain on loan to the school district. The team began its work by meeting with school safety committees, to ascertain each site's needs in violence reduction. During crises, the team serves as consultants when requested, helping school staff members plan and carry out an effective response. The team strongly believes that local personnel are best equipped to deal with site emergencies because of their rapport with students and parents and knowledge of local conditions.

LBUSD's school violence reduction efforts, however, predate the formation of the Violence Prevention Team. McBride (n.d.) promoted a comprehensive approach to violence reduction and supported early implementation efforts. Hilburn (1996) constructed a strong, proactive high school and police partnership. The Safe and Drug Free Schools Program provided materials and training for curricula with positive outcomes, such as Second Step (Grossman et al., 1997), Think First (Larson, 1992), and Anger Coping (Lochman, Dunn, & Klimes-Dougan, 1993).

CRITICAL INCIDENT STRESS MANAGEMENT AT WILSON HIGH SCHOOL

In May 1997, Woodrow Wilson High School (LBUSD) students and faculty were stunned that a senior, Jeremy Strohmeyer, had been arrested for murder. The former honor student was charged and eventually convicted of sexually molesting and murdering 7-year-old Sherrice Iverson in a Nevada casino restroom. While Sherrice Iverson's family, friends, and teachers struggled to cope with the tragedy, the reactions of those close to Strohmeyer ran the spectrum of disbelief, revulsion, anger, and grief. After Strohmeyer's arrest, media vans circled the high school, and reporters approached students and staff for their reactions as they entered and exited.

The Wilson High School counselors immediately began to formulate a plan to help the school community cope with the many and complex emotions evoked by the events. Fortunately, a Critical Incident Stress Management Plan (Tortorici Luna, 1997) had just been completed. Using the plan as a guide, the counselors helped to lead the school through the crisis.

Their first step was to arrange a strategy meeting with school administrators, to develop a schoolwide response to the incident. Counselors recommended that an after-school faculty meeting take place that same day. At the faculty meeting, the administrators and counselors provided information, listened to concerns, and informed staff about the emotional responses they could expect in themselves and their students. The counselors distributed handouts to help teachers respond to distressed students and get additional help if needed.

The following day, counselors set up a crisis center in the Media Center, where teachers and students could go to receive additional care. School counselors and a small number of mental health workers from a partner clinic staffed the center. The group triaged those sent to them: They counseled some immediately and sent others to speak with their own counselors on campus. To avoid hysteria contagion, they sent the most distressed students home after a counseling intervention, with referral information for follow-up care. In the regular guidance counseling center, the staff relaxed the usual pass requirements, allowing distraught students to be seen on a walk-in basis during class time. Meanwhile, the two senior student counselors went to Strohmeyer's classes to provide more extensive debriefing (Mitchell & Everly, 1995). These special measures continued for a few days, with occasional follow-up visits to Strohmeyer's classrooms for 2 weeks.

After the crisis at Wilson High School, the counseling staff distributed an outcome questionnaire to all staff and the students who received services (see Table 21.1) to evaluate client satisfaction with the counseling interventions, similar to the recommendations of Granello and Granello (1998) and Whiston and Sexton (1998). A total of 117 students responded to the questionnaire, and 78% agreed or strongly agreed that the counseling actions around the crisis were timely and effective, 75% felt that the counseling interventions benefited the students who received them, 84% said that counselors were available for students and staff who needed them, and 64% felt the counselor interventions helped to prevent a more widespread campus crisis.

The school faculty and staff also had a positive appraisal of the interventions (see Table 21.2). Of the 34 people who responded, 91% felt the counseling interventions were timely and effective, 88% said that the information that counselors and administrators provided at the defusing meeting was useful to them, 91% said that counselors were available for students and staff who needed support during the crisis, and 79% believed that the counselors' interventions helped to prevent a more widespread crisis. Some respondents gave helpful suggestions, including that those who answered the telephone inquiries also be able to attend future informational faculty meetings during crises.

THE CRITICAL INCIDENT
STRESS MANAGEMENT PLAN:
MENTAL HEALTH COMPONENT

Senate Bill 187 (The Safe Schools Act) mandated that all California schools have a safety plan. However, the mental health or stress management aspects of crisis management are often overlooked by schools. The Critical Incident Stress Management Plan: Mental Health Component is meant to be a companion document to the school safety plan. Its format and terminology are in accordance with California's Standardized Emergency

Table 21.1 | Counseling Outcome Survey Critical Incident Management

MAY 1997
Senior Student Survey (N = 117)

For the following questions, read the statements and indicate whether you strongly agree, agree, disagree, or strongly disagree with each statement. Circle the response that corresponds most closely to how you feel. (NR = no rating.)

1. The counseling actions organized around the recent crisis last week (events leading to and resulting in the arrest of a senior student) were timely and effective.
18% strongly agree   60% agree   12% disagree   5% strongly disagree 5% NR

2. The counseling interventions in the classes of the student who was arrested benefited those students.
14% strongly agree   61% agree   22% disagree   3% strongly disagree 0% NR

3. Counselors were available for students and staff who needed support during the crisis.
28% strongly agree   56% agree   13% disagree   3% strongly disagree 0% NR

4. Teachers provided information and helped students cope with the crisis.
17% strongly agree   52% agree   20% disagree   10% strongly disagree 1% NR

5. Counselors were available for students and staff who needed counseling during the crisis.
28% strongly agree   58% agree   10% disagree   3% strongly disagree 1% NR

6. During the crisis, I felt that the school staff cared about my feelings and well-being.
18% strongly agree   49% agree   21% disagree   12% strongly disagree 0% NR

7. Counselor interventions helped to prevent a more widespread crisis on campus.
10% strongly agree   54% agree   24% disagree   9% strongly disagree 3% NR

Management System, making it easy for schools to integrate it into their documents.

This manual, provided below, is meant to be a generic guide for school teams and should be customized by each school. Rather than offering a static response to each potential crisis as many manuals do, this plan provides an organizational framework as a response tool for a wide spectrum of circumstances. Even with emergency procedures in place, each crisis must be evaluated as it occurs because unknown risks emerge, as evidenced during the mass killings at Columbine High School in Littleton, Colorado. This tragedy raised some questions for those who work in school crisis response: If gunshots are heard outside the building while school is in session, should students be evacuated or locked in? The answer will depend on an evaluation of circumstances that should lead to the safest, least costly (in terms of human life) response.

Table 21.2 | Counseling Outcome Survey Critical Incident Management

MAY 1997
Staff Survey ($N = 34$)

For the following questions, read the statements and indicate whether you strongly agree, agree, disagree, or strongly disagree with each statement. Circle the response that corresponds most closely to how you feel. (NR = no rating.)

1. The counseling actions organized around the recent crisis last week (events leading to and resulting in the arrest of a senior student) were timely and effective.
38% strongly agree 53% agree 6% disagree 3% strongly disagree 0% NR

2. The counseling interventions in the classes of the student who was arrested benefited those students.
27% strongly agree 35% agree 3% disagree 3% strongly disagree 32% NR

3. The faculty meeting which provided information and ways to help students and staff to cope with the crisis was useful.
41% strongly agree 47% agree 3% disagree 3% strongly disagree 6% NR

4. I was able to effectively use the written and verbal information presented at the faculty meeting.
26% strongly agree 50% agree 6% disagree 0% strongly disagree 18% NR

5. Counselors were available for students and staff who needed support during the crisis.
62% strongly agree 29% agree 0% disagree 3% strongly disagree 6% NR

6. Counselor interventions helped to prevent a more widespread crisis on campus.
38% strongly agree 41% agree 9% disagree 6% strongly disagree 6% NR

CRITICAL INCIDENT STRESS MANAGEMENT: MENTAL HEALTH COMPONENT

What Is a Critical Incident? It is any event that has a stressful impact sufficient enough to overwhelm the usually effective coping skills of either an individual or a group. They often are sudden, powerful events that are outside of the range of ordinary human experiences.

Possible Examples of Critical Incidents. Civil unrest, gang/ethnic group-related assaults, sexual assaults, campus-related death or suicide, war, natural disasters.

Purpose of the Critical Incident Management Plan. There are two purposes for the plan. The first intent is to minimize and mitigate damage to survivors, and to help restore previous coping abilities to the affected individuals and groups. Second, this plan will assist survivors in resuming normal operations after the incident and by providing defusing and debriefing sessions.

What Is Defusing? Defusing is a brief meeting that takes place very soon after the critical incident and is led by a member of the Critical Incident Response Team. *All on-campus* adult school personnel should attend.

In the meeting, be sure to state the facts of the incident and dispel rumors. Tell survivors they may have reactions such as anxiety, sleep disturbance, and other signs of distress that will most likely decrease in a period of weeks. Inform survivors about how to get additional help if they need it. Provide any other needed information.

What Is Debriefing? Debriefing is a meeting or discussion about a distressing critical incident. It is used to help people who remain distressed after defusing. It is also used to help people who have histories or current situations that put them at high risk for extreme emotional distress. It is designed to mitigate the impact of a critical incident and to assist people in recovering as quickly as possible from the stress associated with the event. The debriefing is run by a specially trained team that includes a mental health professional and peer support personnel. The meeting should include the following.

- *Introduction:* Explain the purpose of the meeting.
- *Facts review:* Ask each person where he/she was when the incident occurred, what he/she saw, thought, heard, smelled during the incident.
- *Feelings review:* Ask each person what he/she felt during the incident, what meaning the incident had/has for him/her, what he/she feels now.
- *Symptom review:* Ask each person if any unusual sensations have occurred on or away from the incident site or are occurring at this moment.
- *Teach* (mental health professional): Review stress *coping* strategies, *validate* feelings/sensations, emphasize *similarities* of group members' reactions. Emphasize that reactions are *normal* stress responses to abnormal situations. Answer questions.
- *Close:* Thank the participants. Provide mental health community resources.
- *Follow-up:* Set up individual or group appointments as needed.

QUESTIONS TO GUIDE A CRITICAL INCIDENT STRESS MANAGEMENT PLAN

Who should be on our school's Critical Incident Stress Response Team?

Name	Title	Assignment
	Counseling and Psychology Staff	
	School Nurse	

_____Peace Program Staff_____

_____Peer Mediator/Counseling Rep._____

Who will coordinate the mental health component of our response?

_____Backup_____

_____Backup_____

How will the staff be informed of the incident?_____

How will the students be informed of the incident? _____

How will parents be informed of the incident?_____

Who will speak with the media?

Name	Assignment	Backup
_____Public Information Officer_____

Who will write a statement for those answering the phone?

Name	Assignment	Backup
_____Public Information Officer_____

Who will activate the telephone tree?

_____Incident Commander_____

What communications system will we use if phone lines are not working?

_____

Who will contact transportation services?

Name	Assignment	Backup
_____Logistics Chief_____

Who will present the initial stress defusing meeting for staff? (mental health professionals and peer support personnel)_____

Who will present the initial stress defusing meetings for students?

Teachers: _____

Who will present stress debriefing meetings for students? (mental health professionals and peer support personnel)

Counselors: _____ Psychologists: _____

How will stress debriefing meetings be organized?

Teacher/staff referral?_____ Self-referral?_____

Where will stress debriefing meetings be held?_____

Who will provide specialized on-site psychological/medical interventions if needed?_____

What buddy school could we contact if we are overwhelmed by the crisis?

_____

Who will debrief our debriefers, if necessary?

_____

What district support is available to our team?

Name   Telephone #
_____

_____

What city support is available to our team?

Name   Agency   Telephone #
_____

What community resources are available to our team?

Name   Agency   Telephone #

What county support is available to our team?

Name   Agency   Telephone #

What federal support is available to our team?

Name   Agency   Telephone #

Who will contact the above resources if needed?

Name   Assignment   Backup

_____Incident Commander_____

_____Logistics Chief_____

PREVENTION/PREPAREDNESS PLAN OF ACTION

Before crisis:

- Form a Critical Incident Stress Response Team—Operations Chief
- Form and approve plan
- Review plan with entire school staff
- Practice plan
- Identify training needs
- Train staff as needed

During crisis:

- Adults increase visibility in hallways and outdoor areas during passing periods and lunch as notified by memo or faculty meeting.
- Faculty lead classroom discussions to avert emergencies and to continue gathering relevant information.
- Buildings closed, classrooms locked at discretion of Incident Commander.
- Activities canceled, postponed at discretion of Incident Commander.
- Safety Officer monitors the response team and survivors for stress defusing/debriefing needs. Consults with Medical Team Leader.

Reports to Incident Commander and activates/reactivates the Critical Incident Stress Management Team.
- Incident Commander and Safety Officer organize meeting of key players to avoid confrontations, if appropriate.
- Faculty and staff provide structure and reassurance for students.

EMERGENCY ACTIONS

- Incident Commander gathers facts.
- Incident Commander calls emergency response teams if needed (paramedics, police, gang task force, fire department, etc.).
- Incident Commander notifies faculty and staff of needed emergency actions through bells or other emergency signals.
- Incident Commander activates phone tree or other emergency communication system.
- Safety Officer and Medical Team Leader meet to formulate further response recommendations to Incident Commander.
- Critical Incident Stress Response Team reports to Medical Team Leader for direction.
- Critical Incident Stress Response Team meets to coordinate defusing/debriefing actions.
- Incident Commander provides initial information and notifies teachers of preventive and follow-up actions (defusing and/or debriefing) through memo or faculty meeting.
- Operations Chief sets up Crisis Center (if needed) in _____ (where).
- Public Information Officer handles all media contacts.
- Incident Commander contacts LBUSD central office.
- Faculty and staff cooperate with others to treat/evacuate casualties.

Emergency signals:

1. Emergency in progress: _____

2. Evacuate signal_____

3. Lock down signal_____

   What to do:

   Before first period:_____

   During class time:_____

During lunch or nutrition:_____

During teacher's conference period:_____

After last period:_____

4. Student "hit the deck" signal_____

5. Shelter in place signal_____

6. Teacher's "room clear" signal to students_____

Where should students go?_____

7. Teacher's (secret) signal to designated student(s) to leave quietly and get help

_____

8. All-clear signal_____

What to do_____

Other emergency procedures:

Administrators/Staff Assistants:_____

Maintenance/Ground Personnel:_____

Teacher buddy teams:_____

Counselor/Psychologist teams:_____

Emergency early-out procedures:

_____

REHABILITATION RECOVERY

(On as-needed basis, designated by Critical Incident Stress Response Team)

1. Coordination Center set up (where)_____

2. _____ announces faculty meeting same day or morning after incident.
3. Defusing provided for faculty/staff _____ as soon as possible after the incident.
4. Defusing/debriefing procedures for students reviewed at faculty meeting.
5. Teachers conduct defusing sessions in class.
6. Teachers refer students in deep distress and in need of further intervention (i.e., debriefing) to Coordination Center.
7. Faculty self-refer or request further intervention for distressed colleagues.
8. Counselors/psychologists triage distressed students/staff and decide on possible actions:

   - Debrief on site and follow-up on site
   - Send home with follow-up support
   - Refer for specialized intervention (note: suicidal persons must not be left alone for any amount of time).

9. Critical Incident Stress Response Team meets to evaluate and plan further action.

"DEFUSING" A CRITICAL INCIDENT: CLASSROOM TEACHER SUGGESTIONS

1. Model a calm and supportive attitude.
2. Provide correct, timely information. Discourage/correct rumors.
3. Reassure students that adults are on hand to protect and help them.
4. Allow students to express their thoughts and feelings regarding the incident, without your expressing judgment of them.
5. Explain to students that their distress is a normal response to an abnormal incident and will lessen in time.
6. Discourage revenge fantasies by exploring the consequences of any such actions.
7. Help students to find positive ways to channel their desire to "do something."
8. Refer students who remain distressed to on-site counselors.
9. Arrange rest breaks for yourself by working with a buddy. To manage your own stress and possible distress, talk with a trusted person or designated counselor.
10. Support other staff; provide solidarity for those who are distressed.

HOW TO PROMOTE PSYCHOSOCIAL
WELL-BEING IN EMERGENCIES

1. Provide a safe place and time for the survivors to talk about what happened to them and their peers as soon as possible after the incident.
2. Provide a safe area for caregivers to rest, eat, and talk with a designated counselor, if desired.
3. Focus on coping strengths with survivors, not simply on distress and injury.
4. Do not force people to talk about topics they may wish to remain silent about, and do not allow anyone else to do so.
5. Use supportive interventions that do the least harm and do not retraumatize.
6. Stress culturally appropriate interventions, using familiar, local school site and community resource people whenever possible.
7. Use age-appropriate interventions.
8. Be sensitive to particular meanings traumatic experiences may have in various cultures.
9. Be aware that survivors of past trauma, or those with many unmet needs, may react more strongly to current stressors, may take longer to recover, and may need more specialized intervention.
10. Ensure that the psychosocial needs of all members of the school community are met, regardless of the side of a conflict that they, their families, or their communities may be on.
11. Avoid institutionalization or removal of distressed students from their families or communities for treatments.
12. Help prevent psychosocial difficulties by stimulating social interaction, cultural activities, and by allowing time for supportive religious practices for those who wish them.

EMOTIONAL FIRST AID:
SUGGESTIONS FOR CAREGIVERS[1]

1. Assure basic survival needs.
2. Maintain calm and an attitude of solidarity and caring.

---

[1]This section has been adapted from Tortorici (1994).

3. Care for yourself. Take breaks to eat, rest, and talk.
4. Give survivors frequent, accurate, brief explanations of the events in age- and culture-appropriate language.
5. Express understanding of realistic fears. Do not deny what has happened and what is likely to happen.
6. When gathering facts, minimize the number of times survivors are asked to tell what happened. Do not allow repeated questioning by media or other fact-finding groups.
7. Reassure young people that you and other adults are there to protect and care for them.
8. If there are deaths, explain or re-explain the nature of death. Acknowledge that it is difficult to accept death under unexpected, massive, or cruel circumstances.
9. Give young people the chance to express their feelings about what has happened, through conversations, stories, games, drawings, or songs. Model an accepting attitude; do not express judgment or criticism of what is expressed. Allow tears or other expressions of fear, worry, sadness, guilt, and so on.
10. Emphasize the normalcy of reactions to the events. Do not treat the survivor like a "sick" or "crazy" person, even though their reactions may seem extreme.
11. Help contain feelings of extreme anxiety by subtly focusing attention away from the individual from time to time.
12. If the person, friends, or relatives have done things to survive, mention them to reinforce a sense of self-control and positive self-value, and to prevent feelings of guilt for having survived.
13. Gradually and gently help young people to see that wishes and fantasies of being able to prevent the crisis or of saving loved ones are not realistic and should not be used for self-blame.
14. Help the person to separate the events from an association with the place in which it occurred.
15. Tolerate with patience any temporary return to younger behavior (like sucking on fingers, etc.). Orient parents to help them give their children extra support and nurturance.
16. Accompany young people in activities that have to do with injured or dead members of the school, family, or community.
17. In the case of suicide, avoid idealizing or romanticizing the deceased.
18. Explore any plan for revenge survivors may have. Discuss the real consequence of any such action. Help to identify alternative, positive actions that could satisfy the need to "do something."
19. After a period of mourning, help survivors to remember the good times they once had with those who died.

REFERENCES

Berthold, M. (1998, January 24). *The effects of exposure to violence and social support on psychological and behavioral outcomes in Khmer refugee adolescents.* Poster presented at the International Conference on Research for Social Work Practice, North Miami, FL.

Embry, D. D. (1996). Reasons for hope: Creating a climate for change and resiliency. In W. L. Reed (Ed.), *Violence and childhood trauma: Understanding and responding to the effects of violence on young children.* Cleveland, OH: Urban Child Resources Center.

Granello, P. F., & Granello, D. H. (1998). Training counseling students to use outcome research. *Counselor Education and Supervision, 37,* 224–237.

Grossman, D. C., Neckerman, H. J., Koepsell, T. D., Liu, P. -Y., Asher, K. N., Beland, K., Frey, K., & Rivera, F. P. (1997). Effectiveness of a violence prevention curriculum among children in elementary school. *Journal of the American Medical Association, 277,* 1605–1611.

Hatch, T. (1999, March/April). School guidance and counseling and restoring California's schools. *The ASCA Counselor, 36,* 5, 6, 22.

Hilburn, K. T. (1996, February). *Restructured school policing: An effective school–police partnership.* Paper presented at the California League of High Schools Safety Conference, Lake Tahoe, CA.

Kabar, K. (1999, February 4). City council plans Day of Listening. *Press-Telegram,* p. A3.

Keys, S. G., Bemak, F., & Lockhart, E. J. (1998). Transforming school counseling to serve the mental health needs of at-risk youth. *Journal of Counseling and Development, 76,* 381–388.

Larson, J. D. (1992). Anger and aggression management techniques utilizing the Think First curriculum. *Journal of Offender Rehabilitation, 18,* 101–117.

Lifton, R. J. (1974, Summer). "Death imprints" on youth in Vietnam. *Journal of Clinical Child Psychology,* 47–49.

Lochman, J. E., Dunn, S. E., & Klimes-Dougan, B. (1993). An intervention and consultation model from a social cognitive perspective: A description of the Anger Coping Program. *School Psychology Review, 22,* 458–471.

Males, M. (1996). *The scapegoat generation: America's war on adolescents.* Monroe, ME: Common Courage Press.

Males, M. (1998, May 31). Who's really killing our schoolkids? *Los Angeles Times,* p. M1.

Males, M. (1999). *Framing youth: Ten myths about the next generation.* Monroe, ME: Common Courage Press.

McBride, J. (no date). *Violence prevention in schools.* (Available from Long Beach Unified School District, 1515 Hughes Way, Long Beach, CA 90810)

Mitchell, J. T., & Everly, G. S., Jr. (1995). *Critical incident stress debriefing: An operations manual for the prevention of traumatic stress among emergency services and disaster workers* (2nd ed.). Ellicott City, MD: Chevron.

Morrison, G. M., Furlong, M. J., & Morrison, R. L. (1994). School violence to school safety: Reframing the issue for school psychologists. *School Psychology Review, 23,* 236–256.

Ressler, E. M., Tortorici, J. M., & Marcelino, A. (1993). *Children in war: A guide to the provision of services. A study for UNICEF*. New York: UNICEF.

Sexton, T. L., Whiston, S. C., Bleuer, J. C., & Walz, G. R. (1997). *Integrating outcome research into counseling practice and training*. Alexandria, VA: American Counseling Association.

Tortorici, J. M. (1994). *Promoviendo la paz y el bienestar psicosocial en al comunidad: Manual para promotores y supervisores en situaciones de guerra y post-guerra* [Promoting peace and psychosocial well-being in the community: Manual for promoters and supervisors in situations of war and post-war]. Managua, Nicaragua: UNICEF.

Tortorici Luna, J. M. (1997). *Critical incident management plan (Woodrow Wilson High School)*. Long Beach, CA: Long Beach Unified School District.

Tortorici Luna, J. M. (1998). *Critical incident stress management plan: Mental health component. Emergency preparedness guidelines*. Long Beach, CA: Long Beach Unified School District.

U.S. Departments of Education and Justice. (1999). *Annual report on school safety, 1998*. Washington, DC: Author.

Whiston, S. C., & Sexton, T. L. (1998). A review of school counseling outcome research: Implications for practice. *Journal of Counseling and Development. 76*, 412–426.

22 | School Violence: Implications for School Counselor Training Programs

M. Sylvia Fernandez

The incidence of school violence, particularly shootings, is receiving widespread attention with the incidents that have occurred within a short period of time. This publicity has called into question the preparedness of school personnel to respond to crises of this type and magnitude in the school. School counselors are the front-line crisis responders and have the responsibility for ensuring that there is a crisis response plan in place and for activating the plan if and when the need arises. Most school counselors have not been exposed to this type of crisis responding in their academic training for school counseling. School counselor training programs should reevaluate what they have to offer school counselors in preservice and in-service training as it relates to crisis planning and response. This chapter offers suggestions on issues to consider in training school counselors for crisis response and presents a model for planning and managing a crisis.

In 1998–1999, there was a rash of widely publicized school-based violence, particularly shootings that have resulted in multiple deaths and injuries. The incidents in Pearl, Mississippi; Paducah, Kentucky; Jonesboro, Arkansas; Edinboro, Pennsylvania; and Littleton, Colorado harshly bring home the reality that suburban schools are no longer a safe place for America's children. Violence is becoming a pervasive and unfortunate reality in American schools at all levels (Dykeman, Daehlin, Doyle, & Flamer, 1996). We have assumed that violence only happens in inner-city schools and have been in denial that it can happen in any school in America. As such, school counselors in rural and suburban schools are ill-prepared to intervene in and respond to school-based violence of the nature we are now seeing (Srebalus, Schwartz, Vaughn, & Tunick, 1996). It is a wake-up call and it is time to reevaluate the type, amount, and level of crisis response preparation provided in school counselor training programs.

In most training programs, school counselors-in-training are exposed to program development and planning for the needs of the school when taught how to design a comprehensive developmental guidance program. The typical focus is on a generic program that has all the necessary elements, such as philosophy and rationale of the program including a needs assessment; program goals and objectives with activities and strategies, both proactive and reactive, to be implemented that can be formatively and summatively evaluated; all policies and procedures that govern the program; a section on special topics and concerns, for example, abuse, multiculturalism, sexuality, AIDS, and suicide; and a section on crisis intervention. However, we have not taught school counselors-in-training how to translate the generic program to meet the unique needs of, or to adapt the plan in response to, the multitude of possible crises that may occur in the specific school in which they serve. As a result, too many schools have good comprehensive developmental guidance plans that are not functional and with very little attention paid to addressing crisis response within these plans. School counselor training programs can and should better prepare school counselors-in-training to be capable and effective crisis interveners and responders during their preservice training and through in-service training for school counselors already in the field.

PRESERVICE TRAINING

Infused in the comprehensive developmental guidance program is knowledge about life span development and social and environmental factors that influence development. When talking about life span development as it relates to crisis intervention, attention must be given to addressing developmentally based crisis reactions and appropriate ways to respond to these reactions. When dealing with social and environmental factors that influence development as it relates to crisis intervention, some focus needs to be given to the predictors and precursors to violence. In developing their comprehensive developmental guidance plans, school counselors-in-training have been told that a crisis response plan must be included, but they have not been taught how to develop one or what to focus on in violence prevention programming.

Life Span Development As It Relates to Crisis Intervention

Before one can intervene in a crisis, one has to understand stress and trauma. In a person's daily life, he or she exists in a normal state of equilibrium. In this state, the person is able to maintain his or her equilibrium even in the face of daily and sometimes severe stress. When faced with trauma, which is acute, unexpected stress, this equilibrium is disrupted, and it is difficult for the individual to restore a sense of balance without help. Trauma is typically accompanied by multiple losses, such as control over one's life, of faith in God or others, of a sense of invulnerability, of personal loss of property or loved ones, or of the future (National Organization for Victim Assistance [NOVA], 1994f, 1994g).

Children and adults experience and cope with trauma in very different ways. It is helpful for school counselors to keep this in mind as they deal with students, school personnel, and parents. For children, it is important to rebuild and reaffirm attachments; that is, parents and significant adults need to take extra time and care in letting children know that someone will take care of them. Children need to talk about the critical incident or trauma, they will want factual information, they need issues of death to be addressed concretely, and they need to ventilate their feelings and be validated. Reenactments and play about the critical incident are healthy as they allow the children to feel some control and take away their sense of powerlessness. Parents and teachers should be prepared for and tolerate regressive behaviors in children, such as wanting to be held, not wanting to sleep alone, sleeping with the lights on, or having nightmares; accept aggressive behaviors; and also allow children to talk sporadically about the critical incident. Parents and teachers need to reaffirm the future and talk about it in hopeful terms in order to help the child rebuild trust and faith in the future. Nontalk therapies, such as play, art, music, and dance, are very helpful with preschool and elementary-age children. Adolescents may become more childlike in attitude, be angry or withdrawn, and act out in rebellious ways. Eating and sleeping disorders are common, and children may start using or abusing drugs and alcohol, as well as lose pride in their school. Allowing them to ventilate their thoughts and feelings and validating them would be important (Collison et al., 1987; NOVA, 1994a, 1994e).

Although children and adults experience and cope with trauma in different ways, their basic needs or issues are the same. Adults, too, strive to understand what happened and need to talk about the critical incident, and they need validation of the experience in a supportive environment. With adults, there are likely to be more interpersonal conflicts, minor irritants become harder to accept, and anger is directed frequently at the news media (Collison et al., 1987). Adults too need to regain control and equilibrium, reestablish trust, and look forward to a hopeful future (NOVA, 1994d).

Social and Environmental Predictors and Precursors to Violence

Given the pervasiveness of school-based violence of many types, there must be an understanding of the factors contributing to violent behaviors. In their review of the literature of sociodemographic factors related to violence, Dykeman et al. (1996) cited the following factors:

socioeconomic status (Farrington, 1989), ethnicity (O'Donnell, Hawkins, & Abbot, 1995), gender (Kashani, Deuser, & Reid, 1991; Rigby, Mak, & Slee, 1989), and age (Loeber, Stouthamer-Loeber, Van Kammen, & Farrington, 1989) . . . the nature and quality of both peer relationships (O'Donnell et al., 1995) and of family relationships (American Psychological Association Commission on Violence and Youth, 1993; Tolan, Guerra, & Kendall, 1995). (p. 36)

According to Srebalus et al. (1996), aggression and violent student behavior are also correlated with poor school involvement and community adjustment. Fatum and Hoyle (1996), through their work with peer facilitation and mediation training, repeatedly observed that adolescents today operate from a new code of behavior that promotes a position that if one is shown disrespect then one is expected to take action to regain that respect; that aggression is the only type of unavoidable, clear message and is a viable form of conflict resolution; and that adults are of no help in situations involving their peers. Thus, violence is not perceived as inappropriate.

In light of the growing number of incidents of school-based violence, particularly shootings, counselors, psychologists, sociologists, and other experts have posed multiple hypotheses to explain this phenomenon. Specific contributing factors seem to be the physical violence, in the homes and schools, that is an integral part of many students' lives; the viewing of violence on television and in films; and the cultural–racial violence that surfaces in communities across the United States (Daniels, Arredondo, & D'Andrea, 1999).

IN-SERVICE TRAINING

While training programs introduce school counselors-in-training to comprehensive developmental guidance programming, there needs to be a follow-up with them once they are employed. New counselors can be assisted in modifying the existing comprehensive developmental guidance programs in the schools in which they are now employed or the programs that were developed as part of their training program to meet the needs of the specific school in which they are now employed, especially in the area of school violence. In-service training that focuses on the area of school violence is also useful for school counselors long in the field whose training did not and whose current comprehensive developmental guidance programs do not include crisis response planning. In-service training should include not only crisis response planning but also coping strategies for children, conflict resolution, and helpful styles of relating to victims.

A MODEL FOR PLANNING
AND MANAGING A CRISIS

The following model can be used as part of the training program for pre-service school counselors and as a module for in-service counselors. Schools need to develop tactical and strategic plans for multiple types of crises (Collison et al., 1987). Each of the components addressed needs to be modified to meet the unique needs of the school, as well as take into account what is available in the community in which the school is located.

Prerequisite Knowledge to Developing a Crisis Plan

The crisis plan must be based on the school's definition of crises, knowledge of short-term and long-term reaction to crisis, and awareness of the characteristics of crisis.

Definition of Crisis
Each school has to determine what types of crises they have experienced or anticipate, or are unique to their school. For some it may be natural disasters, for others it may be a weapon being brought on campus, and for yet others it may be violence manifested by fights, suicide, accidents, or shootings. For purposes of this plan, school violence is one of the identified crises.

Reaction to Crisis
At the time of the crisis and trauma, the immediate crisis reaction is of shock, disorientation, numbness, a fight-or-flight response, exhaustion, and a cataclysm of emotion. Typical short-term reactions include regression to childhood, both mentally and physically. Individuals may do things like sing nursery rhymes or call and think of law enforcement or authority figures as "mommy" or "daddy." Individuals may feel very "little" or "weak" and want to be taken care of (NOVA, 1994b, 1994h).

After the immediate crisis is over, it is common for individuals to continue to experience strong emotional or physical reactions in the days, weeks, and even months following the critical incident. These long-term crisis reactions are typically in response to trigger events that remind the individual of the critical incident, which brings back the intense emotion experienced during the critical incident. Trigger events may include seeing, hearing, touching, smelling, or tasting something similar to what the individual was acutely aware of during the critical incident. Long-term crisis reactions may manifest themselves physically, cognitively, emotionally, and behaviorally. The physical signs may include fatigue, muscle tremors, elevated blood pressure and heart rate, and chills. The cognitive signs may include confusion, poor concentration, memory problems, nightmares, and loss of time, place, or person orientation. Emotional signs include anxiety, guilt, depression, and irritability. The behavioral signs include withdrawal, emotional outbursts, substance use (alcohol consumption), and the startle reflex becoming intensified (Baldwin, 1998; NOVA, 1994c).

Characteristics of Crisis
Gilliland and James (1997) identified the following characteristics of crises:

1. *Presence of both danger and opportunity.* It is danger because it is overwhelming to the individual, and it is opportunity because the pain compels the individual to seek help.
2. *Complicated symptomatology.* A crisis is weblike rather than linear based on the environments or system of the individual and the degree of involvement within.
3. *Seeds of growth and change.* The disequilibrium brought about by the trauma provides an impetus for change.
4. *The absence of panaceas or quick fixes.* Help is available through a variety of interventions over a period of time that addresses the initiating stimulus.
5. *Necessity of choice.* Not to choose is a choice that could be negative and destructive, whereas choosing some action may allow the individual to overcome the trauma.
6. *Universality and idiosyncracy.* Crisis is universal because it has the potential to impact everybody, and it is idiosyncratic because it impacts individuals differently and their ability to recover is different.

Components of a Crisis Plan

Once the prerequisite issues have been addressed and there is a common knowledge base about crisis, then the school is ready to go about developing its crisis plan. To do this, schools must clearly state school policies as they relate to crises and must identify the local, state, and national resources.

School Policies
One of the first issues that must be clearly stated is the school policies regarding crisis response and management. The identified crises-related policies to be addressed include (a) the methods for identifying and organizing students immediately after the critical incident, (b) the media boundaries and what type and level of access the media should have, and (c) triage handling and the issue of confidentiality in screening. Policies

should also be determined on how to deal with threats after the immediate crisis is over. For example, in the case of a shooting, if a student threatens to bring a gun or kill somebody, suspending the student is not a good idea. Another issue to be considered here is how the school is going to handle the legal aspects, if there are any, that is, if there is any liability attributed to the school.

Resources

Who are the available resources in the (a) school, such as school counselor, school psychologist, school social worker, and school nurse; (b) community, such as counselors, psychologists, social workers, and inpatient and outpatient mental health agencies; (c) state, such as victim assistance programs, local chapter of the Red Cross, and other crises networks; and (d) nationally, such as National Organization for Victim Assistance and Red Cross.

A crisis plan is dependent on the nature and severity of the crisis. For the present purposes, I use school violence as the crisis for designing a plan.

A MODEL FRAMEWORK FOR A CRISIS INTERVENTION AND MANAGEMENT PLAN

In the aftermath of the shooting at Westside Middle School in Jonesboro, Arkansas, the core crisis management team from the school came together and designed the following framework for developing a crisis management plan based on their experience. The Westside Crisis Management Team (1998) recommended that all crisis plans must have the following:

1. An identified Crisis Management Team Coordinator and Team Leaders who know each other and are designated leaders in areas on the basis of their skills, knowledge, and competence. It is also helpful that these individuals know the school setting and personnel because those in crisis need to see those they already trust, for example, a school psychologist or school counselor from another school or a recognized mental health professional in the community. The organizational structure and the role and responsibilities of the team leaders are delineated in a later section of this chapter.
2. A list of available mental health care workers in the area that includes their names and phone numbers, licenses or certifications, areas of expertise, employment agencies, prior crisis counseling experience or crisis response training, and age level with which they are comfortable or familiar. This serves as a list of "approved" mental health care providers for the school.

3. A list of state agencies that should have representatives on-site as soon as possible, such as Department of Human Services, Attorney General, and State Department of Education.
4. A list of local agencies that should have representatives on-site as soon as possible, such as clergy (especially counseling-trained clergy), a physician (who may be the doctor assigned to the school), mental health personnel, and members of the counseling and social work departments of the local university if applicable.

When a crisis occurs in a school where there are multiple buildings on the campus, there is typically an individual identified; in most cases it is the principal who is responsible for the building. It is recommended that the principal or designee have a Building Crisis Kit equipped with name tags, notebooks, pens, markers, a hand radio or beeper, batteries, and first aid supplies (trauma kits). The Building Crisis Kit will be helpful in identifying and keeping track of students and staff in the building, communicating with identified responsible persons in other buildings, and providing immediate medical assistance. It is also recommended that in each building there should also be an Office Crisis Kit that includes a laptop computer with printer and a list of available clerical assistants. In the days immediately following a critical incident, many more demands are placed on the office. Having a portable computer allows for access to student data and for communication, and additional clerical help will be necessary for answering the phones and assisting the many agencies that may be on campus to assist in various ways.

Crisis Management Protocol

As soon as a critical incident—for our purposes, a shooting—occurs, the first step is to make the 911 call to notify the police and get emergency medical assistance, and then inform the school administration. The school administration, in turn, needs to call the crisis management team coordinator who will mobilize the crisis management team. The next step is to stabilize the situation and provide for the safety of the students by placing them in one location.

Crisis Management Team

As soon as the crisis management team coordinator is called, this person takes charge from that point on and mobilizes the rest of the team. The crisis management team needs to be organized and set up a priori and be ready to mobilize at a moment's notice. It is advisable when identifying the team that more than one person be identified to serve as the team coordinator and as team leaders in the event that someone is unavailable at the time of the crisis. It is also critical that individuals selected to serve on the team know each other, are compatible, are designated as leaders in areas they have expertise, are knowledgeable of how school buildings function, and have the appropriate crisis response training. The Westside Crisis Management Team (1998) suggested an organizational structure in which there is a team coordinator with team leaders in areas such as counselors, outreach, check out of students, assistive groups, law enforcement liaison, media spokesperson, national organizations liaison, communication providers, transportation director, physical plant director, point of contact for all/triage, information resources, aftercare, and resource offers. Each team leader has specific duties and responsibilities.

Team Coordinator

This person should be identified and ratified by school administrators and the school board. It is recommended that at least three people be identified as possibilities. The coordinator *must not* be a member of the administration and preferably outside the school system. The coordinator should have complete charge of the crisis and be allowed wide decision-making authority. Any decisions made by the school administration during this time must be done only after consultation with the coordinator. The coordinator needs to stay in contact with the Superintendent and school board at all times. The coordinator is responsible for (a) assessing needs and risk and prioritizing needs, (b) organizing a plan specific to the crisis and determining services required, and (c) administering to the mental health needs of all parties involved first in the school in which the critical incident occurred and also for the entire school district. The coordinator or the media spokesperson responds to all queries from volunteers and external agencies. The coordinator is responsible for ensuring a swift and smooth transition back to a daily routine. The coordinator plans faculty and community debriefings with the counselor team leader. Once team leaders have been dispatched, the coordinator needs to stay out of their way and run interference for them. The coordinator begins planning short- and long-term aftercare with the aftercare team leader and works with the national organization liaison/team leader to coordinate with national relief organization(s).

Counselor Team Leader

This person needs to organize a sign-in table for volunteer counselors and verify that volunteer counselors are on the school's "approved" list of mental health care workers. Those not on the approved list can work with someone on the list, or a method needs to be in place to check credentials and appropriateness of the volunteer to provide mental health care. This person has to maintain a daily list of volunteer counselors and assess mental health personnel present each day and determine relative usefulness in areas of need. This leader is responsible for (a) determining the direction the process is taking and making assignments accordingly; (b) coordinating and preparing materials for critical incident debriefing of school personnel, students, and parents (a model for critical incident debriefing is presented in a later section of this chapter); (c) providing an overview of critical incident debriefing for those unfamiliar with the process; and (d) assigning volunteer counseling coordinators and volunteer counselors for each building in the school where the critical incident occurred. This person also facilitates transition of individuals experiencing pronounced problems to volunteer counselors available in a central location such as the school library or cafeteria and provides support to volunteer counselors and other helpers. This person must have available building maps and the number of students in each class assigned to volunteer counselors.

Outreach Team Leader

This leader coordinates outreach to victims' families, that is, hospital and/or home visits immediately and in the days following the critical incident. This person ensures volunteer counselors are available to ride the buses the next day back to school and to go to the homes of students absent the next day of school.

Check Out of Student Team Leader

This leader is responsible for accounting for all students, with assistance from the respective classroom teachers, and controlling access to students immediately following the critical incident. Students need to be given name tags to assist volunteers in identifying them. There needs to be one sign-in sheet for students and the person (verify identity) taking them home. It is advisable that this is someone who is on the schoolgrounds during the school day and who knows most of the students because this person needs to take action when the situation is being stabilized.

Assistive Groups Team Leader

This leader is responsible for coordinating the activities of groups such as the Red Cross, victim assistance, and social work to ensure that tasks and responsibilities are not duplicated.

Law Enforcement Liaison/Team Leader

This leader is responsible for crowd and media control and for protection of parents and students from media by having escorts available.

Media Spokesperson

This person handles all communication with the various news organizations. This person is initially briefed on what actually occurred to ensure accurate information is given to any requesting party and to dispel rumors, and he or she is briefed daily by the Crisis Management Team Coordinator.

National Organization Liaison/Team Leader

This leader is a liaison between national organizations, such as National Organization for Victim Assistance or Red Cross, and the team coordinator or local agencies.

Communication Providers (Phone, Public Address) Team Leader

This leader needs to have a contact person at the local telephone company who will be able to install as many additional telephone lines as needed (at least two) and have available at least three cell phones or walkie talkies (with scrambling capability) to ensure secure communication at remote locations. This person also fields all calls from other counselors or media and directs the calls to appropriate individuals. Additional clerical assistance for this leader is helpful.

Transportation Director

This person is responsible for ensuring that transportation is available for students or parents who need to come to the temporary Crisis Counseling Center set up at the school; for volunteer outreach counselors who may need to make hospital and home visits; and for anyone else who has been asked to come in and assist the crisis management team and may need transportation, for example, from the airport. In Jonesboro, the police volunteered a deputy who facilitated safe and ready access anywhere.

Physical Plant Provider

This leader has the master key to all school buildings and coordinates the availability and use of meeting rooms and the maintenance of facilities throughout the crisis round-the-clock if necessary.

Point of Contact for All/Triage Team Leader

This leader needs to have a supply box with name tags and pens for use with those who come in for services. This person greets those who come into the temporary Crisis Counseling Center, which may be set up in the gymnasium, library, or cafeteria, and supervises all activities in the Crisis Counseling Center. This person's primary task is to steer those in need, that is, students, parents, and school personnel, toward appropriate volunteer counselors.

Information Resources Team Leader

This leader needs to identify individuals who can contribute relevant information about trauma and critical incident debriefing as it relates to the specific crisis at hand and coordinate the delivery of this information to the appropriate individuals.

Aftercare Team Leader

This leader has to assess aftercare needs of all parties involved, in consultation with the team coordinator, and is responsible for referring individuals to appropriate agencies for ongoing counseling and for tracking ongoing groups, such as grief support groups for students, parents, and school personnel. This person can also begin working with the school counselor on individual and group healing-oriented activities once the students return to the routine of the school day. These activities may need to continue throughout the rest of the semester and even school year.

Resource Offers Team Leader

This leader needs to be somebody outside the school "in crisis" but familiar to and with the school. This person receives and maintains a log of offers of available resources from experienced volunteers, commercial agencies, and external experts and determines what can be utilized and is aware of limited time offers. This leader also coordinates requests for speaking opportunities about the experience by those involved in the present crisis to share what was learned.

On the practical side, the coordinator should have a badge available for each team leader with designation of area of leadership, and each team leader should have badges available for each member on their team with their designated area of expertise. Some team leaders, such as the counselor and outreach team leaders, will have responsibility over many members or volunteers, and being able to identify who these individuals are becomes very helpful not only to the crisis management team but also to anybody else who may need assistance. Collison et al. (1987), Sorensen (1989), and Schmitt (1999) have proposed variations of the prior suggested model of the role and responsibilities of a crisis management team.

Critical Incident Stress Debriefing

Once the situation has been stabilized and the crisis management team mobilized, team leaders go about completing their assigned tasks, and the team coordinator and the counselor team leader begin preparations for critical incident stress debriefing of school personnel and students, and parents if necessary. A group crisis intervention is a way to integrate the trauma of the critical incident into community life and to work with greater numbers of individuals. It provides an opportunity for release of emotion after the trauma—to validate the feelings, emotions, experiences, and reactions to the critical incident. It is an opportunity to educate participants about the common patterns of crisis reactions they may experience and/or encounter, to help them consider various coping strategies and responses, and to cultivate the seeds of hope for the future with emphasis on a support system.

The following critical incident stress debriefing model was put together by a member of the crisis management team and was the process used by the Westside Crisis Management Team (1998) first with school personnel the day after the shootings with the volunteer crisis counselors facilitating, and then with the students the day they returned to school 2 days after the shooting with the teacher and a volunteer crisis counselor facilitating. This process served as a model for the teachers to use when they were in the classroom with their students.

MODEL FOR CRITICAL INCIDENT STRESS DEBRIEFING WITH A GROUP

This process was used with the entire faculty and staff, separated into small groups based on the building they were in and in group sizes that facilitated plenty of air-time for each person. The key element here is to let people tell their story in their own words because it reflects their perceptions of what transpired.

GOAL: HEALING FOR SELF

Group debriefing
    All members talk, one at a time, all equal
    Each talks all the way through the process (will identify one member to lead)
    Share personal experience before, during, after incident (what happened, what feelings)
    Avoid "why" discussions at this point
    Remind of goal above
Discuss "why" these things happen
    Facilitator guides in a healthy direction (i.e., you're not responsible)
    Focus on justice, not vengeance
    Realize that rumors are rampant
    Remember that victims include people who care about the shooters
    Remind of goal above
Understand normal human reaction
    Avoid survivor guilt
        "Thank God it wasn't me" can cause suicidal guilt
        "Thank God it wasn't you" can cause anger in survivors
        Both thoughts are normal

Stages of reaction
  Outcry/shock
  Denial (blocking the impact, emotional numbing, avoiding the subject)
  Intrusiveness (intense emotional anger, rage, guilt, anxiety, preoccu-
  pation, confusion/disorientation/memory loss, hypervigilance,
  nightmares, startle reactions)
  Working through (airing thoughts, feelings, images, grieving, inte-
  grating "new" realities, with or without help)
Physiological experiences
  Changes in sleep pattern (insomnia or oversleeping)
  Changes in eating patterns (loss of appetite or overeating)
  Change in energy level (loss of energy or overly active/anxious/
  aroused)
Give self permission to experience all feelings, to cry, to laugh, to act
silly
Remind of goal above
When to get help
  Anytime you want
  Unable to function as usual for prolonged period
  Others suggest
  Remind of goal above
How to get help
  Psychologists, counselors, ministers, other helpers on-site
  List of referral sources
  Remind of goal above

This model can be used when working with both the primary and secondary victims. The primary victims are the ones who were on-site when
the critical incident occurred and the families of those involved. The secondary victims are those who were in a different building on the same
campus, those in a different school in the same district, and the community in which the school is located. The school or the crisis management
team may be called to assist in working with secondary victims as well.

CONCLUSION

School counselor training programs have a role and responsibility in helping schools deal with crisis response planning in many ways. One, school
counselor training programs can ensure that their graduates are well
prepared to face crises. This chapter has offered a module that can be
incorporated into the curriculum that serves not only to increase the
knowledge base but also to provide a practical plan that can be easily
adapted to any crisis or any school. Two, facilitate the development of

crisis response plans for school counselors in the field. School counselor training programs are in a unique position of providing current information and training to counselors in the field to ensure best practices are being utilized and the integrity of the profession is being upheld. And, three, school counselors should be resources at the school in the event of a crisis. Faculty and advanced students in school counselor training programs have the basic counseling skills necessary for crisis counseling and can serve as volunteer counselors and, it is hoped, also have some crisis intervention expertise to offer the school in crisis.

REFERENCES

American Psychological Association Commission on Violence and Youth. (1993). *Summary meeting of the American Psychological Association Commission on Violence and Youth.* Washington, DC: Author.

Baldwin, D. (1998). *Critical incident stress information sheet* [On-line]. Available: http://www.trauma-pages.com.

Collison, B. B., Bowden, S., Patterson, M., Snyder, J., Sandall, S., & Wellman, P. (1987). After the shooting stops. *Journal of Counseling and Development, 65,* 389–390.

Daniels, J., Arredondo, P., & D'Andrea, M. (1999). Expanding counselors' thinking about the problem of violence. *Counseling Today, 41*(12), 12, 17.

Dykeman, C., Daehlin, W., Doyle, S., & Flamer, H. S. (1996). Psychological predictors of school-based violence: Implications for school counselors. *The School Counselor, 44,* 35–47.

Farrington, D. P. (1989). Early predictors of adolescent aggression and adult violence. *Violence and Victims, 4,* 79–100.

Fatum, W. R., & Hoyle, J. C. (1996). Is it violence? School violence from the student perspective: Trends and interventions. *The School Counselor, 44,* 28–34.

Gilliland, B. E., & James, R. K. (1997). *Crises intervention strategies.* Pacific Grove, CA: Brooks/Cole.

Kashani, J. H., Deuser, W., Reid, J. C. (1991). Aggression and anxiety: A new look at an old notion. *Journal for the American Academy of Child and Adolescent Psychiatry, 30,* 218–223.

Loeber, R., Stouthamer-Loeber, M., Van Kammen, W. B., & Farrington, D. P. (1989). Development of a new measure of self-reported antisocial behavior for young children: Prevalence and reliability. In M. W. Klein (Ed.), *Cross-national research in self reported crime and delinquency* (pp. 203–225). New York: Kluwer Academic.

National Organization for Victim Assistance. (1994a). *Children's reaction to trauma.* Washington, DC: Author.

National Organization for Victim Assistance. (1994b). *The crisis reaction.* Washington, DC: Author.

National Organization for Victim Assistance. (1994c). *Long-term crisis reactions.* Washington, DC: Author.

National Organization for Victim Assistance. (1994d). *Recovery from immediate trauma*. Washington, DC: Author.

National Organization for Victim Assistance. (1994e). *Some coping strategies for children*. Washington, DC: Author.

National Organization for Victim Assistance. (1994f). *Stress and trauma*. Washington, DC: Author.

National Organization for Victim Assistance. (1994g). *Trauma and loss*. Washington, DC: Author.

National Organization for Victim Assistance. (1994h). *Trauma and regression*. Washington, DC: Author.

O'Donnell, J., Hawkins, J. D., & Abbott, R. D. (1995). Predicting serious delinquency and substance use among aggressive boys. *Journal of Consulting and Clinical Psychology, 63*, 529–537.

Rigby, K., Mak, A. S., & Slee, P. T. (1989). Impulsiveness, orientation to institutional authority, and gender as factors in self-reported delinquency among Australian adolescents. *Personality and Individual Differences, 10*, 689–692.

Schmitt, S. M. (1999). Crisis response plans reviewed following school shootings. *Counseling Today, 41*(12), 28–29.

Sorensen, J. R. (1989). Responding to student or teacher death. *Journal of Counseling and Development, 67*, 426–427.

Srebalus, D. J., Schwartz, J. L., Vaughn, R. V., & Tunick, R. H. (1996). Youth violence in rural schools: Counselor perceptions and treatment resources. *The School Counselor, 44*, 48–54.

Tolan, P. H., Guerra, N. G., & Kendall, P. C. (1995). A developmental–ecological perspective on antisocial behavior in children and adolescents: Toward a unified risk and intervention framework. *Journal of Consulting and Clinical Psychology, 63*, 579–584.

Westside Crisis Management Team. (1998). *Crisis plan protocol*. Unpublished document.

SUMMARY AND IMPLICATIONS FOR PRACTICE

Cheryl Blalock Aspy

He was a troubled child. He walked with a slight limp, and his speech was not clear unless he took the time to form the words carefully. His pale blond hair and brilliant blue eyes gave him the appearance of an angel, but often his behavior did not. He was large for his age, and his size belied his level of development. He was often judged to be mentally slow, but he was really physically fast.

School was never fun. He tried teachers' patience because he was determined to try things his way first. His early punishment by teachers was license to the other children to tease him and they did. He was angry early. Life was not fair, and his attempts to make it so with physical force were not met with success. He became increasingly unsuccessful at school and increasingly angry with the adults who could not make life better for him.

As soon as he could, he dropped out of school. The fight that began at the football stadium was the culmination of years of anger. An old enemy with old taunts triggered the first punch. But this was not a match between school boys, but young men. The injury to the other young man was severe and when the police arrived, that's how they sorted it out. He was standing and the other young man lay wounded on the ground, and he was off to jail. If he'd had a gun, he said later, he would have killed his enemy, so intense was his anger.

This story and so many others like it are the reasons for this book. Interventions are possible, and they can change lives. We have the tools to make a difference before children engage in those behaviors that require juvenile justice intervention or incarceration. We need to make them available to every teacher and counselor so that stories like this will be a thing of the past. What have we learned from this book? Let us review what we know and what we can do as counselors and teachers to prevent violence in our schools.

Section I contained a discussion of the nature of the problem, and the following points emerged:

- Violence in general is on the decline, but youth violence is increasing.
  - ➤ Both teachers and students feel this effect and report that, increasingly, they feel unsafe at school.
- The reasons for violent behavior among youths are multifaceted and interactive, and, therefore, our interventions must be developed to target multiple levels of society.
  - ➤ Children who have been abused are unlikely to form affectional bonds that provide security and allow them to trust others.
- The most effective interventions will be directed by an administration that understands local needs and provides the budget to meet those needs.
  - ➤ Programs should be developed for individuals, families, and the various subgroups within the community to effectively change the climate that supports and promotes violence in youths.

Section II of the book addressed etiology.

- Retaliation appears to be the primary reason that youths use to justify their violent behavior.
  - ➤ This implies that conflict management programs that emphasize peaceful negotiation will be much less powerful if taught in isolation than they would be as part of a comprehensive violence program that includes a victim support component.
- Another source of violence is the engenderment of males by American culture to act in violent ways.
  - ➤ These role stereotypes are perpetuated by families, peers, and the media.
  - ➤ Counselors can serve as an interactive buffer to the alienation that society produces and can effectively advocate for students who are at risk for violence.
- The role of the media in perpetuating stereotypes of youths at risk for violence as coming from minority, low socioeconomic groups was explicated.

Section III provided numerous prevention strategies and noted that primary prevention is the preferred treatment. A selected list of suggestions from these chapters includes the following:

- The PEACE POWER! strategy is a program for constructing nonviolent, noncoercive cultures in community organizations and other networks. It involves:
  - ➤ Recognizing contributions and successes
  - ➤ Acting with respect
  - ➤ Sharing power to build community
  - ➤ Making peace through conflict resolution
- Focusing on asset development encourages youths to assume responsibility for their behavior, practice interpersonal competence, and peacefully resolve conflicts.
  - ➤ Programs such as this are resilience-centered rather than problem-centered.
  - ➤ This approach is student-centered and has a lasting value beyond the school years.
  - ➤ Counselors assume the role of school consultant with an eye for what is best for students and encourage schoolwide changes.
- Violence and virtues are antithetical, and thus virtues development is a viable and preferred strategy for reducing violence.
  - ➤ Developing virtues in youths will result in a decrease in violence.
  - ➤ There are effective methods available for promoting virtues development.
- An ecological approach to violence prevention will involve home, school, and community.
  - ➤ All stakeholders must be committed to reshaping the beliefs and assumptions in a community.
  - ➤ Schools should implement a curriculum that educates the young on how to live principled lives and provides the skills to act on their beliefs.
- Creative strategies for preventing violence include:
  - ➤ Implementing programs that have been tested for success, including the Comer Project and the Building Resiliency and Vocational Excellence (BRAVE) programs.
  - ➤ Using group techniques, such as role reversal, modeling, fishbowl, behavioral reversal, psychodrama and sociodrama, and play therapy.
- School counselors can be effective contributors to a school violence prevention program by preparing themselves with the knowledge and skills required of an intervention consultant.
  - ➤ Counselors can implement prevention programs aimed at primary, secondary, and tertiary prevention.
  - ➤ Counselors have an obligation to implement, evaluate, and restructure services and programs based on ongoing evaluation.
- Anger management programs vary widely in their content and delivery methods.

> As a whole, these programs appear to be a worthwhile endeavor.
> They are particularly effective in reducing the most severe and inappropriate behaviors in classrooms.

- Practical approaches to school violence will involve interventions targeted toward:
  > Administrative practices, such as increasing principal visibility and communication skills and developing a school procedures manual.
  > Teacher-focused practices, such as curriculum development and behavior management.
  > Providing alternative curriculum that is diverse and that addresses life skills.
  > Community collaborations.
  > Physical plant alterations.
  > Student-oriented interventions that include counseling, training, and procedures modification.
- There are programs to prevent violence that are widely available and have been evaluated. Specific examples are thoroughly described.

Section IV was dedicated to violence that is targeted toward special populations, including suicidal adolescents; gay, lesbian, and bisexual youths; and the special category of violence defined as hate crimes. We discovered

- Suicide is one of the top three causes of death in adolescents, ranking just below accidents and about equal with homicides.
  > Adolescent risk factors for suicide have been identified and include family dysfunction, poor problem-solving strategies, psychopathologies, hopelessness, running away from home, multiple stressors, male gender, identity issues, giftedness or learning disabilities, and either a real or a perceived loss.
  > Screening instruments are available, such as the STRESS checklist.
- The harassment of sexual minority students and teachers should not be tolerated.
  > Homophobia, which is the fear of being gay and hatred of gays and lesbians, must be exposed just as racism and sexism have been.
  > Reported consequences of the harassment of lesbian and gay adolescents include a high incidence of acting-out in school; rebelling against authority; abusing alcohol and other substances; feeling depressed, isolated, and confused; engaging in prostitution; and attempting suicide.

- Hate crimes are those offenses that are motivated by hatred of individuals or groups on the basis of their race/ethnicity, religion, sexual orientation, disability, or national origin.
  - ➤ Anger management programs can be effective in reducing hate crimes.
  - ➤ The Multidimensional Model for Prejudice Prevention and Reduction is another tool for counselors to use in reducing hate and the violence associated with it.

In Section V of the book, violence intervention strategies related to individuals, schools, and counselor training programs were described. Our major findings include the following:

- Adolescent violence is strongly correlated with alcohol and other drug abuse.
  - ➤ Common *DSM–IV* diagnoses may include conduct disorder, substance dependence, or substance abuse.
  - ➤ Behavioral family therapy is a recommended treatment for adolescents presenting with these comorbidities.
- Serious violent forms of conduct disorder must be understood as the results of the interaction of person factors and environmental conditions in the home, school, and peer domains.
  - ➤ Effective treatments include family therapy, social and parenting skills, anger management training, and other cognitively based treatments.
  - ➤ School-based interventions may include in-school therapy, behavioral consultation with the teacher, and a more structured and predictable school environment that emphasizes rewards for appropriate behavior.
- Counselors can be leaders in addressing critical incident stress management in the schools.
  - ➤ Counselors have critical roles before, during, and after a school crisis related to violence.
  - ➤ Having a comprehensive plan, modifying the plan to meet the critical incident, and then debriefing teachers, students, and staff are tasks that counselors can perform efficiently and effectively.
- School counselor training programs need to include comprehensive curricula to address the new realities of the school environment.
  - ➤ Crisis management is one area that programs should now include.
  - ➤ These programs can also provide crisis management plans and information to counselors in the field.
  - ➤ Faculty who teach in these programs should also be prepared to provide backup and support to counselors in schools who experience a crisis.

A study released by the Federal Bureau of Investigation in December 1999 identified as many as 50 risk factors that will help recognize the one in a million student who might become a killer. Killings at school are indeed rare, and children are much less likely to be killed at school than they are traveling in a car to school. However, lesser levels of violence in schools are still tremendously destructive to the healthy growth and development of children into productive adults. Any reader of this book should take away five major principles that, if implemented, could make a major difference in the violence experienced by every child in school today.

1. Counselors, teachers, and school administrators should know the precursors or factors that contribute to youth violence and be prepared to intervene in the lives of individual youths who appear to be at risk by forming constructive relationships that can change their lives.
2. Because the cause of violence is multifaceted and interactive, interventions must be equally inclusive of the individual, family, and cultural characteristics that are present in the community targeted for intervention.
3. There are programs to reduce violence that have been evaluated and found effective, but every program should be adapted to the particular needs and characteristics of the target community.
4. Primary prevention of violence is the best treatment, and a focus on asset-building or resiliency in youths is an investment for the entire community but one that will pay dividends beyond the school years.
5. When crises occur, counselors should be prepared to assume leadership during and after the crisis has been resolved to prevent reinjury from posttraumatic stress disorder. Because counselors know the teachers and students in their buildings, have the training and expertise to address the emotional life, and have planned and prepared for these events, they can truly make a difference.

Index